D1571522

Agrarian Reform in the Philippines

DEMOCRATIC TRANSITIONS

AND REDISTRIBUTIVE REFORM

Jeffrey M. Riedinger

Stanford University Press

Stanford, California 1995

Stanford University Press, Stanford, California
© 1995 by the Board of Trustees of the Leland Stanford Junior University
Printed in the United States of America

CIP data appear at the end of the book

Stanford University Press publications are distributed exclusively by
Stanford University Press within the United States, Canada, and Mexico;
they are distributed exclusively by Cambridge University Press
throughout the rest of the world.

To Beverly

Acknowledgments

In the years of fieldwork and research that were instrumental in the preparation of this manuscript, I have incurred considerable intellectual and personal debts. Foremost is the debt I owe to the countless men and women in rural areas around the world who, in sharing their lives with me, provided an extraordinary view of the problems and possibilities of development. Since 1986, Henry Bienen has been an invaluable adviser and colleague. For his guidance and assistance in seeing the dissertation version of this manuscript to completion, I owe him *utang na loób*, a permanent debt of gratitude. I owe similar debts to John Waterbury and Kay Warren: to John for his keen insights into agrarian politics; to Kay for sharing the richness of cultural anthropology with me.

In preparing this manuscript and related articles and papers, I have benefited from the comments and insights of Paul Hutchcroft, Atul Kohli, Stephan Haggard, Gary Hawes, Alfred McCoy, Joel Migdal, James Scott, and David Wurfel. Each has helped me in grappling with Philippine politics and the broader issues of democratic politics and redistributive reform.

My colleagues at Michigan State University have offered encouragement and advice as I have juggled the demands of teaching, field research, and revising the manuscript. I owe particular debts of gratitude to Mike Bratton and Nic van de Walle. The staff of the Department of Political Science have provided ready assistance as I labored to meet class and publication deadlines.

In earlier years, Roy Prosterman afforded me an exceptional opportunity to collaborate in fieldwork on rural-development issues, not only in the Philippines, but in countries from Central America to the Middle East to South and Southeast Asia. The debt I owe him is enormous.

Field research for this study was made possible in part by the generous financial assistance of several foundations, most notably the John D. and Catherine T. MacArthur Foundation and the Joyce Mertz-Gilmore Foundation, as well as the support of the Woodrow Wilson School of Public and International Affairs at Princeton University and the Department of Political Science, the Department of Resource Development, the Center for the Advanced Study of International Development, and the Office of International Studies and Programs at Michigan State University.

In the Philippines I amassed intellectual and personal debts too numerous to list fully. Some whom I do mention might well prefer not to be implicated in the conclusions of this undertaking. I am particularly grateful to the late Serge Cherniguin and the staff and members of the National Federation of Sugar Workers, and to Jaime Tadeo, Rafael Mariano, and the staff and members of Kilusang Magbubukid ng Pilipinas, for facilitating many of my site visits and otherwise taking the time to help me understand their organizations and the sociopolitical environment in which they operated. Congressman Bonifacio Gillego gave unstintingly of his time and hospitality as I probed the legislative dimension of the reform process. Florencio Abad and Victor Gerardo Bulatao provided invaluable assistance as I explored the politics of reform within the executive branch. Others who were instrumental in helping me understand Philippine culture, politics, and the reform process include Heherson Alvarez, Raul Socrates Banzuela, J. Virgilio Bautista, the late Luzviminda Cornista, Antonio Fortich, Violeta Lopez-Gonzaga, Francisco and Cynthia Lara, Horacio Morales, the late Gaston Ortigas, Oscar Orbos, Ma. Agnes Quisumbing, Felipe Ramiro, Isagani Serrano, and Hector Soliman. Members of the international media provided timely insights or introductions. In particular I am indebted to the late Robert Shaplen, as well as to his son, Peter, for the supreme courtesy of sharing sources with me at the critical early stages of my research. Clay Jones and Kim Gordon-Bates provided similar help by sharing their files and perspectives on Philippine events. Although the original version of this manuscript was completed before the publication of James Putzel's exhaustive study of agrarian reform in the Philippines, the current version is richer for that work. I hope I prepaid the favor in the course of our discussions in the late 1980s.

Much as I have tried to do justice to the Philippine people in their quest for an equitable and democratic society, I have doubtless committed errors. For that I beg their forbearance.

Acknowledgments

Portions of this work appeared previously in "Everyday Elite Resistance to Agrarian Reform in the Philippines," in *The Violence Within: Cultural and Political Opposition in Divided Nations*, ed. Kay B. Warren, pp. 181–218 (Boulder, Colo.: Westview Press, 1993), and "Philippine Land Reform in the 1980s," in *Agrarian Reform and Grassroots Development: Ten Case Studies*, ed. Roy L. Prosterman, Mary N. Temple, and Timothy M. Hanstad, pp. 15–47 (Boulder, Colo.: Lynne Rienner, 1990).

I am also indebted to Peter Dreyer for his careful copyediting of the manuscript and to Muriel Bell and John Feneron of the Stanford University Press for their encouragement and ready assistance in bringing this manuscript to publication.

Finally, a few words of thanks to my family. My parents instilled and nurtured my thirst for knowledge. My parents-in-law have helped ease the emotional strain on my wife and children during my long absences for fieldwork. Most important, the constant support and infinite patience of my wife, Beverly, and our children, Stephanie and Christopher, have made this study possible. Their companionship and insistence that there is more to life than scholarship have enriched my life beyond measure.

J.M.R.

Contents

Tables

Abbreviations

AABT	Asociacion Agricola de Bais y Tanjay, Inc.
ADB	Asian Development Bank
AFP	Armed Forces of the Philippines
ALARM	Association of Landowners for Orderly Reform
AMA	Aniban ng mga Manggagawa sa Agrikultura (Union of Agricultural Workers)
AMC	Area Marketing Cooperative
AMRS	Association of Major Religious Superiors
AMT	Aguman ding Malding Talapagobra (General Workers' Union)
ARADO	Agrarian Reform Alliance of Democratic Organizations
BAECON	Bureau of Agricultural Economics
BAYAN	Bagong Alyansang Makabayan (New Nationalist Alliance)
BCC	Basic Christian Community
BISIG	Bukluran sa Ikauunlad ng Sosyalistang Isip at Gawa (Union for the Advancement of Socialist Thought and Action)
CAC	Cabinet Action Committee
CAFGU	Civilian Armed Forces Geographic Unit
CAP	Council of Agricultural Producers of the Philippines
CARL	Comprehensive Agrarian Reform Law
CARP	Comprehensive Agrarian Reform Program
CBCP	Catholic Bishops' Conference of the Philippines
CHDF	Civilian Home Defense Force
CLOA	Certificate of Land Ownership Award
CLT	Certificate of Land Transfer

CNL	Christians for National Liberation
COLOR	Council of Landowners for Orderly Reform
CORD	Coalition of Organizations for the Restoration of Democracy
CPAR	Congress for a People's Agrarian Reform
CPDF	Cordillera People's Democratic Front
CPP	Partido Komunista ng Pilipinas—Marxismo-Leninismo-Kaisipang Mao Zedong (Communist Party of the Philippines—Marxist-Leninist-Mao Zedong Thought)
DAR	Department of Agrarian Reform
DATU-Panay	Democratic Alliance for a Truly United Panay
DLGCD	Department of Local Government and Community Development
DOJ	Department of Justice
EP	Emancipation Patent
FACOMA	Farmers' Cooperative Marketing Association
FFF	Federation of Free Farmers
FFHDF	First Farmers' Human Development Foundation
GABRIELA	General Assembly Binding Women for Integrity, Equality, and Law Foundation
HMB	Hukbong Mapagpalay ng Bayan (People's Liberation Army)
HUK	Hukbo ng Bayan Laban sa Hapon (People's Army Against Japan)
IAS	Institute of Agrarian Studies
ICSI	Institute on Church and Social Issues
IPD	Institute for Popular Democracy
IRRI	International Rice Research Institute
JAJA	Justice for Aquino, Justice for All
KAGUMA	Katipunan ng mga Gurong Makabayan (Association of Nationalist Teachers)
KAISAHAN	Kaisahan Tungo sa Kaunlaran ng Kanayunan at Repormang Pansakahan (Solidarity Toward Countryside Development and Agrarian Reform)
KBL	Kilusang Bagong Lipunan (New Society Movement)
KM	Kabataang Makabayan (Nationalist Youth)
KMP	Kilusang Magbubukid ng Pilipinas (Peasant Movement of the Philippines)
KMU	Kilusang Mayo Uno (May First Movement)

KPMP	Kalipunang Pambansa ng mga Magsasaka sa Pilipinas (National Confederation of Peasants in the Philippines)
LABAN	Lakas ng Bayan (Strength of the Nation)
LAKAS	Lakas ng Magsasaka, Manggagawa at Mangingisda ng Pilipinas
LBP	Land Bank of the Philippines
LDP	Laban ng Demokratikong Pilipino
LP	Liberal Party
LUPA	Land's Utmost Productivity Association
MAKIBAKA	Makabayang Kilusan ng Bagong Kababaihan (Nationalist Movement of New Women)
MNLF	Moro National Liberation Front
MSP	Makabayang Samahang Pangkalsugan (National Association of Health Workers, or Patriotic Health Association)
NACUSIP	National Congress of Unions in the Sugar Industry of the Philippines
NASSA	National Secretariat of Social Action, Justice and Peace
NDF	National Democratic Front
NEDA	National Economic and Development Authority
NFSP	National Federation of Sugarcane Planters
NFSW	National Federation of Sugar Workers
NP	Nationalista Party
NPA	Bagong Hukbong Bayan (New People's Army)
NFSP	New Federation of Sugarcane Planters
NOPA	Negros Oriental Planters' Association, Inc.
NRPA	National Rice Producers' Association
PAKISAMA	Pambansang Kilusan ng mga Samahang Magsasaka (National Movement of Farmer Unions)
PARC	Presidential Agrarian Reform Council
PCGR	Presidential Commission on Government Reorganization
PD	Presidential Decree
PDP	Partido Demokratikong Pilipino
PHILCOA	Philippine Coconut Authority
PhilDHRRA	Philippine Partnership for the Development of Human Resources in Rural Areas
PKP	Partido Komunista ng Pilipinas (Communist Party of the Philippines)

PKM	Pambansang Kaisahan ng mga Magbubukid (National Peasants' Union)
PLADAR	Panay Landowners' Alliance for Democratic Agrarian Reform
PRRM	Philippine Rural Reconstruction Movement
RA	Republic Act
RAM	Reform the Armed Forces Movement
SFAN	Small Farmers' Association of Negros
SN	Samahang Nayon
TUCP	Trade Union Congress of the Philippines
UCPB	United Coconut Planters' Bank
UNIDO	United Democratic Opposition
USAID	United States Agency for International Development

Agrarian Reform in the Philippines

1

Democracy and Redistributive Reform

Inclusive polyarchies are more common among countries with the greatest equality in land distribution. Conversely, countries with the greatest inequality tend to be nonpolyarchies.

Robert Dahl

A basic incompatibility exists between parliaments and land reform.

Samuel P. Huntington

The assassination of Benigno "Ninoy" Aquino, Jr., on August 21, 1983, touched off a wave of antigovernment demonstrations and crystallized a massive pro-democracy movement in the Philippines. These demonstrations culminated in the "People Power Revolution" of February 22–25, 1986, which marked the triumph of a nonviolent populist movement headed by Corazon Aquino, the end of Ferdinand Marcos's authoritarian regime, the restoration of democratic political forms, and—it appeared—a renewed commitment to social and economic reform. The Philippines represents one case in a series of generally nonviolent democratic transitions or processes of political liberalization that marked the 1980s and 1990s. Political liberalization in southern and eastern Europe, much of Latin America, and parts of Asia and Africa has been the subject of global attention, giving rise to a considerable and growing body of scholarship (Bermeo 1987; Diamond et al. 1989; Handelman and Sanders 1981; O'Donnell et al. 1986). Analyses of these events have typically focused on issues of timing, the loss of cohesion among the ruling elite, the role of domestic social organizations, international political and economic conditions, and the terms of the transition. Other analyses have taken these transitions as opportunities to reconsider the question of grassroots mobilization and political participation under authoritarian rule or to explore the persistence of authoritarian features in nominally democratic polities.[1] These transitions also provide new

cases with which to address age-old questions concerning the links, if any, between political liberalization and enhanced equality in the social and economic spheres (Dahl 1978; Marshall 1964).

This book raises the issue of socioeconomic inequality in developing countries and questions the capacity of democratic regimes to effectuate redistributive reform. Is significant redistributive agrarian reform possible under the auspices of a new democracy? Agrarian reform involves both redistribution of landownership (land reform) and the development of complementary credit, extension, infrastructure, pricing, and research programs. By definition, such reform involves curtailment of the power and privileges of influential elements of society. Agrarian reform has been an important part of the political debate surrounding liberalization or regime transition in a number of countries, notably Hungary, the Philippines, Portugal, South Africa, and the former Soviet Union (Bermeo 1986; Brooks 1990; de Klerk 1991; Rutledge 1977; Van Atta 1993). To further our understanding of the processes of political liberalization and attendant social and economic reform, this study analyzes the formulation and implementation of agrarian reform policy in the Philippines under the governments of Corazon Aquino and Fidel Ramos.

In the still predominantly rural settings of the developing world, agrarian reform remains the most politically charged of the redistributive societal reforms and arguably the most important. Land-tenure structures have long been viewed as fundamental impediments to the enhancement of agricultural productivity and the initiation of a process of sustained economic development based on a vibrant agricultural sector. Land tenure–related grievances have been regularly identified as being one, if not the principal, reason for civil conflict and social revolution. At a more general level, agrarian reform has been seen as the principal vehicle for political incorporation and control of the rural poor, a means of promoting peasant political participation tied to a political party or regime (Dorner and Kanel 1971; Lipton 1974; Paige 1975; Prosterman and Riedinger 1987; Tai 1974; Warriner 1969).

This is not to suggest that there is unanimity of opinion concerning the benefits of agrarian reform. Scholars, landowners, and political elites have challenged the premises of agrarian reform, arguing that many earlier reforms occasioned little improvement in production, that reform beneficiaries escalated their demands on government, that the threat of rural insurrection proved more apparent than real, and that the political costs in terms of alienated landed support associated with

these modest achievements were considerable (Grindle 1986; Johnston and Clark 1982; McClintock 1980).

Culture and politics converged in the debates over Philippine agrarian reform. Images of landowner and laborer, agricultural productivity, economies of scale, peasant capacities and aspirations, the contractions of paternalism, and connection to land were advanced and debated in political attempts to influence the design of reform policy. This study highlights elite resistance to redistributive agrarian reform and finds that President Aquino and provincial elites shared political and rhetorical strategies to limit the scope and direction of reform. To do so they concentrated on certain critical issues that legitimized the abandonment of important elements of reform, disempowered rural populations on the threshold of democracy, and revealed contradictions in Philippine elite constructions of paternalism and reciprocity. For the present, those resisting reform have largely prevailed in limiting the scope of the new reform program. Nonetheless, important progress has been made under the Aquino and Ramos governments in implementing earlier reform programs and distributing public lands. One task, then, is to explain the Aquino and Ramos governments' willingness and capacity to undertake certain elements of redistributive reform while resisting other elements of such reform.

A State-Society Analytical Approach

In exploring the politics of redistributive reform in the Philippines, I have adopted an approach akin to Joel Migdal's (1988) state-society analysis. The field of inquiry is the interaction of state and society, the clashes between the state and its institutions, on the one hand, and social organizations, on the other, over "which strategies are to be adopted, who will make the rules, and who will determine the property rights that define the use of assets and resources in the society."[2]

Some of the most important contributions to the political science literature of the 1970s involved analysis of peasant activism and revolutionary behavior. In considerable part, the debate focused on social variables; in particular, moral economy versus political economy explanations of peasant behavior.[3] The early 1980s ushered in a much more explicit emphasis on political variables—namely, the role of the state and state elites in setting the policy agenda and initiating processes of significant socioeconomic change.[4] Neither approach precluded consideration of other variables, yet they raised concerns about the adequacy

of the incorporation of both political and social variables within the political science literature. A state-society approach, by contrast, demands analysis of both political and social variables.

I expect the state to have some degree of autonomy in shaping political and economic development, yet the extent and nature of that autonomy will be strongly influenced by social variables, including the nature of social control, the pattern of landholding, religiosity, and ethnic, linguistic, or regional diversity. The perspective of the state adopted here emphasizes, in part, the role of state elites in policy formulation and implementation. The state is assumed to have identifiable, concrete interests independent of those of any particular group or class in the society. The policy-oriented nature of my concern with reform—how to foster political environments supportive of redistributive reform—initially suggested a state-oriented focus for the research. Such an approach characteristically concerns itself with issues of legitimacy and internal cohesion of state elites, state resources, state control over the policy agenda, and the sequencing and timing of reform implementation.

However, the ongoing nature of the state-building process pointed to the interface between state and civil society as a more appropriate focus for the analysis. The respective roles of state and society are still being contested in the Philippines, as elsewhere.[5] Judged against conventional standards of autonomy (independence from dominant socioeconomic elites) and capacity (the ability to implement policy predictably), the Philippine state is weak. Agrarian and industrial elites have extensively penetrated the Philippine state and have engaged in an intense interfamily competition for control of state resources (Hutchcroft 1991; id. 1992). Provincial and local landowning elites, some of whom maintain private armies, retain considerable influence, stymieing the development of a strong, reform-oriented central state. The communist New People's Army (NPA) and the autonomy struggle of the Muslims of Mindanao and Sulu pose direct, armed challenges to state authority and control.[6] Even apart from these movements, the country has witnessed considerable popular mobilization, most notably in the final years of the Marcos regime. New or more forceful demands are being made on the state and new challenges posed to the dominance of traditional elites. Finally, the Philippines lacks a regularized bureaucracy. Government appointments often reflect the politics of patronage and foster loyalty to individual patrons rather than to the state or the bureaucratic institution (Cariño 1989: 6; Francisco 1969; Wurfel 1988: 78–80). All of these factors suggested that a middle-level analysis of

state-society dynamics was likely to yield the greatest insights into the politics of redistributive reform in the Philippines.

In pursuing development and reform, the Philippine state has been forced to confront the complex relationship between reform and contested control. In other settings, development and reform initiatives by the state have unleashed unintended tensions and pressures that have threatened state control (Grindle 1986: 133–59). Social groups have exhibited unexpected powers, pressuring for new state services or challenging the state's capacity to pursue wider reforms (Herring 1983: 212–16). The issue of control is especially problematic in the Philippines, where geography, history, the private armies of large landowners, and insurgency all limit centralized control.

The autonomy of the Aquino and Ramos regimes in executing agrarian reform was circumscribed by both the organized political power of the landed elite and the economic significance of the agricultural sector. As in other countries, the Philippine agricultural sector has often been looked to as a source of surplus, providing cheap food for the urban sector and appreciable foreign exchange earnings.[7] In an era of acute foreign indebtedness, avoiding any disruption in existing sources of foreign exchange was a high priority in the view of senior government officials. Banana, pineapple, and sugarcane producers played on this concern, repeatedly arguing that land redistribution would sound the death knell for their sectors, with sizable concomitant losses in foreign exchange (Diaz 1987: 16; Nasol 1987: 4; Sabino 1987: 21; Sarrosa 1987: 12). Something of a paradox emerged in the Philippine setting, given the economic and political significance of the agricultural sector. On the one hand, the considerable, albeit reduced, economic importance of that sector was reflected in a willingness to accede to the political demands of the landed elite. At the same time, the significance of the agricultural sector meant that landlessness and inequitable patterns of landownership loomed large in calculations of social equality and the potential for civil upheaval.[8]

Cultural features further defined the Philippine context for democratic rule and state-initiated reform, among them personal and group identifications along regional and ethnolinguistic lines; the principle of *utang na loób* (debt of gratitude) and patron-client relations; and the prominence of peasant grievances in the struggle for independence in the late nineteenth century and in several twentieth-century insurgencies. The changing role of the Catholic Church was also pivotal in recent events.[9] Philippine culture has been shaped by the interplay between

the local cultures of Philippine villages, which are ethnically and linguistically diverse, and a variety of foreign influences (Islam, Catholicism, and Spanish, U.S., and Japanese rule). Colonial policies and the penetration of the world market economy in the late nineteenth and early twentieth centuries did much to shape present-day state-society relations and the politics of agrarian reform. These policies and influences institutionalized dramatic inequalities in landownership and "fragmented" social control.[10] Kinship and ethnolinguistic groups and landed regional and local elites contested the central state in governing the details of everyday life. Although the impact of these social groupings is typically limited to specific regions, their aggregate influence on the state and state policy can be profound (Migdal 1988).

The choice of land reform as the policy topic similarly argued for an intermediate, state-society focus. As a process of potentially sweeping social engineering, land reform involves intimate state involvement with social constituencies. This explicit process of social engineering requires the agreement and often active support of intermediate organizations ranging from regional economic and political elites to local government bureaucrats and other local interest groups.[11] In this respect, land reform is distinguishable from agricultural pricing and economic structural adjustment, for example, which are almost inherently viewed as state policies, originating with, and reformed by, political and technocratic leaders. While these leaders are undoubtedly subject to a wide range of pressures, and may eventually be forced to retract unpopular policies, such policies are, in the first instance, products of the state as shaper and formulator of policy. Frequently, it is only after the announcement and attempted implementation of such policies that the constraints on state autonomy come into play. State action on land reform, by contrast, has often occurred only in response to considerable civilian agitation, outright insurrection, or perceptions of a threat thereof.[12]

The distinction ought not be overdrawn, however. The literatures on both economic structural adjustment and redistributive reform have been properly concerned with the autonomy and capacity of the state qua state to influence and implement policy reform (Evans 1992; Haggard and Kaufman 1989; id. 1992b; Kohli 1987; Nelson 1984; id. 1990; Rondinelli 1979). The distinction is rather one of degree, with intermediate interest groups having a relatively greater role in defining state autonomy in the agrarian-reform context. Thus, in considering such reform, the interest extends beyond the state and political elites to focus

on the characteristics of social organizations and the peasant population that facilitate or hinder the politically volatile reform process.

The continued saliency of organizational affiliation and cultural identities that are constructed as "primordial"—ethnicity, religion, or linguistics—confirms the aptness of an intermediate, interest-group/ social organization focus.[13] These social variables have demonstrated a continuing relevance as determinants of individual political participation, confounding the expectations of earlier political science literature, which suggested that socioeconomic status was the principal determinant of political participation, and that other bases for participation would fade as modernization progressed (Lipset [1960] 1981: 238–70). The religious and tribal-based regional autonomy initiatives in the Philippines, while perhaps not as sensational as the ethnic-related strife convulsing parts of Africa, eastern Europe, and the former Soviet Union, are nonetheless equally at odds with analysis that reduces conflict to class.

In summary, an approach that simultaneously addresses state and societal variables is warranted because: (1) the state-building process in the Third World is ongoing, with continuing contestation over state and societal roles in defining the rules that are to guide society; (2) the very nature of land-reform programs entails intimate state interaction with social constituencies; (3) narrow interest groups and organizational affiliation persist as an important basis of individual political participation; and (4) it facilitates a more holistic examination of questions often treated as separate state-oriented and peasant-oriented research issues.

In adopting a state-society approach, I do not wish to overemphasize a strong state–weak state dichotomy. The dichotomy is not always a useful one; states are relatively strong in some policy and geographic arenas, relatively weak in others. The better approach is to emphasize effective policymaking capacity at a given time, in a given policy domain. Similarly, state-society interaction is not universally a zero-sum struggle for power. However, in the context of agrarian reform in the Philippines, the clash between the state and the landowning segment of society has been *perceived* by many landowners and some reform activists to be a zero-sum game.

Finally, much of the analysis here will concentrate on state-societal relations at the national level, although I often illustrate key points with examples that reflect local-level politics, most notably the politics of the sugar economy of Negros Occidental. The special focus on "Sugarlandia" is warranted, not so much because the province is representa-

tive (for a number of purposes it is not), as because the sugar sector's history of exemption from reform suggests that it can offer important lessons about elite resistance to redistributive reform. Unfortunately, the prolonged, phased implementation of the new Philippine reform program limits our consideration of the dynamics of local implementation to the program's first five years.[14] The long-term dynamics may differ, possibly in important ways, from the dynamics of policy formulation and implementation addressed here.

Democracy and Development: A Cruel Choice?

In a classic essay, T. H. Marshall (1964) traced the centuries-long evolution of the formal rights of citizenship in Great Britain and argued that the expansion of civil and political rights made the preservation of economic inequalities more problematic. The expansion of democratic political "space" increased the opportunities for the disadvantaged to contest gross socioeconomic disparities. This theme is echoed in Seymour Martin Lipset's discussion of the "democratic class struggle," the conflict between leftist lower-class parties and conservative middle- and upper-class parties that typified Western democracies in the 1950s ([1960] 1981: 230–78). The power of the lower classes' political "voice" is evident in the many social programs and initiatives to reduce socioeconomic inequalities in these democracies. However, Marshall noted that there were "limits inherent in the egalitarian movement"; the sense of political belonging, of citizenship, among the lower classes appeared to impede challenges to economic inequality (1964: 117). To similar effect, Robert Jackman (1986) has argued that the institutional requisites of democratic class struggle are rarely met. In this view, democratic political institutions typically favor preservation of the status quo rather than minimization of socioeconomic inequalities.

The sorry history of democratic agrarian reform in the Philippines seemed to bear out the more skeptical view of democracy. This legacy lent credence to Marcos's claim, in partially justifying his imposition of martial law in 1972, that meaningful agrarian reform was not possible given elite domination of Philippine democracy (Marcos 1971: 96; id. 1985: 30). Marcos deemed agrarian reform his cornerstone program. On the first anniversary of martial law, he commented, "Land reform is the only gauge for the success or failure of the New Society. If land reform fails there is no New Society" (*Philippine Daily Express* 1973: 6). Poor performance in implementing the reform was hardly the only ill of the

Marcos regime, but Marcos's comment was prescient: the reform was a failure, so too his "New Society."

While the shortcomings of Marcos's own reform indicated that authoritarian rule was not a *sufficient* condition for effecting redistributive agrarian reform in the Philippines, the question remained whether authoritarian rule was nonetheless a *necessary* condition for such reform. At the time Marcos declared martial law, casual empiricism and a considerable body of scholarly literature suggested that authoritarianism was indeed necessary for redistributive reform. The most noted twentieth-century land reforms—those of Mexico, the former Soviet Union, the People's Republic of China, Japan, Taiwan, and South Korea—were either initiated in the wake of social revolution or in the presence of a dominant military force not tied to the landed elite. In his seminal work *Political Order in Changing Societies*, Samuel P. Huntington argued that centralization of power was a precondition to reform, saying "A basic incompatibility exists between parliaments and land reform" (Huntington 1968: 388). Hung-chao Tai reached much the same conclusion in his work on land reform. He viewed the concentration of political power associated with noncompetitive political systems as essential to preventing frustration of reforms by the landed class (1974: 469).

These conclusions paralleled analysis relating to the broader processes of economic development. The development literature of the 1960s and early 1970s posited a "cruel choice" between democratic governance (or political participation) and economic development (Apter 1965; Bhagwati 1966; Huntington and Nelson 1976; O'Donnell 1973). In Richard Lowenthal's words: "It is not a dilemma of absolutes . . . but a continuous line of alternatives where *every degree of increased freedom has to be paid for by some slowing down of development, every degree of acceleration by some loss of freedom*" (1976: 40; emphasis in original).

If the pursuit of general economic development seemed constrained by democratic politics, the possibility of successfully implementing a thorough agrarian reform under democratic auspices was all but dismissed in the conventional literature.[15] Still, Mark Kesselman has reminded us that while "strong governments may be better able than weak governments to create public interests; they are also, however, better able to *thwart* public interests" (1973: 152). The organizational outlook of the military inspired little optimism about the prospect of military regimes becoming forces for reform.[16] The outcomes of the major communist revolutions offered only decollectivization as a long-term agricultural arrangement, at least until China's essential decollec-

tivization in 1978 and the more recent privatization initiatives in parts of the former Soviet Union and eastern Europe. Collectivized agriculture is at odds with both the initial promises of the revolutionary leadership and the stated preferences of the overwhelming majority of peasant agriculturalists.

Beginning in the 1970s, there emerged growing criticisms of the supposed trade-offs between democracy and development and between development and social equity (Adelman and Morris 1973; Chenery et al. 1974). Efforts to compare economic growth under democratic and authoritarian regimes yielded weak, conflicting results (cf. Marsh 1979 and Weede 1983 with Dasgupta 1990 and Dick 1974). Political studies of macroeconomic stabilization programs also began to call into question the conventional wisdom that authoritarian regimes enjoyed a comparative advantage in imposing austerity measures (Haggard 1985; Remmer 1986; Sidell 1987).

Furthermore, Karen Remmer challenged the analytical underpinnings of these studies, maintaining that for some purposes, the exclusionary or inclusionary nature of a regime was more significant than its authoritarian or democratic trappings. In particular, in explaining regime performance on land reform, Remmer argued: "No exclusionary democracy in Latin America has ever administered a land reform program with a major redistributive impact. All significant land reforms have resulted from inclusionary rule, either of the competitive or noncompetitive variety."[17] Democracy per se may not be incompatible with redistributive reform, but exclusionary forms of nominally democratic governance appear to be.

Even if established democracies are capable of promoting economic development and redistributive reform, Stephan Haggard and Robert Kaufman raise concerns about the sequencing of economic and political liberalization in previously authoritarian polities. In particular, they argue that simultaneous pursuit of economic and political reform is difficult and likely to lead to instability (1992a: 336–38). Groups harmed by the economic reforms are not placated by new political opportunities; they frequently use the political space to protest their government's economic policies. By contrast, groups that stand to benefit from economic reform may be poorly organized and confront significant collective action problems in supporting the government (Haggard and Kaufman 1992b: 18–20). The tensions between economic and political reform are likely to be exacerbated in the case of explicitly redistributive policies like agrarian reform. Haggard and Kaufman expect most regimes

to respond to these tensions by adopting one of two strategies—"economic reform first" or "democracy first." In their view, the Philippine case is something of a hybrid—Marcos implemented some economic reforms before his ouster, but left significant economic and political problems for the Aquino government. At issue was the ability and willingness of the Aquino government to pursue economic and political reform simultaneously.

Democratic Redistributive Reform

Democratic institutions may no longer be seen as an inherent bar to agrarian reform or to economic growth or programs of economic reform. Still, there is continuing recognition that such institutional forms can constrain the range of policy choices and the pace of their implementation. Concerned with redistributive reform in a new democracy, this study identifies a number of the social conditions and the actions of the state and intermediate social organizations that facilitate or hinder agrarian reform. The themes I shall be developing are briefly outlined below.

The Aquino government's resort to the rhetoric and, to a limited extent, the substance, of reform was a response to a series of related factors: a history of tenure-related peasant grievances and a stagnant agricultural sector; the developmental ideologies of Philippine intellectuals; political legitimacy concerns and the related desire to incorporate the rural poor into political life; and international pressures.[18]

Analyses of agrarian reform in other settings suggest that sustained, forceful leadership from a disciplined, reform-oriented political party and continual pressure from a highly mobilized peasantry are essential for accomplishing democratic redistributive reform (Herring 1983; Huntington 1968; Kohli 1987). Party ideology and the dictates of regime legitimacy sustain the commitment to reform, while disciplined organization makes it possible to cope with the pressures both of opposition and for more radical measures. Such parties are more likely to promote or accommodate the widespread organization and mobilization of the peasantry that is essential to ensure that the needs and aspirations of the rural poor command national attention, and that reform programs are effectively implemented (Grindle 1986: 9; Huntington 1968: 394). In late-developing countries like the Philippines, however, the combination of a center-left party backed by a powerful, disciplined labor or peasant movement is often problematic. Organized labor may be too

small to exert serious political influence, and the peasantry, although numerically significant, must overcome the repression of authoritarian rule and substantial collective action problems. Furthermore, the military and private sector groups, particularly the landed elite, are likely to oppose center-left parties and their reformist agenda (Haggard and Kaufman 1992a: 346–48).

I am necessarily, then, concerned with the nature of Philippine political parties and their utility as vehicles of reform. Political parties in the Philippines date from the introduction of elections under American colonial rule in the early part of the twentieth century. Historically, the major parties have been weak and personality-based. To the extent that there were any evolutionary tendencies toward stronger, ideologically oriented party politics in the Philippines, these tendencies were abruptly halted by the authoritarian rule of Ferdinand Marcos, particularly in the years 1972–83. By 1986, however, the stage appeared set for the successful emergence of a reformist, left-of-center party in the Philippines.

Experience in other countries indicated that left-of-center parties could succeed in settings marked by widespread disruption of existing agrarian patterns, resulting radicalism, and the absence of political alternatives (Herring 1990: 54). Historically, commercialization of Philippine agriculture and colonial land policies had created significant disruptions in existing production and landowner-tenant or laborer relations. At various times foreign demand precipitated the introduction or marked expansion of tobacco, abaca (hemp), sugar, coconut, and, more recently, banana and prawn production. Commercialization also led to the concentration of land ownership and absentee ownership. In the 1960s and 1970s increasing population and declining availability of new land exacerbated agrarian relations, turning the "terms of trade" further against tenants and laborers. Finally, sharp downturns in sugar and coconut prices, coupled with the abuses of "crony" marketing monopolies, devastated these segments of Philippine agriculture in the late 1970s and early 1980s. Tenant and landless laborer cultivators bore the brunt of this economic decline as unemployment soared and wages plummeted.[19]

A high incidence of landlessness, extreme inequality in landownership, underemployment, and poverty established the conditions for agrarian unrest. When the Marcos regime failed to act upon these grievances, a political niche opened up for the Communist Party of the Philippines (CPP) and its armed affiliate, the New People's Army (NPA), as

well as for various left-of-center peasant organizations, to make credible, reform-based appeals to voters. The rapid expansion of the CPP/NPA in the late 1970s and early 1980s demonstrated that geographic and cultural barriers to collective action among a differentiated Philippine peasantry could be surmounted. The success of the CPP/NPA also gave new impetus to the democratic opposition and heightened the urgency accorded to the ouster of the Marcos regime and the introduction of meaningful agrarian reform.

By 1986, the Philippine situation appeared opportune for the emergence of a left-of-center political party, and with it a significant program of redistributive agrarian reform. However, the 1987 Constitution set important boundaries on redistributive reform. Moreover, democratic grassroots organizational activities were still in their infancy, a legacy of the years of martial law. At the same time, a substantial violent left had opted out of the ongoing political process. With liberal and radical democratic challenges limited, the legislative elections of May 1987 confirmed the reemergence of a democracy typified by weak parties, politics based on personality rather than ideology, and rural electoral dominance by traditional elites (McCoy 1991). The question remained of whether redistributive reform might nonetheless be possible in the absence of a disciplined, reform-oriented party. Could a popular president, for example, or mobilized and militant peasant organizations, supply the requisite political impetus for reform? The issue was all the more salient because a significant, albeit new, confederation of people's organizations and nongovernmental organizations (NGOs) had emerged in the Philippines. Could it serve as an alternative to political parties at the national level? Even if successful in initiating reform at the national level, would such an arrangement prove too anarchic at the local level?

The Philippine case suggests that where existing parties are weak and nonideological, well-organized labor and peasant groups can create a domestic environment in which reform takes on greater political urgency. However, these social organizations appear incapable of effectuating comprehensive redistributive reform in a hostile political environment. Many of the same social conditions that limit the development of effective parties—dependency relations embodied in patron-client networks, powerful regional elites, private landowner armies, and crosscutting social cleavages that constrain solidarity along class lines—similarly hinder the emergence of mass-based social organizations. However, some cultural traditions and norms have potentially revolutionary connotations. For instance, folk Catholicism, although

traditionally a conservative force, has nurtured a millennial undercurrent that has repeatedly facilitated the organization of peasant protest movements and rebellions in the Philippines (Ileto 1979).

Sustained commitment and leadership from a political elite that enjoys relative autonomy from socioeconomic elites appears to be a sine qua non of effective reform. Furthermore, although their role is more often emphasized with regard to implementation, cadres of skilled and committed administrators and technocrats are also important to the formulation of effective reform policy.[20]

Agrarian Reform in the Post-Marcos Era: A Summary

The advent of the government of Corazon Cojuangco Aquino, following the People Power Revolution of February 1986, was accompanied by heightened rural expectations of comprehensive agrarian reform in the Philippines. More than two years passed before a new reform law was enacted—a law that reflected the successive deliberations of the Constitutional Commission, the cabinet, and the Congress. Although the Aquino government initially touted agrarian reform as the "centerpiece" of its development program, the new law is very circumscribed in its potential redistributive impact. At the time of its passage, critics argued that most of the reform could have been accomplished under a combination of previous legislation, bank foreclosures, and voluntary land transfers.[21] Implementation experience in the program's first five years (1988–93) confirms these criticisms—the reform has primarily involved lands subject to redistribution under Marcos-era reform legislation or public lands. Nonetheless, the Aquino and Ramos governments have substantially exceeded the reform accomplishments of prior Philippine governments. Their success stands in particular contrast to the poor performance of Marcos's authoritarian regime. The willingness and ability of the Ramos regime to implement the more controversial elements of the reform program remains in doubt, however.

The shortcomings of the new reform legislation and the failure to implement its more controversial elements reflect a broader legacy of the presidencies of Corazon Aquino and Fidel Ramos—namely, a failure of political institutionalization and incorporation from the top and the frustration of democratic political mobilization from the bottom. In the end, the events of February 1986 ushered in a political restoration, rather than a revolution, a return to a brand of democratic governance characterized by weak parties, factionalism based primarily on person-

alities rather than ideology, and the dominance of traditional regional elites.[22] What was "new" augured not at all well for peaceful democratic rule. On the one hand, important elements of the military have resisted a return to the less political role of the pre-martial law era; on the other, a substantial, nationwide insurgent movement continues to threaten the Philippine state. In important ways, the reform outcome also reflects the distinctive cultural heritage of the Philippines, a fusion of pre-Hispanic social traditions and the political and economic legacies of Spanish and American colonialism. The more immediate legacy of the Marcos regime likewise influenced the reform process, particularly through its destructive impact on the development of democratic political and social organizations.

Experience with agrarian reform under the Aquino and Ramos governments suggests that nonrevolutionary processes of regime transition and political liberalization may increase government responsiveness to reformist pressures, but are unlikely, in and of themselves, to foster significant redistributive reform. Where the regime transition does not materially alter the political influence of national or regional economic elites, democratizing the electoral process holds little promise of concurrent redistribution of wealth within the society. The obstacles confronting proponents of agrarian reform are particularly acute in settings such as the Philippines, where democratic institutions are superimposed on historic and continuing patterns of fragmented social control and considerable economic inequality.

2

History, Culture, and Philippine Politics

Corazon Aquino is not the first Philippine head of state to confront increasing landlessness, poor agricultural performance, and land tenure–related civil unrest. These are recurrent themes in Philippine history. To understand current constructions of democracy and agrarian reform in the Philippines, we need an overview of colonial and postindependence politics. Of interest are patterns of social organization and control that originated with the expansion of world capitalism and the establishment, under colonial auspices, of the Philippine nation-state.

The transformation of Philippine society occasioned by colonial policies and the penetration of the world market economy, particularly in the late nineteenth and early twentieth centuries, had a lasting impact on Philippine cultural traditions and the nature of state-society relations. Spanish, and later U.S., colonial policies dramatically recast land-tenure patterns. With the commercialization of agriculture came important changes in social mores and institutions, peasant survival strategies, and the strengthening of regional economic elites. The mode of colonial rule—indirect rule through collaborating elites—had equally important implications for elite-mass social relations and for patterns of social control. Although there is continuing fluidity in the composition of the Philippine elite, many of the leading families first prospered under Spanish colonial rule and then consolidated their economic and political power under American colonial rule. While governmental authority was formally concentrated in Manila, local caciques strengthened their influence over local, if not national, behavior, constraining the power of the state.

Philippine peasants have responded to the varying impacts of commercialization and Spanish, American, and Japanese rule with episodic

rebellions, in addition to "everyday forms of peasant resistance."[1] This legacy and its cultural underpinnings are important to our understanding of present-day peasant activism and the role peasant-based organizations have played, and can play, in advancing redistributive reform in the Philippines. One theme that runs through much of the analysis is the existence and persistence of powerful, crosscutting class and group cleavages in Philippine society. These cleavages make national reform of any sort problematic. One concern of this analysis, then, is the salience of various identities and cleavages in explaining the outcome of reform under the Aquino and Ramos regimes.

Philippine National Identity

Philippine history is not characterized by a dominant or unifying cultural tradition of the type found in other Southeast Asian or East Asian countries.[2] Since the fourteenth century, the Philippine people have felt the successive influence of Islamic, Spanish, American, and Japanese cultures. One consequence is the continuing search for a Philippine national identity, reflected both in scholarly work and in the nationalist appeals of a series of Philippine social and political movements.[3] In recent decades, Philippine historians have reexamined their national history, rejected the dominant paradigms of colonial scholarship, and given new emphasis, for example, to the role of the working class in the struggle for independence, and the harmful influence uncritical acceptance of an alien language and values has had on Filipino identity.[4]

Nationalism was a prominent theme in the fight for independence from Spain, in the resistance to American intervention and conquest, in the rise of the Nacionalista Party during the commonwealth period, in resistance to the Japanese occupation during World War II, and, most recently, in the armed struggle of the Communist Party of the Philippines/New People's Army (CPP/NPA). Yet even as Filipinos have sought a national identity, there have been important centrifugal forces—regional, linguistic, and religious—at work.

Spanish Colonial Rule

The Spaniards defined the Philippine nation geographically and introduced a centralized political and administrative system.[5] In the absence of a language common to the entire archipelago, Spanish clerics

translated the Christian doctrine into the various local vernaculars, thereby preserving, albeit with changes, the myriad indigenous languages.[6] In turn, Philippine ethnolinguistic identities have persisted, competing with a national identity.

Although Spanish rule had vast cultural implications, for our purposes, its most important impacts were on the locus of social control and patterns of Philippine land tenure. As the most remote of the Spanish colonies, and in the absence of obvious mineral or other treasured resources, the principal roles of the Philippines in the Hispanic colonial order were as a transshipment point for the galleon trade between Mexico and China and as a military outpost. Apart from Catholic missionaries, few Spaniards settled in the Philippines, and those who did were prohibited from residing outside of Manila until 1768. For much of the Spanish period, there was no appreciable colonial development of domestic industries or agricultural resources. Nonetheless, the Spaniards were to have a profound influence on the evolution of land-tenure patterns.

Political Organization Under Spanish Rule

The Spaniards sought to minimize the administrative costs of colonial governance in the Philippines, Spain's most distant and poorly endowed colony. Colonial rule outside of Manila was founded on a limited bureaucracy, Catholic missionaries, a native constabulary, and the collaboration of traditional *datus* (village chiefs).[7] In the position of precolonial *datu*, we see the historical origins of leadership tied to reciprocity and indebtedness. The *datu* was the "one most capable of securing the surplus with which to engage in a series of reciprocal exchanges with others in the community" (Rafael 1988: 139). Other villagers evidenced their deference to the *datu* through various behavior, including contributing labor for cultivation, ritual, or military activities (Scott 1982: 103). For colonial convenience, the *datus* were accorded appreciably greater political status than had been their traditional right.[8] With Spanish rule, the village social system was resituated in a complex bureaucracy, the authority of which was premised on royal and, in turn, divine patronage.[9]

As part of the *encomienda* system—an arrangement whereby individual Spaniards were granted administrative jurisdiction over specified regions—the *datus* (renamed *cabezas de barangay*, or, more generically, caciques) were made responsible for local collection of the tribute, organization of conscript labor, and administration of justice. *Encomenderos*

and caciques frequently abused these powers for purposes of personal gain, in turn occasioning continual peasant resistance and periodic peasant rebellion. These abuses were at odds with the idealized Spanish ideology of domination,[10] providing a basis for peasant radicalism linked to criticism of that ideology in its own terms.[11] For their part, the colonial and local authorities repeatedly turned to the military for enforcement of the objectionable practices. In the absence of a large Spanish military force, these "police" actions were conducted by local constabularies consisting of native mercenaries from other regions of the country. This hiring practice both reflected and reinforced regional identities at the expense of national or class identities.

The Emergence of Regional Power Centers

Although Spanish rule was administratively centralized, the members of the various religious orders enjoyed considerable de facto autonomy at the village (*barangay*) level, autonomy that increased with time. Until late in the Spanish colonial era, the parish priest was the sole Spaniard in more than half the Philippine villages, the only representative of colonial authority. Where present, the priest became "judge, mentor, landlord, and symbol of foreign power" (Steinberg 1986: 42; see also, Roth 1977; Abueva 1988). At the same time, local elites, whose power increasingly became a function of personal landownership, were able to consolidate their influence at the local and provincial levels (Wolters [1983] 1984: 11–12).

In the Philippines, the regionalized pattern of growth in intra-Asian trade in the late eighteenth century and the explosion in trade with European and American markets in the mid nineteenth century unleashed powerful centrifugal forces, which have fostered fragmented social control and reinforced regional identities at the expense of a strong national identity (McCoy 1982a: 8). Anglo-American trading concerns, rather than the Spanish colonial regime, dominated the development of the Philippine export economy. With the opening of provincial ports to foreign trade after 1855, the Anglo-American trading houses were able to establish direct links with different parts of the archipelago, emphasizing distinct regional crops, and working with a variety of region-specific production systems.[12]

Geography, colonial policy, and the particular nature of commercialization of Philippine agriculture thus assured continued fragmentation of social control. This social organization limited, but did not eliminate, the possibilities for concerted rebellion against the colonial power and

hindered the emergence of Philippine nationalism.[13] Furthermore, it played a prominent role in the undoing of the national revolution (1896–1902). Most important for our current analysis, this regional fragmentation of social control has frustrated the development of a centralized state organization capable of effecting nationwide redistributive reform.[14]

In assessing the present-day capabilities of Third World states, Migdal highlights the role of colonial powers in shaping contrasting patterns of social control:

> Of all the distinctions in the local population these policies fostered, one stands out in its long-term effect on state-society relations. Colonizing rulers could either give preferential access to resources to many local indigenous leaders, each of whom could establish social control in only a circumscribed part of the society, or the foreigners could support those in a position to create central, countrywide institutions capable of forming an eventual, centralized state. (Migdal 1988: 105)

In the Philippine case, we would want to modify the thesis slightly, according greater recognition to international forces and powers distinct from the colonial power. The patterns of economic development and resulting social control that emerged in the nineteenth-century Philippines were arguably more reflective of the influence of Anglo-American trading concerns, and the relative weakness of the central colonial (Spanish) government, than of purposive action by the colonial power.

The Historical Development of Negros Occidental

As part of the regional specialization in agriculture, the province of Negros Occidental became the focus of Philippine sugarcane production. Located 300 kilometers south of Manila, Negros is in the center of the Philippine archipelago. Technological innovations—the introduction of foreign sugarcane varieties and furnaces fueled by *bagasse* (waste cane)—and foreign-financed sugar-mill construction led to the rapid expansion of sugarcane production in Negros Occidental beginning in the mid nineteenth century (McCoy 1982b). In the 1920s, the American colonial government facilitated significant further expansion of Negros sugar production by financing the construction of six centrifugal mills (centrals) through the Philippine National Bank. The provinces of Negros Occidental and Oriental have generally accounted for over two-thirds of Philippine sugarcane production. Sugar exports, primarily to

the United States, supplied roughly 20 percent of Philippine foreign exchange earnings in the 1960s and 1970s (Hayami et al. 1990: 108–9).

Expansion of sugarcane production in Negros was marked by extreme concentration of landownership. Spanish barriers to foreign capital—restrictions on Protestant landownership, inter-island migration, and inter-island travel by foreigners—prompted reliance on part-Chinese mestizos as brokers between European commercial interests and sugar planters. In turn, these mestizos came to dominate the sugar industry in Negros (Wickberg 1964). Sugar production was organized around haciendas employing hired labor.

American Colonial Rule

Three hundred years of Spanish colonial rule ended with the Philippine war of independence in 1896. Philippine independence was no sooner proclaimed than it was lost to the United States—a casualty of the Spanish-American War. The American colonial era saw little change in the patterns of elite-dominated politics in the Philippines (Friend 1965: 20; Karnow 1989: 196–256). American colonial administrators repeatedly acknowledged the poverty and social, political, and economic inequities attendant on the prevailing patterns of landownership and distribution of wealth. Yet they concentrated on less controversial education, public health, and infrastructure programs rather than on fundamental societal reform.

As had their Spanish predecessors, U.S. colonial administrators (1898–1946) relied upon the Filipino landowning elite and their clientelist networks for social control. The contest for relative power continued between Manila and the localities. U.S. introduction of periodic elections facilitated elite penetration of the state by creating a wide range of elective offices at the local and provincial levels. In capturing these offices, the Philippine elites founded many of the political dynasties that dominate present-day politics. The clientelist networks of the landowning elite became the foundation for national political alliances. The sugar bloc was particularly effective in utilizing its considerable economic resources to build patron-client networks and exercise regional and national political power. Many of the bloc's most prominent figures were from Negros Occidental (Lopez-Gonzaga 1989: 78–87). The power of the provincial landowning elite thus continued to frustrate efforts to develop a strong central state. As Willem Wolters notes, "The classic state monopolies known from European history, namely those over

violence and taxation, have never been fully developed in the Philippines" ([1983] 1984: 3).

The stage was thus set for a postindependence Philippine "democracy" in which the vast majority of the population exerted little influence, and from which they derived little benefit. "Electoral campaigns were not mass appeals to voters nor forums for the discussion of societal issues, but negotiations between provincial elites and national political personalities" (Tancangco 1988: 89). In the period 1907–41, Philippine politics in general, and the independence movement in particular, was dominated by the Nacionalista Party, whose members and leaders came from the wealthiest Philippine families.[15] The only calls for agrarian reform emanated from a few radical parties, which were small, underfunded, and operative only in parts of Luzon. In voting, tenants and landless laborers—dependent and new to politics—typically followed the lead of their landlord or patron.

At the same time, the 1938 union of the Socialist Party and the Partido Komunista ng Pilipinas (PKP = Communist Party), under the PKP banner, provided a vehicle for mobilizing a portion of the disgruntled peasantry in Central Luzon.[16] They helped inspire strikes and the Sakdal uprisings in the later years of American rule. These were the precursors to the Huk rebellion of the 1940s and 1950s (Abueva 1988: 42; Pomeroy 1978).

Wartime Occupation and Collaboration

Japanese occupation of the Philippines during World War II brought the issue of elite collaboration with foreign powers into sharp relief. Confronting the dilemma of collaboration with the Japanese or resistance in the name of the Philippine Commonwealth and its colonial ruler, the United States, many members of the Philippine elite opted for collaboration. Among the most prominent collaborators were José Laurel, Sr., and Benigno Aquino, Sr.[17] Wartime profiteering afforded substantial gains to some of the nation's foremost families.[18]

At the war's end, the machinations of General Douglas MacArthur, and President Harry Truman's initial inattention to the collaboration issue and subsequent deference to MacArthur, effectively undermined President Sergio Osmeña's limited resolve and capacity to mete out punishment to wartime collaborators. David Steinberg argues that Filipinos decided against punishment of collaborationists out of concern that thus purging the elite would "decapitate" the society at a time of

extreme destruction and social disruption. This decision was, however, a product of Philippine elite and U.S. policy; the Philippine masses had no voice in the matter (Steinberg 1967: 108–11, 141–42). Four decades later, the Aquino government's treatment of former Marcos loyalists and rebellious military officers would sound a variant on this theme of nonpunishment for the supposed sake of national unity.

Collaboration with the Japanese struck at then-prevailing perceptions of Philippine national identity, an identity closely tied to the United States. Elite collaboration thus called into question the legitimacy of elite political dominance. In their grievances against collaborators, peasants received some support from elements of the Philippine elite and, for a time, from official U.S. policy.[19] The issue of past and present collaboration with foreign powers, and the benefits that have thereby accrued to the Philippine elite, are thus another basis for the gulf between elite and mass in Philippine society.

Philippine Politics, 1946–1972

David Wurfel argues that Philippine governance in the period 1946–72 is most appropriately termed "constitutional," rather than "democratic." This terminology emphasizes the preoccupation of the Philippine political elite with legal processes rather than with widespread sharing of power.[20] Reflecting their common origin, there was little of either substance, composition, or constituencies to distinguish the two leading parties, the Nacionalista Party (NP) and the Liberal Party (LP). Each party was built primarily upon vertically linked patron-client networks. Party-switching was frequent as national, provincial and local leaders (and their coteries) sought advantage in access to government resources. Indeed, both Ramon Magsaysay and Ferdinand Marcos switched parties shortly before their respective nominations and elections to the presidency. The parties were noted more for their personalities than for ideological or issue orientation. Elections were typically marred by violence and fraud.[21]

Martial Law

President Ferdinand Marcos halted the evolution of Philippine democracy with his declaration of martial law on September 23, 1972.[22] Martial law was justified by Marcos as a response to several factors, including widespread lawlessness, much of it the work of local armies

and "goons" employed by politicians and landowners; the incompetence and corruption of Philippine democracy; and the threats posed by two incipient rebellions—those of the communist New People's Army (NPA) and of the Muslim separationist Moro National Liberation Front (MNLF). Marcos also justified martial law as a means of breaking the landed elite's grip on Philippine politics and effectuating redistributive reform.

Conventional history has it that most Filipinos either welcomed, or reserved judgment on, Marcos's announcement of martial law (Bonner 1988: 121–23; Landé 1987a: 10; Noble 1986: 86–88). Overt opposition to martial law was minimal, an unsurprising circumstance given the immediate arrests of thousands of oppositionists. Yet in explaining the absence of opposition, analysts typically point as well to Filipino disenchantment with democratic institutions. In summarizing the international reaction to martial law, William Overholt also captures much of the conventional depiction of Filipino reaction: "To many, the Philippines seemed to be jettisoning its democratic baggage of patronage, corruption, incompetent administration, crime, and inequality and following the lead of more economically and socially successful neighbors" (1987: 92). In this view, what the Philippines needed was something along the lines of what was to be found in Singapore, South Korea, or Taiwan—strong, decisive centralized leadership coupled with a cadre of competent and autonomous technocrats. Together they could restore law and order, initiate an export-oriented strategy of economic growth, and address social justice concerns through redistributive reform. Marcos promised all of this in announcing martial law and his plans for a "New Society."

A Politicized Military, Plebiscites, and Elite Influence

What the Filipinos got from martial law was far different from what Marcos had promised. There were some initial improvements in the law-and-order situation and several years of impressive economic growth, fueled by massive foreign borrowing, and with little positive impact on the poor. Thereafter, the promise of martial law, such as it was, gave way to a reality of human rights abuses, corruption, and economic mismanagement. With few restraints on Marcos's power, his family and their cronies gave free rein to their avarice, bankrupting the country in the process. Cronies profited from state monopolies, state enterprises, and preferential loans and contracts and benefited from tax and tariff exemptions or exclusive import privileges and from state interventions in food marketing, the fertilizer industry, and labor ex-

ports. When crony enterprises proved nonviable in the early 1980s, the state provided substantial loans and equity infusions (Haggard 1988: 101). In other cases, crony businesses—notably in mining and manufacturing—failed and were acquired by the state-owned banking sector, which in turn drew upon government grants and public-sector loans to avert collapse (Hill 1988: 278). To paraphrase Robert Dahl, a strategy of centralization initially justified as a means of reducing inequalities instead facilitated the emergence of a new privileged ruling elite (1978: 203).

In centralizing authority, Marcos further politicized the military.[23] Everything from promotions to troop deployments reflected Marcos's political interests. Loyalty replaced merit as the basis for promotion. Equally important, the roles of the Presidential Security Command and of the National Intelligence and Security Agency were dramatically increased. These forces became a privileged elite within the Philippine military,[24] and along with elements of the Philippine Constabulary, the Integrated National Police, and the army, they constituted an extraordinary concentration of security personnel in and around Manila. Moreover, this concentration came at a time of serious military conflicts, first with the MNLF in Mindanao and Sulu, and later with the NPA throughout the country.

Both trends—loyalty-based promotions and enhancement of the intelligence/Manila security apparatus—came at the expense of sound military strategy and adequate field support. Junior officers dissatisfied with this state of affairs formed the Reform the Armed Forces Movement (RAM) in 1981–82, which catalyzed Marcos's downfall with a preemptive military rebellion in February 1986. This evolution has important parallels to a phenomenon Alfred Stepan (1988) has described in the Latin American context: military reactions to the growing influence of intelligence services leading to the formation of military-civilian alliances, and ultimately precipitating transitions to democratic rule.

To further centralize political control, Marcos also arrogated to himself the power of appointment of provincial and local officials and of judges in the lower courts.[25] The two-party system that had dominated Philippine politics in the postwar era was abolished, with a complete ban on political parties in effect until 1978. After an initial suspension of all media operations, the martial regime permitted most to resume operation under conditions of tight control. With time, self-censorship replaced overt censorship of the media. Concurrently, the once independent and respected judiciary was made subservient to Marcos.

Marcos did, however, find it necessary to create the trappings of

popular legitimacy, scheduling a series of plebiscites and referenda to approve his new constitution and the continuation of martial law. His was a rule of "constitutional authoritarianism."[26] In February 1978, he formed his own party, the Kilusang Bagong Lipunan (KBL = New Society Movement). This party was little more than a vehicle for patronage-based disbursement of government resources. Again regional and local politicos demonstrated their ability to survive the vicissitudes of political dominance from Manila. Many provincial and municipal KBL party functionaries were traditional politicians, members of the very class vilified by Marcos when he established his "New Society."[27]

For all their harshness in particular instances, Marcos's efforts to supplant the traditional Philippine elite were largely ineffectual. To be certain, many prominent opposition leaders were arrested or fled to exile. At the same time, a number of elite families were summarily dispossessed of their economic assets.[28] However, much of the traditional Philippine elite, if somewhat weakened politically, took advantage of Marcos's economic policies to expand their operations,[29] often at the expense of small entrepreneurs, the middle class, and labor.[30] They also benefited from a variety of corporate incentives and exemptions, which eroded the state's already modest corporate tax base. There was considerable interpenetration of industrial and agricultural elites, with many families branching out into industry from their traditional agricultural bases. Publicly at least, only as the devastating consequences of Marcos's greed and economic mismanagement hit home in the early 1980s did much of the Philippine elite join the anti-Marcos forces.

For its part, the middle class lost political power and found economic opportunities limited or closed off to it. One response, facilitated by changes in U.S. policies, was a substantial immigration of middle-class Filipinos to the United States. This immigration vented some of the middle-class frustrations that might otherwise have taken earlier form as centrist pressures for the restoration of democratic rights and the termination of "crony capitalism."

The Demise of the Marcos Regime

The assassination of Marcos's principal political rival, Benigno "Ninoy" Aquino, Jr., in August 1983, prompted the voicing of long-overdue domestic and foreign concerns about the Marcos government and the Philippine economy.[31] The assassination signaled the traditional Philippine elite that no opponent of the Marcos regime was safe

and crystallized the democratic opposition, sparking open political activism among business leaders and professionals and massive anti-Marcos demonstrations in Manila's financial district. Regardless of the realities of his life, in death Ninoy Aquino assumed the stature of a saintlike martyr, not unlike the late-nineteenth-century Philippine nationalist José Rizal. Politics and religion fused in the campaign of Ninoy's grieving widow, Corazon Cojuangco Aquino. "Catholic masses became occasions for rousing political sermons, and Aquino rallies opportunities for partisan benedictions."[32]

The political uncertainty and belated reaction against crony capitalism prompted curtailment of international lending after 1984. Capital flight, a problem even before Ninoy's death, increased markedly thereafter. As Carl Landé notes, these two weapons of resistance—capital flight and communication of doubts concerning the competence and viability of the regime to foreign lenders—were largely beyond Marcos's control (Landé 1986: 118). Predicated as it was on the dispensation of enormous patronage resources, increasingly borrowed from abroad, the regime could ill afford this curtailment of international lending and the flight of domestic capital. Two and a half years later, Marcos was ousted by a coalition headed by Corazon Aquino.

Political Opposition to the Marcos Regime

Important cleavages within the Philippine elite had emerged even before the Aquino assassination. David Wurfel identifies four important divisions: those between the traditional economic elite and Marcos cronies competing for economic dominance and access to state resources; between economic nationalists and Philippine entrepreneurs linked to overseas firms contesting trade policies and the role of the international financial community; between civilian bureaucrats and the military competing for increasingly scarce budgetary resources; and, within the military, between Marcos loyalists and Philippine Military Academy graduates contesting promotions based on loyalty rather than merit (Wurfel 1988: 237–40). The industrialist Jaime Ongpin and the Makati Business Club, founded by Enrique Zobel in 1981, were at the forefront of private-sector opposition to the Marcos regime. Prominent sugar *hacenderos* felt particularly betrayed by Marcos: having contributed to his electoral success, they were increasingly disenchanted with his sugar-marketing monopoly and resentful of the growing influence and land grabbing of his cronies (Lopez-Gonzaga 1989: 80–87).

The divisions within the elite and Marcos's halting liberalization of

Philippine political life in the 1980s afforded new opportunities for political and class-based organization. Reflecting Philippine organizational penchants, the groups were many and ever-changing, although since Philippine politics is dominated by personalities, the leading figures remained much the same.[33] The legal opposition to Marcos can roughly be categorized by ideological type as conservative reformist, social or liberal democrat, and national democrat or militant progressive (Landé 1986: 124–25, citing Fr. Jose Drizon). Lakas ng Bayan (Strength of the Nation, or LABAN ["Fight"]), which later merged with the Partido Demokratikong Pilipino (PDP = Philippine Democratic Party) to form PDP-LABAN, and the United Democratic Opposition, later the United Nationalist Democratic Organization (UNIDO), are best characterized as conservative reformist. Ninoy Aquino figured prominently in both the LABAN and UNIDO organizations, from his prison cell in the first instance, from exile in the United States in the second. Salvador Laurel, after cooperating with Marcos until the late 1970s, emerged as the leading UNIDO figure, using this party base to become Corazon Aquino's (oppositionist) vice president. Although PDP-LABAN and UNIDO were both national organizations, they reflected the Philippine pattern of regional or local power centers. PDP-LABAN's principal support was to be found in Mindanao and parts of Manila and Cebu. UNIDO was most influential in the Batangas and Bicol regions (Clad 1986).

Although they shared many of the nationalist and social aims of the revolutionary left, social democrats pursued their agenda through peaceful reform. Organized in February 1982, the Pilipino Democratic Party (PDP) was the principal political vehicle for social democrats in the later years of the Marcos regime. Social democrats were also prominent in the "Justice for Aquino, Justice for All" movement (JAJA), a coalition formed after Ninoy's assassination. JAJA was headed by a former senator, Lorenzo Tañada, with active leadership provided by Jose Diokno, another former senator and the country's foremost human rights lawyer. This group coordinated many of the anti-Marcos demonstrations in late 1983. JAJA was gradually replaced by another umbrella organization, the Coalition of Organizations for the Restoration of Democracy (CORD), which was led by Agapito "Butz" Aquino, Ninoy's brother, and coordinated most of the rallies and educational seminars associated with the largely unsuccessful campaign to boycott the 1984 legislative elections.

Lorenzo Tañada also chaired the Nationalist Alliance for Justice, Freedom and Democracy. Established in November 1983, the National-

ist Alliance was more nearly aligned with the National Democratic Front (NDF) of the CPP than had been the case with either JAJA or CORD. A major initiative was launched in mid 1985 to unite the communist and noncommunist left in the Bagong Alyansang Makabayan (New Nationalist Alliance = BAYAN), which subsumed the earlier Nationalist Alliance, taking Tañada for its president. BAYAN did succeed in uniting a number of mass organizations, but important figures in the political alliance—including "Butz" Aquino, Jose Diokno, and Jaime Ongpin—withdrew in the face of attempts by the NDF to dominate the BAYAN secretariat. Viewed by some as an instrument of the communists, BAYAN boycotted both the 1984 legislative elections and the 1986 presidential elections, arguing that no meaningful political or social change was possible through Marcos-dominated elections.

Although not a party, the Civil Liberties Union, under the leadership of Jose Diokno, played a leading role in the human rights struggle during the Marcos years. The CLU often tied the U.S. military bases in the Philippines to U.S. support of Marcos's authoritarian rule and called for the abrogation of the agreement on the bases. Diokno also headed the Kilusan sa Kapangyarihan at Karapatan ng Bayan (KAAKBAY = Movement for Philippine Democracy and Sovereignty), a party of independent Marxists.

Finally, the national democrats found expression in the National Democratic Front, the political front of the CPP/NPA. As described at length in Chapter 3, the CPP/NPA experienced tremendous growth in the early to mid 1980s.

The Catholic Church and Popular Organizations

By February 1983, the long-divided hierarchy of the Catholic Church had reached consensus, moving from "critical collaboration" with the Marcos regime to open criticism in the issuance of a joint pastoral letter, "A Dialogue for Peace." Part of the Church's disillusionment with Marcos was institutionally based: priests, nuns, and layworkers were increasingly being harassed, arrested, or killed for participation in Church-sponsored social action programs. One of the more notable initiatives was that of activist priests who had begun promoting Basic Christian Communities (BCCs) in the late 1970s. Initially a mechanism for worship among parishioners not readily reached by parish priests, these groups became potent vehicles for collective consciousness raising and self-help responses to local lawlessness and oppression (McCoy 1984b; O'Brien 1987).

In the broader social arena, the Church's criticism of the Marcos

regime reflected concern with increasing military abuses, fraudulent elections, and deteriorating socioeconomic conditions for the poor majority. A Task Force on Detainees sponsored by the Association of Major Religious Superiors had, since the early days of martial law, documented "salvagings" (extralegal executions) and the maltreatment of political prisoners. Elsewhere, priests became active in the struggles of upland tribal communities, of sugar workers, and of urban squatters. In several notable instances, priests joined the armed struggle of the NPA or the Cordillera People's Liberation Army.[34] Following the Aquino assassination, the Church-sponsored publication *Veritas* (Truth) marked the return of more critical print media. A Church-established radio network provided a valuable communication and monitoring link preceding and during the 1986 presidential election. Radio Veritas played a critical role in mobilizing "People Power" during the February 1986 "revolution."

These same years witnessed a proliferation and growth of "cause-oriented" organizations, some Church-affiliated or inspired, others independent, and still others linked to the National Democratic Front and the CPP/NPA. Among the more prominent organizations are GABRIELLA, an alliance of women's organizations; Kilusang Mayo Uno (KMU = May First Movement), a confederation of militant labor organizations; Kilusang Magbubukid ng Pilipinas (KMP = Peasant Movement of the Philippines), a militant peasant organization; and the National Federation of Sugar Workers (NFSW), an alliance of labor organizations in the sugar industry. These groups evidenced the potential for mass mobilization of the Philippine poor and the possibility of giving voice to the disadvantaged in a society where they had long been ignored. Yet most of these groups were still in their infancy when the Marcos regime collapsed. Their capacity to influence national politics was, as we shall see in the case of agrarian reform, still more promise than reality.

The Growth of the Philippine Military

In the postwar era, the Philippine state increased significantly in size. Most important, the Armed Forces of the Philippines grew from some 58,000 men in 1971 to roughly 113,000 in 1982. In 1982, paramilitary forces and reserves were estimated at 110,500 and 124,000 respectively, putting the total Philippine military forces for that year at about 347,000 men (Miranda 1985: 94–95). Beginning in the mid 1970s, there

was also a rapid buildup in the Civilian Home Defense Force (CHDF), particularly in areas of Muslim separatist activity.[35]

In the tradition of "civilian guards" of the 1940s and 1950s and the Barrio Self-Defense Units of the 1960s, the CHDF are local armed forces that serve as an inexpensive adjunct to the military in conducting counterinsurgency operations.[36] CHDF reservists included prominent landowners, businessmen, and government officials. Their participation in the CHDF legitimized their possession of weapons. Private security guards associated with the CHDF were generally employees of these same businessmen and landowners. The CHDF units thus often served as little more than private armies for local elites. The CHDF units were typically poorly trained, ill-disciplined, and heavily implicated in human rights abuses (LCHR 1988: 2).

The growth in the size of the Philippine military was a sign of the military's increasing influence within the Philippine state. Thus the military would strongly shape the democratic context in the post-Marcos era. Despite the restoration of democratic institutions in 1986, civilian control over the military remained unresolved throughout the Aquino era. The issues of military prerogatives and budget levels figured prominently in the military's relationship with President Aquino and in its repeated challenges to her authority. President Fidel Ramos, a former head of the armed forces, has evidenced greater ability to control the military.

Cultural Systems

The context for democracy and redistributive reform in the Philippines is a function, not only of the country's political evolution, but of the cultural systems that shape Philippine life. The issues of how people identify themselves, and for what purposes, are complex and not readily reducible to single dimensions such as class, ethnicity, or religion. Multiple, crosscutting identities—family, ethnic, region, religion, political party, patron-client, class—operate simultaneously, some changing over time. These identities constitute multiple claims on an individual's loyalty, just as they afford access to a variety of vantage points from which to interpret and respond to a changing economic, political, and social environment. These competing identities are the subject of constant negotiation, and some become more salient at times than others.[37] Moments of economic or political crisis can help select or foreground aspects of individual identities. The very existence of powerful, cross-

cutting class and group cleavages in Philippine society makes national reform problematic. The democratic class struggle presupposes that class is the most politically salient identity (Lipset [1960] 1981). Where it is not, strong, class-based political parties are unlikely to emerge to pursue fundamental redistributive reform.

Linguistic Cleavages

Cultural identifications based on regional origin, language, and ethnicity have long worked against development of a national identity and nationwide peasant action in the Philippines. Reflecting the country's archipelagic landbase, linguistic diversity in the Philippines is extreme, with some 80 languages and dialects in use in the archipelago. No single language is common to all Filipinos. Filipino, a revised form of Tagalog, is the national and most common language and is spoken by some 55 percent of the population. English remains the language of major businesses, the government, and secondary and higher education.[38]

Nationalist sentiment prompted constitutional recognition of Filipino as the national language in 1987. The Constitution further directed the government to initiate the use of Filipino as the medium of official communication and as the language of instruction in the educational system (Art. 14, Sec. 6). The University of the Philippines has already taken steps to introduce the use of Filipino in instruction. The use of Filipino as the medium of instruction at the elementary school level remains more complicated. The initial years of public schooling are typically conducted in the regional languages. As many rural children abandon schooling in the course of grades 1–4, they are largely beyond the reach of instruction in the national language and whatever national socialization is attendant thereto. Linguistic diversity is also an impediment to nationwide dissemination of information concerning peasant rights under various government programs, including agrarian reform.

The national print media are overwhelmingly English. Television is somewhat more varied in its linguistic choice: local dramas, variety shows, and news broadcasts are in Filipino; imported dramas, of which there are many, and at least one nightly news program per network, are broadcast in English. Radio broadcasts are also mixed linguistically, with somewhat greater use of Filipino than is true of television broadcasts.

Linguistic identity remains an important part of Philippine political life. A pre–martial law (1969) survey found dialect to be a much more significant determinant of voter behavior than party affiliation (Averch

et al. 1970, cited in Wurfel 1988: 27). Interprovincial migration, intermar-riage, and urbanization are argued to have reduced the importance of linguistic identity among Christian Filipinos, but regional/linguistic distinctions remain a common theme of Philippine political analysis (Wurfel 1988: 27).

A Clustering of Cultural Forms

Overlapping religious and linguistic cleavages—most notable in the cases of tribal populations and the Muslims of Sulu and Mindanao—are not the only instances in the Philippines in which cultural forms have tended to cluster. In the case of landowners and their tenants or farm-workers, for example, patrons and clients may both be fluent in the regional language, reinforcing other commonalities. However, the land-owner is more likely also to have mastered Filipino, English, or, in an earlier era, Spanish. Access to these other languages has been a signifi-cant advantage in economic and legal affairs. It also intensifies the social cleavage between landlords-cum-patrons and tenants-cum-clients.

Patron-client ties have typically reinforced and been reinforced by regional and religious identities. As a legacy of Spanish colonialism, landowners and their tenants or farmworkers have generally shared the Catholic faith. However, religious identities have recently become more complicated. With the Church's post–Vatican II commitment to social action, elements of the traditional socioeconomic elite have grown dis-enchanted with the Church. There appears to have been a surge in elite membership in evangelical Protestant denominations and the Church of Jesus Christ of Latter-Day Saints (Mormons).[39] If this trend continues, the rural Philippines may witness the emergence of class-based religi-osity, heightening elite-poor tensions, to the extent that religious groups address concerns for social justice.

While the development of nationwide class or group-based organi-zations may be hindered by linguistic and regional attachments, these cultural features appear to pose fewer constraints on—indeed, may encourage—the emergence of local or provincial-level social organiza-tions. The evolution of the Huk movement in Central Luzon in the 1930s to 1950s, of current national-level peasant organizations such as the Kilusang Magbubukid ng Pilipinas (KMP = Peasant Movement of the Philippines) and the Federation of Free Farmers (FFF), and of regional organizations such as the Agrarian Reform Alliance of Democratic Or-ganizations (ARADO) and the National Federation of Sugar Workers (NFSW), evidences an organizational tendency in which local or re-

gional organizations are united in a larger confederation. Local or regional organizations enjoy considerable autonomy in their activities
vis-à-vis national leadership. This phenomenon is also reflected to a
degree in the organization of the Communist Party of the Philippines
(CPP) and its armed wing, the New People's Army (NPA). Although
headed by a central committee, the CPP / NPA has adopted a strategy of
"centralized leadership, decentralized operations" in response to Philippine geography and ethnic and linguistic diversity (Jones 1989: 96).

The Role of Education

Philippine national identity may have been poorly served by it, but
missionary education tended, by its content, if not its medium, to counter regional and linguistic differentiation, creating an educated elite (the
ilustrados) with interests and concerns that transcended local boundaries. With the commercialization of the Philippine economy, there also
began a process of migration to Manila by provincial elites and rural
poor. Thus evolved the "imagined community," or sense of national
identity.[40] The *ilustrados* of the late 1800s were initially more concerned
with their rights as citizens of Spain than with Philippine independence. Yet their appropriation and reinterpretation of the term "Filipino" was part of a phenomenon that persists to the present: Philippine
identity is defined with reference to some foreign other. With the
growth of nationalist sentiment and scholarship in this century, Filipinos have recaptured and rewritten their own history, emphasizing
that which is uniquely Filipino. At the same time anti-imperialist
themes have struck an increasingly responsive chord among the Philippine people, as evidenced by the Philippine Senate's rejection of the
treaty on U.S. military bases in the Philippines. The development of a
national identity and class consciousness among the rural poor has also
been furthered by the nationwide educational system introduced by
American colonialists and expanded since independence, improvements in the communication and transportation networks, and, in recent years, the explosion in social organizations.

The Church and Peasant Organizations

Catholic proselytization gave Philippine peasants a powerful new
idiom, which cut across regional and linguistic differences. Although
the historical impact of the Catholic Church is often, and understandably, seen as conservative, central Christian narratives have potentially
radical implications, as the development of the theology of liberation

attests. In times of acute economic or social crises, the *pasyones*—epic poems detailing the suffering, death, and resurrection of Christ—provided a language for criticism both of wealth and status disparities and of economic and political oppression. Moreover, the *pasyones* provided a vision of liberation from the oppression of peasant life.[41]

Over time the Catholic Church's own construction of the Bible and of Christ's teachings changed. Particularly in the wake of Vatican II, the Church in the Philippines developed a greater social awareness and adopted a more activist role in the struggle for social justice. In turn, the Church provided both a new idiom for, and institutional guidance to, peasant organizational activities. Church functionaries and concerned lay members were instrumental, for example, in the organization and expansion of the FFF and the NFSW. In borrowing the concept of Basic Christian Communities from the liberation theologists of Latin America, the Philippine Catholic Church has also worked to redefine community, stressing the biblical importance of social justice and the necessity of united action among the disadvantaged.

Interpersonal Relations: An Ethos of Social Acceptance

Although there have been numerous outbreaks of rural unrest in Philippine history, these episodes are commonly treated as historical exceptions. The cultural ethos of rural Filipinos is generally portrayed in terms suggesting that it is antithetical to peasant activism or rebellion. This conventional wisdom found scholarly support in several widely cited articles dating from research conducted in the 1950s and 1960s (Hollnsteiner [1961] 1973; Lynch 1961). In the intervening years, scholars have increasingly emphasized the complex dimensions of a cultural ethos. We cannot assume that all members of a society internalize its cultural "norms"; nor can concepts such as "national personality" or "apolitical peasants" be accepted uncritically.

Earlier works have failed to note the many departures from the dominant cultural ethos of Filipinos. Indeed, no Filipino fully internalizes it. Peasants know the dominant ethos and often tailor their behavior to fit it, yet in many instances they do not conform (just as elites do and do not play their assigned role). Peasants have fashioned their survival strategies around everyday forms of resistance; false compliance, feigned ignorance, and the like are their weapons in the everyday class struggle (Kerkvliet 1990; Scott 1985). Apparent deference to landlords, patrons, and village elites can mask acute awareness of (and

hostility to) exploitative relations. This book provides a dynamic case study of elite constructions of an ethos of paternalistic agrarian relations and peasant challenges to those constructions.

The conventional analysis of Filipino national culture stresses the high value placed on social acceptance.[42] This ethos emphasizes smoothness in interpersonal relationships, sensitivity to personal affront (*amor propio*), and reciprocity of obligation (*utang na loób*).[43] Debts of gratitude (*utang na loób*) and the principle of reciprocity traditionally regulated patron-client relations between the village chief (*datu*) and villagers, as well as between landowners and tenants or farmworkers. Where the patron advanced rice (*rasyon*) or credit at times of crisis for clients, the recipients were expected to demonstrate gratitude through gift giving and the performance of services for the patron. Festive occasions and elections have long been regarded as important opportunities for exchanges. By contrast, electoral disloyalty (when discovered) has frequently resulted in the eviction of laborers- or tenants-cum-clients (Fegan 1982; Hollnsteiner 1963). Partly as a result, Philippine electoral loyalty has generally been viewed in patron-client terms.[44]

Identities based on interpersonal linkages crosscut and clash with group- or class-based identities around which cohesive ideologically oriented political parties or policy-oriented activities might be organized. Filipino identity and social responsibility are embedded in a web of bilateral kinship and fictive-kinship relations, the latter "fusing the pre-Spanish custom of blood compacts and the Roman Catholic concept of ritual godparenthood (*compadrazgo*)" (Steinberg 1982: 5; see also Szanton 1979). Although these relations inculcate a powerful devotion to those "within the circle," they tend to distance individuals from the remainder of society (Lynch 1961: 49). In analyzing social structure in Philippine villages, David Szanton concluded, "Horizontal solidarity is not characteristic of traditional lowland society" (1971: 87). Intrastatus alliances are found to be quite fragile. This is not to say that such groups do not exist, rather that the awareness of common interests must be strong and the leadership capacity of the political entrepreneur prodigious. Organizational survival, even among more ideologically oriented groups, frequently turns on the breadth of the leader's clientelist network.[45]

An Ethos of Paternalism

If Philippine cultural values have constrained class-based action among the peasantry by directing feelings of affinity along other axes,

such norms are part of a broader ideology used by elites to justify their status and behavior. Elite paternalism appears central to the dominant elite ethos. Peasants are regularly described as "children" incapable of independent action. Political and economic elites constantly evoke this disempowering imagery to their own political and strategic advantage. To be certain, significant costs are associated with conformance to the paternal role, costs many self-styled patrons are unwilling to bear even as they evoke the language of responsibility for laborers' and tenants' welfare.

The paternal ethos also entails appreciable costs for peasants. Internalization of this ethos involves working within relationships of hierarchical interdependence predicated on peasant deference and passivity. The dominant discourse casts peasants as mirroring the discipline required of their masters. Among other consequences, peasant recourse to violence is thus viewed as irrational—a temporary fury. Despite recurrent episodes of peasant unrest, elites express considerable surprise when peasant grievances give rise to violence and expect that token concessions coupled with forceful reprisals will alleviate the momentary crisis. The structural and behavioral features that belie the paternalistic discourse remain, however, as does the enmity that fueled the violence.

Illustrative of elite attitudes to the rural poor are remarks made by Corazon Aquino in a 1983 interview. Asserting that rural Filipinos were less likely to demonstrate against Marcos, Aquino noted: "My husband always explained to me that these [rural] people's No. 1 concern is to get three meals a day. They don't really care about the freedoms as long as they get the three meals" (*Christian Science Monitor* 1983).

The record of the agrarian-reform debate is similarly replete with remarks bespeaking elite disdain of farmworkers and tenants. The use of paternalistic narratives as a means of diffusing the agrarian-reform initiative is particularly notable. In the words of politicians and landowners, we find expressions of elite cultural resistance to changes in the cultural and political terms of the paternal relationship—in other words, to changes in the paternal "contract." At a time of massive unemployment in the sugar sector of Negros Occidental, occasioned by low world prices and "crony" marketing monopoly abuses, a leading sugar *hacendero*, Hortensia Starke, suggested that the pervasive malnutrition among farm laborers' children was the consequence of parental ignorance, rather than the inevitable legacy of poverty. "The parents are not thin, only the children" (Starke interview, June 16, 1986). The remedy, in her view, was nutritional and family-planning education, rather than

providing families with productive assets through land redistribution. Implicit in the context of her remarks was the notion that farmworkers were intellectually unprepared for the responsibilities of landowner-ship.

Similarly, a prominent representative of the sugarcane sector claimed that farmworkers were profligate spenders and, by implication, incapa-ble of the saving behavior demanded by amortization obligations in the event of reform: "The moment they have extra money, what do they do? They spend it on their daughter so that their daughter will become queen in the barrio. That is their priority. They will buy luxury things like [a] stereo or TV, that is why our people in the farm, they have the transis-tor. They buy all those luxury goods also . . . and if there is anything left, on Sundays, they will go to the cockpit" (Acuña 1987: 79).

Daniel L. Lacson, Jr., then governor of Negros Occidental, in contest-ing the need for redistribution of private agricultural lands, maintained that there were "thousands of workers who are not yet prepared to be farmers, or may not even wish to be peasant tillers held in bondage to small parcels of backward farming."[46] In similarly disputing the need for land reform and farmworker preparedness for the responsibilities of landownership, Joaquin Villarosa, a sugarcane grower, asserted: "Our workers do not love farming. They are paid for their work—by the day or by piecework. But there are people who really love farming—they are us landowners. If you give the workers the farm immediately, it's like giving a baby that has been used to spoonfeeding the real food. He will get indigestion; he will not know what to do with it" (Collins 1989: 46–47).

A variant on this same theme is found in various landowner ac-counts of spurned offers of land to their farmworkers. The narrative of Eduardo Alunan of Negros Occidental was typical: "My workers chose [to receive] a P40 daily minimum wage rather than the 1,000 m² parcels I offered to lend them. I could not afford to pay them the high wage so I gave them the plots. . . . The workers complain that they earn less now because they can't work as much for me since they have to work their parcels. Their productivity [on these parcels] is poor because they have no fertilizers. I will try to finance them this year."[47] In marked contrast, community organizers for the First Farmers' Human Development Foundation, also of Negros Occidental, insisted that farmworkers would accept reduced pay if in return they received secure rights to a portion of the land on their respective haciendas. This judgment was based on FFHDF's work on some 129 haciendas with roughly 7,000

farmworker families (Belarmino et al. interview, June 17, 1986). Widespread farmworker participation in the mid-1980s farm-lot program of the National Federation of Sugar Workers (NFSW) similarly evidenced workers' interest in rights to land, even if only temporary usufruct.

Another offer of temporary intercropping rights was ostensibly rejected by farmworkers out of fear that neighboring workers might steal the resulting produce.[48] This view of uncooperative, dishonest peasants is echoed in a National Federation of Sugarcane Planters (NFSP) document arguing against land reform in the sugarcane sector. The NFSP contended that farmworker-beneficiaries lacked the requisite temperament for cooperative operation of farm machinery or cooperation in the scheduling of sugar milling. They cited what they termed the " '*nakalamang*' or '*nakaisa*' custom" and asserted that "Filipinos have the propensity to take advantage of others" (n.d.: 7). As is almost invariably true of observations by the Philippine elite about Philippine cultural norms or behavioral characteristics, the NFSP comment was phrased in terms ascribing these abusive traits only to Filipino peasants. The historical record suggests, however, that the comment could more aptly be taken as an indictment of landowner-farmworker relations.

Most landowners, as well as some Department of Agrarian Reform (DAR) and union officials, claimed that farmworkers preferred the security of hacienda employment to the vagaries of landownership.[49] In justifying the temporary loan of garden plots to farmworkers, as opposed to a permanent transfer, Alunan stated that his workers preferred this no-cost arrangement to ownership based on a formal sale of property rights. Yet landowners and government officials rarely pose the question of landownership to farmworkers or tenants. Rarer still are the instances in which farmworkers or tenants view offers of landownership as credible, or as offers to which they can respond without being branded as subversive.

In a related vein, some landowners and scholars suggested that Philippine peasants were reluctant to participate in a new reform program for fear of losing those survival resources previously provided by landlords-cum-patrons (Fegan 1972; Herring 1981). The extent of this risk needs to be tested empirically; my own fieldwork has revealed relatively few instances in which landlords were still providing production credit, improved inputs, emergency consumption loans, or similar services by the mid 1980s.[50] The failure of landlords to provide such services appears related both to a general decline in patron-client relations, to which the Huk rebellion and other episodes of agrarian unrest

have been attributed, and to the consequences of earlier tenure-reform programs: the shift from share tenancy to leasehold status has frequently been accompanied by the cessation of landlords' contributions to production costs.

In arguing that farmworkers would derive little or no benefit from landownership, two planters' organizations listed disabilities that render the farmworker incapable of coping with maintenance of farm production: "These are his low educational attainment, deficiency in technological know-how, inferior management ability, no capitalization, coupled with the necessity to provide for daily sustenance, and, *above all, his mentality and attitudinal behaviors which need much room for improvement"* (PLADAR and DATU-Panay n.d.: 2; emphasis added).

In fact, most farmworkers and tenants—long disadvantaged in their access to credit, improved inputs, and managerial training—are less able to bear the risks attendant on agricultural landownership. However, crop insurance, farm credit, and technical and managerial training could do much to address these handicaps. For those activities requiring greater education or experience, the farmworkers can contract for management services, just as most large and corporate landowners employ managerial personnel. Moreover, the risks associated with agriculture are not unique to landownership. Past episodes of massive unemployment provide ample evidence that the risks of farming extend to those engaged as tenants or farmworkers as well.

More insidious in the comments of the various landowners and DAR officials is the implication that farmworkers and tenants are somehow inherently inferior to landowners and bureaucrats. Underlying many of these remarks is a class variant of social ideologies of genetic inferiority-superiority. This depoliticizing and disempowering discourse forms part of the continuum of violence and confrontation practiced by elites in resisting redistributive reform. Frequently frustrated in their pursuit of nonviolent reform, Philippine peasants have repeatedly expressed their grievances through civil unrest.

3

Land-Tenure Patterns and Rural Unrest

Highly unequal distributions of assets and income, particularly severe rural inequalities, pose threats to political stability.
Stephan Haggard and Robert Kaufman

The Aquino government debated proposals for agrarian reform against the backdrop of the historical evolution of Philippine land-tenure patterns and the legacy of land tenure–related peasant activism and rebellion. Yujiro Hayami and his colleagues identify four principal patterns of tenure introduced by colonial or commercial pressures: scattered tenant-operated holdings in the coastal region of Central Luzon; haciendas characterized by tenant-operated parcels in the interior of Central Luzon; traditional plantations on Negros; and modern, commercial plantations, often operated by multinational corporations, on Mindanao (Hayami et al. 1990: 29–32). Regardless of tenurial form, Philippine landownership is highly skewed. Landlessness is acute and growing. One consequence of this landlessness, and its historic evolution, has been episodic peasant rebellion. Frustrated by the unresponsiveness of the colonial and postindependence governments, peasants have periodically turned to violence as a last resort.

The Evolution of Philippine Land-Tenure Patterns

Indigenous land-tenure arrangements in pre-Hispanic Philippine society were characterized by communal ownership of land, with individual families accorded usufruct rights to a particular parcel or parcels.[1] In return families were required to perform various public services, an obligation that attached to the land rather than the person. These services often included assisting the *datu* in the tending of his fields and home.

The most significant Spanish innovation concerning property rights

was the introduction of the concept of legal title to land—that is, private ownership (McLennan 1969: 656). Yet in the absence of extensive Spanish settlement, few Spanish-owned latifundios of the kind that typified much of Latin America emerged in the Philippines.[2] While the Church came to own extensive tracts, and some Spanish settlers were awarded large estates, the typical landholding pattern was one of more modest holdings owned by native elites and part-Chinese mestizos.

The emergence of landlordism was hastened by the commercial operations of the Chinese and Chinese-Filipino mestizos (Wickberg 1964). The expanding consumption demands of Manila and the absence of significant Spanish competition prompted the development of internal trade routes by these entrepreneurs. These proclivities were heightened with the introduction of foreign trade in the late eighteenth century and the attendant demand for export crops. The commercial wealth thus accumulated enabled the mestizos in particular to begin land acquisition through money lending to native landholders. Technically, the law forbade sales of native land rights, but this stricture was poorly enforced and easily circumvented.[3] Members of the religious orders, although hardly objective in their assessment of the *indios* they had come to proselytize, attributed the loss of native lands to the Filipino penchant for elaborate celebrations and conspicuous consumption (McLennan 1969: 660, quoting de Zuñiga 1893: 365).

The pacto de retroventa

Many native cultivators lost their lands through a money-lending system known as the *pacto de retroventa*, under which loans were secured by land.[4] The borrower continued to cultivate the land as a sharecropper of his creditor during the loan period. Affected lands were often forfeited for failure to repay loans amounting to only a third to one half of the land's value (McLennan 1969: 659–60; Hayami and Kikuchi 1982: 71–72). The most notable practitioners of this method of land acquisition were mestizos. Such land acquisitions increased with the growth of commercial agriculture. Spanish attempts to prohibit the use of this device date from 1768.[5] The persistence of this lending arrangement to the present is testimony to the ineffectiveness of such prohibitions (*Business World* 1990c). Small peasants were not the only natives to lose their usufruct rights; many *datu* caciques were similarly rendered landless.

With time, Chinese-Filipino mestizos became quite prominent, both economically and socially. As a group, they were second only to the

religious orders in the extent of their landownership on Luzon. Edgar Wickberg cites a variety of accounts describing the social prestige associated with the mestizo designation, and the emulation of mestizo practices by native elites.[6] Landownership and commercial success apparently facilitated social acceptance of the mestizos by the native caciques. Some of the mestizos and caciques intermarried, creating a landowning elite called the *principalia*, although Wickberg (1964: 83) and McLennan (1969: 660–61) both suggest that the process was less one of fusion than of mestizo displacement of traditional native elites. In turn, these *principalia* intermarried to forge powerful alliances, the basis of a new provincial elite.

Where operative, notably in the long-settled areas of coastal Luzon, the *pacto de retroventa*, involving piecemeal acquisition of land, led to a pattern of landownership marked by scattered holdings. By contrast, property patterns in the interior of Central Luzon were initially dominated by haciendas encompassing hundreds or thousands of hectares.[7] Plantation agriculture, characterized by extensive holdings operated by hired laborers, was, and is, most prevalent in more recently settled areas such as Mindanao and Negros.

The Haciendas of Central Luzon

Marshall McLennan traces the haciendas of Central Luzon to the *inquilinato* system introduced on the friar estates in the eighteenth century. The Augustinian, Dominican, and Franciscan religious orders acquired the earliest haciendas, most of them located in the provinces surrounding Manila.[8] Land was leased by an *inquilino* for a fixed rent (*canon*), with actual cultivation performed by share tenants (*kasama*). The *inquilinato* system was an innovation in Philippine society, a means of relieving the landowner of many of the traditional social responsibilities attendant on land ownership.[9] "It was here on the friar lands that the hacienda system was born and it is not surprising, therefore, that the earliest tenant discontent appeared on the friar estates" (McLennan 1969: 666; see also Bauzon 1975: 6–7). Life as a *kasama* did offer one advantage to Philippine peasants: their labor obligations on the estate exempted them—at the landowner's discretion—from forced labor for the Crown.[10]

The concentration of landownership in the religious orders, and the often illegal means by which that land was acquired, repeatedly made the friar estates the focus of agrarian unrest, most prominently during the 1896 struggle for independence[11] and the 1935 uprising of Benigno

Ramos's Sakdals. However, peasant resistance to the depredations of the friar estates dates at least from 1639, when "large numbers" of exempted Chinese laborers fled the hacienda of Calamba and "scourged" the countryside.[12] Although promptly suppressed, the uprising spawned a violent revolt, involving thousands of estate laborers throughout Luzon (Blair and Robertson 1903–9, 29: 208). Natives also filed periodic legal actions against the religious orders for land usurpation; victories, however, were rare.[13]

Land Registration and Land Grabbing

Land grabbing was by no means the exclusive preserve of the religious orders. As restrictions on Spanish settlement in the provinces were terminated in the nineteenth century, private haciendas were established through royal grants, although these were few in number, and purchases of royal domain (*realengas*). These grants and purchases were often substantially augmented through usurpation of adjacent lands previously cleared and occupied by natives who lacked formal titles (McLennan 1969: 667, citing Sanciano y Goson 1881: 55).

This process was facilitated by land-registration laws. Established ostensibly to protect the rights of existing indigenous cultivators and promote more efficient agricultural production, these laws were abused by the politico-economic elites, allowing them to usurp vast tracts of theretofore untitled communal or individual farmlands.[14] The Spanish land-registration acts of 1880 and 1894 and American introduction of cadastral surveys and the Torrens land-registration system in 1913 each afforded opportunities for large-scale land grabbing.[15] These laws served neither the interests of native cultivators nor, paradoxically, the state that issued them. As often happened in other nations, instead of effecting "more secure central control over a territory, [state leaders] found that they had fostered the growth in power of landlords hostile to state centralization" (Migdal 1988: 58).

The land-grabbing process was most pervasive in the frontier areas, initially in the interior of Central Luzon, and later on Negros and other islands remote from Manila. In such settings, power was unevenly distributed and indigenous property rights were less clearly defined. In many instances, migrant families would take up cultivation in unsettled areas only to find themselves later dispossessed or forced to pay rent by landlords who had registered the property in Manila. Hayami and Kikuchi suggest that many paid these rents because they were so low initially. As population increased and vacant land diminished, rent ex-

actions escalated, as did peasant resistance. "Agrarian unrest . . . was thus deeply rooted in the historical process of land accumulation" (Hayami and Kikuchi 1982: 74).

The enmity engendered by land grabbing and other land-related injustices, including persistent, near-universal noncompliance with rural minimum wage legislation and other agricultural labor code provisions, are undimmed by time, fueling recurrent peasant unrest.

Land Tenure and Rural Unrest

Philippine history is replete with peasant uprisings, with tenure-related grievances providing important impetus for many of the revolts. Scholars typically differentiate between the revolts provoked by Spanish colonial impositions unrelated to land (tribute, corvée labor, and the exclusion of Filipinos from the priesthood), which predominated in the period before the mid eighteenth century, and the agrarian-based uprisings that prevailed thereafter (Constantino 1975: 85–112; Hayami et al. 1990: 45–50; Kessler 1989: 6–17).

Culture and Economics Interact

Religion has long had an important influence on Philippine peasant movements and peasant participation in rebellions. Reynaldo Ileto (1979) argues that folk Catholicism—the grafting of Catholicism onto traditional Philippine religions—nurtured an undercurrent of millennial beliefs that facilitated organization of peasant protest movements in times of economic and political crisis, most notably during the Spanish and American colonial periods. In particular the *pasyones*—epic poems detailing the suffering, death, and resurrection of Christ—provided a language and a vision of liberation from the oppression of peasant life.[16] In describing the Katipunan revolt of 1896, Ileto notes a theme repeated in many Philippine revolts: "The history of the Filipino people was seen in terms of a lost Eden, the recovery of which demanded the people's participation in the pasyon of Mother Country . . . Paradise became *kalayaan*—not only independence . . . but enlightenment, prosperity, and true brotherhood" (1979: 317).

The *pasyon* dismissed wealth or education-based distinctions in social status, measuring a person's true worth in terms of individual *loób* (inner self). Furthermore, the *pasyon* suggested the existence of a divine mission for each individual, a mission that transcended considerations of family and thus posed a significant exception to the primacy of the

Philippine commitment to family and ritual kin. For some Filipinos, the *pasyon*, in its description of Christ's activities, may have suggested a blueprint for revolutionary action. The religious imagery and the narrative forms used by the leaders of peasant movements in the late nineteenth and early twentieth centuries not only attest to the leaders' familiarity with the *pasyones*, but evidence considerable borrowing from them.[17] For most peasants, however, the *pasyon* afforded cultural preparation for such action under the leadership of charismatic, quasireligious figures in times of economic or political crisis, real or imagined. Among the revolts spawned by such movements were those of Apolinario de la Cruz's Cofradía de San José (1841), Julian Baltazar's Guardia de Honor (1884–1902), Dionisio "Papa Isio" Sigobela's Babaylanes (1896–1907), and Felipe Salvador's Santa Iglesia (1894–1910) (Alvarez-Castillo 1988; Cullamar 1986; Ileto 1979; Sturtevant 1976).

David Sturtevant takes the analysis further, arguing that serious cultural tensions, rather than economic or political factors, were the primary source of recurrent agrarian unrest until the 1930s; reemerging as a factor in such unrest in the 1970s (1976: 17). Still, his discussion makes clear that many of the objective manifestations of the "incomprehensible" and "depersonalized" forces besetting the peasantry, and motivating their participation in millennial movements, related to land, notably the dispossession of small farmers, taxation, the emergence of a cacique class, and increasing inequality in wealth (Sturtevant 1976: 264). David Steinberg reverses Sturtevant's order of primacy, characterizing these movements as "economic in nature" but "cloaked . . . in the apocalyptic dream" (1982: 71). The issue is not, however, one of primacy but of the interplay between economic and cultural forms.

By Sturtevant's account, supernaturalism gave way to secularism after the 1930s, notably in the Hukbalahap rebellion of 1946–54, only to reemerge in the form of movements such as the Lapiang Malaya (Independence Party) in the late 1960s. It does appear that the relative importance of religious versus secular discourses in legitimizing (or delegitimizing) certain societal structures has shifted over time.[18] The leaders of the current communist insurgency have adopted a more secular, nationalist discourse than characterized earlier, religious-influenced movements. Yet Richard Kessler argues that peasants join the insurgents for many of the same reasons underlying peasant participation in those earlier movements. "The present uprising has been more effective than previous rebellions because of its ability to draw on the strength of the religious and secular themes of the past" (Kessler 1989: 24–25).

The 1970s witnessed a contemporaneous resurgence of religious and secular-based social organizations in the Philippines, paralleling the concurrent emergence of labor unions, socialist and communist political parties, and peasant millenarian movements (known as *colorums*) in the 1930s. Religion-inspired, militant peasant organizations grew concurrently with the dramatic rise of the secular (and communist) NPA. More recently evident are myriad folk "cults" and cult-based, anticommunist vigilante groups.[19]

Early Land-related Peasant Uprisings

The Philippine literature generally cites a 1745 rebellion as the first significant peasant uprising in which agrarian issues appear to have played a central role.[20] This early revolt in the provinces around Manila was largely *defensive* in nature, a revolt by non-hacienda peasantry directed against land usurpation by the haciendas of the Spanish friars, the closing of hacienda lands to common pasturage and forage, and forced labor requirements for those outside the haciendas.[21] The rebellion thus exhibits many of the features identified in the "moral economy" literature on peasant upheaval.[22]

Precapitalist *barangay*, characterized by social and moral arrangements that provided some measure of subsistence for village inhabitants, were threatened by the introduction of market forces, increasing exactions by the state, heightened demographic pressures on land resources, and the withdrawal of crucial elements of peasant survival strategies. These threats to the subsistence ethic forged a link between objective realities and subjective perceptions of exploitation. Peasant activism and rebellion had their impetus in the defensive reaction to violations of the moral economy, reactions that sought to restore earlier, more equilibrated relations between the landed and the landless. In so analyzing rural social relations, it should be borne in mind that the precapitalist era was far from utopian; life for the disadvantaged was often "demeaning, exploitative, and personally debilitating" (Migdal 1988: 94). What was important was the peasants' perception that, however disagreeable their previous situation, conditions had materially worsened.

The legacy of tenure-related grievances also figured in several uprisings during the American colonial era (Kerkvliet 1971). It is, however, the Hukbalahap rebellion of the mid 1940s and the present insurgency of the New People's Army that best illustrate the role of peasant grievances in shaping civil unrest in the Philippines.

The Huk Rebellion

The Huk organization had its origin in scattered grassroots movements in Central Luzon in the 1930s, many of them coalescing under the banners of the Aguman ding Malding Talapagobra (AMT = General Workers' Union) and the Kalipunang Pambansa ng mga Magsasaka sa Pilipinas (KPMP = National Confederation of Peasants in the Philippines).[23] By conventional analysis, these movements were responding primarily to deteriorating patron-client relations between landlords and tenants, as increasing population and declining availability of new land turned the "terms of trade" further against the tenants. Rice loans (*rasyon*) were halted, gleaning rights were curbed, and landlord-tenant relations became those of a "business partnership, not a family."[24]

In response to these deteriorating conditions, peasants turned initially not to overt rebellion but to everyday forms of resistance. Benedict Kerkvliet describes tenants engaged in midnight harvesting to avoid the landlord and secure what they deemed their rightful share, and in arson, strikes, marches, judicial actions, and elections ([1977] 1979a: 29–39, 258). When more individualistic measures proved futile, the recognition of the need for collective action increased.

Wartime Resistance

Landlord-tenant tensions were exacerbated during the Japanese occupation, when landowners fled to the major cities. Whether they fled or remained, landowners often cooperated with the Japanese. The occupation thus (1) threatened elite solidarity, dividing collaborators from opposition leaders; (2) occasioned a major schism between the collaborating or neutral elite and the opposition masses; and (3) loosened the grip of landlords on their tenants.[25] The abuses during the occupation prompted the formation on March 29, 1942, of a unified peasant resistance movement, the Hukbalahap (Hukbo ng Bayan Laban sa Hapon = People's Army Against Japan). Participating in this movement to varying degrees were elements of the Partido Komunista ng Pilipinas (PKP = Communist Party of the Philippines), the AMT, the KPMP, and a number of other peasant, labor, and political organizations.[26]

There is some controversy in the secondary literature concerning the motivations of the Huk rebels. Kerkvliet emphasizes peasant enmity at the collaboration of local political and economic elites with the Japanese and the peasants' need for collective protection from the repression of

the Japanese occupation.[27] He concludes that "the PKP did not inspire or control the peasant movement in Central Luzon during the 1930s and 1940s, the Hukbalahap, or the Huk rebellion itself" (1979: 264). William Pomeroy disagrees, laying much more stress on nationalist sentiments and the ideological and organizational role of the PKP.[28] Eduardo Lachica's analysis falls somewhere between those of Kerkvliet and Pomeroy, stressing the local origins of the Huks, while portraying the movement as dominated by the PKP in the years during and immediately after World War II. By Lachica's account: "The communists took over at the propitious time when peasant organizations were gearing for a showdown with their enemies. They got a free ride on an essentially indigenous protest movement" (1971: 90).

There seems little dispute that the PKP and the Huks cooperated both during the war and, for a time, during the Huk rebellion of the late 1940s to mid 1950s. What these conflicting accounts highlight is the multiplicity of motivations underlying the peasants' resort to violence. Compounding the impact of the global economic depression of the 1930s, droughts and floods in the years between 1935 and 1940 led to poor harvests and economic crisis for many Philippine tenants. The Japanese invasion brought disaster. A range of possible constructions were available to peasants as they sought to understand and respond to these crises. Some peasants stressed their identities within the deteriorating patron-client system, others emphasized their identities as AMT, KPMP, or PKP members, and still others their identities as Filipinos. For many these cultural identities overlapped.

From an initial 300 or so, the Huk forces eventually grew to some 10,000 combatants. These were not eleventh-hour rebels. Most joined the movement in 1942 and early 1943. The Huks were regarded as the most effective resistance organization operating in Luzon, and were active in Bulacan, Nueva Ecija, Pampanga, and Tarlac provinces. Although ambushes and acts of sabotage were an important part of Huk activities, most guerrillas continued farming and remained active in barrio life. Huk members gathered intelligence, often provided barrio governance, and worked to deny the Japanese the rice harvest. Programs of music and drama were staged to contradict Japanese propagandists and sustain peasant commitment to resistance.[29]

The war took an enormous toll on Philippine economic life. Manila, the economic, social, and political hub of the Philippines, suffered wartime damage second only to that of Warsaw. An estimated 80 percent of Manila was destroyed when General MacArthur retook the city. At

the same time, the 1944–45 crop was only 60 percent of normal, and much of that was destroyed or consumed by the warring armies (Steinberg 1967: 114, 122). Transportation, industrial, health, and sanitation facilities were all in ruins. In short, the "scale of distress" was enormous, while the dominant institutions of Philippine society were dysfunctional.[30]

Even apart from the Huk movement, it is argued, World War II institutionalized violence in the Philippines, leaving behind it the legacy of an armed Philippine society willing to use force (Steinberg 1982: 58; Wurfel 1988: 103). Certainly U.S. war surplus dramatically increased per capita gun possession. Exacerbating postwar tensions were landlord efforts to reassert control and claim back rents. To counter peasant resistance and the Huk movement, many landowners established private armies, which were tolerated, indeed supported, by the central government (Anderson 1988: 15; Wolters [1983] 1984: 16).

Postwar Repression

At the war's end, the Huk movement was denounced as communist-influenced and persecuted by the Filipino and American governments.[31] By contrast, members of the Philippine elite who collaborated with the Japanese went largely unpunished. Huk forces were ordered to disarm, while other guerrilla organizations, including Philippine Constabulary units that had abandoned their support of Japanese rule only as American forces swept across Luzon, were officially recognized by MacArthur and allowed to retain their weapons. In February 1945, in the liberated town of Malolos, Bulacan, over 100 Huks were massacred by Filipino soldiers with the knowledge and consent of American officers (Kerkvliet [1977] 1979a: 113). That same month, the leaders of the Huk organization were arrested by American soldiers and imprisoned. In the ensuing months, other Huk leaders and members were arrested or killed. Still, many Huks cooperated with American demands, disbanding and turning in their arms.

Huk veterans, and tenants generally, faced other problems, notably those associated with the return of landlords to the villages. Claiming that back rents were owed, landlords reduced their contributions to agricultural expenses and stopped providing interest-free loans. The interest rates charged by landlords and moneylenders soared. The Pambansang Kaisahan ng mga Magbubukid (PKM = National Peasants' Union), the successor movement to the Hukbalahap and prewar peasant organizations,[32] advocated improved sharing arrangements, with

tenants to receive 60 or 70 percent of the crop. For their part, tenants were to assume most or all agricultural expenses.

Landlords and other members of the traditional village elite were appointed by American military personnel to mayoral and other local government positions pending elections in 1947. "Civilian guards" were recruited by landowners and local governments alike, and arms were supplied by the Department of the Interior and the Military Police (Kerkvliet [1977] 1979a: 148). These "guards" were particularly ill-disciplined, frequently abusing the local populace in the name of local authorities and landed elites.

In 1946, congressional seats were denied to six duly elected members from the PKM. The candidates ran as members of the Democratic Alliance, an anti-collaborationist party supportive of the unsuccessful Nacionalista Party presidential candidate, Sergio Osmeña. The disqualifications are explained, in part, by quorum requirements and President Manuel Roxas's related inability to obtain approval of amendments to the Constitution of 1935, granting Americans "parity" access to Philippine resources in exchange for preferential trade rights and U.S. foreign aid, in the face of opposition from these members of Congress.[33]

The Huks Rebel

Simultaneously to pursue their agrarian agenda—increased tenant shares of farm output and collateral-free, low-interest loans—and protect themselves from increasing repression, the peasants turned to organized violence under the aegis of the Hukbong Mapagpalay ng Bayan (HMB = People's Liberation Army). Citing interviews with HMB guerrillas, Kerkvliet characterizes them as "reluctant rebels."[34] While there was considerable continuity between the HMB and the earlier Hukbalahap organization, as well as the PKM, some members of the latter groups were deterred from participation by rising government repression. Only in May 1948, when the Lava brothers, Jose and Jesus, had regained control of the party, did the PKP declare a "revolutionary situation" and endorse the "armed struggle" of the HMB (Lachica 1971: 123–24; Kerkvliet [1977] 1979a: 179, 188). Even then, most of the PKP politburo members remained in Manila.

HMB demands initially included the right to retain weapons, a halt to the raids of the Military Police and repression by civilian guards, removal of "fascist" government officials, and the carrying out of social welfare measures and agrarian reform.[35] Soon after the armed conflict began, the demands expanded to include immediate enforce-

ment of the bill of rights, release of political prisoners and dismissal
of charges against all parties to the conflict, and the seating of the six
dismissed congressmen. The demand for agrarian reform was also
fleshed out: the HMB insisted on legislation guaranteeing a 70–30 sharing of production in favor of the tenant and the eventual abolition of
tenancy.[36]

The Huk rebellion lasted from 1946 to 1954. HMB forces grew to
some 5–10,000 combatants. By most accounts, Huk strength remained
concentrated in Central Luzon, with some modest success in southern
Luzon.[37] Where it was active, the HMB afforded tenants some protection from landlord abuses and the repressive acts of the Philippine
Constabulary and the civilian guards. The Huks also provided a measure of protection against other forms of lawlessness, capturing and
punishing those guilty of criminal offenses.

American Policy and Agrarian Reform

American alarm over the strength of the insurgent movement led to
renewed attention to rural problems in the Philippines, culminating in
the Hardie Report of 1952,[38] named for Robert S. Hardie of the U.S.
Mutual Security Agency. Concluding that "the land tenure system
stands as an obstacle thwarting all efforts of the United States to foster
development of a stable and democratic economy" (Hardie 1952: 8), the
report recommended that the Philippine government abolish tenancy
so far as practical and establish a rural economy based on owner-
operated family-sized farms. On average, owner-cultivators were to be
permitted retention areas of six tillable (cultivable) hectares and resident noncultivating owners would be permitted retention areas of three
tillable hectares. Absentee landlords were afforded no retention area.
Recognizing that landlords frequently exercised influence over tenants
in credit as well as land markets,[39] Hardie called for simultaneous action
to assure beneficiary access to rural credit. Similarly, the report urged
the introduction of new marketing facilities, agricultural cooperatives,
and improved production techniques.

Unfortunately for the course of Philippine development, the landed
elite and their representatives in the Philippine Congress rejected these
proposals as "communist-inspired."[40] Nor, after initial approval of the
proposals, was continuing support forthcoming from an increasingly
conservative U.S. government, whose colonial policies had cemented
both political and important personal ties with Philippine elites. In explaining the abandonment of U.S. support for the Hardie Report, Paul

Monk emphasizes the conservative shift in American politics associated with the inauguration of the Eisenhower administration in 1953 (1990: 59). With few exceptions, the Hardie Report had initially been endorsed by both U.S. embassy personnel and the State Department. "The Report is sound, feasible and adequate for that segment of land reform which it deals with, namely conditions of land tenure. . . . It is strongly recommended that the EMB [embassy] and the STEM [Special Technical and Economic Mission] at Manila *support by all possible means the recommendations of the report*," Secretary of State Dean Acheson cabled the Manila embassy.[41] However, in March 1954, the U.S. foreign aid agency issued a new report on Philippine agricultural land tenure that repudiated the recommendations of the Hardie Report without acknowledging its existence. By May 1954, John Foster Dulles, the new secretary of state, was counseling a nonactivist posture, informing the embassy in Manila that "primary emphasis should be placed on uniform and forceful enforcement of existing rice share tenancy legislation."[42]

The mid 1950s also saw McCarthyite recriminations against many "China hands" in the State Department and the dismissal of Wolf Ladejinsky, chief architect of the U.S.-supported postwar land reform in Japan.[43] Although there remained proponents of land reform within the U.S. bureaucracy after Ladejinsky's dismissal and the repudiation of the Hardie Report, the message seemed clear: espousal of land reform was incompatible with career advancement. Since the mid 1950s, the U.S. foreign aid agency has, with limited exceptions, afforded no more than nominal support to the cause of land reform. The exceptions, however, are instructive. In the early 1970s, at private and congressional urging, the U.S. Agency for International Development quite belatedly committed significant administrative and financial resources to land reform in South Vietnam. In the early 1980s, it also committed limited financial, but virtually no administrative, resources to land reform in El Salvador (see Prosterman and Riedinger 1987: 113–73).

Formally, this antipathy toward reform was explained in terms of deference to the sovereignty of other nations. In language equally applicable to the U.S. response to agrarian reform under the Aquino government, Lewis Gleeck of USAID summarized U.S. policy toward Ferdinand Marcos's "New Society" agrarian reform as follows: "It was clear from the Washington [cable] traffic that *the USG* [U.S. government] *wanted to be part of something that looked like real reform, but didn't want to get sucked into appearing to dictate GOP* [government of the Philippines] *policies, or into financing the program*" (1974: 3; emphasis added).

Demise of the Huk Rebellion

"Battle fatigue" among the Huk rebels and their supporters in a context of improved and more humane performance by the Philippine military, modest land grants to some surrendered Huks, initiation of community development programs, and extensive anti-Huk propaganda spelled the effective defeat of the Huks by 1954. Government repression fractured the HMB's alliance with several political parties. The government captured most of the national PKP leadership in Manila on October 18, 1950, severely damaging Huk links to urban supporters. In December 1952, the PKP central committee formally abandoned the Huk rebels, renouncing armed struggle. Curfews and travel restrictions imposed in many villages curbed activities in support of the Huks. Substantial U.S. assistance helped assure the military superiority of the government forces and kept the Philippine government solvent at a time of acute domestic deficits.[44] With American assistance the Philippine military was reorganized, retrained, and expanded.

More important, in the eyes of many peasants, military discipline improved beginning in 1951, with Huks and non-rebels alike giving much of the credit to Secretary of Defense Ramon Magsaysay. If inhumane government behavior had driven many peasants to join or support the Huks, improved military behavior, including the disbanding of civilian guard units, suggested better prospects for nonviolent resolution of other peasant grievances. The relatively peaceful and fair elections of 1951, a marked contrast to those of 1949, gave similar evidence of an improved climate for legal struggle. The government also introduced rural improvement projects—health clinics, new bridges and roads, wells and irrigation canals—and a widely advertised program of resettling surrendered Huks on homestead lands.[45]

In practice, 950 families were resettled in Mindanao at a cost of several million pesos. Of these, fewer than 250 had been involved with the Huks, and many others were not even from Central Luzon. Citing a number of sources, Kerkvliet concludes that the program's intent was never to resettle substantial numbers of Huks. Instead, its aim was "to steal from the PKP and HMB the idea of 'land for the landless' with a well-publicized experiment that was more than the Huk movement itself had been able to do" ([1977] 1979a: 239). Government credit facilities, agricultural extension, the creation of several new agrarian courts to settle tenure disputes, and Magsaysay's pledges to reduce rent levels also worked to defuse agrarian grievances.

With the surrender of the Huk commander Luis Taruc on May 17, 1954, the rebellion was for all intents over. Still, many of the grievances underlying the rebellion persisted, as did remnants of the Huk forces. Moreover, with the end of the military conflict, what little interest the politico-economic elite had in reform largely evaporated.[46] Indeed, the waxing and waning of interest in reform coincident with the fortunes of the insurgency of the moment is a continuing theme of Philippine history, as it often has been elsewhere. New land reform legislation was passed in 1955 at the behest of President Magsaysay, but was so circumscribed in scope as to represent little improvement over existing legislation (Wurfel 1983: 3–4). Land tenure–related grievances and the resort to violence would resurface with even greater intensity in the 1970s and 1980s.

The Current Insurgency

Officially established in late 1968, the Partido Komunista ng Pilipinas—Marxismo-Leninismo-Kaisipang Mao Zedong (CPP = Communist Party of the Philippines—Marxist-Leninist-Mao Ze-dong Thought) had blended and transformed nationalist impulses and agrarian grievances into a potent commitment to Marxist armed revolt by the early 1980s.[47] The CPP was founded by Jose Maria Sison and other urban intellectuals in rejection of the politics of the PKP, the traditional Philippine communist party. By the CPP's account, the principal evils afflicting Philippine society were U.S. imperialism, fascism, feudalism in agrarian relations, and bureaucratic capitalism, as practiced by foreign multinationals, the World Bank and the International Monetary Fund, and their Philippine adherents.[48] Given the "semi-feudal and semi-colonial condition of the Philippines," the CPP visualized a two-stage process of revolution: a national democratic revolution to be followed by a socialist revolution (Sison 1968b: 12).

Illustrating the historical continuity of agrarian unrest in the Philippines, the CPP's military wing, the Bagong Hukbong Bayan (NPA = New People's Army), originated in a remnant Huk guerrilla force headed by Bernabe Buscayno (Commander Dante), the son of a poor tenant farmer and former Huk rebel. In an effort to further tie the NPA to the earlier peasant rebellion, Sison selected March 29, 1969, the twenty-seventh anniversary of the founding of the World War II Huk movement, as the date for the formal founding of the NPA.[49]

The CPP/NPA learned much from the failures of the Huk rebellion

and its own early mistakes: the CPP/NPA dispersed its best cadres to the field, decentralized power and operations, developed full-time combatants trained in propaganda and organizational work, and established a more systematic program of local taxation and international fund-raising.[50] Unlike the Huks, whose activities were confined to Central Luzon, the CPP/NPA has become a nationwide organization.[51]

Although all estimates of NPA strength should be treated with caution, the Armed Forces of the Philippines (AFP) gauged CPP/NPA armed forces at 25,200 at their peak in December 1987.[52] At that time, the military considered over 12 percent (4,993) of the country's 40,761 *barangay* "infiltrated"—that is, "areas where the insurgents stay for long periods of time . . . without fear of being discovered or attacked by government forces" (ROP, Presidency, Office of the Press Secretary 1989: 6). Since 1988, the NPA has experienced significant declines in membership and influence. Mid-1993 estimates put the number of NPA combatants at 10,600, with even greater reductions in the areas influenced or controlled by the NPA (McBeth 1993).

The National Democratic Front

The CPP/NPA has long complemented its strategy of armed struggle ("protracted people's war") with political front work. The principal vehicle for the political struggle has been the National Democratic Front (NDF),[53] which was meant to "win over the middle forces and elements [to the revolutionary cause] in order to isolate the die-hard elements" (Sison 1968a). First planned in 1971, the NDF was formally established on April 24, 1973. The early leaders of the NDF included Satur Ocampo and Antonio Zumel. Horacio Morales assumed prominence in the organization in the late 1970s.[54] In addition to the CPP and NPA, NDF member organizations include Katipunan ng mga Samahang Manggagawa (KASAMA = National Association of Workers), Pambansang Kilusan ng Magbubukid (PKM = National Farmers' Organization), Kabataang Makabayan (KM = Nationalist Youth), Makabayang Kilusan ng Bagong Kababaihan (MAKIBAKA = Nationalist Movement of New Women), Cordillera People's Democratic Front, Christians for National Liberation, Katipunan ng mga Gurong Makabayan (KAGUMA = Association of Nationalist Teachers), and Makabayang Samahang Pangkalsugan (MSP = National Association of Health Workers, or Patriotic Health Association).

The original NDF manifesto spelled out an agenda of nationalist political and social transformation, including support for "a genuine

land reform program that can liberate the peasant masses from feudal and semifeudal exploitation and raise agricultural production through cooperation" (Kessler 1989: 80–81). The NDF program went through several iterations over the years, but the 1985 program of the NDF bore a substantial resemblance to this original charter (see Kessler 1989: 82–84). The foremost themes remain nationalism and opposition to U.S. imperialism. At the same time, the call for a genuine land-reform program has consistently been a central element of the NDF program.[55]

Nationalist and Land Tenure–related Themes

Nationalism and the struggle against imperialism are part of Sison's family heritage. His great-grandfather had supported the Katipunan, a secret society dedicated to ending Spanish colonial rule. Later his great-grandfather diverted grain to forces resisting the imposition of American colonial rule. Sison's great-uncle was killed by American troops for supporting the resistance (Chapman 1987: 49).

Central to the educational development of the CPP founders was the Philippine nationalism of Teodor Agoncillo, Hernando Abaya, Cesar Majul, and Claro M. Recto, which had taken hold among University of the Philippines academics in the 1950s. Philippine nationalists indicted America's colonial intervention for its violent suppression of Philippine independence at the turn of the century. Even after nominal independence, postwar trade and agreements on military bases assured continuing American influence, if not domination. Whatever the benefits of the American colonial era, they were unknown to the new generation of students. In the words of Francisco Nemenzo: "You had a new generation of Filipinos who had no recollection of MacArthur and the war experience. Their recollection of America was a country that was shooting Filipinos inside Clark Air Base, throwing its weight around, bullying little Cuba."[56]

Anti-American sentiment grew and became more radical with the increasing U.S. involvement in the Vietnam conflict, the intervention being viewed as paralleling the earlier Philippine experience. The link was reinforced by the Vietnam-related expansion of operations at U.S. Philippine bases. In September 1966, Philippine ties to the Vietnam conflict became even more direct: at the behest of the United States, President Marcos committed 2,000 Filipino troops for "civic action" duty in Vietnam.

The concurrent unfolding of the Chinese Cultural Revolution also exerted considerable influence on Philippine university students, par-

ticularly on the intellectual development of Sison and the other CPP founders.[57] Most important, the Chinese experience and Mao's writings focused the attention of these urban intellectuals on the problems of the Philippine countryside and stimulated a variety of student contacts with the rural populace. Tenure-related grievances are at the heart of peasant support for the CPP/NPA. "The peasant struggle for land is the main democratic content of the present stage of the Philippine Revolution," Sison wrote (1968b: 9). Victor Corpus, a former military strategist for the NPA, sounded the same theme: "It is the problem of the peasant farmers—the issue of agrarian reform—which is the most urgent and primary. . . . It is this issue that the CPP/NPA primarily uses to arouse the people in the countryside to join and fight for their cause. Like cogon grass with a deep taproot, the taproot is unequal distribution of landownership in the country; all other issues are mere lateral roots."[58] Peasants displaced by the expansion of sugar plantations in Negros Occidental in the 1960s, the (often foreign-financed) expansion of banana plantations in Mindanao in the 1970s, and other forms of land grabbing rallied to the CPP/NPA's promise of land to the landless. Other peasants turned to the insurgent movement as a means of strengthening their negotiating position vis-à-vis landlords and moneylenders.[59]

In response, the CPP/NPA enacted a land-reform program, which has typically involved well-enforced rent reductions coupled with reductions in money-lending interest rates.[60] There are rarer instances in which landowners have been driven off their property and the laborers given individual or communal usufruct rights. In cases of land redistribution, beneficiaries are required to pay 5 to 10 percent of their net annual income to the NPA. Military estimates put the area so distributed as of December 1988 at over 31,000 hectares. Personal observation suggests that insurgent activity has also indirectly facilitated abandonment of other properties, leaving the permanent labor force in a position to negotiate with the banks or the Department of Agrarian Reform (DAR) for acquisition of the land. The NPA reform provides a benchmark against which peasants can measure the government's commitment to agrarian reform.

The success of the CPP/NPA lies in its ability to link tenure-related grievances to the international arena, thereby melding nationalist themes with peasant demands for agrarian reform. CPP/NPA educational and recruitment programs stress these links, rather than communist doctrine.[61] In analyzing the peasants' social conditions, CPP/NPA organizers cite foreign multinational firms that have usurped substan-

tial tracts of land for export crop production, the denuding of Philippine forests for export markets, foreign corporate domination of the agricultural input markets, and government efforts to attract foreign investment, including suppression of agricultural (and urban) wage demands (Chapman 1987: 140; Hawes 1990: 293–94; Kessler 1989: 67). Prior to 1992, military abuses were similarly explained in terms of Philippine–U.S. relations, notably U.S. preoccupation with military basing rights and U.S. provision of military assistance.

The Locus of Early CPP/NPA Successes

Although the NPA was based on Buscayno's Huk organization, the CPP/NPA found early success, not in Central Luzon, the traditional seedbed for Philippine rural unrest, but in the peripheral, mountainous areas of the country, including eastern and northern Mindanao, Samar, Bicol, and the Cordillera mountains of northern Luzon. Increased militarization, improved transportation and communication, and substantial government investment had combined to make Central Luzon a less hospitable site for peasant revolution. Furthermore, continuing commercialization of rice agriculture, programs of partial land reform, population growth, and new labor and land-tenure arrangements occasioned considerable differentiation among peasant cultivators. This increased stratification and the varying, sometimes conflicting, interests of different segments of the cultivating population deterred organization or collective action.[62]

By contrast, in many upland areas, lawlessness and land grabbing were more extensive, while patron-client networks were weak or nonexistent, and landlord and government authority was tenuous. Human rights abuses were frequent in many of these regions, as local CHDF detachments served as private armies for landowners bent on expanding their holdings by illegal means and maintaining a compliant labor force.[63] In some areas, ethnicity—traditional tribal identity—created a further basis for the perception of common interests.[64] The conditions of exploitation were plain, and the relative isolation of these regions was conducive to revolutionary organization. The entrepreneurial or leadership role of the CPP/NPA then provided the critical catalyst for collective action. Notably, the CPP/NPA linked peasant experience of oppression and the Marcos regime.

Martial Law and Human Rights Abuses

Marcos was by general agreement the NPA's "best recruiter."[65] His declaration of martial law and attendant repression of opposition, while

initially crippling many CPP/NPA operations, proved an eventual boon to the movement. Martial law shattered the legal opposition. Threatened by the repression and viewing the traditional elite as discredited by its inability or unwillingness to thwart Marcos, politicized elements of the younger generation fled the cities to join the armed struggle.[66]

Martial law, and the militarization and human rights abuses attendant on it, also drove many peasants into tacit, if not direct, support of the CPP/NPA. Echoing Kerkvliet's characterization of the Huks as "reluctant rebels," Gregg Jones argues that "by the late 1970s, the effects of militarization and government human rights abuses by government soldiers had become a primary, if not the single most important, reason that thousands of rural Filipinos joined or supported the NPA."[67] Similarly, Gary Hawes argues that the absence of alternatives—for protection from government abuses and pursuit of social reform—explains why many peasants turned to the CPP/NPA (Hawes 1990: 288–90).

The actions of government soldiers were not the only abuses from which peasants sought protection. In many areas, the early recruiting successes of the CPP/NPA related to its law-and-order role. Protection was (and is) afforded against abusive landlords, moneylenders, and land grabbers. Striking laborers were protected from harassment, urban squatters from eviction. Punishment was also meted out to those guilty of excessive drinking, theft, rape, and wife-beating.[68] By contrast, in many of these regions the government either had no effective law-enforcement presence or local elites were able to manipulate the legal apparatus through direct control, bribery, legal delays, and the like. Richard Kessler argues, however, that the government's principal shortcoming was (and is) not its ineffective administration of justice, but its refusal to address the more fundamental distributive conflict in Philippine society.[69]

The Catholic Church and the CPP/NPA

The growth of the CPP/NPA in the late 1970s and early 1980s was further facilitated by elements of the Catholic Church. The Church's post–Vatican II posture on social justice, and the creation of Basic Christian Communities (BCCs), focused attention on existing inequities and abuses, gave new voice to critiques of social ills, and legitimized direct peasant action to redress social grievances. Although much of the Church hierarchy is vehemently anticommunist, elements of the Church participated directly, or indirectly, in the activities of the CPP/NPA,

lending legitimacy to the CPP/NPA and helping the insurgents overcome some of the anticommunist sentiment among peasants. Radical
priests and nuns joined the Christians for National Liberation (CNL), a
member organization of the National Democratic Front (NDF). Some
rural priests provided field support to the CPP/NPA, others joined the
armed struggle. Supporters within the Church also afforded the CPP/
NPA additional links to the urban middle class.[70] Gregg Jones suggests
that support for the CPP/NPA from within the Church reflected two
phenomena: frustration with other means of effecting social justice, and
the "incendiary union" of resurgent nationalism and theologies of liberation (1989: 202).

The CPP/NPA also capitalized on Church-sponsored organizational work, including that of the Federation of Free Farmers (FFF), the
National Federation of Sugar Workers (NFSW), and the Basic Christian
Communities. These organizations stressed legal action, offering peasants a nonviolent alternative for pursuit of social reform, with the FFF
adopting an explicitly anticommunist posture. The insurgents, however, saw the members of these groups as attractive recruits: already
politicized, and often experienced in the frustrations of efforts at peaceful reform, these peasants were considered more amenable to the call
for armed struggle.

Martial Law Fractures Elite Solidarity

The emergence and growth of the Huk movement reflected the ex-
acerbation of the elite-peasant schism and the fracturing of elite solidarity occasioned by the Japanese occupation during World War II. The
explosive growth of the CPP/NPA in the later years of Marcos's rule
was similarly facilitated by a split in the Philippine elite. Under martial
law, Marcos deliberately set out to dismantle oppositional elements of
the traditional Philippine elite. Indeed, part of the justification for martial law was the need to overcome elite opposition and create a "New
Society."[71] Selective enforcement of land-reform legislation, forced sales
of enterprises at a fraction of their value, and the creation of "crony"
marketing monopolies for sugar and coconuts, and their abuse for personal gain, were but some of the instruments Marcos employed to this
end. On the one hand, these policies, coupled with downturns in world
sugar and coconut prices, weakened landlord control in the countryside
at a time of increasing grievances among tenants and laborers, who bore
the brunt of both economic retrenchment and human rights abuses. At
the same time, Marcos's policies eventually prompted some well-to-do

business leaders and landowners to lend tacit moral, if not direct financial, support to the CPP/NPA and its affiliates as the only effective alternative to the Marcos regime (Overholt 1987: 95).

This break in elite solidarity aided the growth of the CPP/NPA by creating political space for peasant mobilization.[72] The aims of the anti-Marcos elite and those of the CPP/NPA should not be mistaken, however. The former sought only the ouster of Marcos and the restoration of their privileges; the latter sought a fundamental restructuring of Philippine society, including the eventual elimination of the elite class (Kessler 1989: 21).

Boycott of the 1986 Elections: A CPP/NPA Setback

By 1985, the CPP/NPA appeared poised to exert appreciable influence over the course of Philippine politics. Its ranks had swelled with Filipinos reacting to land-related grievances and the repression and abuses of martial law. The radicalization of the Catholic Church and schisms within the elite had further facilitated the CPP/NPA's rapid growth. Even conservative estimates indicated that the CPP/NPA was operating in one-fifth of the villages in the Philippines (Nemenzo 1985: 57; Porter 1987b: 19). The CPP/NPA claimed an "organized" mass base of 1 million, and a "general" mass base of 10 million people variously influenced by the movement.[73] Yet two months into 1986, the CPP/NPA found itself marginalized.

The CPP/NPA lost significant political ground because of its boycott of the February 1986 presidential elections.[74] In 1978, 1981, and, to a lesser extent, 1984, the CPP/NPA had been vindicated in its decision to boycott elections. As the CPP/NPA and several other opposition forces predicted, Marcos so limited the opportunities afforded legal oppositional parties and so distorted vote tabulations in these elections as to make participation meaningless. Yet the turnout for the 1984 National Assembly elections suggested limited public sympathy for the boycott policy, and participants felt confirmed in their decision when the opposition parties made a strong showing, notwithstanding Marcos's manipulation of the results.

There was even less popular support for the call to boycott the 1986 elections. It was in misjudging the depth of popular sentiment favoring electoral participation that the CPP/NPA erred most seriously in 1986. The boycott decision was not lightly taken. It occasioned extensive internal debate preceding the election. Although BAYAN, the NDF-influenced political alliance, hewed to the CPP/NPA boycott decision,

prominent members of BAYAN, including its chairman, Lorenzo Tañada, opted to participate in the electoral process. "The issue in 1984
and the issue in the coming elections are different. Even if the opposition is able to elect a majority in the *Batasan* [National Assembly]
Marcos could repeal any law they pass or even dissolve the *Batasan*
itself. If we win the elections on February 7, we can terminate the
Marcos dictatorship," Tañada argued (Petitjean 1986a: 10).

In the immediate aftermath, the CPP/NPA could point to Marcos's
theft of the election as confirming the appropriateness of the boycott
decision. What the CPP/NPA leaders did not anticipate—although in
this they were hardly alone—was the military revolt that precipitated
Marcos's ouster. The success of this rebellion turned on popular involvement, but the CPP/NPA was positioned to play only a marginal
role in galvanizing mass support. Having been at the forefront of the
opposition to Marcos for so long, the CPP/NPA was on the sidelines
when the denouement came.

CPP/NPA Human Rights Abuses

Increasing CPP/NPA human rights abuses also served to reduce
public support for the insurgents. By most accounts, the CPP/NPA was
quite selective in its political assassinations and in other punishments
meted out to "enemies of the people," at least until the mid 1980s. The
movement also enforced a rigid code of discipline, banning drinking,
gambling, and a range of "inappropriate" social behavior.[75] However,
atrocities increased in the late 1980s, tarnishing the movement's reputation. Particularly egregious were a series of internal purges in Mindanao
stemming from concerns about government deep-penetration agents.
There have also been reports of reprisals, including execution, against
villagers who refused to pay CPP/NPA tax assessments. The taxation
policy itself appears to have alienated many middle-class businessper-
sons and, in some cases, villagers. The CPP/NPA issued guidelines in
February 1988 to regularize and legitimize tax collections.[76] An NPA
massacre of a group of anticommunist religious "cultists" in June 1989
prompted further negative publicity and was widely condemned.[77]

Current Assessments of the CPP/NPA

Since late 1991, a major factional split has emerged within the
CPP/NPA. The Manila-Rizal Regional Committee and regional committees in the Visayas and Mindanao, together representing as much as
60 percent of the CPP membership, have broken from the Maoist line of

CPP-founder Jose Maria Sison, who remains in exile. Sison loyalists remain committed to protracted people's war based in the countryside; the breakaway groups give greater emphasis to an urban struggle.

Reacting to the strife within the CPP/NPA and the collapse of the socialist states of eastern Europe and the former Soviet Union, Philippine government officials, members of Congress, and business leaders express a markedly reduced sense of urgency concerning the need for redistributive reform. Others dismiss the link between landlessness and the insurgency altogether. Illustrative of these patterns of denial is a 1987 joint statement of two sugar-planters' organizations:

It has been said by some quarters that the present state in sugarlands breeds agrarian unrest because of the great disparity between the rich and the poor. But it can be said without fear of contradiction that in the area of Bais, Tanjay, Manjuyod and Mabinay, Negros Oriental—the sugarland areas of Negros Oriental—there is no agrarian unrest. In fact, communist insurgency in these places is minimal and "imported." This proves that agrarian unrest is *not caused* by the simple fact that the farm workers do not own the lands they till but by some factors more fundamental than that. And the most important factor is the *treatment* the farm workers get from their landowner-employers.[78]

The phrasing of this passage is instructive. On the one hand, the very existence of agrarian unrest is denied; on the other, the existence of agrarian unrest is acknowledged, but it is deemed minimal. The planters apparently intend to suggest that such insurgent operations as occur in their districts are the work of outside agents provocateurs who are disrupting the districts' harmonious agrarian relations.[79]

In this view, the existence and success of insurgent agents is due, not to land hunger per se, but to the failure of other, outside landowners in their patronal role. This passage implicitly recognizes that within the named districts, farmworkers are receptive to calls for armed rebellion, and that at least some farmworkers are actively soliciting the assistance of the insurgents. The remarks of NPA rebels and supporters and the Philippine legacy of recurrent land tenure–related rebellions belie suggestions that land hunger is irrelevant to the current insurgency.[80]

Some landowners denigrate the NPA by alleging that the insurgents have taken the "easy way," that they are unwilling to work hard for personal and national advancement.[81] Others, however, acknowledge the appeal (and dedication) of the NPA, even as they minimize the peasant aspirations underlying that appeal. "The NPA will only give up when the poor are given economic opportunity, equality, and justice" (Starke interview, June 16, 1986).

Where it exists, elite optimism about the insurgent threat and the waning perception of urgency in addressing land-tenure relations seem at considerable odds with firsthand impressions of rural life. Whatever the current setbacks suffered by the insurgents, most of the underlying conditions—land-tenure grievances, human rights abuses, and U.S. influence in the Philippines—against which their struggle is aimed, and around which they have so successfully organized in the past, remain fundamentally unaltered. The grievances are real; the question remains whether Filipinos can meaningfully redress these grievances in a peaceful, democratic fashion.

Nonrevolutionary Peasant Organizations

If extended attention has been accorded the activities of rebellious or revolutionary movements, that is not to suggest that Philippine peasants have entirely wanted for alternative social organizations and alternative means of pursuing their agrarian agenda. Social activists within the Catholic Church have played a special role in the organizational lives of two of the more prominent peasant groups, the Federation of Free Farmers (FFF) and the National Federation of Sugar Workers (NFSW). Let us consider them in turn.

The Federation of Free Farmers

The FFF was founded in 1953 as a Christian democratic response to the radical, communist-oriented organizations allied with the Huk movement. The importance of religion and religious idiom in peasant movements is evidenced by the instrumental role of Jesuit priests such as Fr. Walter Hogan and Fr. Hector Mauri in the organization of the FFF, the frequent service of parish priests as FFF advisers and proponents, and the leadership of the Jesuit-educated Jeremias Montemayor, president of the FFF since its inception.[82] The FFF views agrarian relations primarily in terms of social justice, with the national leadership giving legal, and occasionally political, definition to that concept. The organization experienced rapid growth in the late 1960s after a prolonged period of slow but steady growth. The late 1960s also saw the radicalization of an appreciable part of the younger FFF membership, radicalization that reflected the poverty and exploitation of the peasantry, reaction to increasing persecution of FFF organizers by landowners and the growing influence of the theology of liberation in the Philippines in the wake of Vatican II. In particular, religiously based Philippine groups

borrowed from the organizational techniques developed by Paolo
Friere, Gustavo Gutierrez, and others in Latin America (Chapman 1987:
200–201; Po and Montiel 1980: 51–53).

The FFF achieved maximum effect in 1969, when it collaborated
with a student group, the Federated Movement for Social Justice and
Reform, to organize a nearly three-month-long protest at Agrifina Circle in Manila, fronting the Department of Agriculture. Coupled with a
storming of the presidential palace, this demonstration resulted in the
immediate resolution of numerous grievances involving land grabbing
and failure to deliver promised land titles. The demonstrations also
catalyzed the passage of new agrarian-reform legislation in 1971. However, this legislation was effectively superseded by martial law and
Marcos's presidential decrees.[83]

The process of radicalization led to a split in the FFF. In the months
preceding the declaration of martial law, Montemayor began purging
radical members. During martial law, government crackdowns struck
further at radical leaders and local affiliates, with the acquiescence of
the established FFF leadership. All told, some 30 percent of the FFF
membership was purged.[84] Under martial law, Montemayor and the
remaining FFF leadership supported Marcos and his reform initiatives,
compromising the independence of their organization in the process.
FFF identification with Marcos is nowhere better illustrated than in a
passage from an FFF press release issued on January 10, 1986, at the
height of the "snap election" campaign between Marcos and Aquino.
Responding to an order by Marcos expanding agrarian reform to public
lands and private lands other than those planted to rice and corn, Montemayor is quoted as saying: "This recent act of the President is an
indication that President Marcos continues to run true to form as the
greatest champion of social justice in the history of the Philippines"
(FFF 1986a: 1).

The National Federation of Sugar Workers

As the militancy of the FFF waned, activist priests set about establishing other farmers' organizations, among them the National Federation of Sugar Workers (NFSW). Founded in 1971, the NFSW was the
brainchild of Fr. Luis Jalandoni, scion of a wealthy landowning family
and social action director of the Bacolod diocese, and Fr. Hector Mauri,
an Italian Jesuit. Mauri had earlier, in March 1956, established a chapter
of the FFF on Negros. Six years of negotiations, legal action, and strikes
yielded little more than frustration for the FFF chapter. Negros's largest

sugar mill, the Victorias Milling Company, colluded with sugarcane growers to deny farmworkers their statutory share of sugar profits.[85] Strikes, some involving as many as 4,000 farmworkers, were met with violence and large-scale arrests. The chapter's militancy prompted the termination of FFF funding from the papal nuncio and the Asia Foundation and Fr. Mauri's eviction from the Bishop's Residence in Bacolod (McCoy 1984b: 115–18).

With Vatican II and the 1966 appointment of Bishop Antonio Fortich to the Bacolod diocese, social reform endeavors received new impetus. It was in this spirit that the NFSW was established, led by Ed Tejada, a Catholic student leader, Fr. Edgar Saguinsin, and Fr. Mauri. Subsequent leadership changes evidenced the continuing influence of the Church. Robert Ortaliz, a government official active in the Church's Sa Maria movement,[86] replaced Tejada as NFSW president. Ortaliz later became an executive in the militant labor federation, Kilusang Mayo Uno (May 1st Movement). The late Serge Cherniguin, national vice president of the NFSW, similarly cited the Church and the theology of liberation in shaping his decision to resign his position as *encargado* (overseer) on a sugar hacienda to work with the union.[87]

Cherniguin also attributed the NFSW's early organizational success to the Church. The Church's Basic Christian Communities served to organize sugar workers and other peasants. Through the BCCs, workers were made aware of biblical condemnations of oppression. The BCCs redefined community, stressing the importance of united action in confronting social injustices. The groundwork thus laid, union organizers then approached BCC members and began to focus more specifically on the legal rights of farm and mill workers and the inequities in Philippine landownership. At the same time, the Church endeavored to arouse the consciences of the landowners. Yet, in words attributed to Bishop Antonio Fortich, "Three hundred years of Catholic education in the Philippines has been a waste; it only ended up educating exploiters and oppressors."[88]

Nuns took up the union cause during a bitter contest over a union-certification election at the Binalbagan-Isabela Sugar Company (BISCOM) mill. As the election approached, workers were threatened with loss of various hacienda benefits and employment opportunities. Zoilo de la Cruz, president of the rival union federation, the NACUSIP (National Congress of Unions in the Sugar Industry of the Philippines), wrote the secretary of defense, charging NFSW leaders with seditious behavior. Moreover, de la Cruz claimed that the "foreign priests" aiding

the NFSW threatened the "peace and order of Negros Occidental."[89] Church and union activists were branded communist with little regard for their ideological orientation. Efforts to enforce existing laws were identified as subversive.

The Association of Major Religious Superiors (AMRS) also became active in the struggle for farmworkers' rights on the sugar haciendas. In the mid 1970s, the AMRS released an exhaustive study of the sugar industry on Negros, documenting widespread noncompliance with labor laws and condemning the "outdated feudal system of dependency" found on the haciendas.[90]

Over time, the NFSW has shifted to a more militant posture. Initially, the union emphasized the legal rights of the farmworkers, challenging violations of the labor code. Innumerable cases were filed, but "so many were dismissed that DOLE [the Department of Labor and Employment] began using a mimeograph form. They had only to fill in the blanks. Each day stacks of dismissals were delivered to the NFSW office."[91] This so discouraged farm workers that NFSW membership fell from "30,000 to 1,000."[92] Although legal advice and judicial proceedings remain prominent parts of the union's work,[93] the union's educational work now emphasizes the need to restructure the entire sugar industry and the importance of landownership. Union membership later rebounded, and by 1989 the NFSW was reporting a membership of around 85,000 workers.[94]

During the height of the sugar crisis in the mid 1980s, the NFSW introduced a farm-lot program for utilizing idle land—with the landowners' consent—to produce foodstuffs and thereby ameliorate the extensive hunger among the sugar workers, several hundred thousand of whom were unemployed. The NFSW typically signed three-year land-use contracts for its farm-lot program, agreeing thereafter to return the parcels involved. Around 4,000 hectares were made available for food lots, which was barely 1 percent of the farm area in Negros. Large landowners were resistant to land sharing, fearing—despite union assurances to the contrary—that farmworkers would lay permanent claim to the land.[95] Viewed by union leaders as a breakthrough in early 1987, the program represented the first instance of land sharing for many landowners, and the first time farmworkers had been entitled to their entire production. With the upturn in domestic sugar prices in the late 1980s and early 1990s, the farm-lot program came under attack. Many landowners reclaimed the farm lots, often without complying with labor laws or offering their workers a livelihood capable of meeting basic needs.

Labor relations remain a source of constant conflict. Harassment, torture, and assassination of union organizers and sympathizers continues. Many of the abuses are committed by vigilantes and private landowner armies financed by the Negros Democracy and Peace Foundation, a fund established by *hacenderos* and mill owners through an assessment on milled sugarcane. The opening of political space for union activities attendant on the transition from the Marcos to the Aquino regime, which saw popular demonstrations involving tens of thousands of peasants in Bacolod (the provincial capital of Negros Occidental) in 1986, has now narrowed appreciably.

4

Landlessness, Low Productivity, and Failed Reforms

The land . . . has a value far beyond its economic benefits. It provides social security, community status, and other non-monetized benefits.
—John Osmeña

When she assumed the presidency in 1986, Corazon Aquino had to be concerned with three related agrarian issues: extensive and increasing landlessness; poor agricultural performance; and a history of Philippine land-reform initiatives that were limited in scope and impact. Assessments of all three issues varied markedly. Empirical data were scarce and their interpretations disputed. Cultural and structural factors established the context for the debate over agrarian-reform policy; the competing claims concerning the benefits of reform were the heart of that debate.

Although political outcomes may ultimately reflect the relative power of competing personalities, parties, or interests, the debate is typically framed in terms of purported facts and their interpretation. The deliberations over Philippine agrarian-reform policy were characterized throughout by contested meanings and contested histories. To evaluate the need for agrarian reform, it was essential that the nature of existing land-tenure patterns and the extent of landlessness first be determined. In the Philippine case, the data on landlessness were extremely poor, and the debate was less concerned with the extensiveness of landlessness than with the extent of land concentration.

A second element in assessing the need for agrarian reform involved the relationship between prevailing tenure patterns and agricultural performance. At issue was the prospect, if any, that agrarian reform would result in improved Philippine agricultural performance. The issue of farm size and agricultural productivity, although relatively

settled internationally, was the aspect of the tenure-productivity relationship most disputed in the Philippines. Meanwhile, the more complicated and unsettled empirical link between tenure type and productivity elicited relatively little debate.

Finally, the Philippine experience with past reform programs fueled a variety of debates as the Aquino administration formulated its reform program. At issue were, among other things, the appropriate scope of reform in terms of crops and farm size, the past failure and present ability or inability of the government to recompense owners of expropriated properties, and the past failure and present ability or inability of reform beneficiaries to pay land amortizations.

Contested Terminology, Contested Meanings

The paternal construct of Philippine landowners notwithstanding, agrarian relations are not characterized by a hegemonic ideology, if by that we mean a widely embraced construct of agrarian relations.[1] Debates over the proper interpretation of theoretical and empirical materials relating to agrarian reform in the Philippines begin with contested terminology and meanings—that is, differences over the very terms with which to describe Philippine "reality." The discussions over land reform in the Philippines involve debates about historical and current events and their meanings. In an important sense, there is no objective "reality" waiting to be discovered; instead, there are conflicting versions of past and present realities. The Philippine reform debate became a contest over which of these competing paradigms would dominate policymaking.

Both laborers and landowners use language to describe their centrality to agriculture rather than the particulars of their role in usual forms of production. Tenants, landless laborers, and other nonlandowning cultivators term themselves "farmers" to emphasize their central role in agricultural production. For their part, landowners typically term themselves "planters" as a means of similarly signaling an essential role in the production process, although they are frequently absentee landowners or otherwise manage their holdings indirectly (NOPA and AABT 1987).

The concept of agrarian reform has been the subject of contested meanings, ranging from the introduction of Green Revolution technological innovations to tenancy regulation, from land resettlement to land redistribution. Those wishing to minimize the redistributive core

of agrarian reform have, however, frequently promoted technological interventions under the guise of agrarian reform and as a substitute for land redistribution (cf. Ledesma 1980). Landlords attempt to shape the reform discourse in other ways, and some characterize their relationship with share tenants as one of profit sharing (Sawit 1987: 41). This is a technically accurate description of share-tenancy: the name denotes a sharing—to a degree unspecified—of crop output as well as inputs to production. However, terming the relationship "profit sharing" tends to defuse the negative connotations associated with share-tenancy. It also speaks to those who extol profit sharing (or stock distribution) as an alternative to—and the equivalent of—redistributive reform. By a turn of phrase, share-tenancy might be transformed from a tenurial form that is to be abolished by agrarian reform to agrarian reform itself.

In a similar fashion, the terminology used to denote larger Philippine landholdings is the subject of orchestration. Landowners often explicitly reject terms such as "hacienda," which suggests the existence of large farms. "Only 12 percent of the planters own more than 10 hectares. Even the large holdings are getting smaller because of inheritance," asserted a group of Negros elites.[2] These claims are flatly contradicted by census and survey data that in 1988 showed operational farm holdings in excess of 100, 200, even 500 hectares.[3] When pressed, large landowners will acknowledge the existence of sizable farm holdings. However, the landowners emphasize how few large holdings there are in number, ignoring the significant portion of farm area encompassed by such farms.[4] For the landless, by contrast, it is the issue of land concentration in the hands of the few that elicits such determined reformist sentiments.

The debates over meanings and terminology are not simple semantic exercises; they have been central to Philippine policymaking. Conflicting constructions of past and present agrarian relations occupied a significant part of the agrarian-reform deliberations. Although the Aquino government's reform legislation suggests the continuing dominance of a particular paradigm—one that is purveyed by large commercial landowners—challenges to that paradigm are considerable and mounting.

Agrarian Structure and Poverty

In 1985, the Philippine archipelago was home to 56.8 million people, or roughly 10.2 million families. Nearly 43 percent, around 4.4 million

households, of all Filipinos made their living from agricultural cultivation.[5] As of 1980, about 7.85 million hectares (1 hectare = 2.47 acres) were planted in annual or permanent crops, out of a total farm area of 9.73 million hectares.[6] Most of the remainder was equally divided between temporarily idle, but arable, land (0.84 million hectares) and nonarable meadows or forests (0.87 million hectares). This agricultural land base provided a ratio of 1.8 cropped hectares per farm family; inclusion of idle arable land raised the ratio to 1.99 hectares. These ratios were appreciably higher than those in countries such as China or South Korea but much lower than those in most Latin American or many African settings.

The Philippine government estimated that in 1987, *64 percent of the rural population nationwide was living below the poverty threshold.* Of the total population, 59 percent were similarly situated (ROP, NEDA 1986b: 33). Rural underemployment—defined as working less than 40 hours per week—was extreme, estimated at over 40 percent in 1987, with some estimates exceeding 60 percent.[7] The pressures of high population growth rates and limited rural employment opportunities—agricultural or nonagricultural—were also reflected in stagnant or declining real wage levels for most agricultural laborers during the 1960s and 1980s.[8]

In the sugar sector, periodic sharp downturns in world and domestic prices in the 1970s and 1980s were accompanied by massive unemployment, and by labor displacement through mechanization and diversification to alternate, capital-intensive products (Lopez-Gonzaga 1983; McCoy 1984b: 61–73; Rutten 1982). On Negros, the retrenchment in sugarcane production also caused a decline in employment opportunities for the traditional harvest labor force composed of migratory laborers (*sacadas*) from other islands. Even in the best of times, sugar workers were among the most impoverished members of the Philippine labor force. The crisis in the sugar sector in the early 1980s meant that *in the Western Visayas region, which includes Negros Occidental, nearly three-quarters of the total population was living below the poverty threshold in 1986* (ROP, NEDA 1986b: 51).

The 1980 agricultural census confirmed the trends of growing population pressure and diminishing availability of land suitable for agricultural expansion (ROP, NCSO 1985a). While there were increases in both the number of farms (from 2.4 to 3.4 million)[9] and the area in farms (from 8.5 to 9.7 million hectares), average farm size declined from 3.6 to 2.8 hectares over the 1971–80 period.

Table 1 details the national pattern of farm-holding size as of 1980,

TABLE 1

Distribution of Philippine Farms by Number and Size, 1980

Farm size (hectares)	Number	Percent	Area (1,000 ha)	Percent
Under 0.5	289,962	8.5%	68.9	0.7%
0.5– 0.99	485,829	14.2	300.1	3.1
1.00– 1.99	964,220	28.2	1,189.9	12.2
2.00– 2.99	613,824	17.9	1,332.3	13.7
3.00– 4.99	588,151	17.2	2,066.7	21.3
5.00– 7.00	283,585	8.3	1,612.1	16.6
7.01– 9.99	76,421	2.2	630.8	6.5
10.00–24.99	103,723	3.0	1,406.4	14.5
25.00 & Over	14,608	0.4	1,117.8	11.5
TOTAL	3,420,323	100.0%	9,725.2	100.0%

SOURCE: National Census and Statistics Office, *1980 Census of Agriculture* (Manila, 1985).
NOTE: Data are for operational holdings. Columns may not add up to total because of rounding.

giving evidence of persisting concentration of landownership.[10] Farms of less than 2 hectares accounted for 50.9 percent of Filipino farms, yet their aggregate area was only 16 percent of total farm area. Farms of 10 hectares and above included 26 percent of the land in farms, while representing a mere 3.4 percent of all farms.

Provincial-level figures revealed instances of even greater regional concentration of landownership. The province of Negros Occidental, one-third the size of New Hampshire, was home to just over 2.1 million people, or 351,100 families, as of 1985. Forty-nine percent (some 172,000 households) of the province's residents made their living from agriculture. As of 1980, some 249,200 hectares were planted in annual or permanent crops, with sugarcane occupying much of this land. The increasing population pressure on the province's agricultural land base was exacerbated by severe concentration of landownership (Table 2). Farms under 2 hectares accounted—as nationally—for roughly half (50.2 percent) of all farms in Negros Occidental, while encompassing markedly less farm area (8.9 percent) than the national average. Farms of above 10 hectares, by contrast, made up 8.7 percent of all farms, yet included fully 59.8 percent of the provincial farm area.

The 1980 census figures represented the best available data at the time the Aquino government deliberated agrarian reform. Data gathered subsequent to the passage of the reform law, as part of the Listasaka land-registration program, suggest an even greater concentration of landownership than that shown in the 1980 census. James Putzel

interprets the preliminary Listasaka data as demonstrating that fewer than 1 percent of all Philippine families owned 50 percent of the agricultural land reported in 1988 (1992: 28–29).

The continuing skewed distribution of land is evidence of the ineffectiveness and limited scope of previous Philippine land-reform initiatives. These reforms were limited to redefining or eliminating tenancy on rice and corn holdings. To avoid the reforms, large landowners often displaced tenant farmers in favor of hired laborers and shifted out of rice or corn production. Although illegal, such actions enabled landlords to evade application of the reform law.[11] Other policies such as subsidized credit for imported farm machinery, particularly in the sugar sector (bankrolled in substantial part by the World Bank, especially in the years 1974–79 [McCoy 1984b: 60–73; id. 1985: 180–82]), and the high costs of supervising hired labor exacerbated the substitution of capital for labor. Production was biased toward capital-intensive operations with few hired laborers.

Landlessness

Although the data on landlessness in the Philippines are imprecise, there is general agreement that it is extensive and growing. The term "landless" refers throughout to *all* cultivating relationships in which cultivators work land without having ownership or ownerlike rights in that land, whether they are called "tenants," "agricultural laborers," or

TABLE 2

Distribution of Negros Occidental Farms by Number and Size, 1980

Farm size (hectares)	Number	Percent	Area (1,000 ha)	Percent
Under 0.5	4,012	6.7%	987	0.3%
0.5– 0.99	9,710	16.2	5,878	2.0
1.00– 1.99	16,371	27.3	19,587	6.6
2.00– 2.99	9,461	15.8	20,228	6.8
3.00– 4.99	8,143	13.6	28,262	9.6
5.00– 7.00	5,481	9.1	20,813	7.0
7.01– 9.99	1,604	2.7	13,306	4.5
10.00–24.99	3,608	6.0	48,729	16.5
25.00 & Over	1,593	2.7	128,129	43.3
TOTAL	59,983	100.0%	295,919	100.0%

SOURCE: National Census & Statistics Office, *1980 Census of Agriculture: Negros Occidental*, vol. 1: *Final Report* (Manila, September 1985).

NOTE: Data are for operational holdings. Columns may not add up to total because of rounding.

TABLE 3
Number and Area of Philippine Farms by Tenure, 1980

Tenure	Number	Percent	Area	Percent
Total holdings	3,420,323		9,725,200	
Owned or held in ownerlike possession	1,993,293	58.3%	6,496,200	66.8%
Rented or leased from others	871,536	25.5	1,806,900	18.6
Rent free	65,376	1.9	96,700	1.0
Other single forms of tenure	37,462	1.1	104,700	1.1
More than one form of tenure	452,655	13.2	1,220,700	12.6
Of which:				
owned			544,900	5.6
rented			604,800	6.2
rent free			37,700	0.4
other			33,400	0.3

SOURCE: National Census and Statistics Office, *1980 Census of Agriculture* (Manila, 1985).
NOTE: Columns may not add up to total because of rounding.

something else. Table 3 delineates land-tenure patterns as of 1980. A conservative estimate for 1980[12] suggests that of the then nearly 3.9 million agricultural families, at least 1.8 million (46 percent) made their living entirely or primarily from land they did not own.

Even apart from possible underestimation of the 1980 figures, the number of landless families is certain to have increased substantially during the 1980s. Among the contributing factors were continuing rapid population growth, the diminishing availability of new farmland, and limited nonagricultural employment opportunities. These factors, and the displacement of tenants in favor of hired laborers by owners evading the Marcos-era land reform, have disproportionately increased the number of laborer families relative to tenant families in recent years (Kikuchi 1983).

It appears that of the roughly 4.4 million agricultural families in 1985, around 2.2 to 2.8 million made their living entirely or primarily from land they did not own.[13] Of these, some 1.0–1.3 million families were on holdings entirely or predominantly rented, and a further 0.9–1.8 million families were dependent on performing agricultural labor for hire without simultaneously farming land as tenants. (The higher estimate for each group correlates with the lower estimate for the other group.) *Landless families represented 50–64 percent of the agricultural population, and 22–27 percent of the total population.*

Mirroring the national trend, landlessness in Negros Occidental was significant and increasing. A conservative estimate for 1985 suggests

that, of the then roughly 172,000 agricultural families, about 136,900 made their living wholly or primarily from land they did not own. Of these, some 19,100 families were on holdings wholly or predominantly rented, and a further 117,800 families were dependent on performing agricultural labor for hire without simultaneously farming land as tenants. By 1985, landless families constituted nearly 80 percent of Negros Occidental's agricultural population and almost 40 percent of its total population.

At the time of the reform debates, other estimates of Philippine landlessness were significantly higher than the figures I have developed. In 1980, Antonio Ledesma used a figure of 3.4 million landless laborer households, citing several census-based studies (Ledesma 1980: 327). A 1987 Institute of Agrarian Studies (IAS) study, by contrast, listed some 4.2 million agricultural and animal-husbandry workers, out of some 9.9 million persons employed in agriculture.[14] With just under two economically active members per household, the IAS data would suggest that the number of landless laborer households was 2.1 million. The Department of Agrarian Reform estimate of 2.0 million share and leasehold tenants in 1985, if taken to be synonymous with tenant households, would likewise be notably higher than my estimate. However, this figure is too high to be consistent with 1985 agricultural population data. The variance in these estimates underscores the need for accurate data on landlessness as part of a rational planning process. Unfortunately, the 1988–89 Listasaka land-registration program only partially addressed this need (and the not-yet-available 1990 agricultural census holds little promise of significantly improving on earlier censuses).

The political impact of the higher estimates was double-edged. On the one hand, they suggested that the landlessness problem was much greater than had been thought, and therefore that much more deserving of remedial action. On the other hand, as landowners and their representatives repeatedly stressed, these higher figures carried the implication that land reform was futile. In combination with assertions of economies of scale in Philippine agriculture, the argument was made that redistributing land to all the landless would result in nonviable "postage stamp" parcels.[15] Others used the higher estimates to emphasize the need for nonagricultural employment opportunities, implying that industrialization was more labor-intensive and would absorb the surplus rural labor.[16] Although labor-intensive industrialization is an essential element of economic improvement in the Philippines, experience strongly suggests that industry has a quite limited absorptive capacity

relative to the existing and projected labor force. Agriculture will, of necessity, remain the economic activity of a plurality of the population for the foreseeable future. The issue then becomes one of maximizing equity and efficiency.

Land Tenure and Agricultural Productivity

A central element of political and scholarly debates over agrarian reform has been the relation, if any, between tenure forms and productivity and between farm size and productivity. In this area, the reform debate in the Philippines was no exception. Somewhat curiously, the latter relation was the subject of considerably greater debate than the former. This focus is explicable less in economic than in political terms, a reflection of the influence of large plantation owners and the political marginalization of rice and corn landlords.

Rice and corn are the primary staple crops in the Philippines, and coconuts and sugarcane are the principal cash crops. In 1980, some 3.65 million hectares were devoted to rice production, inclusive of multiple cropping. Corn production accounted for another 2.47 million hectares, again inclusive of multiple cropping.[17] Sugarcane cultivation occupied a further 0.3 million hectares. Coconut data are reported in terms of trees rather than cultivated area; the total area of farms devoted primarily to coconut production was 2.84 million hectares, or 29.2 percent of the 9.73 million hectares in farms.

Historically, cheap food imports from the United States, trade and exchange rate policies,[18] and relatively abundant land, at least into the 1950s,[19] all served as disincentives to intensification of Philippine agriculture. Furthermore, Philippine agriculture had not benefited from the technological innovations in small-scale food-crop production that the Japanese introduced during their pre–World War II occupation of Korea and Taiwan.[20] The import and pricing-related disincentives to production persisted until well into the 1970s. The modest nature of improvements in Philippine rice and corn yields in more recent years, and the decline in sugarcane yields, suggest the continuing existence of other structural impediments to production, including land-tenure arrangements.

The relationships between landlords and tenants and between landowners and hired laborers are part of a class of principal-agent relationships. As generally stated, the principal-agent problem is this: how to give necessarily decentralized agents (tenants or laborers, for example)

incentives to pursue the objectives of some central actor (in this case, the landlord or landowner). Problems of "adverse selection" and "moral hazard" plague principal-agent relationships. In the case of adverse selection, the prospective tenant (laborer) has information about his or her skills and work habits that is unknown, or largely so, to the prospective landlord (landowner). Lacking such information, landlords (landowners) may have to engage in costly screening of potential tenants (laborers) to assure that they are willing and able to apply the desired level of effort. The problem of moral hazard arises when the actions of the tenant (laborer), notably his or her work effort or use of various inputs, are not directly observable by the landlord (landowner) and agricultural output is a function of both the tenant's (laborer's) effort or use of inputs and uncertain factors, such as the weather, that are outside the tenant's (laborer's) control. In the event of low output, the landlord (landowner) is unable accurately to attribute responsibility for the shortfall between the tenant's (laborer's) effort and poor weather. Knowing this, the tenant (laborer) can exert less effort than the principal would like, since the tenant (laborer) can reduce his or her work effort with some degree of impunity.

While the debate is far from settled, and the empirical results are far from uniform, farm-level studies seem to sustain the proposition that, other things being equal, share and fixed-rent tenancy are less efficient than owner-operated farming.[21] The relative efficiency of owner-operated farms appears fairly clear in terms of crop mix and output value per hectare. While more ambiguous in terms of output for a given crop, the evidence, on balance, points to the same finding, particularly in the absence of efficient mechanisms for contract enforcement. Perhaps the most important advantage of owner-operated farms concerns conservation and permanent improvements to the land.[22] The multi-year investments that can be made include terracing, land leveling, irrigation/drainage improvements, and the introduction of tree crops in appropriate settings. Many can be realized, in large part, through "sweat equity" put in by the farmer and his family, rather than through cash outlay; all require a farmer who is sufficiently motivated and who anticipates a fair return over time on the investment to be undertaken.

There are relatively few farm-level studies of the relationships between tenurial status, technology choice, and productivity in the Philippines, particularly studies that control for land quality and access to support services (see BAECON 1972; Estanislao 1965; Mangahas et al. 1976; Ruttan 1966; Sandoval and Gaon 1971; Von Oppenfeld et al. 1957).

TABLE 4

Comparative Crop Yields for Selected Asian Countries

(Yields in metric tons per hectare)

Country	Rice	Corn	Sugarcane
Bangladesh	2.24	—	45.15
China	5.33	3.66	53.79
India	2.23	1.33	58.98
Indonesia	3.94	1.79	75.15
Japan	6.32	—	—
Korea, South	6.38	4.72	—
Philippines	*2.64*	*1.10*	*47.57*
Taiwan	4.81	3.76	87.14
Thailand	2.01	2.52	39.98
Vietnam	2.79	1.46	39.91
World	3.26	3.67	58.57

SOURCE: UN Food and Agriculture Organization, *1986 FAO Production Yearbook*, vol. 40 (Rome, 1987); Foreign Agricultural Service, U.S. Department of Agriculture, "History of Sugarcane" (computer printout, Aug. 16, 1989); and id., "Rice: Area, Yield and Production" (computer printout, Sept. 15, 1988).

NOTE: Yields are area-weighted average of crop years 1984–86. Yield data are included for countries planting 25,000 hectares or more of that crop.

Among the studies available, the results are not uniform, but upon closer analysis they appear consistent with the "Marshallian" argument (Riedinger 1991: 183–85). However, several prominent Philippine economists interpret the available evidence as indicating that there is little difference in productivity that can be traced to tenure status alone (Mangahas et al. 1976: 7).

Table 4 provides comparative productivity data for the major Philippine crops. These data illustrate the relatively poor performance of Philippine agriculture as of the mid 1980s and suggest that tenant-based agricultural systems are less productive.[23] The primarily tenant-operated rice farms of the Philippines produced only two-fifths to one-half as much rice per hectare, on average, as the owner-operated rice farms of Japan, South Korea, or Taiwan and the ownerlike farms of China, operated since 1978 under the "household responsibility system."[24] Similarly, the predominantly tenant-operated Philippine corn farms produced less than one-third as much corn per hectare, on average, as in South Korea, Taiwan, or China. Finally, average Philippine sugarcane yields, with plantations accounting for much of the production, were less than two-thirds those of Indonesia. More important, in light of oft-heard arguments about "economies of scale" in sugarcane production, Philippine sugarcane yields were, on average, little more

than one-half those of the small (1 to 2 hectare) owner-operated farms of Taiwan, and only one-quarter the yields obtained on small owner-operated farms in Maharashtra state in western India.[25]

The average yield data for other countries in which tenant farmers and agricultural laborers predominate in the agricultural sector, notably Bangladesh and India, mirror the low productivity experience of the Philippines. By contrast, of the countries with predominantly owner-operated agriculture, only Thailand continues to experience low yields. Thailand, however, has the luxury of producing a significant grain surplus and is a major exporter of rice.[26]

The small owner-operator farming system thus appears to demonstrate the greatest productivity potential, and the tenant/laborer system appears to show a striking and consistent lack of potential.[27] However, evidence presented in other studies, particularly data on African agriculture, makes it clear that ownership alone is not sufficient to realize this potential. Owners who lack access to improved seed, fertilizers, pesticides, a regular credit system, technical advice, storage, and reasonable marketing facilities, and who confront very low prices, whether as a result of state controls or of private marketing or milling monopolies, will produce at a very low level.[28]

Although the evidence linking tenurial status and productivity was controverted among Philippine and foreign scholars, there was relatively little debate on this topic during the reform deliberations. In marked contrast to earlier reform programs, landlords in the rice and corn sectors were conspicuous by their absence from the policy deliberations. They had apparently lost their ability to influence the political process. By the mid 1980s, the political debate over the desirability of cultivator ownership versus sharecrop (or leasehold) tenancy had been settled in the Philippines.[29]

Economies of Scale in Agriculture

The issues of economies of scale in Philippine agriculture remained a matter of considerable contention in the political arena, however, although it was largely settled among scholars (see Hayami et al. 1987: 13–16). It was (and is) an article of faith among large landowners that agrarian reform means subdivision of their holdings, with a concomitant decrease in agricultural output (Acuña 1987: 62; NFSP n.d.: 1; NOPA and AABT 1987: 3; PLADAR and DATU-Panay n.d.: 1–2; Sabino 1987: 17). Sugarcane farmers, in particular, argued repeatedly for higher

retention limits, if not outright exemption from reform legislation, on the basis of supposed economies of scale inherent to that crop.[30] Large landowners typically expressed themselves, not as opponents of all reform, but as acting out of concern for the welfare of their nation and their farmworkers, both of which, in their view, would suffer a decline in income in the event of farm fragmentation.[31] Evidence of the centrality of this issue to the reform debate is to be found in the name of an antireform landowners' organization established as the reform debate unfolded, the Land's Utmost Productivity Association (LUPA).[32]

So persistent were the arguments suggesting the existence of economies of scale in Philippine crop production that some representatives of landless cultivators accepted the notion. Jerry Montemayor, of the Federation of Free Farmers, argued that in contrast to large plantations, "The moment you go on a six or five hectare [coconut] plantation, that plantation will become inefficient. That is also true with sugar, banana and other plantations."[33]

Some Philippine scholars of agrarian relations similarly posited the existence of economies of scale in counseling against subdivision of existing estates (Lopez-Gonzaga interview, June 17, 1986). Scholars and analysts evaluating agrarian relations from a Marxist paradigm also accepted the premise of scale economies; their prescription was typically for comprehensive agrarian reform along collectivist lines. Other proreform activists sought to dispel the idea that economies of scale existed in Philippine agriculture (or elsewhere), viewing scale economies as an argument by which redistributive agrarian reform might be defeated (ICSI 1987: 2–3).

What was the available evidence on the issue of economies of scale in agricultural production? Internationally, small farms generally demonstrated an ability to make more efficient use of scarce land and capital resources than did large farms, primarily through more intensive use of relatively abundant labor resources and of the land resources that were available.[34] These findings were largely uncontroverted in settings of traditional foodcrop agriculture, where land and labor were the principal inputs. Some studies of the "Green Revolution" in South Asia cast doubt on the superiority of small farms in the face of technological innovation (Khan 1975; id. 1977; Patnaik 1972). There was limited early evidence that adoption of technological innovations was more rapid on large farms. Even then, the lag time in adoption by small farms was not more than a few years.[35] Other studies suggested that, on average, small farmers adopted new seed varieties, fertilizer, and insecticide, as, or

even *more*, rapidly.[36] Most international data thus belied notions of economies of scale in agricultural production.

Economies of scale existed in the purchase of inputs (seeds, fertilizers, and pesticides) and the marketing of production, where processing, transport, and storage equipment costs are relatively fixed and indivisible. Agricultural credit also exhibited certain economies of scale—loan processing and servicing costs were largely fixed regardless of loan size. Individualized agricultural extension similarly involved relatively fixed costs regardless of farm size. Finally, farm mechanization, often—although inappropriately—associated with the Green Revolution, entailed large, indivisible ("lumpy") investments such as tractor combines. As a consequence, some analysts argued, there were reasons to expect that individual small farms would be disadvantaged relative to large farms in the present era of technological change (Ghatak and Ingersent 1984: 139–41; Herring 1983: 246–47).

Yet in principle, input, credit, and marketing cooperatives will enable small farmers to enjoy the same scale and cost advantages available to large farmers.[37] In the case of credit, cooperatives or similar groups can mobilize members' savings for lending and joint investments. Such organizations can also play a role in the administration of government-provided credit, by assuming responsibility for screening loan applications and insuring loan repayments. Cooperatives can be a vehicle for extension outreach, bringing groups of farmers into direct contact with extension agents. This approach reduces the extension costs per farmer served, while circumventing the barriers that have often confounded efforts to diffuse innovations through "progressive" farmers.[38] These types of cooperatives entail minimal compromise of member individualism and avoid many of the "free rider" problems that have often plagued production cooperatives.[39] Furthermore, cooperatives facilitate exertion of group bargaining power, empowering small farmers in the competition for scarce government and institutional resources.

This latter point is particularly important, because large farmers have historically enjoyed preferential access to government-provided resources and services. The most egregious examples of this typically concerned access to subsidized agricultural credit intended to benefit "small" farmers (Adams and Graham 1981; Adams and Von Pischke 1992; Braverman and Guasch 1986; Gonzalez-Vega 1977; Von Pischke et al. 1983). The exercise of political and institutional influence by large farmers, and their consequently enhanced access to credit resources and extension information, should not be mistaken for evidence that techni-

cal change is no longer scale-neutral, or that the comparative productivity advantage of small farms no longer exists. Rather, these farm size–related inequities in access to scarce productive resources, and the evidence of greater social-factor productivity on small farms, argue all the more forcefully for redistributive agrarian reform.

Scale Economies and Philippine Agriculture

Consistent with findings in other settings, the available Philippine data showed no scale economies in the case of rice or corn. The 1980 agricultural census, for example, revealed a consistent and marked decline in average rice productivity by farm size for farms of less than 0.5 hectares (2.61 metric tons per hectare) to farms in the 10–24.99 hectare range (1.98 mt/ha) (NCSO 1985a). Farms in the largest size category, those over 25 hectares, showed some recovery in rice yields (2.20 mt/ha). Corn yields were fairly stable across farm-size categories, with moderately higher productivity on farms in the 3.0–4.99 hectare and 10–24.99 hectare ranges (1.19 mt/ha and 1.24 mt/ha respectively) than on either the smallest or largest farms (1.06 mt/ha and 1.14 mt/ha respectively).[40]

Similarly, data from the Philippine agricultural census and informal surveys suggested that no scale economies existed for crops such as coconuts, coffee, and cacao (ROP, NCSO 1985a: 36–37; Hayami et al. 1987: 14). For coffee and cacao, the highest yields per tree were achieved on farms of less than 0.5 hectares. Productivity was markedly lower on farms of 0.5–1.0 hectares, and lower still—although essentially constant—across the remaining farm-size categories. Coconut yields peaked on farms in the 2.0–2.99 hectare range (35.59 nuts per tree), tapering off slightly on both smaller and larger farms—29.0 nuts per tree for farms under 0.5 hectares, 29.87 nuts per tree for farms of 25 hectares or more. Furthermore, it has been observed that small coconut farmers make more intensive and diverse use of their available land area, with papayas, coffee, or pineapples grown underneath the coconut canopy (Dominguez 1987: 49).

Only sugarcane appeared to be an exception to the rule that land-related scale economies did not exist in Philippine agriculture. The 1980 agricultural census showed sugarcane yields generally increasing with farm size, with significantly higher yields on the largest farms. As of 1980, farms of 25 hectares or more had average yields of 60.79 mt/ha. Farms in the 7.01–9.99 hectare range followed with average yields of 43.77 mt/ha, while the various farm-size categories below 5 hectares in size were associated with yields of 22.84–28.44 mt/ha.

However, data from the Philippine Sugar Commission indicated that small sugarcane farms were more efficient in terms of total-factor productivity. As of 1985, farms under 10 hectares produced a picul[41] of sugar at an average cost of 107 pesos. On farms of over 50 hectares, production costs averaged 120 pesos per picul (Guevarra 1987: 8).

An Institute of Agrarian Studies (IAS) review of Philippine sugar-sector research found contradictory results in terms of the link between productivity and farm size. "It is now a common observation that economies of scale [are] more critical in sugar processing than in farm production. . . . Where economies of scale in production [are] indeed critical, a reform program that democratizes control of the land without disrupting operational units can be evolved," the review concluded (1987a: 2).

Planters claimed that scale economies existed in the sugar sector—at least on farms of up to 50 hectares, the area planters deemed necessary to support efficient use of the large tractor needed for the more productive deep plowing and related soil preparation operations.[42] In arguing against land redistribution in the sugarcane sector, planters typically decried the production losses they argued would be attendant on parcelization of existing sugarcane farms. Furthermore, the planters argued, the resulting parcels would be too small to support farm worker–beneficiary families.

Where tractor rental or custom-plowing markets were found, as in Batangas and Bukidnon provinces, this basis for scale economies did not exist.[43] Such markets did not then exist in Negros Occidental—the nation's main sugar-producing province—because most sugar plantations were large enough to justify ownership of a tractor. This situation posed no inherent barrier to agrarian reform, however. Even in the event that agrarian reform beneficiaries opted to subdivide affected sugarcane plantations, the advantages of deep plowing could be realized through cooperative ownership and use of the plantations' tractors or through the development of a market in custom-plowing services.

This assumes that reform beneficiaries would continue to plant sugarcane, an assumption at odds with the preferences of some potential beneficiaries who faced capital constraints and recalled the significant downturns in the sugar market in the preceding decades.[44] While some economists and sugar-mill workers' union officials counseled continued production of sugarcane on properties subject to reform, other scholars, farmworkers' union officials, and development institutions argued the importance of scaling back sugar production and emphasizing food security or nontraditional export crops.[45] In the event the farm-

workers elected to grow sugarcane, they were required to make a contribution of P5.00 per picul to a sugar-planter's fund—the Negros Democracy and Peace Foundation—that has been used to finance vigilantes and private armies. Farmworker members of the militant NFSW were in effect helping to underwrite the costs of union harassment, an irony not lost on the union.[46]

Another supposed scale economy related to sugar milling.[47] Large plantations were argued to be better suited to coordinated delivery of cane to sugar mills, maximizing efficiency of mill use and minimizing the loss in sugar content of the harvested cane.[48] Observations of mill operations by the author and others confirm, however, the almost complete absence of effective scheduling of cane deliveries.[49] The one notable exception is the Central Azucarera de Don Pedro (CADP) in Batangas. The third-largest mill in the country, CADP coordinates deliveries from around 4,000 planters. Because the actual sugarcane cultivation is done by about 20,000 share tenants, this experience suggests that coordination of harvesting by smallholders is possible on a massive scale.[50]

In the context of Philippine deliberations over agrarian-reform policy, what was most important about the ongoing theoretical and empirical debate over the relative efficiencies of various farm-tenure arrangements and scales of operation was the very existence of that debate. The contradictory empirical results and increasingly complex analysis in the literature on economic theory made economic-based decision making problematic for the executive and legislative branches of the Philippine government. With both pro- and antireform political forces able to cite scholarly support for their positions, political considerations—rather than Pareto efficiency—drove the decision-making process.[51]

A History of Philippine Land Reform

Since the turn of the century, there have been repeated—although ineffectual—initiatives to address landlessness, underemployment, and poverty in the Philippines through land reform. These reform programs were limited to tenanted holdings devoted to grain-crop production. The political influence of the large sugar, coconut, and tobacco growers assured the exemption of holdings devoted to export crops (Bautista n.d.; Starner 1961; Wurfel 1969: 216). The land-reform programs have also provided liberal landowner retention limits, reducing the area landowners could retain from 300 hectares in 1955 to 75 hectares in 1963, 24 hectares in 1971, and 7 hectares in 1972.

The primary enactments regarding Philippine land reform are the Friar Lands Act of 1903 (Commonwealth Act 1120); the Rice Share Tenancy Act of 1933; Commonwealth Act 539 (1940); the Agricultural Tenancy Act of 1954 (Republic Act 1199); the Land Reform Act of 1955 (Republic Act 1400); the Agricultural Land Reform Code of 1963 (Republic Act 3844); the Code of Agrarian Reform (Republic Act 6389, 1971); and Presidential Decree 27 (PD 27, 1972).[52]

The Friar Lands Act of 1903

Introduced by the American colonial government in an attempt to defuse agrarian unrest, the Friar Lands Act provided for the acquisition of roughly 166,000 hectares held by the Catholic Church, at a price of $7.2 million. In the redistribution of these holdings, preference was given to roughly 60,000 tenants. Still, over half of the area acquired under the law passed directly, by sale or lease, to American and Filipino business concerns. Moreover, the requirement that the full acquisition price, plus interest, be repaid by beneficiaries apparently put the land beyond the financial reach of most tenants. Lacking access to institutional credit, marketing facilities, or improved agricultural techniques, most of the tenants who did acquire property soon lost it to local moneylenders and *hacenderos*.[53]

The Rice Share Tenancy Act of 1933

The next significant reform law, the Rice Share Tenancy Act of 1933, was an attempt to regulate the landlord-tenant relationship rather than to redistribute property. The law required that share contracts be written, provided in most cases for 50–50 sharing of the crop, set an interest ceiling of 10 percent per annum on loans made to the tenant, and prohibited arbitrary dismissal of tenants. However, the law only required one-year rental terms, providing tenants little assurance of tenure security. More important, the law directed that a majority of the municipal councils in a given province petition for application of the law before it was to be effective in that province. With local landed elites dominating these councils, this proviso rendered the law ineffective from the outset.[54]

The Agricultural Tenancy Act of 1954 and the Land Reform Act of 1955

Reacting to the peasant discontent expressed in the Huk rebellion, Ramon Magsaysay campaigned for the presidency in 1953 on vague promises of agrarian reform. His Nacionalista Party's platform in-

cluded a pledge to "execute a more liberal and expeditious plan for the disposition of our public agricultural lands . . . [and] embark on a large-scale campaign to purchase, subdivide and distribute large landed estates to their tenants at cost" (Tai 1974: 149, citing Coquia 1955). For seven months the charismatic Magsaysay carried his reformist message to remote Philippine villages, stressing his humble background and his commitment to clean government and reform.[55]

The Nacionalista Party was not alone in touting agrarian reform. President Elpidio Quirino's Liberal Party highlighted its government's reform accomplishments, however limited. These accomplishments consisted of revisions to the Rice Tenancy Act that nominally increased tenant crop shares, and a negligible program of distribution of landed estates. Sounding themes that have been repeated by Philippine agrarian-reform advocates through the years, the Democratic Party argued: "The land is under God the property and the source of life of our people. . . . No society can thrive, no people can be happy or even moderately secure, unless there is an equitable distribution of the national patrimony of the land" (Tai 1974: 150).

After his electoral victory—in which overwhelming rural support was decisive—Magsaysay introduced two pieces of reform legislation, which would become the Agricultural Tenancy Act of 1954 and the Land Reform Act of 1955. However, landowner resistance in Congress, and the reduced political urgency attached to land reform as the Huk insurgency declined, resulted in a substantial watering down of Magsaysay's reform proposals. The original tenancy-reform proposal would have transformed share tenants into leasehold ("fixed" rent)[56] tenants and extended the scope of the law to include tenants on sugarcane lands. As adopted, the 1954 legislation recognized the leasehold concept but did not require a shift to leasehold tenancy; nor was the law extended to sugar lands. The law limited rent to 30 percent of the crop, capped annual interest rates at 8–10 percent, and increased tenant exemptions from creditors' liens. Congress voted few resources for enforcement of the new law, and for a year the House derailed Magsaysay's effort to establish a new forum, a Court of Agrarian Relations, for adjudicating agrarian disputes. In the end, the program's modest aims went largely unrealized. Given the difficulties inherent in enforcement of tenancy regulations, it is unlikely that even a significant commitment of government resources would have materially improved tenant conditions. In the event, the Philippine government made little effort at enforcement.

The Land Reform Act of 1955 was to provide for the expropriation of

large estates and their redistribution to landless agriculturalists. The debates over the legislation are instructive, because they foreshadow much of the reform debate under the Aquino government. In what might appropriately be termed an "everyday form of landowner resistance," most opponents of the reform challenged, not the idea of agrarian reform, but the particulars of Magsaysay's proposal. They identified themselves as concerned with improving peasant welfare, but argued that subdivision of large estates would cause production to decline, thereby worsening peasant and national welfare. It would be better for all, the reform opponents suggested, if the government focused on the development of virgin public lands.[57]

Other opponents were more direct in their condemnation of agrarian reform. Manuel V. Gallego, president of the National Rice Producers' Association (NRPA), argued that the proposed reform represented a variant of the "Chinese communist land reform system under the guise of democracy."[58] Gallego denounced the reform as unconstitutional and un-Christian—the proposal would reward those who coveted the property of others. Furthermore, he denied the seriousness of tenure-related rural unrest, terming it "more imagined than real" (Starner 1961: 163). The most incredible of Gallego's remarks was made in an exchange with the proreform chairman of the Philippine Code Commission, Jorge Bocobo: "Don't we take pride in the fact that our countrymen, who are generally poor, can point with pride to foreigners that we have also a little of 'the landed gentry' who live a little bit better like they do, and that we are not a nation of peasants as you would like to have them?" (Starner 1961: 163).

Although making it clear that the NRPA exerted important influence over the legislative deliberations, Francis Starner noted that the rice producers "doubt seriously the efficacy of their own arguments" (1969: 232). Few critics of reform publicly identified themselves with Gallego's remarks. In the differing—albeit all extraordinarily high—retention limits we see evidence of the greater political influence of corporate and export-crop growers vis-à-vis owners of rice land.[59] Committed to industrialization, the Philippine government put a premium on export earnings, exempting all but the largest export-crop landholdings. As introduced by Magsaysay, the law would have covered all private agricultural lands in excess of 144 hectares. Congress chose to limit the scope of the reform to lands in excess of 300 contiguous hectares in the case of private rice farms, 600 hectares for corporations, and 1,024 hectares for private farms devoted to crops other than rice.

The proposed reform also came in for criticism from within Magsay-

say's party. Senator Claro M. Recto, an ardent nationalist, condemned the reform as a U.S.-inspired initiative designed to perpetuate an agriculturally based Philippine economy and, in turn, a dependency relationship with the United States. Later he endorsed the reform program, although cautioning that it must remain subordinate to the goal of industrialization (Tai 1974: 157–58).

Apart from the issue of retention areas, Tai identifies the principal points of legislative contention as: (1) the scope of the reform—some bills required repeated violations of tenancy laws before landowners would be subject to the reform; (2) land valuation and the form of compensation—cash, negotiable land certificates, and exchanges of government properties were the forms of payment preferred by landowners; (3) the authorization of funds for compensation—Congress sought to curtail the proposed allocations substantially; and (4) the size of the farms to be redistributed—at issue was the size needed for viability and the possible displacement of some tenants in order that others be given "viable" farms (1974: 160–62; see also Murray 1973: 158).

Although Magsaysay was ultimately instrumental in securing passage of the legislation, he provided little leadership in the early deliberations. During the initial formulation of the Land Reform Act, he remained aloof, appointing several committees to review tenure conditions and make legislative recommendations. Then, having seen Congress balk at redistributive reform in the 1954 session, he was silent for four months after the draft legislation was reintroduced in January 1955. A falling-out with senior members of the Nacionalista Party early in his presidency—he had only joined the party to become its standard-bearer on the eve of the election campaign—meant that Magsaysay had no effective party base from which to mobilize his considerable popular support in furtherance of a reform agenda. As we shall see, Corazon Aquino adopted much the same detached approach to the reform debates in 1986–88 and likewise lacked an effective party organization, all to similar effect: as adopted, the legislation bore little resemblance to the original government drafts.

The final law, although noteworthy for embracing the concept of compulsory expropriation, contained several critical flaws. The high retention limits meant that less than 2 percent of the nation's agricultural land was even potentially subject to redistribution.[60] Absent explicit provisions to the contrary, it appeared that each individual family member could claim a retention area, if only on the basis of belated, nominal transfers of title to relatives and straw men, reducing the po-

tential scope of the program even further. Under the terms of the law, the government could initiate action to purchase or expropriate a particular property only upon petition by a majority of the tenants on that holding. In the event of expropriation, the law provided little guidance in determining valuation. Payment was to be wholly in cash unless the landowner chose otherwise. The law authorized only a small fraction of the funds requested by the Magsaysay government. Faced with these various restrictions, the government acquired less than 20,000 hectares—less than four-tenths of one percent of the nation's then total farm area—in the first six years of the program.[61]

Philippine Land Reform, 1963–1985

I have discussed the 1955 legislation at some length because of the many parallels between the Magsaysay reform experience and the dynamics of the agrarian-reform process under the Aquino government. These were not the only Philippine reform initiatives in the postwar era. To correct the deficiencies of the 1955 law, a series of enactments were introduced under both democratic and authoritarian auspices in the period 1963–85. The achievements, as of the end of 1985 (shortly before Marcos's ouster), under the three principal reform programs introduced since 1963 are detailed in Table 5.

Operation Land Transfer

Although Operation Land Transfer dates from the 1963 Agricultural Land Reform Code (RA 3844), it was only with the adoption of Presidential Decree 27 (PD 27) in 1972 that the program was to have national effect. Pursuant to PD 27, tenants of rice and corn land whose landlords held more than seven hectares were permitted to purchase the parcels they tilled. By executive fiat, eligible tenants were deemed "owners" of "family-size farms," which the decree set at three hectares of irrigated land or five hectares of unirrigated land.[62] In theory, tenants needed do nothing to initiate the reform process. Department of Agrarian Reform (DAR) personnel were to determine the existence of a tenancy relationship and identify the tenant-cultivators and their respective landlords. DAR personnel were also responsible for identifying the parcel involved and determining its soil classification and the average gross production for the three years preceding announcement of the law. The tenanted parcel was then to be surveyed and mapped by Bureau of Lands and DAR personnel. Once reviewed and approved at the local

TABLE 5

Summary of Accomplishments Under Philippine Land-Reform Programs, December 31, 1985

Program	Program Scope		Cumulative Progress	
	Beneficiaries	Area (ha)	Beneficiaries	Area (ha)
PD 27 (1972)				
Operation Land Transfer[a]	587,775[b]	822,000[b]		
(i) EPs[c] generated			137,931	183,592
(ii) EPs distributed			17,116	11,197
(iii) Payment Verified			179,285	286,922
(iv) Payment Approved			134,371	258,638
(v) Direct Payments[d]			27,269	34,750
RA 3844 (1963; as amended)				
Operation Leasehold[e]	527,667	562,230	533,808	566,444
CA 539 (1940; as amended)				
Landed Estates				
(i) CLT[f]	56,302	88,143	33,503	54,986
(ii) Deed of Sale	43,130	62,965	12,270	19,611
Resettlement	78,450	565,079	16,998	94,977

SOURCE: Department of Agrarian Reform, *Accomplishment Report CY-1986* (Manila, n.d.).

[a]Operation Land Transfer provided for the redistribution of tenanted rice and corn holdings to landless tenant cultivators.

[b]As of December 31, 1988. The original program goals were 520,000 beneficiaries and 1,000,000 hectares. The Department of Agrarian Reform, *Accomplishment Report CY-1986* cites goals of 427,623 beneficiaries and 716,520 hectares.

[c]Emancipation Patents (equivalent to final title).

[d]These are beneficiaries who chose to make amortization payments directly to the ex-landlord rather than through any government agency.

[e]Operation Leasehold provided for the transformation of share tenancy to leasehold (fixed rent) tenancy.

[f]Certificate of Land Transfer (preliminary documentation of tenant entitlement to land).

and regional agency levels, the map was sent to DAR/Manila for final approval and transfer to the National Computer Center (NCC). The NCC would thereupon print a Certificate of Land Transfer (CLT), which then had to be registered and annotated by the Register of Deeds and returned to the local DAR office.

Only upon proof of membership in a *samahang nayon* (village-level associations organized by the Ministry of Local Government and Community Development) and of current cultivation of the subject parcel would the prospective beneficiary receive his or her CLT. Receipt of the CLT did not signal the termination of beneficiary rent obligations. Land valuation and landowner compensation had to be completed before

beneficiaries could begin amortization payments. Valuation of affected properties was set at 2.5 times the value of average annual production,[63] with the beneficiary repaying the land costs to the government over fifteen years at 6 percent interest. Upon completion of their amortization payments, beneficiaries would receive final title, an Emancipation Patent (EP).

Shortly after the enactment of PD 27, the Department of Agrarian Reform estimated the number of tenants on rice and corn lands at 914,000. Other observers believed actual tenancy to be as much as 50 percent higher (Hickey and Wilkinson 1977: table 1). That the program initially embraced little more than one-half of the government-estimated number of such tenant families reflected the program's 7-hectare retention limit.

The successful postwar land reforms of Japan (1947–49), South Korea (1949–52), and Taiwan (1953–55) all featured much lower retention limits.[64] The Japanese reform allowed no ("zero") retention of tenanted land owned by landlords not resident in the village. Resident landlords were permitted one hectare of tenanted land. The South Korean reform allowed no retention of tenanted land regardless of landlord residency. Taiwan, under conditions of scrupulous administration of land registries and the disallowance of land transfers in the year preceding adoption of the reform, permitted landlord retention of three hectares in the case of average land.

The 1972 law was flawed in other ways. While introducing a significant tension between tenant and landlord interests, the law did not sever the legal nexus between the two parties (World Bank 1987a: 33, 36–37). CLT recipients were required to continue their rent payments until the land valuation and compensation process was complete, although some beneficiaries refused to do so.[65] For real property tax purposes, however, CLT recipients were deemed owners of the lands they tilled and were therefore liable for such taxes. All tenant farmers on tenanted rice and corn estates of 100 or more hectares were similarly liable for real property taxes, whether they had received their CLT or not (ROP, DAR 1973; ROP, DOJ 1973).

Rather than adhere to the law's valuation formula, landlords were permitted to negotiate the land price directly with tenants.[66] Landlords alternately pressured tenants to agree to overstated valuations and delayed valuation agreements. Some DAR field officials sided with landlords, and those who sided with the tenants found themselves harassed and subject to landlord-initiated legal actions. By 1977, tenant-

beneficiaries were paying an average of almost P7,000 per hectare, some 44 percent higher than average valuations based on the crop-multiple formula.[67]

Field interviews suggest that implementation of Operation Land Transfer was also very uneven: in many areas, no tenants benefited, in others, 20–30 percent of the tenants had received CLTs. Of those who received CLTs, many were involved in protracted disputes with their ex-landlords over land valuation; some were still paying rent, others had stopped paying either the landlord or the government. Not surprisingly, the extent of implementation was strongly influenced by political considerations. Although concerns about rural unrest appear to have been a factor in implementation in areas of past Huk activity, for instance, the more important explanatory variable appears to have been Marcos's desire to target elements of the traditional elite and political enemies. Thus, for example, the Aquino family holdings were among the first to be expropriated.[68]

Keijiro Otsuka (1991) cites peasant demand as an additional factor explaining differential implementation of the reform. In this view, tenants in irrigated and favorable rain-fed areas were more insistent on implementation, as they stood to benefit most from the Green Revolution. As yields increased, rent levels diverged from the law's amortization (or leasehold) payment schedules, which were fixed as of 1972. This divergence increased the incentives for share tenants to change their status to owner (or leaseholder). Although this may explain peasant participation in the reform program, it cannot explain the adoption of the program in the first instance. Otsuka, following other scholars, attributes the latter to the government's interest in suppressing rural unrest and punishing wealthy landlords. By implication, these same political considerations explain the differences Otsuka found in DAR staffing and resource allocations across regions. These differences, in turn, are significantly correlated with implementation of the reform (Otsuka 1991: 349–50). Left unclear is the relative importance of the economic incentives and DAR staffing allocations in explaining peasant demands for reform. From the peasant's viewpoint, the former increase the benefits of participating in the reform, whereas the latter reduce the perceived cost of pursuing reform by increasing the prospect of protection from landlord reprisals.

Apart from tenants on rice and corn lands excluded from redistribution by the high retention limit, PD 27 excluded tenants on lands devoted to crops other than rice and corn, as well as all landless laborers.

Yet even judged against the modest program goals of Operation Land Transfer, Marcos-era performance was dismal, although admittedly better than that of earlier reforms (see discussion below). By year-end 1985, Emancipation Patents (EPs) had been generated for less than one-quarter (23.4 percent) of the targeted beneficiaries. Under the most pessimistic reading of program accomplishments, only 3 percent of the targeted beneficiaries had actually received Emancipation Patents in the first fourteen years of implementation of Operation Land Transfer.[69]

The compensation figures are not easily reconciled with the data on Emancipation Patents. The area in holdings for which payment by the Land Bank of the Philippines had been approved was much greater than the area covered by the Emancipation Patents (258,638 versus 183,592 hectares). At the same time, the number of beneficiaries associated with that 258,638 hectares seems low. No explanation of these discrepancies is offered in DAR reports. While the issue cannot be resolved here, the figures suggest that an additional 75,000 hectares, not titled, may have been acquired under the program.

Ongoing monitoring of the accomplishments under Operation Land Transfer was complicated by the deliberate efforts of the Marcos regime to blur the distinction between CLTs, which were provisional titles, and EPs, final titles. Over time, government press releases touting the program's accomplishments began to treat the number of CLTs printed in Manila as synonymous with the number of erstwhile tenants who had received ownership of the land they tilled.[70] This characterization was misleading on several levels: CLTs were not final titles; there was a substantial divergence between the number of CLTs printed in Manila and the number distributed to erstwhile tenants; and delays in the payment of compensation to former landowners meant that even fewer tenants were "amortizing owners."[71] This myth was perpetuated in a U.S. Agency for International Development presentation before a U.S. congressional committee in 1981 (Schieck 1981, cited in Wurfel 1983: 9–10).

The distinction between CLTs and EPs was further obscured when Marcos, and later Aquino, effected changes in the procedures governing distribution of EPs. Initially, EPs were issued only upon completion of amortization payments. Beginning in 1982, EPs were awarded after two successive amortization payments by the farmer-beneficiary. Then, as a final desperate election bid on January 14, 1986, the Marcos government began issuing EPs without any payment having been made, although amortization obligations were noted on the back of the title document.[72] Furthermore, the requirement that farmer-beneficiaries

make payment of 90 percent of their back taxes has been waived as a precondition to the issuance of EPs since 1987.[73] Despite these changes, EPs are correctly seen as representing final title, albeit subject to significant amortization and tax obligations.

Operation Leasehold

Operation Leasehold—which dates from 1963, with revisions in 1971—was designed to convert share tenancies to fixed-rent leaseholds, on the supposition that leaseholds afforded tenants greater incentives to increase production.[74] A rent ceiling was set at 25 percent of the average harvest, after deducting various production costs.[75] On paper the program had exceeded its goals by 1985. However, informal surveying by the author and the observations of other researchers suggested that the provisions of this program were often ignored.[76] Share tenancy continued to be practiced, and rent levels, whether determined on a share or leasehold basis, often exceeded the rent ceiling. Efforts by local DAR personnel to enforce leasehold regulations were often undermined by landowners with access to senior DAR personnel or higher political authorities.[77] Tenancy regulation, particularly in a developing country, is a largely futile endeavor, fraught with administrative pitfalls and opportunities for evasion.[78]

The Landed Estates Program

The landed estates program had its inception in Commonwealth Act 539 (1940).[79] Its aim was government acquisition of large private estates for redistribution to the tenant cultivators. As of 1955, individually owned estates of 300 hectares or more and corporate-owned estates of 600 hectares or more were, upon petition by a majority (later reduced to one-third) of the tenants, subject to expropriation. In 1963, the scope of the program was expanded to include holdings over 75 hectares, regardless of mode of ownership. Under the 1963 reform code, the program focused on tenant-operated rice and corn estates. Lands under "labor administration"—that is, land cultivated by hired labor—such as sugarcane and coconut plantations, orchards, and commercial farms were exempted from government acquisition. The exemptions illustrated the political clout of this segment of agricultural producers and their ability to convince legislators that economies of scale and foreign exchange earnings would be jeopardized by the reform program.

As of 1985, the program had delivered CLTs to only 33,500 beneficiaries, covering some 55,000 hectares. Nearly half of the program's lim-

ited achievements occurred under the Rural Progress Administration in the period 1940–50. In explaining the failure to issue deeds of sale to nearly two-thirds of those who received a preliminary certificate, DAR pointed to beneficiary difficulties in meeting amortization repayment obligations.

Resettlement Programs

Finally, some 95,000 hectares of public land had been subject to government resettlement programs as of 1985. Most of the program achievements date back to the years following the Huk rebellion, notably 1950–54. Dwindling public land resources and the high financial, social, and environmental costs of resettlement argued against the DAR committing any substantial part of its resources to further resettlement efforts.[80]

Cumulative Land Reform Achievements

Prior to the Aquino administration, fewer than 315,000 hectares[81] of private land had been acquired under Philippine land reform, or only 4 percent of the country's 7.8 million cultivated hectares. Associated with this land were just over 168,000 beneficiary families,[82] a figure equal to roughly 6–8 percent of those landless nationwide in 1985. This record of accomplishment had neither appreciably furthered the cause of social justice nor been adequate to catalyze significant improvements in national agricultural performance.

Very few of the reform beneficiaries—no more than 10 percent, and perhaps as few as 5 percent—were current in their land amortization payments in the mid 1980s.[83] While the introduction of high-yield rice varieties generally increased production, rising input costs and low output prices undermined beneficiaries' capacity to pay for their lands. In some cases, amortization obligations were greater than previous rent levels, making repayment that much more difficult. In other cases, the absence of credible sanctions allowed beneficiaries to refuse repayment regardless of their financial status (Cornista et al. interview, Mar. 24, 1986). At year-end 1986, about P1.5 billion in delinquent payments were owed (ROP, ITFAR 1987b: 15).

Reform proponents cited this poor repayment experience to argue that repayment obligations be capped and the government introduce a significant and deliberate element of subsidy. This subsidy would create an "affordability wedge" between beneficiaries' repayment obligations and the amount of compensation paid the erstwhile landlords. Reform

opponents, by contrast, saw the poor repayment rate as further evidence of the inappropriateness of modeling Philippine agriculture along small-farm lines (Hernandez 1987: 26; Starke interview, June 16, 1986). In their view, the resulting holdings would be economically nonviable, and would simply lead to further farmer-beneficiary indebtedness and forfeiture of the reform parcel.

Other Legacies of Marcos-era Agricultural Policies

In addition to its limited scope and glacial pace of land redistribution, agrarian reform under the Marcos government was seriously flawed in several regards. Marcos initiated a poorly conceived program of beneficiary "pre-cooperatives" (*samahang nayon*, or barrio associations). After rapid early expansion, the government's agricultural credit program collapsed in the face of inadequate technical assistance, corruption, and poor repayment experience. The process of compensating affected landowners was marked by lengthy delays. Finally, there was a substantial element of "reverse land reform" associated with the promotion of corporate and export agriculture.

Of the comparatively few tenants who received land rights, some lost their parcels through indebtedness, while others apparently abandoned self-cultivation in favor of leasing the land out to sharecroppers bereft of legal status.[84] Both phenomena elicited considerable criticism from landowners potentially affected by reform. In some instances, land-reform critics phrased their remarks so as to suggest empathy for tenants and farmworkers. Tadeo Villarosa, a sugar-industry consultant, condemned previous land-reform schemes as having "discouraged the [sugar *hacenderos'*] historic practice of loaning lowland areas with poor drainage [to farmworkers] for rice cultivation during the 'dead season.' "[85]

Administrative Delays and Landowner Resistance

The complex administrative processes of beneficiary, landlord, and parcel identification, land survey, valuation, and payment of compensation gave rise to lengthy delays in the implementation of PD 27 and earlier Philippine reforms. Norms of administrative simplicity were violated in a number of ways: the application, review, and valuation procedures required multiple state-beneficiary and state-landlord contacts; time-consuming traditional metes-and-bounds ground surveys were used for property identification and titling rather than aerial

photography–based identification and titling; and dispute resolution frequently involved recourse to formal court proceedings rather than making effective use of village-level dispute-resolution mechanisms.[86]

Facing few credible penalties for malfeasance, landowners affected by the reform were often uncooperative, if not engaged in overt efforts to thwart the reform process, including intimidation or eviction of tenant-beneficiaries. In the case of land valuation, it is estimated that 85 percent of the landowners affected by PD 27 failed to participate in the valuation process, either boycotting the proceedings or being unwilling or unable to produce the necessary documentation in support of their compensation claims (David 1987b: 5; ROP, ITFAR 1987a: 6). The obverse of this noncooperation was the claim by some representatives of landowner interests that only 15 percent of the landowners affected by PD 27 were paid for their land.[87] Other landowners cited official data indicating that 32 percent of affected landowners had been paid (Caparas 1987: 55). Yet to hear landowners tell the story, responsibility for the delayed payment of compensation lay entirely with the government, notably through its failure to appropriate adequate resources.[88] This blaming of government was a recurrent theme of the Aquino-era reform deliberations.

Landowners further challenged the legal bases of valuation, arguing that the three-year crop-multiple formulation was too mechanistic, making little provision for potential capital gains associated with enhanced Green Revolution yields and grain-price increases (ROP, ITFAR 1987b: 12; cf. Otsuka 1991). The claim had some superficial plausibility. Landlords might have made investments in the land prior to announcement of the reform law, the full benefits of which would not be realized for several years thereafter. More often these claims rested on the protracted processes of land valuation and payment of compensation and on intervening increases in farm yields or profits. Where, as was frequently the case, the valuation delays were attributable to landlord obstructionism, it was hardly appropriate that such landlords should profit from government or tenant-beneficiary investments or price increases that boosted the yields or profit of the farm operation during the period of delay.

Landlords also considered the proffered compensation to be unattractive in form, with 80 percent of the award consisting of 25-year bonds earning 6 percent per annum. The long maturation and relatively limited convertibility of these bonds made them a poor vehicle for prompt redeployment of landlord resources into industry. By 1986, land

bonds were trading at only 30–50 percent of their face value (Alunan interview, June 16, 1986).

Reverse Land Reform

The agrarian-reform program itself occasioned "reverse" land reform; landlords evicted tenants on rice and corn land in favor of hired laborers as one means of avoiding application of PD 27. In addition, a series of other government policies had the effect of displacing significant numbers of erstwhile tenant, landless laborer, and even small landowner households. In particular, beginning in 1974, the government, seeking to alleviate food-crop shortages, required that all large corporations (those with 500 or more employees) directly provide rice and corn for their employees, either through corporate production or direct importation.[89] Corporate production arrangements, direct and contracted production, extended to over 52,000 hectares by January 1977.[90] As many as 20,000 hectares of this total may have come from tenant recipients of CLTs under PD 27 and from erstwhile owners. Typically, these corporate farming operations were conducted on a capital-intensive basis, with a net loss in employment on the affected farms (Wurfel 1988: 173). These operations did achieve often substantial increases in grain yields, however, meeting the central government's objective (Ofreneo 1987: 80). President Aquino terminated the corporate food-crop production program in May 1987, with a three-year phase-out (Executive Order 176, May 28, 1987, repealing General Order 47).

Similarly, Presidential Decree 472 required timber licensees and pasture lessees on public lands to produce rice, corn, and other basic staples. The favored lands for such production were typically occupied by squatters who had been denied title to these parcels because the land was formally classified as unsuitable for agriculture. David Wurfel estimates that corporate concessionaires drove squatters off more than 26,000 hectares (1977: 30).

Export-crop production also expanded dramatically in the 1970s. In the early 1970s, skyrocketing world sugar prices, combined with (illegal) crop shifting by landowners wanting to avoid land-reform programs that affected rice and corn holdings, resulted in a substantial increase in the area devoted to sugar production. The period of peak sugar prices in the mid 1970s saw some 550,000 hectares of sugarcane harvested annually, up from just over 326,000 hectares in 1971 and less than 196,000 hectares in 1958.[91] This expansion occurred at the expense of tenants, squatters, small owner-cultivators, and food crops. With the collapse of sugar prices in 1976, the trend was reversed, and the area

harvested declined to under 300,000 hectares by 1980. However, sugar planters who "temporarily" turned to rice and corn production were specifically exempted from the agrarian-reform program by presidential decree in 1976.[92] The expansion-contraction cycle was repeated in the early 1980s, with the harvested area reaching nearly 414,000 hectares in 1982–83 and falling to 282,000 hectares in 1986–87. Domestic price increases in the late 1980s and early 1990s again resulted in an appreciable expansion of sugarcane planting. Yet relative to the boom years of 1974–75, tens of thousands of hectares of sugar land lie abandoned.

Production of bananas, principally for the Japanese market, also expanded markedly beginning in the late 1960s, as did coconut and pineapple production. During the 1970s, the areas devoted to production of these crops increased 35 percent (83,000 hectares), 66 percent (1,242,000 hectares), and 117 percent (34,000 hectares) respectively.[93] It is argued that much of the expansion again took place at the expense of existing, insecure food-crop cultivators. Mindanao was the principal site of the expansion of banana, coconut, and pineapple production, exacerbating the land-related tensions that have fueled the Muslim-Christian conflict on that island.[94]

While acknowledging the difficulty of precisely quantifying the extent of reverse land reform—that is, the displacement of existing tenants, squatters, and small owners through the expansion of corporate export-crop production and the corporate rice- and corn-farming program—Wurfel suggests that by 1980 those deprived of land might well have outnumbered those who had received Emancipation Patents under PD 27 (Wurfel 1988: 174). Although complete and reliable data are unavailable (the Marcos government understandably had little interest in disseminating data on reverse reform), the accomplishments under PD 27 were modest, whether measured in 1980 or 1985, and Wurfel may well be correct. In any event, critics of Marcos-era land-reform accomplishments abound, landless tenants and laborers prominent among them. The rapid growth of the NPA in the late 1970s and early 1980s bears witness to the depth of peasant disenchantment with the reform issue (among others).

The Agricultural Performance of Land-Reform Beneficiaries

It is axiomatic among Philippine landowners that earlier land-reform programs have not resulted in appreciable improvements in

agricultural yields (Starke interview, June 16, 1986). The empirical findings are at odds with this view. Although one prominent Philippine study of tenure and productivity suggested a priori that the productivity impact of land-tenure reform would be neutral (Mangahas et al. 1976), two studies of pre–martial law agrarian reform found "modest" production increases in reform areas, and two 1978 studies of reform-induced changes in tenure status showed "significant" increases in production among reform beneficiaries.[95]

A study of Plaridel municipality, Bulacan—although a pilot area for implementation of the Agricultural Land Reform Code of 1963—confirmed the limited scope of land (ownership) redistribution (Angsico et al. 1978, discussed in Carroll 1983). While 283 of the 437 farmers surveyed had shifted from share tenancy to leasehold status as of 1974 (53 farmers remained share tenants), only 17 of the farmers surveyed had received a CLT under PD 27; of these 13 still considered themselves lessees. The study was thus concerned primarily with the impact of a change from share-tenant to leasehold status.

In a form of linguistic "weapons of the weak,"[96] the tenants-cum-beneficiaries had apparently demystified the change wrought by PD 27. They correctly understood that receipt of a CLT did not constitute an irrevocable transfer of title. Pending completion of the land-valuation process and payment of compensation to the affected landowner, there was little to distinguish CLT recipients from tenants; both were obliged to make rent payments to their landlords. The recall of thousands of CLTs for reasons of bureaucratic ineptitude or landlord challenges to beneficiary claims lent further uncertainty to the status of CLT recipients.

In the baseline year, crop year (CY) 1962/63, yields per hectare were not significantly higher for farmers who would later shift to leasehold status, when compared with those who would remain share tenants. By CY 1974/75, the new leasehold tenants were obtaining yields per hectare that were significantly higher (at the 0.05 percent confidence level) than those of the share tenants. The principle explanation for the productivity differential was the more intensive application of labor, seeds, and fertilizers by leaseholders. The Plaridel study attributed this to the leaseholders' greater investment motivation, a function of the enhanced security of tenure assumed to be associated with leaseholding and the lower share of output paid as rent.

In analyzing the survey data, John Carroll notes that those who shifted tenure status did enjoy higher, although not significantly so,

yields at the outset (1983: 17). Moreover, prior to the reform, "shifters" employed significantly more labor per hectare than did "nonshifters." Carroll interprets this as suggesting that the reform process "selects" more "energetic" farmers; that is, those tenants already marginally better-off, and thus less likely to be constrained by considerations of risk, were self-selected participants in the tenure-reform process.[97] Not all reform participants benefited equally from the reform; income inequality among reform beneficiaries increased over time. For reasons not identified in the study, some beneficiaries were able to take far greater advantage of the opportunity the reform afforded them.[98]

A second study covered the Bicol River Basin of Camarines Sur (San Andres and Illo 1978). Implementation of land reform in this region was even slower than in Plaridel. By 1977, only 66 of the 332 erstwhile share tenants identified themselves as amortizing owners under Operation Land Transfer (that is, as recipients of CLTs); a mere 10 farmers identified themselves as leaseholders. Another 142 farmers were listed as leaseholders by the Department of Agrarian Reform, but did not so consider themselves (a further reflection of tenant "demystification" of the reform process).[99]

While overall rice production increased 30 percent in the Bicol study area from 1974 to 1977, the largest yield increases were realized by the few farmers who shifted from share tenancy to leasehold, followed by the new amortizing owners. Rice productivity was most influenced by levels of labor, fertilizer and chemical input, although irrigation, tenure status, and education also played a role. At a time when the percentages of farmers in the study area applying fertilizers or chemicals—pesticides and herbicides—were declining (for reasons not given), intensity of fertilizer application increased among users, most significantly among amortizing owners.

Again those who shifted tenure status under the reform program experienced higher yields from the outset, reinforcing the notion that such farmers are self-selected participants in the reform process. And again not all participants benefited equally from the reform; income inequality among reform beneficiaries increased over the study period (1974–77). Furthermore, despite increases in production and in the operator's share, average farm income for amortizing owners and share tenants remained essentially constant over the study period. Although these groups experienced increases in household income, the increases were a consequence of nonfarm and off-farm employment. Only the 10 leaseholders realized significant increases in farm incomes.

Underscoring the central theme of *agrarian* reform (as opposed to *land* reform alone), Carroll concluded from these two studies that tenurial improvement had been one element in a package that had enhanced rice production. He was, however, much less sanguine about the equity impact of reform. The reforms had permitted beneficiaries to increase their share of farm output appreciably, but the price structure operative in the early to mid 1970s had resulted in declining or stagnant incomes from rice production, and income inequality among reform beneficiaries had increased over time (Carroll 1983: 20, 22).

In contrast, Mangahas et al. (1976) predicted that reform of tenancy arrangements would have little impact on productivity, whether alone or in concert with technological improvements, yet expected such reform to have a positive impact on social equity. By their calculations, the shift to amortizing owner status would reduce the land-related payments of erstwhile leaseholders and share tenants. Land redistribution would increase beneficiary income streams, those of former share tenants most significantly, while reducing those of former landlords.

It was against this background of acute landlessness, poor agricultural performance, recurrent tenure-related civil unrest, slow implementation of past reforms, and contradictory theoretical constructs and empirical findings that Corazon Aquino came to power in February 1986. The responses of the Aquino and Ramos governments to the challenges of Philippine land-tenure arrangements are the subject of the next three chapters.

5

Campaign Promises: Democracy and Agrarian Reform

We are determined to implement a genuine land-reform program.

Corazon Aquino

The willingness of landowners to lose their property through land reforms short of revolution varies directly with the extent to which the
only alternative appears to be to lose it through revolution.

Samuel Huntington

The government of Corazon Aquino began on a triumphal note. An
essentially peaceful "People Power Revolution" had brought to an end
the twenty-year rule of Ferdinand Marcos. Laden as it was with religious symbolism, Aquino's ascendance to the Philippine presidency
appeared to promise a new economic, political, and social order. During
her presidential campaign, Aquino had criticized the Marcos land-
reform program as a "mockery of the age-long aspiration of the vast
majority of Filipinos for land they can call their own and from which
they can draw a dignified existence."[1] She pledged to undertake "genuine" agrarian reform (1986a: 7) and identified her top priority as the
"efficient utilization and equitable sharing of the ownership and benefits of land" (1986b). Two months after assuming office, Aquino described agrarian reform as "the most fundamental and far-reaching
program of government for it addresses the economic well-being and
dignity of many Filipinos" (IBON Databank Philippines 1988: 59;
Bulatao 1987: 3). Had Aquino chosen to act quickly on agrarian reform,
the "freedom" constitution empowered her to act unilaterally—to mandate reform by decree.

Yet judged against the energy devoted to her various tasks, Aquino
saw her principal duty in assuming the presidency of the Philippines as
the reestablishment of democratic institutions.[2] She used the consider-

able political capital available to her in the early months of her presidency to effectuate the restoration of the writ of habeas corpus and release of political prisoners; the drafting and adoption of a new constitution; initiation of local, congressional, and ultimately presidential elections; and, at the outset of her tenure, negotiations aimed at a peaceful resolution of a two-decades-old communist insurgency and several regional autonomy movements. In all but the latter, she was successful, at times demonstrating forceful leadership—notably in the release of prominent political prisoners and in initiating negotiations with the insurgents despite stiff military opposition.

On the economic side, her campaign speeches evidenced a strong commitment to renewed economic growth, principally through the elimination of the "crony capitalism" and other restraints on free-market activity that had marked the Marcos era:

We shall dismantle those structures of privilege, of which the monopolies are only the most glaring examples, that have stifled the spirit of enterprise in our country and robbed our people of their just share of the nation's wealth. . . . I look on the private sector as the engine of the economy and shall count upon it to be the prime mover of the effort towards national recovery. What I offer principally to private business is an enhanced environment for private initiative. (Aquino 1986a: 6)

Remarks such as these suggested a commitment to democratizing access to productive resources and opening markets to competition. In executing this commitment, however, Aquino and key advisers focused their attention on Marcos-era abuses rather than on the systemic inequities in the Philippine economy and politics.

Aquino believed that much of the support for the insurgent Communist Party of the Philippines/New People's Army consisted of "soft" recruits. In her view, these Filipinos could be persuaded to renounce violence through a combination of negotiations and amnesty, respect for human rights, restoration of democratic institutions, expanded employment opportunities, and some measure of agrarian reform:

I am convinced that, apart from gross violations of human rights and the persistence of certain structural injustices, much of the appeal of the [communist] armed struggle is rooted in our present economic conditions, rather than in ideological conviction. (Aquino 1986a: 8)

Of course, I know I won't get the real hard core NPAs. But I would like to get the majority . . . who are not really Communists or who do not espouse violent methods. Maybe we can still win them over. (*New York Times* 1985)

The urgency she attached to the communist insurgency and the social problems on which it was built—notably land-tenure relations, poverty, and human rights abuses—would wane noticeably over time. This diminished commitment was a function of the exclusionary nature of Philippine democracy, of the disarray of the CPP / NPA in the wake of its unsuccessful boycott of the February 1986 "snap" presidential election, and of the increasing threat to the Aquino presidency posed by elements of the Philippine military.

Factors Conducive to Significant Agrarian Reform

When Corazon Aquino became president of the Philippines in late February 1986, there was reason for judicious optimism concerning the prospects for comprehensive redistributive agrarian reform. Her electoral movement spanned most segments of Philippine society, although the alliance drew its principal strength from its opposition to Ferdinand Marcos. Among the groups likely to challenge land-reform initiatives, the traditional political and economic dominance of the sugar and coconut planter blocs had been appreciably undermined by Marcos-established marketing monopolies and by declining world prices. Indeed, the precariousness of the planters' economic position revealed itself in estimates indicating that a substantial portion of the sugar land of Negros Occidental—the principal sugar-producing province—was either foreclosed or technically foreclosable.[3] For their part, some prominent representatives of the sugar sector expressed a willingness to participate in some form of land reform in exchange for a restructuring of both the industry and their personal debt.[4]

Other factors indirectly pointed to an atmosphere more conducive to reform. Aquino pledged to abolish Civilian Home Defense Force units and disband private armies, both of which were heavily implicated in human rights abuses.[5] Both represented instruments of local domination, the removal of which would increase the political space for peasant political activism. A top government strategy team identified the "dismantling of private armed groups (which have been used by land lords to intimidate the peasantry)" as one of the "minimum requirements for a successful land reform" (ROP 1986b, quoted in Rosenberg 1990: 166).

Meanwhile, the explosive growth of the New People's Army in the early 1980s, coupled with the prominent role of land tenure–related grievances in explaining this growth, gave the Aquino government and landowners good reason to be attentive to demands for land reform. To

similar effect were the land-related grievances fueling the autonomy struggles of the Muslims of Mindanao and Sulu and the tribal populations of the Cordillera region of Luzon.

Finally, the Catholic Church had become increasingly progressive and politically active during the martial-law era.[6] The evolution of the Church was mirrored by the emergence of "people's organizations" and politically active nongovernmental organizations. Prominent elements of the Church and many of these new social organizations were pressing for land reform.

Factors Mitigating Against Significant Agrarian Reform

On the other hand, previous Philippine experience with agrarian reform, characterized by programs limited in scope and implementation, gave cause for considerable skepticism concerning the prospects for meaningful reform. This skepticism seemed all the more warranted given Aquino's landed-class background and that of key advisers and cabinet appointees.[7] The belated political conversions of some elements of the Aquino coalition were further cause for suspicion about the intentions of the new government.[8] Moreover, the "People Power Revolution" that formally ousted Marcos was considered an urban, predominantly middle-class, phenomenon. In this view, the "revolution" owed relatively little to the left or the rural poor.[9]

Equally important, Aquino believed that the rural poor cared little for politics or political and personal freedoms, so long as they received "three meals a day" (*Christian Science Monitor* 1983), a view revealing Aquino's elitist background, and that of her martyred husband, to whom she attributed this insight. Born into a wealthy Chinese-mestizo family, Aquino became accustomed to life among the Philippine and international elite, a reflection of the deep involvement of her family and husband in Philippine politics.[10] By contrast, she reportedly remained ill at ease when directly interacting with Filipino peasants. The exclusively middle- and upper-class composition of the crowd attending Aquino's inauguration ceremony at Club Filipino on February 25, 1986, was one sign of the distance between the new president and the Philippine masses.[11]

Although the movement that propelled her to power had populist attributes, Aquino was not a classic charismatic figure. To a considerable degree her electoral support reflected public reaction to the abuses of the Marcos years. Aquino's ability to unite the anti-Marcos

forces seemed to stem more from her veneration as an almost religious figure than from personal charisma. Her sacred symbolism was intimately linked to the "Christ-like, Passion-like quality of her husband's death."[12] To the extent her following was populist, that populism did little to erode Aquino's distance from Philippine peasants. Moreover, much of the populist social-justice rhetoric used by the Aquino regime was not the president's, but that of others within her coalition.

The imagery of political transition masked both important continuities with the authoritarian rule of Ferdinand Marcos and the exclusionary legacy of earlier "democratic" rule in the Philippines. Aquino confronted a military that had become much more politicized under Marcos. The specter of prisoner releases that included the founder of the CPP/NPA, campaign promises of negotiations with the insurgents and punishment for human rights abusers within the military, and the exclusion of the military from the early cease-fire negotiations with the NPA all antagonized a military whose loyalty was suspect from the start.[13] By the summer of 1986, conservative critics of the Aquino government were arguing, if wistfully, that "the military is simply biding time until [the political situation] gets out of hand, then they will move in to restore order."[14]

The social configuration of the Philippines and the insurgency posed other potential challenges to the Aquino regime. Regional and provincial "strongmen" retained considerable power and influence. Faced with an ongoing insurgency and a poorly led, ill-equipped and ill-trained military, the Aquino government turned to vigilante groups and, less explicitly, to the private armies of local bosses to ensure a semblance of stability in the countryside once negotiations with the insurgents broke down. Among the agricultural poor, dependency relations, cultural norms, and differentiated interests stood as obstacles to effective mobilization in favor of a common program of agrarian reform.[15] It has been argued that the socialization apparatus of hierarchical societies—upper-class penetration and control of religious, educational, and informational institutions—serves to divert attention from class cleavages.[16] At least as important, it would appear from rural fieldwork and the scholarly literature, are the multiple social identities—kinship, patron-client, village, region, ethnolinguistic, religion—and individualism that fashion peasant behavior. There is no single exploited peasant class, only various peasant groups, with often divergent interests.

By some standards, the Aquino regime had established an *inclusion-*

ary democracy: nearly 40 percent of the population voted in the February 1987 constitutional plebiscite and the May 1987 legislative elections.[17] However, rates of electoral participation disguised the continuing importance of "guns, goons, and gold" in Philippine elections, despite improvements in the post-Marcos era. Upper-class control was maintained through the manipulation of rural voting blocs by large landowners and formal or informal restrictions on popular mobilization (cf. Remmer 1985–86: 74–75). Philippine democracy under Aquino was most appropriately characterized as *exclusionary*, electoral turnout notwithstanding. Alternatively, one might use Benedict Anderson's apt phrase "cacique democracy" to describe Philippine politics (Anderson 1988; see also IPD 1987; McBeth 1989a).

Meanwhile, the technocrats in Aquino's inner circle, among them Vicente T. Paterno, Vicente R. Jayme, Jose S. Concepcion, Jr., and Jaime V. Ongpin, were primarily from banking and manufacturing backgrounds.[18] To the extent that these men concerned themselves with agriculture, they seemed more interested in the Malaysian estate-farm model than in redistributive reform.[19] They feared that redistributive reform might result in production declines and crop shifting that would exacerbate the critical shortage of foreign exchange. In light of the financial constraints confronting the new government, compensatory land redistribution was viewed as something the nation could ill afford.[20] Some believed that gains in productivity were possible without tenure changes. The cautious attitude of these technocrats toward redistributive agrarian reform was doubtless reinforced by the knowledge that the private business sector, which exercised considerable strength within the Aquino coalition, had long-standing investments in agricultural land. In other countries, urban and industrial interests have on occasion supported redistributive agrarian reform, viewing "feudal" relations in the countryside as an obstacle to economic development. In the Philippines, however, there has been considerable overlap between urban industrialists and large agricultural landowners. There appeared to be little promise of strong urban support for agrarian reform.

Prominent agrarian scholars were further concerned that the free-market orientation of the Aquino government would be misread by landlords. Absent early, substantive policy pronouncements in support of agrarian reform, landlords might subject tenants to intimidation or eviction (Adriano et al. interview, Mar. 20, 1986). These concerns reflected reports from peasant organizations that reform beneficiaries

were being evicted by (ex-)landlords who claimed that the demise of the Marcos regime had invalidated all Marcos-era reform laws—a claim reportedly corroborated by some local and regional DAR officials.[21]

Another development that boded ill both for reform and for the survival of the Aquino regime generally was Aquino's unwillingness to consolidate her grassroots support in a reform-oriented political organization, despite calls for her to do so.[22] Aquino's commitment to the restoration of democratic institutions and democratic decision-making predisposed her to leave major social-policy decisions to a constitutionally elected body. Past Philippine experience suggested that any legislative body would be strongly influenced by landed interests.[23] Aquino appeared to have the power to change this script, to lead a reform-minded, populist party to legislative victory. She chose instead to repay old debts and backed candidates with little apparent regard for their ideological bent.

There was little to balance the political strength of the traditional elite. The Church was under instructions from the Vatican to be less overtly political in the wake of Marcos's ouster.[24] Notwithstanding a proreform pastoral letter issued by the Catholic Bishops' Conference of the Philippines (CBCP), there was evidence that some elements of the Church hierarchy were ambivalent toward the reform process. The Church provided what one observer termed "diluted advocacy" of agrarian reform (Gillego interview, June 17, 1989).

The CPP/NPA's decision to boycott the February "snap election" left the political field open to other, late-arriving, opponents of Marcos, while excluding the left from any role in influencing the government's policy agenda. "Now instead of a NDF [National Democratic Front] faction in the Aquino government we have the 'born again' Marcos loyalists, 'balimbings.'"[25] For their part, prominent planters viewed their participation in the anti-Marcos movement, however belated, as legitimizing their claims to resumed political influence. Given the predominantly anticommunist orientation of the Aquino coalition, it is doubtful whether the radical left would have had significant policy influence even had it lent its support to the Aquino campaign.[26] However, the CPP/NPA would likely have enjoyed much greater public legitimacy in its advocacy of political and social reform. Instead, the internal disarray of the CPP/NPA occasioned by the boycott debate gave the impression of a much-diminished insurgent threat. This reinforced Aquino's belief that the ouster of Marcos and the restoration of

economic growth and democratic institutions would bring many of the insurgents back into the "democratic fold" (Youngblood 1987: 1251; Jones 1989: 165).

Finally, Washington was preoccupied with the insurgency and with preserving U.S. military bases in the Philippines, and remained unconvinced of the economic merits of land redistribution. Most U.S. government officials accorded agrarian reform a relatively low priority in their policy dialogue with the new government,[27] and Philippine landowners reminded Americans that many of those urging agrarian reform were also calling for removal of the U.S. bases (Alunan interview, June 16, 1986).

Aquino's Construction of Democracy

Aquino's campaign organization was a diverse coalition, combining a family-dominated personal organization, traditional opposition parties such as the United Nationalist Democratic Organization (UNIDO) and the Pilipino Democratic Party (PDP), and the Catholic Church. Aquino's campaign apparatus relied in part on traditional Philippine elites, many of whom were tardy critics of the Marcos regime. Contact was also established with the dissident Reform the Armed Forces Movement (RAM) within the military.[28]

Aquino's First Cabinet

Aquino's first cabinet featured conservative reformists, social democrats, and soldiers (Bello 1986; Landé and Hooley 1986: 1091–92; Putzel 1988: 44–45; Wurfel 1988: 305–8). This composition reflected Aquino's personal debts (*utang na loób*) far more than it did considerations of ideology or competency (*Economist* 1988). The conservatives, the dominant group, endorsed a generally restrained approach to issues of social reform. The social democrats had long favored a nationalistic economic policy and basic social reforms. The military members were late participants in the anti-Marcos struggle, but their contribution to the ouster of Marcos—the rebellion of February 22–25—was undeniable. These officers were concerned primarily with military prerogatives and a military approach to the NPA insurgency, although the dissident cabinet member Juan Ponce Enrile's larger political ambitions were evident.[29] The disparate viewpoints represented in the Aquino cabinet promised a prolonged and fractious debate over issues as politically charged as land reform.

It appears that in her choice of cabinet members Aquino insisted on neither allegiance nor ideological unity.[30] Perhaps it was impossible to do so at the outset of her presidency, with so many divergent viewpoints and personalities involved, however belatedly, in the anti-Marcos movement. Aquino did reward social democrats and other noncommunist progressives, the heart of the nonviolent opposition to Marcos, with a number of cabinet and other government appointments.[31] She also evidenced considerable political savvy in her eventual ouster of Enrile from her cabinet.

However, the November 1986 coup attempt that led to Enrile's discharge also precipitated the dismissal of two of the most progressive cabinet members: Labor Minister Augusto S. Sanchez and Local Government Minister Aquilino Q. Pimentel. The firing of these two progressives was one of the prices of military loyalty.[32] The military was not alone in its criticism of Sanchez, however—senior U.S. officials had similarly made known their displeasure with him.[33] Military loyalty to Aquino during an August 1987 coup attempt carried a similar price: Executive Secretary Joker P. Arroyo, Aquino's closest adviser, and her special legal counsel, Teodoro L. Locsin, Jr., were both dismissed from their positions, tarred as leftists by military and business leaders, notwithstanding that Arroyo had been a leading critic of redistributive reform within the cabinet (Gillego interview, Nov. 20, 1992; Putzel 1992: 232–33, 247–48).

Aquino resisted all calls for the institutionalization of her popularity and movement. Disdainful of traditional politics, she headed no political party, commanded no systematically organized political apparatus. Rejection of the Marcos legacy of single-party rule and "personality cult" politics may partially explain her refusal to consolidate her popularity in a political organization. Like many in the anti-Marcos movement, Aquino appeared determined to curtail the powers of the presidency, relative not only to those exercised by Marcos, but to those exercised by earlier Philippine presidents under the 1935 Constitution.[34]

Aquino's predisposition to nonparty politics may have been reinforced by the contentiousness surrounding the appointments of new local government officials. In its early months, the new Aquino administration systematically removed Marcos-era provincial and local officials from office, replacing them with appointed officers-in-charge (OICs). The selection process was conducted primarily by Minister of Local Government Pimentel. As head of the PDP-LABAN, Pimentel used this opportunity to place party members in government positions.

This process disadvantaged and upset Salvador Laurel's UNIDO party, bringing an end to the alliance between UNIDO and PDP-LABAN (Tancangco 1988: 107–8). Even apart from this intracoalition conflict, the process of replacing local officials generated considerable controversy. The Philippine military was among the foremost critics of the OIC appointments (Sacerdoti 1986a). The displaced officials had been elected to their offices—however flawed the Marcos-era elections—and, it was argued, many of them enjoyed sufficient local popularity to make their victory likely in the event new elections were held. Local military commanders and the leadership of the armed forces argued that the incumbents better understood local issues, and were thereby able to afford greater aid to the military in combating the insurgency. In the view of other critics, summary replacement of local officials by the central government was not only antidemocratic, it raised disturbing parallels with Marcos's assumption of the power of local appointment in the early years of martial law.

The Constitutional Commission

Aquino also used her executive powers to appoint all of the members of the Constitutional Commission. Reflecting her democratic disposition, she chose to make the commission reasonably representative.[35] No known communists were appointed, but the 48-member commission included progressives, important figures from the pre-Marcos era, Catholic Church clergy and laity, and five members of Marcos's Kilusang Bagong Lipunan party.[36] Despite this diversity, the commission included only one representative of the peasant sector. Once the commission had begun its deliberations, Aquino adopted a hands-off policy, refusing to use it to push through a specific economic, political, or social agenda. Criticized in some circles for forgoing this opportunity to mandate a specific reform program, Aquino apparently sought to contrast her actions with those of Marcos in 1972–73.[37]

Congressional Elections: The Return of the Traditional Politicos

The 1987 Constitution separated executive, judicial, and legislative functions and restored a bicameral Philippine legislature. Members of the House of Representatives were to be elected from single-member districts, while senators were to be elected at large (i.e., in nationwide contests). The May 1987 congressional elections presented the best opportunity for President Aquino to democratically institutionalize "People Power." Whether in reaction to the OIC controversy, in reflection of

her general antipathy to party politics, or as a function of inadequate preparation, Aquino neither formed nor joined a political party for these elections. Nor did she use the elections to install legislators who were both loyal and reform-oriented. Instead, Aquino again repaid old favors and backed candidates with little regard to their ideological bent. Consistent with the results of previous Philippine elections, between one-half and three-quarters of the winning candidates in the House of Representatives owned agricultural lands.[38]

Formation of this new political alliance was left largely to the president's brother, Jose "Peping" Cojuangco, Jr., just as he had earlier been responsible for campaign financing in Aquino's bid for the presidency (Mydans 1986a). He justified his role saying, "My sister is not a politician; she does not know about these things" (Clad 1987: 71). What Peping fashioned was a rebirth of the premartial law network of provincial bosses, relying on them to restore the economy and address the local law-and-order situation. Among those recruited to Cojuangco's PDP-LABAN banner were many Marcos loyalists (Anderson 1988; McBeth 1989a; id. 1990). One measure of the influence of these former Marcos supporters within the Aquino congressional coalition is provided by the progressive Institute for Popular Democracy.[39] Using political affiliation as of the 1984 national assembly elections as the benchmark, the IPD identified 18 (of 56) heretofore Marcos-supporters as having run under the banner of an Aquino-affiliated party. Had political affiliation been defined as of 1980, the IPD claimed that the number of "blue wearing yellow"—Marcos supporters turned nominal Aquino backers—would be "overwhelming" (IPD 1987: 4).

Another report parses congressional membership somewhat differently, emphasizing the influence of the traditional elite, regardless of affiliation. By this account, over two-thirds of the members of the new House of Representatives had previously been elected to national office or belonged to "political dynasties"—that is, they were the second or third generation of their family to hold national office.[40] Even apart from the elections, the ouster of Marcos afforded traditional elite families important opportunities to strengthen or reassert regional influence.[41] Her elite alliance gave Aquino precious little political space vis-à-vis rightists and the military, while so shaping the composition of the Philippine Congress as to all but doom measures of redistributive reform.

To be sure, the largest political party, the Laban ng Demokratikong Pilipino, was identified primarily by its commitment to passage of legis-

lative initiatives in Aquino's name.[42] However, Aquino held no office in the party. Furthermore, the party lacked any defining ideology or agenda (Orbos interview, June 22, 1989). Most important for our purposes, the LDP was generally left to its own devices on the reform question; at several key junctures, it failed to honor Aquino's wishes.

The Political Impetus for Reform

If Philippine politics has been a relatively hostile ground for effectuating redistributive reform, why have Philippine politicians so frequently promised agrarian reform? Why would Aquino, a member of one of the country's wealthiest landowning families, even purport to be committed to agrarian reform? Aquino's resort to the rhetoric of reform was a response to the history of tenure-related peasant grievances and a stagnant agricultural sector, the sentiments of her martyred husband,[43] the developmental ideologies of Philippine intellectuals, the government's concern with political legitimacy, the related desire to incorporate the rural poor into political life (motivated by both rural unrest and a commitment to participatory democracy), and nominal international pressure. Aquino's campaign commitment was premised on the belief that such reform would accomplish the following policy objectives: (1) increase the peasants' stake in Philippine society; (2) defuse the NPA insurgency; (3) shift rural resources from land to rural industrialization; and (4) rationalize and increase agricultural production.

In other settings a similar combination of factors has typically been operative in the reform decision (Grindle 1986: 139; see also Herring 1983; Prosterman and Riedinger 1987). Illustrative are the reforms announced throughout Latin America in the early 1960s.[44] These reforms were responses to varying combinations of concern about potential rural unrest in the wake of the Cuban revolution, recognition of the potential political base in rapidly expanding rural electorates, acceptance of the prescriptions of structuralist economists, and the influence of the United States in the guise of the Alliance for Progress.

Some members of the Aquino coalition deemed agrarian reform central to the creation of a new social order based on social justice, political empowerment and incorporation of the rural poor, and economic development. In the words of the National Economic and Development Authority, social justice was to be the "primary consideration in the pursuit of development objectives."[45] Agrarian reform would sweep away the vestiges of feudalism in Philippine agrarian

relations. Early in her tenure, President Aquino expressed her commitment to strengthening and expanding the agrarian-reform program as designed to "truly liberate the Filipino farmer from the shackles of landlordism and transform him into a self-reliant citizen who will participate responsibly in the affairs of the nation."[46] Tenants were to benefit from agrarian reform and incorporation into a new democratic political and social order; Aquino made no mention of hired laborers on plantations, however.

Senator Heherson Alvarez, Aquino's first minister of agrarian reform, sounded this same theme of incorporating tenants into democratic society in a speech to the Senate in support of agrarian-reform legislation: "Farmers who continue to live as tenants under the present system are in effect denied their role as citizens in a democratic society. They are outside the market system because of their poverty. They are outside the political system because they vote and decide the way their landlords want them to. Indeed, Mr. President, the limited political power of our farmers is both uneconomic and anti-democratic" (1988: 10).

Jerry Bulatao, an Aquino-appointed undersecretary in the DAR, elaborated on the premises of a more inclusive vision of reform:

Agrarian Reform is expected to lead also to the creation of a broader base democracy and the recognition of the human dignity of our farmers and farm workers. This should lead to heighten[ed] consciousness, social concern and civil involvement and the greater participation of our people in political affairs in order to broaden the base of our democracy.

Ultimately, Agrarian Reform will make a very important contribution to national development in the formation of a more dynamic democracy.[47]

In his homily celebrating the second anniversary of the "EDSA Revolution" of February 1986, Jaime Cardinal Sin, the person most responsible for brokering the Aquino presidential candidacy, remarked: "We cannot bring an effective political democracy into being without an underlying economic democracy in operation, at least in some true measure. . . . We have to bring about a more equitable distribution of wealth throughout our country. Only then can our nation survive and go forward. Only then can the house of a genuine democracy built on social justice rise up securely in our land" (1988).

Aquino's desire to more fully incorporate, and control, the rural poor into Philippine social and political life was of a piece with the nominal policies of her presidential predecessors. Earlier in this century,

concern with the political and social incorporation of the Philippine rural population prompted extensions of the voting franchise and central government investments in education and basic infrastructure. In 1916, the requirement of property ownership as a qualification to vote was eliminated. The voting franchise was further liberalized with the adoption of the 1935 Constitution and the Election Code of 1939 (Commonwealth Act 357).[48] The increasingly literate and accessible rural electorate became a potential new base for national power. As a campaign rallying cry, "land reform" has had particular symbolic value; it strikes at the heart of existing patterns of power and prestige in an agrarian society.

"It is precisely because ruling elites come from privileged groups that dramatic illustration of good faith and dedication to the masses is necessary to establish their legitimacy," Ronald Herring contends (1983: 226). During her campaign for the presidency, Aquino sounded the noblesse oblige theme: "The very fact that I was born privileged carries with it certain obligations."[49] In this light, the government's position on agrarian reform was a litmus test of its commitment to redressing poverty and income inequality, rural and urban. The symbolic role of reform is all the more pronounced in the wake of a political crisis such as that which preceded Aquino's presidency. The early promulgation of a land-reform program could serve as evidence both of government capacity and commitment to fundamental societal reform.

Agrarian reform afforded the Aquino regime an opportunity to forge new links with the rural masses as a means of consolidating regime and state power. Both as a function of the anticipated land reform–related disruption of old landlord-tenant relations and to redress historic shortcomings in the agricultural sector, the state prepared to assume significant new responsibilities to assure the timely and adequate supply of credit, inputs, marketing, and extension services. The regime also made provision for greater state-beneficiary interaction in consideration of pricing, taxation, and the like.

At the same time, there were significant political risks attendant on agrarian reform, not least of which was the possibility of a backlash from a reactionary coalition of the landed elite and the military. During the consolidation of the Aquino regime, in a setting of ongoing economic and political crises, the risk of failure in implementing a reform program was considerable. The combination of lost popular credibility in the wake of such failure and antireform backlash from landed interests might well have precipitated the ouster of the Aquino regime.

Economic Motivations for Agrarian Reform

In analyzing reform motivations, Alain de Janvry (1984) alerts us to the possibility that the loci of reform-related political and economic benefits may differ. He argues that antifeudal reforms have typically been designed to serve primarily political ends within the reform sector—that is, to foster political stability by satisfying peasant demands for land. The principal economic results were to be achieved in the nonreform sector, with the now-credible threat of expropriation, complemented by inducements to investment (subsidized credit, infrastructure construction, and extension services), facilitating the transformation to capitalist agriculture.

Many of those espousing agrarian reform in the Philippines, however, expected it to result in important productivity gains *within* the reform sector when heretofore landless cultivators acted upon the incentives of private ownership to increase short- and, more important, long-term investments in the land. In turn, these newly efficient small producers would both supply cheap foodstuffs for the burgeoning urban workforce and provide a dynamic new market for consumer goods. Jun Medina, then acting secretary of the DAR, summarized this rationale as follows:

State policy on agrarian reform is to establish [the] owner-cultivator and the economic size family farm as the basis of Philippine agriculture, and as a consequence, divert landlord capital in agriculture in[to] industrial development. . . . It has been proven not only here but abroad that where the farmer becomes the owner of the land he is tilling, he spends more hours in the land. He intensifies cultivation; he diversifies crops and he increased [sic] productivity, and by attaining that, the purchasing power of the farmers—which are the great majority—increases. And when we have effective purchasing power among the farmers, among the rural areas, then this will lead certainly to industrialization.[50]

Signing the reform program into law, President Aquino shared this view, citing as its goals "a radical leap in agricultural productivity and, therefore, a significant contribution by the agricultural sector to Philippine progress and the upliftment of the Filipino masses from their ancient poverty. . . . Let us see the program not as a taking of property from some and a giving of it to others, but rather as a way of liberating hitherto suppressed energies and creativity" (Balingcos 1988).

Civil Unrest as Impetus for Reform

Aquino came to office at a time when the communist insurgency appeared to threaten the very existence of the Philippine state. This threat, in turn, was a principal impetus for her administration's advocacy of agrarian reform. In the words of her government's task force on agrarian reform: "An analysis of the land distribution problem in the Philippines shows that its roots lie in the abuse of state prerogatives to grant land to the powerful and, hence, socially undeserving few. Thus, the land reform issue has given the subversive movement its most alluring talking point to attract the landless poor. The new regime, in its bid for peace and reconciliation, has made genuine land reform a high priority" (ROP, ITFAR 1987a: 1).

Although economic and social-justice arguments for reform figured prominently in the ideology of proreform Philippine intellectuals, the issue of potential rural unrest was central to the reform debate.[51] It was the latter argument that weighed most heavily in the calculus of the landed elite and their representatives. In writing about reform generally, Herring captures the essence of many political discussions when he notes, "Reforms are frequently defended by the promulgating regime, almost as an apology to landed groups, as the only alternative to bloodshed and revolution."[52] The economic rationales for reform were clouded by contradictory interpretations of the empirical evidence concerning land tenure and agricultural performance in the Philippines. The irrelevance of social-justice concerns was almost axiomatic for much of the landed elite. Were it otherwise, compliance with social legislation (minimum-wage laws, rent ceilings, and the like) and voluntary sharing or transfer of land would have been much more in evidence. Yet the promotion of reform as a means of defusing potential or actual insurgencies was understandably viewed with suspicion by the political left and peasant movements. The counterinsurgency motif thus threatened to alienate part of the mass base that might otherwise pressure the government to formulate and implement effective reform.

Samuel Huntington saw no prospect in general for significant reform absent violence or the imminent threat thereof.[53] In Herring's words, "Reforms are taken most seriously and implemented most effectively when landowners and governing elites alike realize that the alternative is rural violence" (1983: 236). Yet we would do well to recall Joan Nelson's comment—made with reference to economic stabilization—

that "commitment that grows out of desperation will fade if any aspect of the situation becomes less binding" (1984: 986). To the extent that counterinsurgency concerns drove the Aquino regime's espousal of agrarian reform, perceptions that the threat posed by the communist insurgency was abating were likely to be accompanied by reduced commitment to reform.

The International Dimension to Agrarian Reform

International variables can also exert significant influence on the reform calculus. The Alliance for Progress and U.S. concern about the Cuban revolution were integral to the introduction of reform programs throughout Latin America in the early 1960s. Even more direct was U.S. involvement in the postwar agrarian reforms in Japan, Taiwan, and South Korea.[54] In the case of Japan, U.S. support received considerable impetus from General MacArthur on the advice of Wolf Ladejinsky. The postwar Huk rebellion in the Philippines occasioned calls by U.S. advisers for sweeping redistribution of hitherto tenanted rice and corn holdings. Resistance among the Philippine political elite and Washington's reluctance to see the recommendations through effectively eviscerated the reform initiative. More recently, concern over the fallout from the Nicaraguan revolution and the insurgency in El Salvador prompted direct U.S. support of the Salvadoran reform process and landowner compensation and, for a time, the conditioning of all economic and military assistance on progress in agrarian reform.[55]

In the case of the Aquino government's agrarian-reform program, the international signals were mixed. It has been suggested that Aquino was playing in significant part to an international, particularly American, audience in her espousal of agrarian reform. Yet in the crucial early months of her administration, the U.S. posture on agrarian reform was low-profile and reactive. Official U.S. policy held that any reform initiative should originate with the Aquino government and represent an internal decision based on the merits of reform, rather than one based on considerations of external financial assistance.[56] This approach was in some ways commendable, evidencing sensitivity to Philippine nationalist sentiment and the considerable residual hostility to U.S. support of Marcos.[57] The U.S. position in effect increased the autonomy of the Aquino administration vis-à-vis external actors in this crucial policy domain.[58]

In important ways, however, the U.S. stance simply begged the

question. The Aquino government had inherited some $26 billion in foreign debt from the Marcos years. The amount and terms of further foreign assistance, and debt rescheduling or debt forgiveness, were understandably of extraordinary importance to the Aquino administration. The negotiations on foreign debt and foreign assistance consistently involved an array of externally prescribed fiscal and structural reforms as part of a program of economic stabilization and recovery. For creditors-cum-donors such as the U.S. government to remain largely silent on the agrarian-reform issue was to proclaim the insignificance of such reform for Philippine economic (and political) development.

To the surprise of many observers, the World Bank—or at least a World Bank mission—took a position strongly supportive of a comprehensive and immediate agrarian reform.[59] In May 1987, the World Bank issued a report sharply critical of the Aquino government and many features of its draft reform program, features it saw as defeating the aims of agrarian reform with respect to social equity and economic development. However, the World Bank coupled its support of nonconfiscatory reform with a refusal to finance the land-transfer process directly, a position that has been common among the international donors in recent decades.[60] The multilateral donor agencies and most bilateral donors have instead opted for support of complementary measures such as credit and agricultural research and extension services (Martokoesoemo and Tacke interview, June 1986). While the fungibility of resources should permit donors to underwrite other portions of government budgets and thereby free up domestic resources for payment of compensation and the like, the mixed signals communicated by donors doubtless lent encouragement to the antireform forces.

Campaign Promises: How They Were Understood

A variety of political, economic, and social considerations led Aquino to make agrarian reform a cornerstone of her rural social and economic program in a campaign that otherwise substituted religious symbolism for substance.[61] In the first major policy address of her presidential campaign, delivered before the Manila business community, Aquino promised to undertake "genuine" land reform.[62] She later tempered this to "viable" land reform.[63] The specifics of such reform received scant consideration in the Aquino inner circle during the campaign, nor were they debated much in public.[64] Aquino's pledge to "explore how the twin goals of maximum productivity and dispersal of

ownership and benefits can be exemplified for the rest of the nation" on her family's 6,000 hectare sugar estate Hacienda Luisita was characteristic of her public statements (1986b: 6). Even this pledge was accompanied by remarks suggesting ambivalence about the extension of reform to crops other than rice and corn or to farms operated under arrangements other than tenancy.

In agitating for reform, peasant activists regularly stressed Aquino's campaign rhetoric. Her promise of "genuine" agrarian reform echoed the phrasing used by more militant peasant organizations and the Communist Party of the Philippines in their calls for free distribution of land to landless and near-landless cultivators.[65] Some reform proponents interpreted her pledge concerning her family's Hacienda Luisita to be a firm commitment to redistribute the hacienda's lands, to lead by example on the reform issue. For their part, landowners cited another Aquino campaign pledge, "I shall ask no greater sacrifices than I myself am prepared to make" (1986a: 7), to argue against any agrarian-reform initiatives that might affect their landholdings.

In citing Aquino's proreform campaign pledges, peasant activists argued, if sometimes only by implication, that her rural support was in substantial measure a function of her call for agrarian reform, and radical reform at that.[66] However, several prominent Filipinos otherwise supportive of agrarian reform have questioned the extent of public awareness of Aquino's reform pledges, particularly at the village level (Bernas interview, July 10, 1989; Gillego interview, June 17, 1989). As a general matter, Philippine villagers still have rather limited access to mass media. Given Marcos's effective control of the Philippine media and the resulting near-absence of coverage of the Aquino campaign (Mydans 1986a), the question is appropriately raised as to how many Filipinos knew of, and voted on, Aquino's reform promises.

There has long been considerable grassroots demand for agrarian reform, variously defined, in the Philippines. Nonetheless, my interviews suggest that only the more politicized landless farmers—for example, those who were members of peasant organizations or Basic Christian Communities—were aware of Aquino's proreform campaign pledges or the later pledges of various congressional candidates.[67] Inasmuch as the vast majority, perhaps 90 percent (Montemayor 1987: 4), of Philippine peasants were not organized, one might reasonably conclude that peasant electoral behavior was premised more on their (or their patrons') rejection of Marcos and his policies than on reliance on Aquino's position vis-à-vis reform.

There are scholars who believe political awareness and politicization among tenant farmers was relatively high (Cornista et al. interview, Mar. 24, 1986). Whether in February 1986 the number of voters who knew of, and acted upon, the candidates' positions on agrarian reform was sizable enough to have a material impact on the outcome of the election is another question. Unfortunately, we have no direct data on this issue. Most of the indirect evidence that is available, however, suggests limited public awareness of the politics of agrarian reform. Even after some eighteen months of often-heated political debate, and the attendant, near-daily media coverage, only 46 percent of those surveyed nationally were aware of the Comprehensive Agrarian Reform Law of June 1988. Public awareness was greatest in Metro Manila (68 percent) and lowest in rural Mindanao (35 percent). In all regions, public awareness was lower in rural areas than in urban areas (Mangahas 1989: 3).

Peasant activists concede that public awareness of the new reform law was initially quite limited. They have exerted considerable effort to overcome that informational shortcoming (Ramiro interview, Feb. 21, 1989). The importance that organizations such as the National Federation of Sugar Workers (NFSW) attached to basic land-awareness training for their members bore similar witness to limited peasant awareness of the terms and nature of the national-level reform debate (Cherniguin interview, Mar. 3, 1989). These results are perhaps unsurprising, given limited rural access to media sources and government outreach. Still, these findings denote both a notable ignorance concerning one of the most important political initiatives dealing with rural life and a profound failure to incorporate rural inhabitants into the reform debate.

Even where Philippine peasants were aware of the various pro-reform campaign promises, there remains the question of how these pledges were understood. Certainly there has been no universally accepted definition of agrarian reform in the Philippine context.[68] Indeed, the very vagueness of the agrarian-reform concept made it attractive as a campaign slogan, for it encompassed a wide range of agendas: from free-market pricing and termination of Marcos-era marketing monopolies to subsidized credit and agricultural inputs, from voluntary land sales to confiscatory land redistribution. Landowner candidates could promise reform, then seek refuge in these ambiguities, at the same time as radical reform candidates used these ambiguities to mask their larger agenda. Agrarian reform had often been discussed and was embodied in numerous legislative enactments, but these did not a consensus make. The one issue on which there seemed to be general agreement

was that the Marcos-era reform had not worked,[69] although there was considerable disagreement as to the reasons for that failure.

The elaboration of "genuine" agrarian reform embodied in the KMP's *Program for Genuine Land Reform*, and similar pronouncements from other peasant organizations and the CPP/NPA, appeared months after Aquino assumed office. These documents and speeches were intended to give definition to Aquino's campaign promise. They constituted the opening salvo in what became a highly contested search for a definition of agrarian reform appropriate to the Philippines. At stake was not merely semantics, but executive and legislative embodiments of that definition.[70]

I am unable reliably to establish the extent to which rural Filipinos' understanding of "genuine" agrarian reform at the time of the 1986 election comported with the KMP definition.[71] My field interviews date from March 1986. Informants' reconstructions of their understanding of Aquino's promise of reform, and of the concept of agrarian reform generally, as of some earlier date were influenced by their understanding at the time of the interview, the latter often reflecting intervening educational and mobilizational efforts of the KMP, NFSW and other peasant organizations. It is worth noting that in contrast to "genuine agrarian reform" as here defined, agrarian reform as then *practiced* by the CPP/NPA was most often limited to rent and interest-rate reductions. The longer-term CPP/NPA objective was, however, to "confiscate and redistribute lands and . . . eliminate land rent completely."[72]

Aquino's Early Inactivity on the Reform Issue

Following the February "revolution," relatively little was said or done about land reform until the convening of the Constitutional Commission in early June 1986. Aquino reiterated her pro–land reform stance in early April and in her Farmer's Day speech on May 30. On April 12, she appointed Heherson T. Alvarez minister of agrarian reform.[73] Whether symbolic of the divisions within her advisory group or of ambivalence on the reform issue, Alvarez was the last appointee to the new Aquino cabinet. The considerable concern this long delay had occasioned among reformists was hardly assuaged when Alvarez, a person with little agricultural background, was appointed.[74] Landowners distressed by Aquino's reform pledges were likewise further concerned by this appointment. Alvarez was not an outspoken reformist, but it was feared that in his relative ignorance, he might fashion a

reform program that failed to make adequate allowance for—that is, exempt most of the land of—productive landowners (Benedicto interview, June 18, 1986; Locsin et al. interview, June 14, 1986).

Shortly after taking office, Alvarez did suggest that agrarian reform be expanded to the sugar and coconut sectors, an announcement that was applauded by peasant organizations (FFF 1986e). However, Ramon Mitra, then minister of agriculture (and owner of sizable cattle and coconut holdings), took immediate and strong public exception to Alvarez's remarks. Mitra argued for a completion of the Marcos-era reform (PD 27), the awarding of upland stewardship contracts, and the distribution of idle and public lands before initiating reform in the sugar and coconut sectors. Moreover, Mitra was quoted as claiming that average sugarcane and coconut farm holdings were only three and five hectares respectively, and thus inappropriate targets of reform. The president appeared to side with Mitra in this dispute, cautioning against redistribution of productive lands.[75] Instead, she called for prompt completion of the reform of tenanted rice and corn lands and redistribution of public lands (Gilding 1993: 6).

Aquino's "Freedom Constitution," announced on March 25, 1986, preserved previous constitutional provisions regarding agrarian reform and existing reform legislation, ending (at least in theory) confusion about the continuing validity of Marcos-era reform decrees and allaying some related peasant concerns.[76] The only substantive proposal introduced at the time was a draft Executive Order extending the reform program to lands foreclosed by government banking and financial institutions, which was shelved. So too was a proposed order, drafted in August, extending reform coverage to idle and abandoned private agricultural lands.[77] The Aquino government's decisions to defer redistribution of foreclosed and idle and abandoned farm properties did little to allay fears that yet another Philippine administration would fail to implement the more controversial reform measures—for example, expropriation of profitable commercial farm holdings.[78]

The convening of the Constitutional Commission marked the first significant consideration of agrarian reform under the Aquino government. The drafting of a new constitution afforded Aquino a rare opportunity to further an agenda of social reform. Rather than put her stamp on the commission's deliberations, she chose to remain silent. Aquino's silence at this and other critical junctures raised serious questions about the depth of her commitment to agrarian reform. Indeed, a member of her cabinet, Secretary of Agriculture Carlos G. Dominguez, would later

almost apologetically cite the Constitution in justifying the taking of private lands under the Aquino government's reform program: "I do recognize, though, that the landowners will look at the [injustice of] forceable coercion to sell their property. But unfortunately, as I said, this is what we have in the Constitution. . . . We *have* to give land to the tillers" (1987: 30; emphasis added). The implication of Dominguez's remarks was that the Constitutional Commission acted beyond the control, and against the desires, of the Aquino government.

Explanations for Aquino's inactivity on the land issue during the early period of her presidency are varied. Some observers pointed to the reluctant nature of her candidacy / presidency and her predisposition to laissez-faire.[79] This proclivity was reinforced in the early months of the Aquino regime by her perception that the problems of the Philippines were Marcos-related, and that simply ridding the country of Marcos would in large measure right the course of Philippine economic and political development (Ortigas interview, June 22, 1989). Other observers argued that Aquino viewed her role only in terms of the restoration of democratic institutions.[80] Others cited Aquino's class background and that of her principal advisers in explanation.[81] In a March 1986 speech, Bernabe Buscayno ("Commander Dante"), former commander of the NPA, noted positive and negative features in Aquino's background. Although a member of the "hacendero-comprador class," Aquino was influenced by "Western liberalism and the free enterprise ideology of the bourgeois-capitalist class." Her background thus revealed dimensions both antithetical and hospitable to "genuine land reform" (1986: 25).

Meanwhile, the CPP / NPA, having boycotted the February election, had effectively dealt itself out of a role in influencing government policy. The various "cause-oriented" and peasant organizations became increasingly active in promoting agrarian reform in these months, but their access to, and influence on, the Aquino administration remained limited.

Observers more sympathetic to Aquino explain her inaction on land reform in terms of other, and in their view more pressing, issues. She had to address the imperatives of consolidating her presidency, drafting a new constitution and restoring democratic institutional forms, dealing with the debt situation and the ill-gotten wealth of Marcos and his cronies, releasing political detainees, and working toward negotiations with the CPP / NPA and several regional autonomy movements.[82] Finally, her political survival became increasingly problematic in the face

of rightist threats from within her military, leading to substantial concessions to the military and the avoidance of any measure, including land reform, viewed as potentially destabilizing (insofar as they threatened her middle-class support).[83]

Landowner Response to Reform Initiatives

Rhetorical Support for Agrarian Reform

Such was the perceived threat of the communist insurgency in 1986, and hence the political urgency of reform, that few went on record as being *against* agrarian reform, although some argued that there was no need for it. For the most part, resistance was couched instead in terms of support for the concept of reform but opposition to program specifics.[84] Practicing a landowner version of "everyday forms of resistance," Philippine landowners manipulated language to mask their antipathy to reform and their efforts to subvert the reform process. The following remarks are illustrative:

We are not against reform, just against drastic reform.[85]

We do agree that land reform must be implemented, but the same must exempt private agricultural lands from the concept and scope of its operation. (Barcelona 1987: 15)

I was not against land reform, I was in favor of it. It can uplift the people and make the land more productive. . . . [But] all the way I was against [the Comprehensive Agrarian Reform Law]. (Guanzon interview, July 1, 1989)

We are not against the land reform program. In fact we would like to support whatever we can. It is only in the implementation that we would like to see some clarification. (Caparas 1987: 6–7; accord, Hernandez 1987: 29–30)

As a Congressman of this First Congress, I would like to inform people that I am willing [*sic*] land reform myself, that I will not go around the law. . . . I want to give example of the real meaning and objectives of this CARP. But for justice sake, now if you can increase . . . the cash portion. (Monfort 1987: 33–34)

We are not against the Program *per se*. We only wish to seek equitable treatment in the Program's implementation with respect to agro-industrial private lands. (Sebastian 1987: 39)

One description of the Philippine agrarian reform debates of 1955 was just as applicable in 1986–88: "The favored tactics of the reform opponents . . . were to delay and weaken legislation rather than oppose it outright" (Tai 1974: 152). Wurfel puts it more forcefully: "Public praise

for the principle of reform [was] combined with the sponsorship of emasculating amendments."[86]

Landowner Organizations and Resistance

Among the standard bearers in the fight against agrarian reform were a number of crop-specific planters' organizations, the Council of Agricultural Producers of the Philippines (CAP),[87] and the Movement for an Independent Negros, a sugar-planters' organization that threatened armed resistance—even secession—in the event of land reform.[88] Threats of violent resistance and secession continued through the congressional deliberations, many of them made in open testimony before congressional committees. For these landowners, agrarian reform was synonymous with communism. Tadeo Villarosa, a sugar-industry consultant, condemned a proposal to redistribute 10 percent of sugar lands in exchange for debt relief, arguing that it was a "ploy of the NPA" that would only serve to "create friction between the planter and his workers" (interview, June 19, 1986).

Other critics adopted a less militant, if no less damning, stance: "The CARP is a program drawn up by government technocrats out of touch with reality and promoters of noble causes, to be implemented by the inefficient and underfinanced, supposedly for the unaware and the ungrateful," said one.[89]

Landowners used a variety of strategies to resist reform. Although violence and electoral machinations figured in this resistance, rhetorical strategies of resistance dominated the formal deliberations in the Constitutional Commission, the executive branch, and the Philippine legislature. Consider the way in which landowners attempted to shape the nature of the debate by the very names they selected for their organizations. Among the various organizations prominent in the reform debate were the Council of Landowners for *Orderly* Reform (COLOR; an outgrowth of a Marcos-era organization, ALARM, or the Association of Landowners for Orderly Reform), the Panay Landowners' Alliance for *Democratic* Agrarian Reform, and the Democratic Alliance for a Truly *Unified* Panay (my emphases). Could even the staunchest reformist deny the desirability of orderly or democratic reform or of a unified Panay?

Landowners Deny Need for Agrarian Reform

Some landowners denied the need for agrarian reform, arguing that tenants and farmworkers were better served either by existing arrange-

ments or by nonreform alternatives. Hortensia L. Starke, a congresswoman and sugar *hacendero*, argued that "land was not necessarily the
answer," that farmworkers should be "emancipated from the soil"
through the creation of industry.[90] Another landowner suggested that
the law of family succession obviated the need for reform, with generational subdivision of farm holdings having essentially eliminated large
estates from the Philippine agricultural scene (Benedicto interview,
June 18, 1986). Still another landowner suggested that equity-based
rationales for reform were misplaced: "In the history of mankind . . .
there have always been the rich and the poor, the ruling class and the
peasants, the farm workers. It is impossible to eradicate poverty"
(Acuña 1987: 62).

Rather than redistributing a portion of their farmland and leaving
their workers to care for themselves, Tadeo Villarosa maintained that
planters should be "directly concerned" with the betterment of their
workers' conditions, working to create small-scale industries to provide
off–milling season employment. In terms of farm activities, the emphasis, in his view, should be on livelihood projects not involving competition with the landowner over land rights.[91]

Sugarcane and coconut growers blamed the policies of the Marcos-
era "crony" monopolies in sugar and coconut marketing for the impoverished state of the agricultural economy.[92] "There was no hunger,
no insurgency [in Negros Occidental] before Marcos," one landowner
claimed (Alunan interview, June 16, 1986). The planters argued, in effect, that all would be right with the rural economy, and that the well-
being of the rural poor would be assured, once these monopolies were
eliminated (coupled, in the case of sugar, with an increase in the U.S.
import quota—something the United States was "duty bound" to provide the Philippines in the view of many planters).[93]

Many sugarcane landowners emphasized the benefits farmworkers
supposedly enjoyed under current agricultural arrangements. As these
landowners would have it, farmworkers had little cause to complain or
to agitate for reform; nor by their account did farmworkers aspire to
landownership, preferring instead the security of employment as farm
laborers (Acuña 1987: 76). Sugarcane growers characterized the benefits they gave farmworkers as "womb to tomb"—including medical,
housing, educational, and recreational services.[94] The landowner-as-
benevolent-patron line of argument is well represented, as is the standard rationale for landowners' failure to pay minimum wages, in the
remarks of the then president of the largest sugar-planters' association:

The farmers in the sugar farms in Negros are provided with free housing, free electricity, free water, free medicines, free hospitalization. Well, it is true perhaps that in some instances there are landowners, sugar landowners who have been remiss in their duty and obligation to pay their laborers the minimum wage. But, Mr. Chairman, that is more of an exception than the rule. And in fairness to those planters who are unable during certain crop years to meet their obligation to their farm laborers . . . it was because they themselves had great difficulty making both ends meet. . . . During the time of President Marcos, the industry was plundered. Besides that, Mr. Chairman, we had this depressed world market prices. Now, on top of that, the high interest rates in the banks.[95]

What remarks of this sort evaded was the considerable evidence that a substantial minority, if not the overwhelming majority, of landowners did not pay the minimum wage. Few haciendas provided hospitals or medical clinics, schools, garden plots of any consequence, or the other services cited by landowners as typical benefits. The conditions under which most permanent hacienda laborers (*duma-ans*) lived and worked little resembled those portrayed by landowners; the living conditions of the migratory laborers (*sacadas*) were often abominable.[96] Yet in the contest over the symbols and language of agrarian relations, the exceptional hacienda became the norm cited in landowner discourse. Ironically, in so doing, landowners indirectly lent legitimacy to peasant grievances: the owners established a rarely met standard by which peasants could measure and criticize landowners' behavior.

Landowners' Concerns About the "Middle Class" and Philippine Democracy

Throughout the reform deliberations, large landowners successfully phrased their concerns and objections in terms calculated to establish common cause with small landowners, particularly on the crucial issue of retention limits (Modina interview, Oct. 17, 1988). Retirees, teachers, and government employees who had invested their savings in 7–10 hectare farms identified completely with the interests of much larger landowners. Large landowners had effectively redefined the common good, the area of mutual interest among all landowners.

These mid-range landowners were among the most vocal opponents of the reform program in the view of Bonifacio Gillego, chairman of the House Committee on Agrarian Reform during the reform deliberations (interview, Feb. 22, 1989). While agreeing that middle landowners were "staunchly opposed to the reform," the chairman of the Senate Committee on Agrarian Reform, Heherson Alvarez, deemed the

outspoken sugar *hacenderos* of Negros the most prominent landowner group attempting to influence Senate deliberations (interview, Feb. 24, 1989). The differing perceptions may simply reflect differing landowner tactics for influencing the two legislative bodies. With their leading members elected to the House of Representatives, the sugar-planter organizations may have felt less need for overt politicking on the House side.

Landowner groups also offered political justifications for limiting the scope of the reform program. CAP argued for exemption of the "88 percent" of private agricultural holdings below 24 hectares, deeming these owners "the middle class who constitute the bulwark of any democracy."[97] Not to be outdone, Senator John Osmeña proposed, immediately after the June 1988 enactment of the reform law, that farms of 50 hectares or less be exempted from redistribution. He contended that such farms were owned by the rural middle class—teachers, merchants, small farmers, and professionals.[98] To deprive these owners of the economic benefits, social security, and community status associated with landownership would be to destroy the middle class (Ronquillo 1988).

By one account, the probable response of middle-class landowners, in the event their holdings were subjected to agrarian reform, would be nothing short of social revolution:

I do not believe that peasants will lead the revolution. History tells us that revolution is led by the middle class. It is only the middle class, they have the power, the brains and the capacity. If we alienate the middle class . . . once they feel they have been dispossessed, that they have been betrayed, then Gentlemen, you plant and nurture the seed of resentment in their hearts, that seed of betrayal and it will cry redress and we will have in our hands a social volcano. (Dizon 1987: 94)

In further defense of the exemption of farms of 50 hectares or less, Osmeña claimed, in an idiom much used by large landowners: "Usually, owners of these lands [50 hectares and below] are not exploiters of their tenants, but *are like fathers of big families whom farm workers can run to when they have problems*. They are not oppressive and thus, to destroy the system is to destroy the rural middle class" (Cruz 1988; emphasis added).

Landowners Divided on Some Issues

Landowners should not be mistaken for a monolithic interest bloc, however (Salcedo interview, Mar. 15, 1989). Indeed, on some issues,

landowner groups were at pains to distinguish themselves. Land-owners involved in sugarcane, prawn, and livestock production all argued that the unique nature of their crop or their relationship with their tenants or farmworkers warranted their exemption from the reform process.[99] A prominent sugar landowner from Central Luzon contended that agrarian reform should not include tenanted sugarcane holdings, because there was little evidence of peasant unrest on such farms. By his account, the problem of insurgency was limited to those areas of sugarcane production typified by hired farmworkers. The relative absence of insurgency in tenanted areas was explained by the relationship between landlord and tenant: "We do not treat our tenants as workers. We treat them as members of the family. And that's the value which I highly appreciate in [the] Filipino's way of life" (Sawit 1987: 40).

Although Luzon sugarcane growers were seeking exemption from the reform process because they had tenants, sugarcane growers in Negros Occidental sought exemption from the reform precisely because they did not employ tenants (Acuña 1987: 61). Similarly, representatives of the coconut sector sought exemption from the reform by redefining "tenancy":

There is not tenancy in coconut plantations as practiced in rice and corn regions. The coconut worker families are mere "guardians" of the trees. . . .

The primary reason for land reform i.e., the emancipation of the tenant from the bondage of the soil, cannot be accomplished in coconut areas for the simple reason that there are no tenants in coconut lands.[100]

Other landowners argued for exemption from the reform by redefining the "tiller"—they portrayed their operations as being so highly mechanized that their farmworkers did not qualify as tillers, and thus should not be entitled to land redistribution.[101]

A prawn producer from Negros Occidental cited a variety of the reasons for exemption from the reform. Variants of several of these themes were also proffered by representatives of other sectors of Philippine agriculture:

We are earnestly requesting, Your Honors, to exempt fish ponds and prawn ponds from the coverage of the proposed [agrarian reform] for the following reason:

The prawn industry requires a big amount of capital and high technology which are beyond the reach of ordinary tenant-farmer-laborer. . . .

The industry has existing and present international and local contractual commitments to comply with. . . .

The wages of prawn farmers are the highest in the agricultural sector. And there is an existing industry practice of profit-sharing with employees and workers. . . .

Land is less than 20% of the total investment cost. . . .

We submit, therefore, that the prawn industry should be classified as agro-industrial instead of agricultural, and should therefore, not be included in the proposed agrarian reform program. (Larrosa 1987: 8–9)

The policy thrust of the new reform law suggests that congressional deliberations were strongly influenced by domestic corporate and commercial farmers, at the expense of traditional rentiers and, to a lesser extent, multinational corporations.

Paramilitary Organizations and Private Armies

Another part of the political equation, as regards both constraints on peasant activism in support of agrarian reform and government implementation of the reform measures adopted, were the many local private armies operating in the Philippines. One reporter put the number of such armies at 260 (Mydans 1987a; id. 1987c). Some of the armies were controlled by Marcos loyalists, others by ostensibly pro-Aquino local landed elites. In settings such as El Salvador, such groups have seriously impeded reform efforts through intimidation and assassination of farmer-beneficiaries, peasant organizers, and government land-reform officials (Mason 1990: 12–13, 22–23; Prosterman and Riedinger 1987: 158; Union Communal Salvadoreña 1981).

In the Philippines, the private armies of local landowners and the Civilian Home Defense Forces (CHDF) were widely regarded as the worst violators of human rights. CHDF units, created during martial law, were often indistinguishable from the private armies. Marcos cronies such as Eduardo Cojuangco (Corazon Aquino's cousin) and Armando Gustillo maintained huge private armies (1,600 and 1,200 men, respectively).[102] On September 25, 1985, members of the CHDF unit of Escalante, Negros Occidental—a unit on Gustillo's payroll—opened fire on peasant demonstrators, killing some 30 and wounding dozens more.[103]

In March 1986, Jaime Tadeo argued: "The machinery of the previous fascist dictatorship is still in place [in the countryside]. The political warlords still reign there. So the [February 'revolution'] has had no liberating impact on the countryside" (Tadeo 1986: 20).

These private armies are prohibited by the 1987 Constitution (Art.

18, Sec. 24), but little effort was made to disband them.[104] Indeed, after the breakdown in negotiations with the NPA, Aquino adopted a policy of "total war" and offered conditional praise of vigilante groups.[105] This policy shift reflected both frustration with the NPA response to the negotiations and the growing autonomy of the military in waging the counterinsurgency campaign. However, her praise was taken by some as carte blanche approval of abusive vigilante groups and private armies, as well it might be in the absence of effective enforcement of government guidelines on the operation of anticommunist civilian groups. As of June 1988, there had not been a single successful prosecution of a member of a vigilante group. Furthermore, as of March 1989, there had not been a single human rights case even brought against a member of the armed forces, despite widespread reports of abuses by both groups (Thompson 1989: 7; LCHR 1988: xvii).

As with other controversial issues in the Philippines, the terminology used to describe the rise of armed civilian groups is the subject of debate. The Aquino government preferred that these groups be termed "civilian volunteer self-defense organizations." The New York-based Lawyers Committee for Human Rights (LCHR) rejected the government terminology, arguing that membership in many of these groups is not voluntary, nor are the groups' operations limited to self-defense functions. The LCHR adopted the term used by most Filipinos: "vigilantes" (1988: v n. 1).

Aquino did order the disbanding of the CHDF in March 1987. However, in response to strong reaction within the military, the directive was immediately changed, calling for recommendations from the military as to the future of the CHDF. In the end, the CHDF was essentially converted into the new Civilian Armed Forces Geographical Units (CAFGUs).[106]

Other Political Actors: the Church and Cause-oriented Organizations

Arrayed against the landowner organizations (and the private armies) in the reform debate were elements of the Catholic Church and myriad sectoral and cause-oriented groups. The former had slowly evolved into a powerful opposition force in the years following the 1972 imposition of martial law, playing an instrumental role in the events of February 1986 (Giordano 1988; Ofreneo 1987; Shoesmith 1985; Youngblood 1981; id. 1987; id. 1990). The Church hierarchy and Church-

affiliated organizations such as the Institute on Church and Social Issues and the Bishops-Businessmen's Conference for Human Development played an active, proreform role in the debate on land reform.

Most democratic grassroots organizational activities were curtailed for much of the Marcos authoritarian era (1972–86). However, the formal, albeit nominal, lifting of martial law in 1981 began to open political space for legal grassroots organizing. More significant, the assassination of Benigno "Ninoy" Aquino, Jr., in August 1983 fractured whatever elite solidarity still existed in support of Marcos, giving rise to a dramatic upsurge in oppositional political activity and organization. Sectoral and cause-oriented groups began to proliferate, which sought to defend members' interests and, in many cases, to pursue a broad agenda of social and political reform.[107] In the absence of large, ideologically oriented political parties, these groups (and the Church) served as the principal vehicle for democratic articulation of the interests and demands of the poor, although they remain politically weak.

Prominent among the new cause-oriented organizations were the Kilusang Magbubukid ng Pilipinas (KMP = Peasant Movement of the Philippines), a militant peasant organization founded in July 1985 and claiming some 750,000–800,000 members in the early 1990s,[108] and the Congress for a People's Agrarian Reform (CPAR), a unique confederation of twelve peasant organizations founded in May 1987, claiming to represent some 1.5 million peasants and fisherfolk (inclusive of the KMP), and fourteen nongovernmental organizations (Ramiro interview, Feb. 21, 1989; see also CPAR 1987). These groups, and more established organizations such as the Federation of Free Farmers, prepared draft legislation and worked to educate and lobby members of both the executive branch and Congress concerning the desirability of agrarian reform.

In sheer numerical terms, landless and near-landless peasants ought to have dominated the Philippine competitive political system and, in turn, the reform agenda. Such was not the case. As Ronald Herring notes of democratic polities generally, "the agrarian system fosters the imperfect translation of numbers and interests into political power through the mediation of patron-client relations, 'vote banks,' dependence, and ideology" (1983: 217). Given their dependent relationship, the intended beneficiaries of reform typically posed little threat to the electoral prospects of either local or national political figures. If not voting at the specific behest of a local patron, many of the rural electorate continued to vote in terms of actual or perceived patronage.[109] These

voters were often physically isolated, making it difficult to be informed about rural policy, let alone reach or influence state leaders. They generally lacked the contacts and wherewithal to publicize their positions independently (Chambers 1983; Esman and Uphoff 1984).

Samuel Huntington attributes the legislative dominance of landed elements in competitive polities to the absence of effective political organizations. Absent such parties, elections are nothing more than a "conservative device which gives a semblance of popular legitimacy to traditional structures and traditional leadership" (1968: 402).

Still political parties are not the only vehicle for expressing peasant aspirations and furthering peasant agendas. In the absence of such parties, Philippine peasant interest in agrarian reform was expressed primarily through the peasant organizations mentioned above. In the next chapter, I explore the tactics these organizations employed to influence political events and the success or failure of those tactics.

The CPP / NPA and Agrarian Reform

For much of its existence, the insurgent CPP / NPA enjoyed a popular, Robin Hood–like image and appeared to be much more discriminating in its use of force than either the Philippine military or private armies. By the late 1980s, however, a number of notable CPP/NPA human rights abuses had received widespread media attention, occasioning considerable public condemnation. These abuses included the massacre of a group of anticommunist religious cultists, several regional purges of the CPP / NPA's own ranks, and assassinations of police, military personnel, and civilians under the guise of "revolutionary justice."

Particularly important in terms of the politics of agrarian reform was the NPA's enactment of its own, increasingly publicized, land-reform program. This reform program typically involved well-enforced rent reductions coupled with reductions in money-lending interest rates, but there were instances in which landowners were driven off their property and the laborers given individual or communal usufruct rights. Insurgent activity also indirectly facilitated abandonment of other properties, leaving the permanent labor force in a position to negotiate with the banks or the DAR for acquisition of the land. In the battle for "hearts and minds," the NPA reform served as a potential counterpoint against which peasants could measure the government's agrarian-reform program.

Summary

Corazon Aquino's ascendance to the Philippine presidency reflected her commitment, and that of the Filipino people, to restore democratic political institutions and build a more just Philippine society. One element of that commitment was a pledge to carry out a program of "genuine" agrarian reform. That pledge reflected Aquino's belief that serving the cause of agrarian social justice would simultaneously increase the stake of the rural masses in Philippine society; defuse a nationwide communist insurgency fueled in considerable part by land-related peasant grievances; introduce a new dynamism in Philippine agricultural performance; and occasion the redeployment of (erstwhile) landowner resources into rural industrialization. The combination of decree-making authority vested in the new president and the relative economic weakness of important sectors of the landed elite suggested new opportunities for significant redistributive reform.

Confronted with myriad responsibilities and opportunities in the transition from the Marcos authoritarian era, President Aquino devoted herself primarily to the restoration of the institutional trappings of democracy. However, the democracy that she and her appointees fashioned represented a restoration of the political influence of traditional Philippine political and economic elites. Repaying old favors, Aquino opted against both a forceful leadership role in shaping the new Constitution and institutionalizing her popular support in the form of a political party. Past experience suggested that democratic institutions in the Philippines would be elite-dominated and relatively hostile to meaningful agrarian reform. As the reformist and antireformist forces squared off, the Philippine masses remained, to a considerable degree, marginal to the political life of the country. Their ability to influence public debate was limited, a function of their limited resources and the difficulties attendant on forming and sustaining independent social organizations during the Marcos era.

6

Agrarian-Reform Legislation:
Contested Constructions

So long as class privileges do not jeopardize economic health or political stability, those privileges have been left largely in place, though whittled at the margin as exigencies arise. In times of crisis, regime interests have prompted more fundamental interference with property.

Ronald J. Herring

I shall ask no greater sacrifices than I myself am prepared to make.

Corazon Aquino

The issue of agrarian reform was successively deliberated in three fora: the Constitutional Commission, the cabinet, and the Philippine Congress. The terms of the debates highlighted alternative constructions of democracy and agrarian reform, affording insights into the motivations of the various political actors; the outcomes of the debates reflected the political strengths and weaknesses of the various actors and the paradigms they espoused. In examining these debates, we improve our understanding of the dynamics of redistributive reform in democratic polities.

In its reform calculations the Aquino government appeared to pursue something of a "minimax" strategy: maximizing the number of reform beneficiaries while minimizing the number of landowners adversely affected by the reform process. Although generally unstated, this calculation was particularly important to the determination of ceilings on landholding size, as evidenced by the discussion of the trade-offs during the reform debates.

Peasant Organizations Define Agrarian Reform

In the months before the June 2, 1986, convening of the Constitutional Commission, the Aquino government issued no major policy

directives on agrarian reform. In the absence of government action, peasant organizations attempted to shape deliberations by setting the policy agenda. In March 1986, Jaime Tadeo, head of the Kilusang Mag-bubukid ng Pilipinas (KMP = Peasant Movement of the Philippines), commented that "it would seem too radical to speak right away of free distribution of land, regardless of the crop to which it is planted" (1986: 17). The KMP's immediate demands included confiscation and free distribution of lands owned by Marcos and his cronies; prevention of any further expansion of multinational landholdings; termination of the repayment obligations of beneficiaries of Presidential Decree 27 (PD 27) and distribution of titles to the same; and reduction of land rents to 10 percent of the net harvest.[1]

The KMP then submitted a six-point proposal for agricultural and rural development to the government in April 1986.[2] The KMP's National Council convened in early June 1986 and approved several additional documents (1986a; 1986b; 1986c) aimed at giving definition to the government's promise of "genuine agrarian reform," to wit: (1) confiscation and free distribution of lands owned by Marcos and his cronies to the actual tillers; (2) expansion of free distribution to all croplands, with selective compensation to former landowners; and (3) nationalization of transnational agribusiness plantations and the abolition of feudalism (KMP 1986d; id. 1986a).

Echoing the call for genuine agrarian reform was the Bukluran sa Ikauunlad ng Sosyalistang Isip at Gawa (BISIG = Union for the Advancement of Socialist Thought and Action), an alliance of academics, community activists, trade unionists, and former communists committed to a democratic transition to socialism (Thompson 1990: 4, citing Petitjean 1986b: 18). At its May 1986 founding congress, the BISIG pledged its support for the adoption and implementation of genuine land reform, defined to include all agricultural lands regardless of crop, farm size, or tenure. Ownership and control of farms operated by hired labor were to be passed to "duly constituted workers' cooperatives or collectives." In the case of tenanted lands transferred to individuals, the program was to "introduce cooperative forms in specific aspects of production and marketing" (Tadem 1987: 26). Finally, all foreign-owned or controlled agribusiness operations were to be nationalized.

The center-right Federation of Free Farmers (FFF) announced its own list of ten agrarian reform priorities in early May 1986 (Montemayor 1986a). The directive evidenced the substantial agreement between the FFF and more militant peasant groups concerning the scope

of the needed reforms. The FFF called for the immediate completion of the processing of all Certificates of Land Transfer (CLTs) under the Operation Land Transfer (PD 27) program; reform of all tenanted rice and corn lands previously overlooked; immediate augmentation of the incomes of reform beneficiaries (through credit and pricing policies); expansion of agrarian reform to include idle and abandoned lands; expansion of agrarian reform to sugar, coconut, and other lands not planted in rice and corn; and recovery of all lands unfairly taken over by domestic and multinational corporations.[3]

Beginning in March 1986, peasant and nongovernmental organizations held a series of national conferences on agrarian reform. On March 14, 1986, 22 nongovernmental organizations (NGOs) convened the National Consultation on Agrarian Reform and Rural Development (NCARRD I) to map out an advocacy role in support of reform and the consolidation of democracy. NCARRD II was held August 7–8, 1986, to review the results of village, regional, and national consultations with roughly 10,000 grassroots representatives. More than 70 peasant, nongovernmental, Church, and business organizations convened May 29–31, 1987, to forge a unified position on agrarian reform. This conference launched the Congress for a People's Agrarian Reform (CPAR),[4] a unique alliance of ideologically diverse peasant, fisherfolk, and nongovernmental organizations. The 12 peasant and fisherfolk organizations claimed a combined reach of 1.0–1.5 million people (Ramiro interview, Feb. 21, 1989). The CPAR's founding members included militant peasant organizations such as the KMP and NFSW, as well as social democratic organizations such as the Katipunan ng mga Samahan ng Mamamayan (KASAMA) and Pambansang Kilusan ng mga Samahang Magsasaka (PAKISAMA). The more conservative FFF was also a founding member of the CPAR, but soon withdrew from the coalition. The CPAR's roster of nongovernmental organization members included the Center for Agrarian Reform Transformation (CARET), the Center for Community Services (CCS), the Forum for Rural Concerns, the Philippine Partnership for Development of Human Resources in Rural Areas (PhilDHRRA), and the Philippine Rural Reconstruction Movement (PRRM). CPAR articulated an eight-point "authentic people's agrarian reform program," which included implementation of a land-to-the-tiller program, abolition of absentee landownership, comprehensive coverage of all agricultural lands, a preference for cooperatives and collective farms, and landowner compensation that took account of farm size and mode of acquisition. Unlike the KMP, its largest member

organization, the CPAR rejected the notion of free land distribution, declaring instead that the terms of land transfer should not be burdensome to the beneficiaries (CPAR 1987c).

Biblical and spiritual references were a recurrent feature of the arguments of many agrarian reform proponents (see Bascog 1987: 44; Dominguez 1986; Montemayor 1986a; id. 1988; Tadeo 1986). Land was a gift from God; not being a creation of man, it could not properly be owned by man. Those having control over the land had an obligation to assure that the land served a social function.

Government Pronouncements on Economic Policy

Initially, the peasants' demands were well received by elements of the Aquino government, the regime's inactivity notwithstanding. A Presidential Commission on Government Reorganization (PCGR) task force issued a series of proposals relating to agrarian reform in June 1986, as the Constitutional Commission began its deliberations. Adopting the principle of "land to the tiller," the task force urged a program that would "democratize ownership and control over all agricultural lands."[5] The reform was not to be limited by crop, farm size, or tenurial status. Landowners would not be permitted any right of retention. Compensation was to be based on crop production or on declared or assessed land value. The reform process was to include support services for reform beneficiaries. To implement this program, Department of Agrarian Reform (DAR) staffing was to be increased 50 percent (Bulatao interview, Mar. 15, 1989).

Agrarian reform was also addressed in *Policy Agenda for People-Powered Development*, a publication of the National Economic and Development Authority (NEDA) expressing the development goals of the new Aquino administration,[6] which reflected both social concern and free-market values: "respect for human rights, promotion of social justice and poverty alleviation, attainment of growth and greater efficiency, and minimum government intervention" (NEDA 1986a: 1). "Social justice" was to be the "primary consideration in the pursuit of development objectives" (ibid.: 2). The supposed choice between growth and equity was rejected as a false one; both objectives could be simultaneously pursued. "The development of agriculture will be given the highest priority in keeping with the goals of alleviating poverty and increasing employment opportunities and incomes in the rural sector" (ibid.: 23–24). Exchange rates, tariffs, and quota levels were all to be

adjusted to remove existing biases against agriculture.[7] "Increased incomes in the rural areas stimulate investment and change consumption patterns towards products and industries that are more labor-intensive and enterprises that are small and medium scale," NEDA argued echoing one of the traditional justifications for redistributive agrarian reform (ibid.: 4–5).

NEDA distinguished between promoting agricultural productivity and the promotion of rural justice. Agrarian reform was intended primarily to accomplish the latter:

The previous land reform program shall be reviewed and redirected to accomplish its original objectives. Genuine agrarian reform shall, therefore, be pursued to serve justice to those who till the land. . . .

Agrarian reform shall eventually be expanded to include natural resources and other crops. The reform shall be intensified to benefit the greatest number of small farmers. Alienable and disposable lands under the public domain shall be the priority target for land justice. (Ibid.: 20–21)

Furthermore, subsistence farmers and landless rural workers were to be permitted to lease sequestered properties and lands heavily indebted to government financial institutions. "Agrarian reform will ensure that the gains from agricultural growth are fully transmitted to small farmers" (ibid.: 25).

There was clearly much in the NEDA policy agenda from which those agitating for reform could take heart. NEDA was committed to "genuine agrarian reform," including expansion of the reform process to lands devoted to crops other than rice and corn and maximization of the number of reform beneficiaries. Provision was made for improved agricultural price supports, research and extension, marketing infrastructure, and crop diversification. To facilitate agrarian reform, law and order was to be improved: private armies were to be disbanded, and a democratic system of electing local officials was to be established.

NEDA, the government's principal economic planning body, subscribed to a number of the traditional economic rationales for agrarian reform, but some important ambiguities and problems remained. The policy agenda was not a program of implementation. It made neither recommendations nor commitments as to the timing of expansion of the reform or completion of earlier reform programs. The restoration of peace and order was to take precedence over agrarian reform. Sequestered and foreclosed properties were to be leased out rather than transferred to landless tillers. Those familiar with the internal politics of the

Aquino cabinet also understood that Solita Monsod, NEDA's director general, was predisposed to favor agrarian reform. This disposition was not shared by more conservative cabinet members such as Minister of Finance Jaime Ongpin and Minister of Trade and Industry Jose S. Concepcion, Jr. NEDA's policy agenda was thus a welcome, but not dispositive, sign of the Aquino administration's posture on agrarian reform.

Land Reform and the Constitution

The drafting of a new constitution represented the earliest, and arguably most important, stage in the process of constructing Philippine democracy and a program of agrarian reform. Peasants and their representatives were largely excluded from this process. Of those appointed to the Constitutional Commission, only Jaime Tadeo of the KMP could be characterized as a bona fide representative of the tenant and farmworker sector. Nonetheless, with the backing of liberal democrats and Church figures, Tadeo introduced a series of progressive, even radical, agrarian reform provisions in the Committee on Social Justice.[8]

Reflecting Tadeo's input, early drafts of Article 13, Section 4, of the Constitution provided, in part, that the state undertake a *"genuine* agrarian reform founded on the *basic* right of farmers and regular farmworkers, who are landless, to own directly or collectively the land they till" (ROP 1986a, 2: 651; 3: 6; emphasis added). The terms "genuine" and "basic" had important legal implications, as did the eventual omission of these terms. Although the definition of the term "genuine" was, by Commissioner Tadeo's account, still a subject for legislation, its meaning as defined by the KMP was known to the commissioners and explicitly considered during commission deliberations (ROP 1986a, 2: 651, 653–54). Had the phrase "genuine agrarian reform," thus interpreted, been retained, the Constitution would have mandated a program of radical redistributive reform unparalleled in Philippine history or that of other democratic polities. In the event, the phrasing was dropped by the Committee on Social Justice.[9]

The phrase "basic right" was interpreted by Commissioner Teodoro Bacani as implying an "unqualified and plenary right" of landless tillers to receive the specific parcel they then cultivated.[10] The commission agreed that landless agriculturalists were to have a preferential right to the land they were then cultivating, but refused to make that right absolute. The tiller's preference right would be superseded where the particular parcel was, for example, within the retention area permitted

the owner. In such cases, the commissioners expected, alternative land would be made available to the farmer-beneficiary (ROP 1986a, 3: 6–10).

The New Constitution

Although the most progressive provisions had been watered down, the new Constitution made unprecedented provision for "comprehensive rural development and agrarian reform" (Art. 2, Sec. 21), albeit with important qualifications. Article 13 asserted, inter alia:

§ 4. The State shall, by law, undertake an agrarian reform program founded on the right of farmers and regular farmworkers, who are landless, to own directly or collectively the lands they till or, in the case of other farmworkers, to receive a just share of the fruits thereof. To this end the State shall encourage and undertake the just distribution of all agricultural lands, subject to such priorities and reasonable retention limits as the Congress may prescribe, taking into account ecological, developmental, or equity considerations, and subject to the payment of just compensation. In determining retention limits, the State shall respect the rights of small landowners. The State shall further provide incentives for voluntary land-sharing.

§ 5. The State shall recognize the right of farmers, farmworkers, and landowners, as well as cooperatives, and other independent farmers' organizations to participate in the planning, organization, and management of the program, and shall provide support to agriculture through appropriate technology and research, and adequate financial, production, marketing, and other support services.

§ 6. The State shall apply the principles of agrarian reform or stewardship, whenever applicable in accordance with law, in the disposition or utilization of other natural resources, including lands of the public domain under lease or concession suitable for agriculture, subject to prior rights, homestead rights of small settlers, and the rights of indigenous communities to their ancestral homes.

The State may resettle landless farmers and farmworkers in its own agricultural estates which shall be distributed to them in the manner provided by law.

§ 8. The State shall provide incentives to landowners to invest the proceeds of the agrarian reform program to promote industrialization, employment creation, and privatization of public sector enterprises. Financial instruments used as payment for their lands shall be honored as equity in enterprises of their choice.[11]

It is significant that the key provisions appeared in the article on Social Justice and Human Rights, signaling the primacy of social justice as the impetus for agrarian reform, at least in the view of the constitutional commissioners.[12] The commissioners' deliberations made clear their intention that farmers (tenants) and regular farmworkers should

have the right to own land, and that the government should guarantee that right. Moreover, this right encompassed *all* agricultural land, without regard to the crop. Provision was made for free choice of ownership mode, be it individual, cooperative, or collective, with the decision left to the beneficiaries. Although primarily a program of social justice, agrarian reform was also seen by the commissioners as a means of promoting economic development and political stability.

Peasant Dissatisfaction with the Constitution

The Constitution thus enshrined many peasant demands. On the issues of "just compensation," beneficiary repayment, retention limits, and implementation priorities, however, strenuous objections were heard from militant and moderate peasant organizations alike (see Tadem 1986). In reaffirming the landowners' right to "just compensation," the commission rejected outright confiscation, as well as "selective" or "progressive" compensation. Selective compensation would take account of past landowner behavior—for example, compliance with labor and tenancy legislation—in determining the amount to be paid. Progressive compensation would be based on a declining proportion of land value with increasing farm size.[13] Previous legislation had tied compensation to productive capacity (PD 27), or to annual legal rent capitalized at 6 percent per year (RA 3844). Little reference was made to these definitions during commission deliberations. Just compensation was interpreted by some commissioners as fair market value (ROP 1986a, 2: 647–48; 3: 17–19). In the end, no categorical agreement was reached on the meaning of just compensation.[14] The FFF argued that compensation based on fair market value would represent an increase of 500 percent or more over the PD 27 formulation, making agrarian reform unaffordable to the beneficiaries and the government alike.[15]

Similarly, the Constitutional Commission failed to adopt specific language concerning beneficiary repayment obligations. The commission appeared to reject calls for free land distribution in favor of a principle of "affordable cost," whereby beneficiaries would pay what they were able and the government would bear the monetary difference (ROP 1986a, 2: 648). However, the Constitution contained no language on beneficiary repayments.

The provision on retention limits, and, more generally, the scope of authority left to Congress, caused further consternation among peasant organizations. Most were distressed to find the concept of retention limits accorded constitutional recognition (see Montemayor n.d.; id.

1986b). As to the particulars, arguments that the right of retention be limited to owner-cultivators were rejected by other members of the commission, and, apparently, by the Committee on Social Justice.[16] In determining retention limits, the Constitution directed the state to "respect the rights of small landowners" (Art. 13, Sec. 4). The appropriate definition of "small landowners" was debated by members of the Constitutional Commission, but final determination was left to the state (ROP 1986a, 3: 10–11).

The Commission also deferred to Congress in setting priorities for implementation of the reform, despite arguments that this "would open the floodgates to more restrictions and limitations, thereby seriously impairing . . . agrarian reform."[17] The decision to leave this matter to Congress was based on the presumed agricultural expertise of representatives of the major crop-growing regions and the greater public mandate enjoyed by members of Congress as elected officials (remarks of Commissioners Rodrigo, Villegas, and Nolledo in ROP 1986a, 3: 24–27).

Upset by the watering down of the reform provisions (and inadequate safeguards for national sovereignty), Jaime Tadeo was one of the two constitutional commissioners to vote against the draft Constitution (Tadeo interview, July 11, 1989). So disappointed were the leaders of the FFF that they urged rejection of the Constitution by the organization's membership in the February 2, 1987, plebiscite. As interpreted by the FFF, the new Constitution would, among other things, increase landowner compensation and the amortization obligations of beneficiaries fivefold, as well as greatly expanding retention areas and concomitantly abolishing the rights of tenants on the retained lands. Constitutional commissioners and senior government officials alike denied the FFF's interpretation of the Constitution, assuring the FFF and the nation that the Constitution would expand and accelerate the reform process.[18] Thus assured, the Philippine electorate overwhelmingly approved the Constitution.

Cabinet and Congressional Deliberations on Land Reform

Once the Constitutional Commission had completed its deliberations, attention shifted to the president. There remained the possibility that Aquino would preempt congressional action by issuing an agrarian-reform decree under her executive powers. The new Constitution (Art. 18, Sec. 6) gave her executive-decree authority pending the convening of the new Congress. An Executive Order (229) was issued on

July 22, 1987, but it left the determination of the key elements of the reform program to Congress.[19] The story of the evolution of EO 229 and the subsequent enactment of Republic Act 6657, the Comprehensive Agrarian Reform Law, is most easily told by subject area. Before turning to specifics, however, a brief description of the chronology of events is appropriate.

Peasant Activism and Cabinet Deliberations

When repeated demonstrations in the July–October 1986 period failed to arouse any apparent government action on agrarian reform, the KMP initiated a series of land occupations.[20] Initially, these were limited to idle and abandoned properties, but they were expanded to include the cultivated lands of "despotic" landlords in late March 1988 (Tangbawan 1988a; id. 1988b). Several other peasant organizations, notably the Aniban ng mga Manggagawa sa Agrikultura (AMA = Union of Agricultural Workers), the Katipunan ng mga Samahan ng Mamamayan (KASAMA), and the Pambansang Kilusan ng mga Samahang Magsasaka (PAKISAMA = the National Movement of Peasant Organizations) also began land occupations.[21] On October 21, thousands of KMP members from across Luzon marched to the Mendiola Bridge—which leads to Malacañang, the presidential palace—to mark the fourteenth anniversary of Marcos's reform program (PD 27). The KMP launched a new series of demonstrations in front of the Department of Agrarian Reform in mid January 1987. These rallies culminated in a January 22 march on Malacañang that ended in tragedy; at least thirteen participants were killed and more than ninety others were wounded when police and military forces opened fire on the demonstrators as they approached the Mendiola Bridge (KMP 1988; Maglipon 1987; Mydans 1987a).

This bloodshed—the "Mendiola Massacre"—galvanized the establishment of a special cabinet action committee (CAC), and with it meaningful government consideration of agrarian reform.[22] For the next six months this committee deliberated, drafting and redrafting a proposed decree.[23] With each ensuing draft, the scope of the reform was narrowed. There was no permanent secretary of the Department of Agrarian Reform during most of these deliberations, because Heherson Alvarez resigned in February to run for the Senate, and the DAR was thus unable to provide forceful leadership within the CAC (Bulatao interviews, Mar. 15, 1989 and June 27, 1989; Ortigas interview, June 22, 1989;

Vistan interview, June 23, 1989). Alvarez's replacement, Philip Juico, was not named until EO 229 was announced in July 1989. Recognizing that not all viewpoints were represented in Manila, the CAC conducted two rounds of public consultations in various regions of the country, in May and June 1987.

Cabinet and Landowner Objections

Even as the CAC conferred, those with private access to President Aquino were making their case for revisions in the land-reform agenda. In early May, Jaime V. Ongpin, secretary of the Department of Finance, urged that the reform program be subjected to "serious cost-cutting" and that beneficiaries be made to understand that the land and accompanying financial support were not an "unconditional gift." Ongpin argued that it might be "impractical to break up some large estates" and that "some commercial agricultural projects may require common management of large tracts of land" (1987). In early June, Ongpin and Deogracias Vistan, president of the Land Bank of the Philippines, made known their opposition to several key features of the program then under consideration by the CAC, preparing their own draft of a "genuine" agrarian-reform decree.[24] Trade and Industry Secretary Jose Concepcion, Jr., warned against a 7-hectare retention limit as discouraging foreign and domestic investment in aquaculture (*Manila Bulletin* 1987). Justice Secretary Sedfrey Ordonez argued that the Constitution precluded the executive from setting retention limits or determining just compensation by decree.

The June–July 1987 period also witnessed an extraordinary private and public campaign by antireform landowners. Most conspicuous was an antireform pledge signed in blood by Negros sugar planters, accompanied by threats of armed resistance and secession in the event of land reform (see *Newsweek* 1987; Palacios 1987; Sa-Onoy 1987). Threats of violent resistance and secession continued through the congressional deliberations, many of them made in open testimony before congressional committees.[25] The banking sector cautioned the administration about the reform's potential for disrupting agricultural production. Bankers then assured this outcome by withholding agricultural loans pending resolution of the reform debate (Gilding 1993: 10). One thousand members of the Council of Agricultural Producers of the Philippines (CAP) convened in March 1988 to denounce agrarian reform, predicting it would reduce the nation to poverty.

In the end, the decree issued by Aquino, Executive Order No. 229, was not the product of the CAC, but of a select group of presidential advisers.[26] The result was an amalgam of the CAC draft, the Vistan/ Ongpin draft, and position papers submitted by various outside groups. Excluded cabinet members were told to acquiesce or resign.

Executive Order 229 was issued five days before the scheduled opening of the new Congress. The new decree left the crucial determinations of implementation priorities and retention limits to the landowner-dominated Congress (Sec. 2). Compensation was to be based on the owner's declaration of current fair market value, subject to controls to be subsequently adopted by the Presidential Agrarian Reform Council (Sec. 6). Corporate landowners could meet their reform obligations by giving workers the right to purchase stock commensurate with the relative value of the land assets (Sec. 10). Finally, the decree permanently disqualified as beneficiaries any "persons, associations, or entities who prematurely enter the land to avail themselves of the rights and benefits" provided by the law (Sec. 22). As the decree deferred to Congress on the most important and controversial issues, its promulgation, it would seem, was intended, not so much to preempt congressional action, as to give the appearance of Aquino personally fulfilling her agrarian reform pledge.[27]

Proreform Activists and the Legislative Process

Thereafter, the legislative process substantially mirrored that of the cabinet deliberations—that is, progressive or radical draft reform provisions were successively watered down. Proponents of agrarian reform in both houses of Congress were quick to introduce their legislative drafts, attempting to shape the policy agenda and ensuing debate. In this endeavor they were assisted directly and indirectly by peasant organizations, most notably through the work of the Congress for a People's Agrarian Reform (CPAR), which provided technical assistance to the House Agrarian Reform Committee chair, Bonifacio Gillego, and other proreform legislators. The CPAR staged a series of mass demonstrations inside and outside of the congressional hall, forwarded petitions and position papers to legislators, lobbied key members of Congress, and engaged in a variety of public education activities. Its legislative assistance was most evident in House Bill 65, introduced by the "nationalist bloc" led by Florencio Abad.[28] In mid April 1988, frustrated by the continuing delays in Congress, the CPAR launched its "Agrarian Reform Express." Week-long caravans from across Luzon

culminated in 20,000 peasants and reform advocates converging on Manila to demonstrate their support for "genuine" agrarian reform.

It was during the legislative consideration of agrarian reform that the Catholic Church hierarchy and Church-affiliated organizations such as the Institute on Church and Social Issues (ICSI) and the Bishops-Businessmen's Conference for Human Development became most involved in promoting the reform cause.[29] Through its monthly publication, *Intersect*, the ICSI kept the Church community and other concerned observers up-to-date on legislative developments concerning agrarian reform and related lobbying initiatives by peasant organizations. The analysis was avowedly proreform, taking considerable pains to illustrate the deficiencies of various legislative proposals (see CPAR 1988; *Intersect* 1988a; id. 1988b; Tejam 1988a; id. 1988b; Wong 1987a; id. 1987b; id. 1987c; id. 1987d; id. 1988a; id. 1988b).

The senior body of the Church, the Catholic Bishops' Conference of the Philippines (CBCP), issued a pastoral letter that—while acknowledging differences of opinion among the bishops—lent the Church's official, albeit qualified, support to agrarian reform:

We are for as *comprehensive* a program of agrarian reform as possible—one that will make it possible for all, the 70% who live below the poverty line especially, *to have* more in order *to be* more. (Cf. Paul VI, *Populorum Progressio*, 6)

We believe furthermore that a genuine agrarian reform program must be *realistic*. No program can be successful if it transcends the capabilities of government to manage and finance. (CBCP 1987; emphasis in original)

Building on this commitment, the CBCP's National Secretariat of Social Action, Justice and Peace (NASSA) worked in support of significant reform, organizing a "Campaign for a Genuine Agrarian Reform Program" within the Church community, circulating information about the respective House and Senate bills, and urging a letter-writing campaign directed at members of the House-Senate Conference Committee (Wong interview, Oct. 12, 1988).

In his homily celebrating the second anniversary of the "EDSA Revolution" of February 1986, Jaime Cardinal Sin remarked:

As we stand here this afternoon, asking if EDSA was worth it, if EDSA had meaning, can we not answer: We *will make sure* it *had* and *has* meaning! We will gather together around the common purpose of building a nation of freedom, of participation, of justice, of democracy, of faith. And we will give a point to that purpose—an *immediate point*. It will be genuine, far-reaching, effective land reform. This is the next miracle on our agenda.[30]

Although he had used what by this time amounted to a term of art—"genuine" land reform—Cardinal Sin went on to qualify his remarks, saying, "It is not for the Church, or me as a churchman, to lay down the exact shape and detail of a reform program we need and want" (1988).

Multiple Legislative Proposals on Agrarian Reform

The more progressive bills were those introduced by the nationalist bloc, by Bonifacio Gillego, then chairman of the Agrarian Reform Committee of the House of Representatives, and by Senator Agapito "Butz" Aquino, brother of the president's late husband.[31] The landowner bloc in the House was led by Romeo Guanzon and Hortensia Starke of Negros Occidental and the Tarlac representative Jose Cojuangco, Jr., the president's brother. Starke introduced a bill (House Bill 319) in committee that would have exempted a wide range of commercial farms from reform. This initiative was circumvented by Gillego. Guanzon attempted to introduce the "landlord's" bill on the House floor, but was defeated on procedural grounds.[32] The landowner bloc then shifted its focus to amending the committee bill. Such was their success in amending the House bill that Congressman Gillego and thirteen other original co-sponsors eventually withdrew their sponsorship of that bill (HB 400).[33]

On the Senate side, Heherson Alvarez, now a senator and chairman of the Senate Agrarian Reform Committee, introduced several bills,[34] which served principally to flesh out Executive Order 229. Senator Agapito Aquino offered a more radical Senate bill, sharply contesting Alvarez's rendering of reform. As between the final House and Senate bills, the latter—having lower retention limits and fewer exemptions—was marginally more progressive, although each had important flaws. It has been argued that the more progressive outlook of the Senate reflected its national electoral constituency, whereas members of the House were elected by district and were thus more directly answerable to local landed elites.[35] Although many Senate members were landowners, they were more likely than House members to have diversified interests in business (Illo interview, Oct. 11, 1988; Modina interview, Oct. 17, 1988). That earlier commentators should describe the respective chambers of the 1955 Congress in precisely these terms suggests just how little the politics of Philippine democratic institutions had changed.[36]

House-Senate conferees then engaged in several weeks of often-heated debate. In the end, the House conferees largely prevailed on such crucial issues as retention limits. On June 10, 1988, Aquino signed into law Republic Act No. 6657, the Comprehensive Agrarian Reform

Law. In fact, the law held relatively little promise of comprehensive agrarian reform.

The Scope of the New Agrarian Reform Law

Table 6 illustrates the systematic reduction in program scope that characterized the deliberative process in the cabinet. The January 23, 1987, *Accelerated Land Reform Project* report of the government's Inter-Agency Task Force, prepared before the Mendiola Massacre and hastily released after it, established a four-part schedule for implementation: (1) program A during 1987–89 would complete the distribution of tenanted rice and corn land on holdings of more than seven hectares and provide for administrative reforms geared to expediting the land valuation and compensation processes; (2) program B would implement reform on expropriated, foreclosed, and idle and abandoned lands, as well as on lands made available through "voluntary offers" (again during 1987–89); (3) program C, in the years 1989–92, would extend land redistribution to haciendas under labor administration (subject to a 24-hectare retention limit), to tenanted holdings devoted to crops other than rice and corn (ultimately subject to a 7-hectare retention limit), and to tenanted rice and corn holdings of less than seven hectares (with a *zero* retention limit for such holdings); and (4) program D (not included in Table 6) would implement land reform on public lands suitable for agriculture during the period 1987–92 (ROP, ITFAR 1987a).

Most notable in this initial draft is the relative scale of the various programs affecting private holdings: *Program C was projected to involve fully two and a half times as much farmland as Programs A and B combined.* Together the three programs were expected to affect over 5.3 million hectares, or 55 percent of all land in farms.

Additionally, Program D was slated to involve the transfer of some 1.35 million hectares of public lands.[37] In practice this program was expected to primarily entail regularizing the status of existing squatters on public lands. Expansion beyond that was likely to be constrained by limited land availability, environmental protection concerns, and the high cost of resettlement on marginal lands.

By March 1987, the scope of the reform, specifically Program C, had been significantly curtailed. The CAC had decided against reform of all tenanted rice and corn lands, reinstating the 7-hectare retention limit on such lands and thereby excluding an estimated 562,000 hectares from the reform program (ROP, ITFAR 1987b).

TABLE 6
The Scope of Philippine Land-Reform Proposals
(Area in hectares)

Program	1/23/87	3/13/87	4/27/87	12/1/87
Program A	557,000	557,000	557,000	727,800
Program B:	939,000	939,000	600,000	560,000
(i) Voluntary offers of sale	300,000	300,000	50,000	—
(ii) Idle & abandoned lands	189,000	189,000	200,000	—
(iii) Foreclosed & foreclosable lands	300,000	300,000	200,000	—
(iv) Sequestered lands	50,000	50,000	50,000	—
(v) Expropriated lands	100,000	100,000	100,000	—
Program C:	3,852,000	2,138,500	1,280,000	1,280,000
(i) Haciendas under labor administration	2,333,000	1,516,450	1,199,000	1,199,000
(ii) Tenanted croplands other than rice and corn	957,000	622,050	81,000	81,000
(iii) Tenanted rice and corn lands within the retention limit	562,000	0	0	0
TOTAL	5,348,000	3,634,500	2,437,000	2,567,800

SOURCES: Republic of the Philippines, Inter-Agency Task Force on Agrarian Reform, "Accelerated Land Reform Program," (drafts, Quezon City, Jan. 23, 1987; Mar. 13, 1987; Apr. 27, 1987); DAR Planning and Project Management Office, "Policies, Priority Concerns and External Assistance Needs" (Quezon City, Dec. 1, 1987).

With the April 1987 draft came further reductions, primarily in Program C, but embracing Program B as well. The overall program had by then been reduced to 2.4 million hectares, or only 25 percent of farm area (ROP, ITFAR 1987c). This, of course, was the theoretical scope of the program. All previous Philippine experience suggested that the area actually subject to reform would be substantially less than the target. By comparison, the land reforms of Japan, South Korea, and Taiwan actually redistributed 41, 30, and 33 percent of all cultivated land, respectively.[38]

By June 1987, Secretaries Ongpin and Vistan were arguing for deferral of Program C pending development of crop-specific retention limits. Measured against the standards of "social justice" and "continuity of agricultural productivity," they considered the CAC draft unacceptable, because it "absolutely ignores crop characteristics and instead uses only a time schedule of coverage strictly by land size."[39] Citing the glacial pace of reform implementation under previous administrations, Ongpin and Vistan argued that the implementation of programs A, B, and D would fully occupy Philippine administrative capacity. In their

view, implementation of programs A, B, and D would fulfill Aquino's promise to deliver a meaningful, comprehensive reform program, while entailing "manageable or zero landowner resistance."[40] In their judgment: "Program C in terms of land area and number of farmer-beneficiaries is estimated to account for only 23.6% and 23% respectively of the total program. And yet, Program C accounts for perhaps 99% of the furor, controversy, resistance[,] all of which could contribute to a total program delay if pre-determined, uniform retention limits for Program C were included in the executive order" (Ongpin and Vistan 1987: 3).

Ongpin and Vistan also took exception to CAC's recommendation of 17-year, interest-free terms for beneficiary repayments. The zero-interest provision violated "simple credit fundamentals. There is a certain consciousness level that Land Bank [sic] wants the farmers to maintain and that includes the notion that there is a cost of money."[41]

In December 1987, the DAR appeared to increase the scope of Program A (ROP, DAR 1987). This reflected only the changed view of the Marcos-era accomplishments. Earlier estimates assumed that the area still to be reformed was that not covered by previously *generated* Emancipation Patients. The new estimates reflected the larger area not covered by previously *distributed* Emancipation Patents.[42]

Official estimates of the program scope for RA 6657 as enacted are detailed in Table 7. These projections document some fundamental changes in the conceptualization of the reform, in particular the acceptance of landowners' claims that vast tracts of public lands were available for distribution. Over two-thirds of the reform program—6.95 million out of 10.3 million hectares—would involve public lands: the distribution of alienable and disposable public lands, grants of usufruct rights in forest areas, and resettlement of landless peasants. The various elements of Phase I were either covered by statutory authority predating RA 6657 or required no new legislation. The new reform law provided initial authority only for the compulsory acquisition components of Phases II and III, which represented less than one-fifth of the anticipated program. Nonetheless, compulsory acquisition of 1.9 million hectares would be an extraordinary accomplishment. However, retention limits, exemptions, and landowners' evasions were likely to thwart attainment of this goal.

At the time of its passage, two foreign reform specialists put the scope of RA 6657, as it was likely to be implemented, as follows: 200,000–300,000 hectares under Program A; another 200,000–300,000

TABLE 7

The Scope of the 1988 Philippine Land-Reform Program

(Area in hectares)

Phase	Area	Beneficiaries
Phase I:	1,454,800	765,009
(i) Rice & corn lands	727,800	522,675
(ii) Idle & abandoned lands	250,000	83,332
(iii) Voluntary offers of sale	400,000	133,335
(iv) Sequestered lands	2,500	833
(v) Government-owned lands	74,500	24,834
Phase II:	7,487,900	2,685,302
(i) Public lands & lands under leases	4,595,000	1,721,000
(ii) Integrated social forestry	1,880,000	626,667
(iii) Resettlement	478,500	159,500
(iv) Compulsory acquisition—private lands over 50 hectares	534,400	178,135
Phase III:	1,352,900	450,966
Compulsory acquisition		
(i) Private lands 5.01–24 hectares	1,049,800	349,932
(ii) Private lands 24.01–50 hectares	303,100	101,034
TOTAL	10,295,600	3,901,277

SOURCE: Presidential Agrarian Reform Council, *Comprehensive Agrarian Reform Program of the Philippines*, vols. 1 and 2 (Manila, 1988).

hectares under Program B; and less than 100,000 hectares under Program C. Since the legal authority for Programs A and B predated RA 6657, the new law would, in their judgment, involve the incremental distribution of less than 100,000 hectares, barely 1 percent of cultivated farmland, to fewer than 100,000 families, or 3 percent of the presently landless (Prosterman and Hanstad 1988b).

Implementation Priorities

Throughout the reform debates, it was the position of private landowners, including some in their capacity as public officials, that all public lands should be distributed, and the success of the reform demonstrated, before there was any resort to expropriation of private lands.[43] Romeo Guanzon spoke for many landowners when he urged the government to "first distribute all government lands before disrupting the heritage of planters" (interview, June 19, 1986). In support of this policy, landowners typically cited figures to suggest that there remained vast areas—thousands, if not millions, of hectares—of unoccupied, arable public land.[44]

Landowners and their representatives were not alone in arguing that public lands as well as foreclosed, idle, and abandoned lands ought to be redistributed before the state expropriated any productive private holdings. As he had in the case of scale economies in Philippine agriculture, the FFF's president, Jeremias U. Montemayor, accepted the landowners' argument, stating: "The prime sugar lands the present owners may keep because there are other lands. There are public lands in Negros. Thousands and thousands of public lands. And some forest lands—maybe they can be reclassified."[45]

Among those arguing to the contrary and urging priority redistribution of larger landholdings were an array of religious, business, and union organizations.[46] Some argued that the reform should concentrate initially on the very large holdings acquired through questionable, if not fraudulent, means by Marcos cronies and "sequestered" by the Aquino government's Philippine Commission on Good Government, and on foreclosed properties held by government banking institutions (Lopez-Gonzaga interview, June 17, 1986).

Evidence that the availability of public lands was quite limited was presented to Congress in the course of its deliberations. For example, Violeta Lopez-Gonzaga noted that while 8.62 percent of the land area of Negros Occidental (676,813 hectares) was denominated public land, "except for the very steep land areas, the few remaining public lands have already been cleared and settled by displaced peasants."[47] "Case studies have shown, the chances for a successful independent agricultural production of recipients in said [logged-over and public land] areas are nil" (Lopez-Gonzaga n.d.: 4–5).

Those seeking to delay or defeat all-inclusive land redistribution also argued that the Marcos-era reform of tenanted rice and corn holdings first be completed and "perfected" (Abaya 1987: 59; Caparas 1987: 8). This element of the reform program was, in any event, a top priority of the Aquino government, with completion initially targeted for the end of 1988 (Monsod 1987: 62). Where private lands were at stake, even proposals for immediate implementation of the reform program on lands classified as "idle or abandoned" drew congressional fire.[48]

The new law provided for a protracted, three-phase reform process, with implementation to be completed in not more than ten years (Sec. 7). Exemptions for commercial estates would push back completion for another five years or so, assuming such estates were reformed in practice. The successful land reforms of Japan, South Korea, and Taiwan were all carried out in much shorter time frames, in no instance involv-

ing more than four years of implementation. Provision is made for the PARC to declare certain provinces or regions "priority land reform areas," in which case implementation may be expedited (Sec. 7).

Ten-Year Exemption of Commercial Farms

Section 11 of the new law deferred application of the reform for a period of ten years in the case of commercial farms. Such farms include those devoted to "commercial livestock, poultry and swine raising, and aquaculture . . . fruit farms, orchards, vegetable and cut-flower farms, and cacao, coffee and rubber plantations." In the case of "new farms," the deferment period runs from the first year of commercial production and operation, extending the deferment another three to seven years for newly planted crops such as coffee and mangos. Moreover, the legislative language is ambiguous, leaving open the possibility that lands might be converted to commercial crops *after* the effective date of the reform. Indeed, shortly after passage of the reform law, Senator Osmeña effectively invited landowners to circumvent the law, saying: "The CARP law exempts [for ten years] cattle and orchard, so you can raise cattle and *plant* mango trees. And since mango trees start to bear fruit on the seventh year, you practically have 17 years before your lands can be expropriated" (quoted in Cruz 1988, emphasis added).

Section 73(e) of the law does prohibit the "sale, transfer, conveyance or *change in the nature* of lands . . . after the effectivity of this Act" (emphasis added), language that can be read as proscribing belated conversions to commercial crops, although this may require judicial clarification.

President Aquino's subsequent approval of guidelines implementing this 10-year exemption was roundly criticized by proreform groups. A KMP spokesperson argued that Aquino's action was "proof that she and her administration is [*sic*] a government of landlord class interests and cannot in any way institute a genuine agrarian reform law" (Simon Sagnip, quoted in Melencio 1988).

Stock Distribution on Corporate Farms

Consistent with the provisions of EO 229, the new law permitted corporate landowners to satisfy their reform obligations by giving their farmworkers the "right to purchase such proportion of the capital stock

of the corporation that the agricultural land, actually devoted to agricultural activities, bears in relation to the company's total assets."[49] Peasant organizations strongly opposed this legislative provision as violative of the Constitution, arguing instead for direct transfer of land-ownership (Bascog 1987: 56). Meanwhile, many landowners incorporated their properties in anticipation of this provision (Lopez-Gonzaga interview, Oct. 28, 1988). The provision created obvious incentives to dilute the value of the workers' shares by either undervaluing the land assets or overvaluing the non-land assets. The workers were guaranteed but one seat on the corporate board of directors.

This provision appears to be a prima facie violation of the 1987 Constitution, Article 13, Section 4,[50] which provides: "The State shall, by law, undertake an agrarian reform program founded on the right of farmers and regular farmworkers, who are landless, to own directly or collectively the lands they till or, in the case of other farmworkers, to receive a just share of the fruits thereof." This section carefully and clearly distinguishes between two categories of agrarian reform beneficiaries—(1) "farmers and *regular* farmworkers, who are landless" (emphasis added); and (2) "*other* farmworkers" (emphasis added)—and their corresponding constitutional entitlements.[51] The importance of this distinction was underscored in a colloquy among constitutional commissioners Bacani, Rodrigo, Tadeo, Monsod, and Bennagen during the commission's deliberations on August 7, 1986. At issue was the possibility that landowners might attempt to subvert the reform process and deny "farmers" (tenants) or "regular farmworkers" (permanent laborers) their entitlement to "*own* directly or collectively the lands they till" (emphasis added). The commissioners were concerned that landowners might change the status of such farmers and regular farmworkers to that of "other farmworkers" after ratification of the constitution (ROP 1986a, 3: 12–13).

"Other farmworkers" (temporary laborers) are constitutionally entitled only to a "just share of the fruits" of the land they work. Congress in effect rewrote the Constitution by extending this "just share of the fruits" provision to refer to *all* farmworkers, "regular" as well as "other" farmworkers. That which the constitutional commissioners expressly sought to prevent landowners from doing, Congress did for the landowners. In turn, the DAR has sided with the landowners and Congress in upholding the validity of Section 31 of RA 6657.[52] Undersecretary Corazon Paredes del Rosario summarized the DAR's position:

The Congress deemed it proper to include the subject provision in the law because they were fully aware of the constitutional mandate and that certain corporate farms might be better left to continue their proven and viable operations with their lands unfragmented for as long as this would result to [sic] increased income and greater benefits to the farmworker beneficiaries (FB's) than if the lands were divided and distributed individually to them.[53]

There is, however, no necessary reason why adherence to the constitutional mandate, properly interpreted, should result in the fragmentation of "proven and viable operations." Nor, given Philippine and international experience, is it necessarily the case that individual parcelization will result in decreased production and decreased beneficiary incomes.

There are a variety of means by which both to meet the constitutional requirement that regular farmworkers receive direct or collective ownership of the land they till and permit the continued operation of such corporate farms as are proven to be efficient in their present scale of operation. For example, separate corporate entities could be established, with one corporation having ownership of all land assets, coupled with distribution of *all* the stock of that corporation to the worker-beneficiaries. Assuming existing operations were maintained; existing management retained, or comparable management hired; and wage and benefit levels remained constant, farm profitability would not differ significantly from previous levels. However, the land-related portion of those profits would now benefit the farmworkers.

Anticipatory Transfers

Equally troubling in terms of their potential impact on the reform program was the recognition accorded transfers of land up to the effective date of the law. It appears that transfers to relatives, friends, and straw men, in anticipation of the reform law, were massive. Such subdivision of ownership, if recognized, could drastically reduce the amount of land owned in excess of the relevant retention limit. Section 6 of RA 6657 validates transfers executed *prior* to the effective date of the law if registered within three months of that date. This provision raises the additional problem of possible postlaw execution of fraudulently predated land transfers. Section 73(e), by contrast, recognizes only those transfers duly registered or the subject of the issuance of a tax declaration as of the effective date of the law. No resolution of the apparent conflict between these provisions has been forthcoming.

Landowner Retention Limits

Perhaps the most heated debate in the deliberations over the Philippine agrarian-reform program concerned retention limits—that is, the amount of land existing landowners and their heirs could retain.[54] At the heart of these debates were three contested issues: the appropriate definition of "small landowner"; the economies of scale, if any, associated with the production of various agricultural commodities; and the historical origins of present land rights.

The state was constitutionally obliged to respect the rights of "small landowners" in determining retention limits, although the Constitution provided no direct guidance as to what constituted a small landowner. In some cases, owners of 50-hectare farms were termed "small farmers," although their holdings were among the top 0.4 percent of all Philippine farms by size (Senator John Osmeña, quoted in Ronquillo 1988). A Department of Labor study defined "small farms" to be all those with less than 40 hectares (Inocentes et al. n.d.). Others defined small farmers as those having 24 hectares or less (Belarmino et al. interview, June 17, 1986).

A variant on the "small landowner" theme was the "widows with children" exception: small tenant-operated holdings of widows with children, the disabled, or other similarly situated owners should be exempted from the reform process.[55] The (superficial) appeal of this exception was apparent in the question posed to Laurentino Bascog, a CPAR spokesperson, by Milagros German, while testifying before a Senate committee:

Now, if a person, a retired employee who is almost nailed to a wheelchair for one reason or another and the only means, source of income is that derived from the sugarland, now because that person can no longer work the land, he cannot be an owner-cultivator in the legal sense, do I understand from you that you are also depriving that paralytic man, sick man of his land, the use of his land and to profit therefrom without retaining something? (German 1987: 53)

Bascog replied that the rule should be zero retention for noncultivating landowners, although he indicated that in extreme cases flexibility was appropriate. He further noted that CPAR's recommended policy of selective and progressive compensation would reward small landowners with compensation based on fair market value, to be paid 50 percent in cash and 50 percent in bonds maturing in five years (1987: 53).

The hypothetical case posed involved a situation that was extremely rare. Furthermore, as policymakers began to appreciate the important role women play in agriculture, the notion that widows were perforce incapable of direct cultivation should have been summarily rejected. Moreover, it is clear from tenant interviews that in circumstances of obvious inequity, the tenants were very unlikely to apply for reform of the particular holding.[56] For those limited cases where landlords who are otherwise incapable of direct cultivation do lose their holdings to the reform process, special compensation arrangements could be made to assure them a comparable income flow.[57] The real question was whether beneficiaries could be trusted to self-administer certain limited exclusions or whether the law should, instead, exempt all "small" land-holdings in the name of averting a potential injustice to a rare type of landlord.

Economies of Scale in Philippine Agriculture

We explored the economies-of-scale issue in some detail in Chapter 4. The empirical data cast considerable doubt on the existence of any scale economies in Philippine agriculture, with the possible exception of sugar. In the case of sugar, there were data to suggest that apparent economies in crop production could be explained by correctable market failures or disproportional access to certain complementary services and inputs.

This is not to say that landowners agreed with my interpretation of the data; quite the contrary. It was an article of faith among large land-owners that agrarian reform meant subdivision of their holdings, with a concomitant decrease in agricultural output.[58] Indeed, by the account of one sugar-sector representative, even the NPA objected to land redistribution in Negros Occidental, believing that fragmentation of the holdings would mean the collapse of the sugar industry, causing massive unemployment (Acuña 1987: 62).

Concerns that land redistribution would disrupt economies of scale were clearly inapposite in the case of small tenanted rice and corn holdings—one reason, perhaps, that this element of the reform program drew little criticism. By the same logic, reform of coconut, banana, and pineapple farms should have generated relatively little controversy, at least from an economic standpoint. In the case of coconut production, many large holdings had long been effectively subdivided, with farm operations conducted by small tenants. In the banana and pineapple sectors, many small farmers leased their lands to Philippine and multi-

national firms, which thereby operated hundreds or thousands of small farms on an integrated basis. The Aquino government anticipated that in the event of individual parcelization of larger banana and pineapple holdings, the farmworker-beneficiaries would lease their new holdings back to larger operators for purposes of integrated management. Even granting the possibility of scale economies in production of these crops, lease-back arrangements, as well as collective or (appropriately tailored) corporate stock ownership, would likely assure that the reform occasioned no significant disruption in production.[59]

Parcelization, Sugar Production, Mill Operations, and Foreign Exchange

In the view of large sugar landowners, fragmentation of their holdings would not only result in reduced sugar yields but would occasion a diversification of production away from sugar to the detriment of foreign exchange earnings, sugar-mill operations, and mill-related employment (Hernandez 1987: 33; Sabino 1987: 17–19; Sawit 1987: 40). In 1986, at the height of the sugar crisis, many landowners acknowledged a need to permanently reduce the area planted to sugar, by as much as 50 percent.[60] As domestic sugar prices began to rise in 1987 and 1988, however, lands that had been shifted to rice and corn production, as well as idle and abandoned lands, were brought back into sugar production, and earlier plans to diversify were forgotten (ADB 1988: 81–89). By the time of the legislative debates over agrarian reform, sugar growers were expressing great concern that reform would mean curtailment, if not termination, of sugar production, with a variety of attendant negative consequences.[61]

Land Development: Whose Sweat and Blood?

As with the argument about economies of scale, it was an article of faith among landowners that the land was theirs—not simply in legal terms but in a more metaphysical sense. Indeed, judging from the arguments proffered by landowners and tenants or landless laborers alike, the justness of their respective claims to a given parcel of land turned on their respective contributions to making that land productive. To emphasize their roles in the process of agricultural production, landowners, tenants, and laborers described themselves as "planters," "farmers," and "farmworkers" respectively. At issue, however, was not merely who had paid for or provided particular services or inputs in recent crop years. The debate frequently dated from the original clear-

ing of the land and encompassed the relative contributions of each party (and his or her ancestors) from that date to the present. The argument was over who had shed more "blood, sweat, and tears" in the nurturing of the land.

"Most sugarcane landowners acquired their lands, not through inheritance, but by the sweat of their brow through the years," one planters' organization argued.[62] The president of another planter's organization prefaced his remarks to Congress saying, "I just want to present the feeling of the landowners who really worked hard, through sweat and blood, just to acquire these lands" (Caparas 1987: 54). A representative of the Land's Utmost Productivity Association (LUPA) argued that land redistribution would trigger violent resistance. This, he indicated, was particularly likely in the case of "pioneers who, having been encouraged by the government to take advantage of homestead laws, acquired, developed and nursed their farms from the virgin jungles of Mindanao, Palawan, Luzon and Visayas thru [sic] the sweat of their brows" (Marasigan 1987b: 116). In urging that the landless be resettled on public lands rather than becoming the recipients of redistributed private lands, Congresswoman Starke sounded this same theme: "And they will not just be getting somebody else's land because that is developed already. They should start from zero, like the rest of us did. I started from zero, why should they not start from zero."[63]

By contrast, peasants and their representatives emphasized both their contribution to the productive value of the land and the unjust means by which their forebears were dispossessed of land. The KMP's president, Jaime Tadeo, claimed: "Those pieces of land were handed down to us by our forefathers, and for centuries have been tilled by the peasants. If the landlords have been able to buy those lands, we have more than paid for them—five times, ten times, twenty times we have paid for them" (1986: 14). Similarly, in attacking free-market value as a basis for determining landowner compensation, the FFF's president, Jeremias U. Montemayor, wrote: "The free market does not consider the special relationship of the tenant or tiller to the land which he has conserved and made productive for the benefit both of himself and of the owner for many years" (1988).

In his presentation to the Philippine Congress, Germelino M. Bautista argued that tenants shouldered a disproportionate share of current operating costs, suggesting that at present it was the tenants' sweat and capital that was making the land productive.[64] The issue of "sweat equity" in the land was also reflected in calls by peasant organizations for a zero retention limit for noncultivator landowners.[65]

Legislative Provisions Concerning Landowner Retention Limits

Reviewing the protracted, phased implementation of retention limits (with a final retention limit of 24 hectares for Program C) contemplated in the March 13, 1987, CAC draft, a World Bank land-reform mission concluded:

Potentially most damaging to the ultimate goals of the land reform are both the step-wise introduction and the high levels of the retention limits on private lands. The proposal to phase in the retention limits in three successive steps . . . would encourage evasion, leave out a high proportion of tenants and landless [laborers], and add to the administrative burden. . . . *The Government should decide on the ultimate retention limit and enact it from the start . . . the Mission recommends that the Government consider adopting a uniform land ceiling of 7 ha for all Programs and implementing Programs A, B, and C simultaneously.* (World Bank 1987a: vi–vii; emphasis added)

Legislative proposals concerning retention limits were, as might be expected, quite varied. Radical provisions set the general retention area at 2 hectares (the nationalist bloc's HB 65), and several drafts established a *zero* retention limit for absentee landlords (Gillego's original HB 400, Sec. 5; Aquino's SB 123, Sec. 5). As passed out of the House, the retention limit was set at 7 hectares, with an additional 3 hectares permitted each legal heir (HB 400, Sec. 5, Third Reading copy, as approved Apr. 21, 1988). This provision was attacked by a Philippine analyst as exempting nearly 90 percent of private agricultural lands (Guieb 1988: 2). Landowners who had received title under homestead or free patent were entitled to retain up to 24 hectares.

On the Senate side, Senator Alvarez initially adopted a 7-hectare retention limit, then introduced a variant of crop-specific retention limits, an approach that enjoyed some support in the proreform scholarly community as well as the support of various planters' organizations.[66] Even the CPAR, while insisting that retention limits be limited to owner cultivators and in no event exceed 5 hectares, argued that "the land retained should vary according to the following factors which govern a viable farm size . . . commodity produced, terrain, infrastructure, and soil fertility" (Cuizon 1987: 6–7). The central argument in favor of variable retention limits was that the land area needed to realize productive efficiency varied by crop, soil type, elevation, and climate. Whatever the agronomic merits of this argument, the administrative complications and potential distortions in production incentives attendant on such a reform approach would be staggering.[67] In the event, the Senate set a 5-hectare limit, with owners who had already

been the subject of reform under PD 27 entitled to retain seven hectares (SB 249, Sec. 5, Third Reading copy, as approved Apr. 28, 1988).

While the Senate provision was more advantageous to erstwhile landless cultivators than the retention limit adopted in the House, the provision was, like the House version, attacked as a departure from the principle of owner-cultivatorship and zero retention. Furthermore, the Senate provision was argued to exclude 60 percent of private agricultural holdings (Guieb 1988: 4).

The compromise struck in the conference committee, and embodied in RA 6657, provided for retention areas that would "vary according to factors governing a viable family-sized farm . . . but in no case shall retention by the landowner exceed five (5) hectares."[68] An additional 3 hectares could be awarded to each child of the landowner provided the child was at least 15 years old (as of what date is not stated) and was actually tilling the land or directly managing it.[69] Landowners whose lands had been previously taken under PD 27 were allowed to keep their original retention area (7 hectares). Homestead grantees or their direct compulsory heirs were permitted to retain their homestead areas (24 hectares).

The Effect of RA 6657's Retention-Limit Provisions

Understandings as to the effective retention limit created by the legislative provisions varied. During the course of congressional deliberations, there was explicit consideration given to the number of landowners who would be affected by reform depending on the retention limit adopted.[70] A representative of the coconut sector questioned the propriety of "dispossessing millions of middle class landowners" for the sake of satisfying some "50,000 armed dissidents." "If we become dissidents ourselves in our own ways, you [members of Congress] must realize that you have made us such" (Barcelona 1987: 27).

Citing an average of four children per family (and implicitly arguing that, on average, three of these children would qualify for retention rights), Congressman Florencio Abad claimed that the law created an effective retention limit of 15 hectares. By his account, only 10–15 percent of private arable land in the Philippines would be subject to the new agrarian reform law.[71] Jaime Tadeo, the KMP's national chairperson, was (perhaps unintentionally) more generous, estimating that the retention provisions would exempt all but 25 percent of private agricultural land (Lazaro 1988).

Inclusive of the retained areas of landowners with farms in excess of

the retention limit, a universal 5-hectare retention limit would exempt over 75 percent of total farm area in the Philippines from the reform. If, on average, one to two heirs per landowning family also receive the maximum retention rights, the effective retention limit will be 8 to 11 hectares. Under this scenario, farm holdings with some two-thirds to three-quarters of all land in farms will be completely exempt from the reform. Of those farms that remain subject to the reform, only the excess above 8–11 hectares would be available to the reform. When such retention areas are netted out, even without evasive landowner behavior, *only 13 to 16 percent of the land in private farms nationwide will be available for redistribution under the combination of preexisting and new legislation, and much of this may not be subject to reform for a decade or more.*[72]

Unimodal Farm Strategies and Viable Farm Size

Part of the explanation for a 5-hectare retention limit can be discerned in Table 1. Farms in the 2.00–4.99 hectare range account for 35.1 percent of all Philippine farms by number and 35.0 percent of all land in farms. This group of farmers would appear to be the nucleus of a commercial smallholding stratum for a "unimodal" pattern of agricultural development.[73] Unimodal strategies have been utilized, most notably in Japan, South Korea, and Taiwan, to achieve significant nationwide increases in agricultural productivity and income. To a considerable degree, these successes have featured labor-intensive, capital-saving technologies. By contrast, countries emphasizing "bimodal" development patterns—Mexico is a classic example—have relied upon labor-saving, capital-intensive technologies to achieve productivity increases in the large-farm sector, while perpetuating poverty in the small-farm sector.

Closer examination of the East Asian cases suggests that from an agronomic standpoint, a unimodal landholding pattern with a median farm size of under *one* hectare is feasible, indeed can be quite successful. Some 95 percent of Japan's farms are under three hectares in size; two-thirds are under one hectare. Farms under three hectares account for just under 80 percent of farm area; those under one hectare contain one-third of Japan's farm area (Barker et al. 1985: 34). South Korean farms are similarly concentrated in the small size categories: 89 percent of the farms are under two hectares in size; 63 percent are under one hectare. Farms under two hectares in size account for over 80 percent of the land in farms in South Korea (Powelson and Stock 1987: 181). In Taiwan, 82 percent of the farm units are less than two hectares in size; two-thirds are under one hectare. Farms under two hectares contain 55 percent of

Taiwan's farm area. Another 15 percent of Taiwanese farms are in the two-to-three hectare size category. These farms contain just over 30 percent of the land in farms.[74]

Philippine landowners rejected efforts to infer viable farm size from the experiences of their East Asian neighbors, arguing that the Philippines lacked comparable rural and industrial infrastructure, and that the scope of the proposed Philippine reform program was markedly greater.[75] Landowners' estimates of viable farm size ranged from five hectares for mangoes to fifty or more hectares for sugar (Dizon 1987: 95). The remarks of a representative of coconut landowners were not atypical of the arguments offered against low retention limits: "In the event that the seven-hectare retention limit is implemented, banks and other lending institutions will tighten, if not completely abolish, their agricultural credit or lending transactions since the risk of default would be greater because of insufficiency in terms of productivity due to inadequate planting area and poor farm management practice" (Barcelona 1987: 16). Peasants typically estimated much smaller viable farm sizes, in the range of one to three hectares.[76]

A Word of Caution on Determinations of Viable Farm Size

Determination of "viable" farm sizes is fraught with complications. It involves consideration of myriad variables bearing on the productive potential of land, predictions about input and crop prices, judgments as to the relative adequacy of given income levels, and the like. Moreover, redistribution of some predetermined viable farm holding can have a pernicious impact on the reform. In the case of Marcos's PD 27, distribution of the "family-sized" farms of three hectares of irrigated lands or five hectares of unirrigated land provided for in the law would have resulted in the *displacement* of at least two tenants for every one tenant benefited.[77]

Any distribution involving a minimum or optimum or so-called economically viable holding, in which some tenants were ousted so that the remaining beneficiaries (at the former's expense) met some abstract ideal of farm size, would be widely perceived as unfair by the beneficiaries and would require enormous administrative effort as well. Clearly, no true easing of population pressure on land would thereby occur. The ousted *minifundistas* would still have to be fed by the products of the society's land resources. Paradoxically, their very small holdings could be expected to produce more per square meter—given anything close to proportionate access to inputs—than any idealized somewhat larger

holdings. The same reasoning suggests the desirability of accommodat-
ing substantially all hired laborers, whether permanent or temporary, in
the redistribution of plantation lands on which they had worked rather
than wholly excluding some in order to meet an abstract ideal as to per-
family holding.

If many tenanted holdings in a given country are today smaller than
some idealized size or if the same is true of the quotient of all plantation
land divided by all plantation laborers, that is a reflection of an existing
agricultural population pressing on a limited land resource. Land reform cannot create land to ease this pressure. It can make every beneficiary family significantly better off relative to its existing situation,
whatever size parcel or aliquot share of plantation land that family now
farms, by assuring the beneficiary the full benefit of production and
replacing onerous rent obligations with modest amortization payments
or augmenting wages with land-related profits.

Land Valuation

The March and April (1987) CAC drafts adopted a market-oriented
valuation scheme for compensation purposes, with the latter draft basing market value on the owner's latest tax declaration (ROP, ITFAR
1987b: 18–19; id. 1987d: 15). The drafts were silent as to a cut-off date for
such declarations, leaving open the possibility of new, inflated declarations. Average fair market values were estimated at P25,000 (about
$1,200) per hectare for Programs B and C, subject to further consider-
ation of land productivity, location, and proximity to transport. The
land-value figures used for planning purposes were subsequently revised to P37,000–45,000 per hectare, about $1,800–2,000.[78]

Again the more radical provisions were introduced in the House.
The nationalist bloc's House Bill 65 provided for outright confiscation
of property and free distribution to farmer-beneficiaries. The original
Gillego bill (HB 400) adopted CPAR language that proposed a scheme
of selective and progressive compensation. Compensation as a percentage of market value (determined from the owner's tax declaration, subject to some controls) would decline with increasing farm size, as would
the cash portion of that compensation.[79] Owners of more than 50 hectares were to receive *no* compensation. The landowner bloc argued instead for valuation based on the owner's declaration of fair market
value, with payment entirely in cash or cash equivalent.[80]

As reported out, the House bill would have the DAR and the land-

owner determine land value (HB 400, Sec. 13, Third Reading copy, as approved Apr. 21, 1988). The various Senate bills generally set valuation at the owner's tax-declared value, subject to PARC controls.[81] Senate Bill 249 was revised, however, to incorporate an array of additional valuation considerations: the cost of acquiring the land; the current value of like properties; the nature, use and income of the property; the owner's sworn valuation; and assessments made by the government. Also to be considered were the social and economic benefits contributed by the farmers, farmworkers, and the government, as well as the land-owner's nonpayment of taxes or loans secured by government financial institutions (SB 249, Sec. 18, Third Reading copy, as approved Apr. 28, 1988).

As passed, the law valued tenanted rice and corn lands of more than seven hectares at 2.5 times the value of average crop production, the valuation formula of PD 27. For other lands, compensation was to be based on the valuation variables introduced in SB 249, as amended (RA 6657, Sec. 17). The complexity of the valuation process lends itself to abuse and protracted administrative and judicial proceedings. Equity and administrative efficiency have been far better served in other Asian land reforms through the use of a multiple of average annual productivity in calculating land values.

Note that reliance on a multiple of crop production is no assurance of a valuation process free of administrative complications. Philippine landowners have historically resisted or challenged valuation determinations as one means of obstructing agrarian reform. The Aquino government's ITFAR took the position that all valuations should be completed "with or without landowners' cooperation." It would then be left to the landowners to accept the valuation and provide legal evidence of their claim to just compensation (ROP, ITFAR 1987a: 6). The new law embodied this principle. In the event landowners rejected or failed to reply to the DAR's valuation and offer of corresponding compensation, the DAR was to conduct summary compensation proceedings and thereafter deposit the compensation award in a bank and take immediate possession of the land.[82]

Landowner Compensation

The compensation packages associated with earlier Philippine reforms were generally criticized by landowners as being inadequate both in amount and in form. There were those who insisted that "just compensation" required full payment in cash for any land taken, in the

knowledge that such compensation was well beyond the means of the Philippine government (Acuña 1987: 62).

As it began its consideration of agrarian reform, the Aquino government had at least one new tool for addressing landowners' complaints: the fairly extensive array of public and "sequestered" properties that were available for privatization.[83] The 1952 Taiwanese agrarian-reform program provided a model for privatizing ownership of publicly held properties or industries through distribution of stock shares as part of the compensation package for landowners affected by agrarian reform. Philippine landowners otherwise ill-disposed toward agrarian reform were notably interested in this potential feature. They were similarly interested in possible provisions to make compensation bonds preferred collateral for use with the Philippine banking system, whether to invest in new industries or to repay outstanding landowner indebtedness (Starke et al. interview, June 16, 1986).

The new law provided cash payments as an inverse function of farm size: 25 percent for lands in excess of 50 hectares; 30 percent cash for lands of 24–50 hectares; and 35 percent cash for lands below 24 hectares. In all cases the balance was to be paid in government bonds maturing in equal annual installments over a 10-year period. Generous provisions were made for transferability and negotiability of these bonds.

Beneficiary Repayments

In the initial CAC drafts, the beneficiary amortization schedule was extended to 30 years (previous laws set it at 15 years) with 6 percent interest to meet affordability concerns. Further, an "affordability wedge" was envisioned for Programs B and C, under which beneficiaries were to be responsible for repaying only 80 percent of the cost of the land.

The World Bank mission recommended a one-time nominal payment of P600 per beneficiary. The mission concluded there was little prospect of an immediate improvement in the disposable family income of reform beneficiaries if beneficiaries were required to repay land costs over 30 years at 6 percent interest. Elimination of further amortization obligations was urged in order to effect an instant and significant increase in beneficiary income.

House Bill 65 provided for free land distribution, echoing the demand of the KMP. Eventually the House adopted a 17-year amortization schedule with zero interest, coupled with a 2-year deferment of initial repayment. Payments were not to exceed 10 percent of the net

value of current production. Furthermore, all previous land rentals and uncompensated labor—defined as the difference between actual wages and the government-mandated minimum wage, including other benefits provided by law—were to be deducted from the resale price of land to the beneficiary (HB 400, Sec. 22, Third Reading copy, as approved Apr. 21, 1988).

The Senate opted for 30-year repayment at 6 percent interest. Payments in the first three years were to be reduced, while the first five payments were in no event to exceed 5 percent of the value of annual gross production. Thereafter adjustments were to be made in the event amortization obligations exceeded 10 percent of annual gross production, where the failure of production was not the fault of the beneficiary. Prompt payment of amortization amounts entitled beneficiaries to a 2 percent interest rebate (SB 249, Sec. 26, Third Reading copy, as approved Apr. 28, 1988).

The Senate provisions were adopted in toto in RA 6657. Nonpayment of an aggregate of three annual installments will be grounds for foreclosure by the Land Bank of the Philippines. Peasant groups have objected to the repayment provisions, arguing that the high cost of inputs, most notably chemical fertilizers, renders amortizations equivalent to 10 percent of *gross* production value onerous, if not unaffordable. While these claims seem overstated—the amortization payments appear to be lower than typical rent payments—they do underscore concerns that the reform will effect only a modest immediate redistribution of income.

Penalties for Noncompliance by Landowners

Section 74 of the new law provided for imprisonment for one month to three years or a fine of P1,000–15,000 (roughly $40–715) in the event of willful or knowing violation of the terms of the act. Imprisonment of recalcitrant landlords is not, in the Philippine context, a credible penalty and will not serve as an effective deterrent. The maximum monetary penalty is roughly equivalent to the value of 0.5 hectare of average farmland. Inasmuch as this fine is set without regard to the number of hectares affected by landowner misconduct, it too will have little deterrent effect, particularly in the case of larger landowners. Higher, but credible, penalties are important to successful reform. Sanctions commensurate with those applicable to reform beneficiaries who prematurely enter lands subject to agrarian reform—namely, permanent dis-

qualification from the benefits of the reform—would, in the case of landlord misconduct, call for forfeiture without compensation of holdings subject to such misconduct. Landowners' attempts to obstruct the reform process might also be treated as separate and multiple, with each offense subject to the statutory fine (Prosterman and Hanstad 1988a: 11).

Complementary Measures in Support of Land Reform

From the earliest drafts, provision was made for complementary services such as liberalized credit, marketing, extension, infrastructure, and research. As enacted, RA 6657 mandates the provision of beneficiary support services, as well as support services for affected landowners. The law further requires the setting aside of at least 25 percent of all agrarian-reform appropriations for support services. It leaves all details of such support services to the determination of the PARC, however.

In arguing the importance of support services to the success of the reform process, Congressman Narciso Monfort made remarks quite revealing of elite landowners' attitudes to the prospective reform beneficiaries: "You give them five hectares or seven hectares without support, with the Filipino habit of mañana habit [sic], with their gambling, with their habit in dancing in disco. . . . I regret this will fail," (Monfort 1987: 38).

Program Costs

While estimates of the cost of the reform program fluctuated, most of those available at the time of the congressional deliberations placed the cost over the first five years at P60–70 billion ($2.9–3.3 billion), while life-of-program costs were estimated at P160–170 billion ($7.6–8.1 billion). In each case, land-transfer costs were the largest single component. Subsequent to passage of the reform law, estimates of the life-of-program costs increased considerably, ranging from P221.1 billion ($10.4 billion) to P402.7 billion ($19.2 billion) (USAID 1989: 21; Putzel 1992: 347).

Foreign Donor Assistance

Government estimates suggested that roughly one-half to two-thirds of the financing would have to come from foreign sources.[84]

While the language is susceptible of other interpretations, the law appears to limit the use of foreign resources to financing production credits, infrastructure, and other support services. If this provision, thus interpreted, is enforced, and if foreign donors are willing to provide the necessary funds, foreign donors will effectively be paying *all* program costs not related to land transfers.

In any event, the multilateral donors, as well as most bilateral donors, appeared predisposed to limit their funding to activities other than land transfer.[85] The inconsistency of donor signals, arguing for nonconfiscatory land reform, yet refusing to finance compensation directly, is not lost on the Philippine government or on those hostile to reform. Indeed, the unwillingness of the World Bank and the Japanese government to finance landowner compensation directly was explicitly cited by antireform organizations as one reason to exempt *all* productive agricultural land (private and public) from the reform process (PLADAR and DATU-Panay n.d.: 3). The fungibility of government resources, however, should permit donors to underwrite other portions of the government budget and thereby free up domestic resources for payment of compensation.

Other Issues

The 1987 Constitution mandated that temporary laborers receive a "just share of the fruits" of the land. Yet the various CAC drafts made no provision for temporary or seasonal workers, particularly those who have regularly worked on specific farms near their residence. The new law includes them as qualified beneficiaries, according them priority behind agricultural lessees and share tenants and regular (permanent) farmworkers. Wherever possible these laborers should be accommodated on the land.

The CAC drafts also gave few details concerning Program D. Particularly notable was the absence of provisions regarding indigenous communities or long-settled cultivators, both of whose rights are protected under Article 13, Section 6 of the Constitution. The new law corrected the earlier oversight, making explicit provision for ancestral lands, protecting them to ensure the "economic, social and cultural wellbeing" of the indigenous communities. The indigenous systems of landownership, land use, and the modes of settling land disputes were likewise to be recognized and respected.

Landowner Reactions

For all the provisions that limit the scope of the reform, landowners and their representatives in Congress viewed the new law as anathema. Despite voting for the reform law, Congresswoman Hortensia L. Starke denounced it as "extremely faulty . . . the most radical and encompassing agrarian reform law in the history of the world" (Gob 1988). Apart from evasive actions such as introduction of commercial crops and the establishment of corporate agricultural entities, the present strategy of the antireform forces is twofold: legislative and electoral.

On the legislative side, they have offered various legislative amendments that would permanently exempt certain commercial farms and all lands suited for tourist development.[86] Meanwhile, President Aquino's brother, Congressman Jose "Peping" Cojuangco, Jr., offered an amendment to decentralize implementation of the reform program to the regional and provincial levels, on the premise that "the people are familiar with their own economic and social conditions, and they are in a better position to decide what is best for them."[87] By its reference to "the people," this argument deliberately obscured the dynamics of local politics in settings such as the Philippines.[88] Without forceful administrative arrangements to the contrary, provincial and local economic and political elites can be expected to dominate the decentralized deliberative process at the expense of the landless and other marginal elements of local society.[89] Cojuangco's proposal was thus widely viewed as an attempt to emasculate the reform (*Business World* 1990c).

Most of the crippling amendments have remained bottled up in committee, but political balances can change. In a September 1988 speech before the Council of Agricultural Producers of the Philippines, Vice President Salvador Laurel condemned the reform law as "unjust" and called for use of the initiative process to reject the law and the very idea of agrarian reform (Gob 1988). Landowners also looked to the 1992 elections. "There will be another election. . . . we will be careful not to re-elect these [pro-reform] people. They are all leftists or are out for themselves."[90] Noting that 1992 was also the year in which landholdings of 50 hectares and less were targeted for redistribution, Senator Osmeña urged affected landowners to organize themselves in support of appropriate candidates. "There is an indirect referendum built in this CARP law. Just organize yourselves" (Cruz 1988).

Peasant Reactions

Militant and nonmilitant peasant organizations denounced the new law for its provisions on retention limits, as well as for deferring reform of commercial farms, permitting stock distribution in lieu of land transfer on corporate farms, and establishing beneficiary repayment obligations they deemed unaffordable. The Philippine Peasant Institute editorialized that "the CARP law protects the interests of the landed class in the Philippines and their US masters" (*Farm News & Views* 1988b). Several peasant organizations responded by initiating land invasions.

Summary

Dissatisfied with the slow pace of the Aquino government, peasant organizations actively sought to define the reform agenda and promote their vision of redistributive agrarian reform in the deliberations of the Constitutional Commission and later of the cabinet and the Philippine legislature. They were aided in this endeavor by a variety of nongovernmental organizations and important segments of the Catholic Church. The 1987 Constitution did embody significant new provisions on agrarian reform, albeit with important qualifications.

After protracted cabinet debates, President Aquino elected not to use her decree-making powers to mandate a sweeping reform process. Instead, she deferred to the Philippine Congress on the central issues of implementation priorities and retention limits, a decision justified by, and consistent with notions of representative government (i.e., democracy). As had been anticipated by many observers, in the absence of forceful direction on the part of President Aquino to establish a new political order, the legislature was dominated by members of the traditional Philippine political and economic elite. At each stage in the deliberations over the reform, the scope of the proposed program was successively reduced. Perhaps the greatest triumph of the antireform forces was in getting Aquino to defer to the legislature. Once the reform debates took place within the legislature, landed interests were particularly effective in exercising direct and indirect influence to weaken the reform program and tailor exemptions and exceptions to the program. The result is a program limited in scope, to be implemented over a decade or more—ample time for further weakening or reversal of the reform process.

7

Implementation:
Scandal, Subversion, and Success

Private property has triumphed over democratic rights.
Bonifacio Gillego

We don't want to be drown[ed] in the emotion of land-to-the-tiller.
Deogracias Vistan

Following the June 1988 passage of the Comprehensive Agrarian Reform Law (RA 6657), the Philippine government has encountered, and
abetted, significant abuses of the reform program, most notably in the
areas of land valuation and conversion of agricultural lands to nonagricultural uses. The Department of Agrarian Reform (DAR) has been
plagued by leadership problems as well as congressional and landowner resistance. Philippine peasants have frequently been frustrated
in their efforts to accelerate implementation of the reform, and they
have had even less success promoting more progressive reform legislation. Philippine politics continues to be exclusionary; peasants still find
it difficult to make their voices heard. The cause of peasant mobilization
and unity has been dealt a number of serious setbacks. Yet for all these
problems, President Corazon Aquino and her successor, Fidel Ramos,
have made substantial progress toward completing the Marcos-era reform of tenanted rice and corn lands. The Aquino and Ramos governments have also distributed significant amounts of public and government-owned lands. These results reflect both continuity and change in
Philippine cultural and political dynamics.

Valuation Scandals

A major scandal concerning overvaluations of land in the Voluntary
Offer to Sell (VOS) program marked the first anniversary of the new

reform law.[1] The most notable instance involved the 1,888-hectare Garchitorena estate in Camarines Sur, a hilly property largely unsuited to cultivation. In April 1988, Sharp International Marketing Inc. purportedly purchased the foreclosed estate from the United Coconut Planters Bank (UCPB) for P3.014 million. In May 1988, Sharp International offered the estate to the DAR for P56 million. In November 1988, DAR officials increased the valuation of the estate. Following a December 28, 1988, meeting of the joint DAR–Land Bank of the Philippines (LBP) Compensation Clearing Committee, the DAR issued a bill of sale in the amount of P62.725 million. The valuation was challenged by LBP staff, and in early April 1989 the LBP's president, Deogracias Vistan, rejected the order for payment.[2]

The fallout from this episode included a series of congressional and independent investigations, the resignation of Secretary of Agrarian Reform Philip Juico, and a shake-up in DAR personnel. The threatened criminal proceedings came to naught, however, and most of the implicated DAR officials resumed their duties. Attributing DAR's problems to corruption, President Aquino named Miriam Defensor-Santiago—best known for her "graft buster" image as commissioner of immigration and deportation—as DAR secretary-designate and ordered her to "start cleaning up the department" (Balana 1989: 1). Santiago's appointment was greeted with cautious optimism by peasant organizations. KMP and CPAR officials and other reformists identified the flawed reform law as the real problem and argued that Santiago's anticorruption image was no guarantee against future anomalies (Bulatao interview, Feb. 16, 1994; *Philippine Daily Inquirer* 1989: 6). The scandal occasioned a near-paralysis of the reform program for months, a situation exacerbated by congressional refusal to confirm Defensor-Santiago's appointment.

The Garchitorena scandal and similar overvaluations of VOS lands illustrated several serious defects in the VOS program and in the reform program generally. Most of the VOS lands were remote, unproductive, and often in "conflicted" (insurgency) zones (Adversario interview, Jan. 29, 1992; Vistan interview, Feb. 20, 1991). In several cases, there were few, if any, families cultivating the subject properties.[3] The complicity of local DAR officials in the overvaluation of such properties confirmed the potential for abuse of the complex valuation criteria. The problem was not simply corruption or fraud within the DAR, however. In June 1990, Aquino issued Executive Order 405 transferring responsibility for land valuation from the DAR to the LBP. Yet in the case of the

Garchitorena estate, even the LBP's 1989 valuation—P28.32 million—reflected a nearly tenfold increase over Sharp International's purchase price, suggesting fundamental flaws in the valuation formula. The process by which Sharp International acquired the Garchitorena estate raised further issues of fraud. Had Sharp International finalized its purchase of the estate from the UCPB in April 1988, as it initially claimed, the transaction would have skirted application of the new reform law, which was then still mired in congressional debate. However, Sharp International's purchase was not finalized until December 5, 1988. The transaction thus violated the new reform law and suggested UCPB cooperation in the fraud.[4] The transaction, which involved a prominent businessman with close ties to the president and her family, also hinted at a broader pattern of influence-peddling within the Aquino government and exposed a pattern of overvalued land purchases by the DAR that predated the Aquino administration.[5]

The Garchitorena scandal confirmed peasants' and critics' concerns that the valuation provisions of the new reform law were excessive (see Cruz 1989; Hanstad 1988). Were it to adopt an aggressive proreform posture, the DAR could, through selective emphasis of the valuation variables, effectuate a significant redistribution of wealth.[6] The Philippine Supreme Court appeared to validate the constitutionality of such an approach in its 1989 ruling in *Association of Small Landowners* v. *Secretary of Agrarian Reform*. Instead, the DAR compounded the legislative flaws by adopting valuation regulations in March 1989 that effectively set the total land value at *133 percent* of market value.[7] During the summer of 1989, the DAR considered a valuation formula tied to the income produced by the property, with the aim of both simplifying and rationalizing valuation. Since that time, the DAR has issued a series of administrative orders aimed primarily at making compensation more attractive to affected landowners.[8] Administrative Order No. 6 of 1992 "recalibrated" the valuation formula. Although still based on comparable sales, owner-declared value, market value, income from the land, and cost of acquisition, the new formula was expected to increase land valuations by as much as *50 percent*. This change was credited with resolving "75–80 percent" of the valuation disputes pending before the LBP. Some landowners, however, remained dissatisfied with the valuation formula (Millar 1993). Peasant organizations criticized these valuation formulas as further burdening reform beneficiaries and undermining any redistributive impact in terms of beneficiary incomes (Bacsain interview, Jan. 25, 1992).

One simple check on excessive valuations would be to treat the valuation of President Aquino's family plantation as establishing a ceiling on Philippine land values. Hacienda Luisita's lands are among the finest in the country; they are well irrigated, level, and fertile. For purposes of stock distribution, these lands were valued at P40,000 ($1,900) per hectare in 1989. If this valuation is correct, it should act as a cap on land valuations nationwide. By contrast, in 1988, the DAR adopted working figures for the reform program that assumed *average* land values of P37,000–45,000 per hectare.[9] In 1993, compensation payments averaged slightly less than P18,600 per hectare. Prime private agricultural lands had not yet been subjected to compulsory acquisition, however, so compensation payments can be expected to increase substantially as (if?) that component of the reform is more forcefully implemented (ROP, DAR 1993a: 5).

Stock Distribution on the Cojuangco Family Estate

The new law's provision on corporate stock distributions appears to violate the constitutional mandate that ownership of agricultural lands be redistributed to the regular farmworkers cultivating them. Aquino's family plantation, Hacienda Luisita, has been the most prominent subject of such stock distribution.[10] Hacienda Luisita has been frequently cited, by Aquino and others, as a model both of efficiency and of benevolent labor relations.[11] The latter characterization is disputed, however (Tavanlar interview, June 13, 1986). Of Hacienda Luisita's 6,000 plus hectares, 4,915.75 hectares were deemed to be agricultural for purposes of the reform. As of 1989, this land was valued at P196.63 million ($9.36 million at P21=$1). The non-land assets were valued at P393.92 million ($18.76 million), or two-thirds of the total value of corporate assets.[12] The worker-beneficiaries are to receive, at no *apparent* cost, their one-third minority stock shares in 30 equal annual installments, a further dilution of their benefits that seems without basis in the law. Analysis suggests that the workers would be no worse off, indeed might be substantially better off, if they were to purchase the land assets of Hacienda Luisita under the terms of the reform law rather than accept the proposed "no cost" stock distribution (Riedinger 1989; id. 1990).

Throughout her presidency, both landowners and peasants looked to Aquino's actions regarding Hacienda Luisita as a symbol of her commitment (or lack thereof) to agrarian reform. Landowners argued that, consistent with her campaign remarks, the president could not expect

them to relinquish their farm holdings if she was unwilling to redistribute her own property. Peasant representatives viewed Aquino's decision to exercise the stock-distribution option on Hacienda Luisita as further evidence of her insincerity on the reform issue.

Land Conversions

In the absence of reliable land registration and classification systems, the Philippine agrarian reform is open to potential abuses as landowners alter their landownership records and cropping patterns in an effort to avoid the reform. The issue of conversion of agricultural land to nonagricultural use came to a head coincident with the nomination of Florencio Abad to be DAR secretary. In particular, Abad attempted to block conversion of the 232-hectare government-owned Langkaan estate in Dasmariñas, Cavite, to nonagricultural uses. The government's National Development Corporation (NDC) had leased this prime agricultural land to the (Japanese) Marubeni corporation for a joint venture to develop the site for industrial use. In 1980, the Housing and Land Use Regulatory Board (HLURB) reclassified the property as industrial. During the 1990 controversy, Trade and Industry Secretary Jose Concepcion, Jr., and Justice Secretary Franklin Drilon strongly supported the conversion. In a February 14, 1990, legal opinion for Executive Secretary Catalino Macaraig, Jr., and Presidential Executive Coordinator for Economic and Financial Affairs Vicente Jayme, Drilon concluded that the DAR had no jurisdiction over land conversions that predated the reform law.[13] Drilon conceded that under several prior laws, the DAR had similar authority, but argued that this earlier authority was not exclusive—that is, it was always subject to coordination with other government agencies. Drilon went on to argue that the earlier enactments in question merely affirmed whatever prior (i.e. even earlier) authority the DAR had; they were not sources of that authority.[14] Drilon failed to identify either the original source of DAR's authority or the explicit abrogation of that authority. The shortcomings and tortured logic of Drilon's opinion notwithstanding, the Aquino and Ramos governments have treated it as dispositive on the land conversion issue.

Two referenda were held to determine the preferences of the farmers on the estate. In the first instance, those voting rejected conversion. The second referendum involved more of the farmers, and by a vote of 94 to 28 they approved the conversion on the understanding that they would receive P55,000 per hectare in disturbance compensation.[15] The 28

farmers who favored redistribution of the land under the terms of the reform program were to receive 45 hectares on the Langkaan estate and 39 hectares on the adjoining Ramos estate, as well as P8,000 in assistance. Although the government made good on the 45-hectare allotment, the land of the Ramos estate was subject to the competing claims of 100 farmers who were cultivating it. As of mid 1991, the 28 Langkaan farmers had received neither the Ramos estate allotment nor alternative land.[16] In terms of the larger reform process, however, the more important casualty of this affair was Florencio Abad's nomination for the post of DAR secretary. The withdrawal of Abad's nomination was widely regarded as symbolic of Aquino's antipathy to agrarian reform.

Another prominent instance of land conversion involved 275 hectares of agricultural land in the Cavite Export Processing Zone tilled by 200 peasant-occupants. As with the Langkaan estate, the lands in question had been reclassified as an industrial zone by proclamation of President Marcos in 1980 (CPAR 1991: 6). Other landowners sought exemption from the reform program by belatedly converting their agricultural parcels to industrial and residential sites. To facilitate government approval of the land conversion, landowners were bulldozing the parcels or dumping construction materials on them, rendering them unusable for agriculture (Cruz 1991a). Casual observations from the air also confirm concerns that large swatches of agricultural land outside of Metropolitan Manila are being prepared for residential and commercial uses. As many of the more distant conversions involve little more than paving potential residential roads, it would appear that their primary purpose is to avoid application of the agrarian reform. Land speculators are apparently willing to wait, perhaps for years, to profit from the continuing residential and commercial sprawl out from Manila. Some observers describe a major decline in area planted to rice occasioned by land speculation and conversions (Serrano interview, Feb. 21, 1994).

Of even greater concern to the peasant movement is the provision (Sec. 20) in the Local Government Code giving authority over land conversions to local governments. Citing a memo from DAR Secretary Leong to Aquino, the Kilusang Magbubukid ng Pilipinas (KMP = Peasant Movement of the Philippines) has estimated that the provision is likely to result in the reclassification of 371,000 hectares of agricultural land, which will then be exempt from the reform process (Mariano interviews, Jan. 21, 1991, and Nov. 24, 1992). Reports from the field suggest that considerable pressure is being brought to bear on munici-

pal agrarian reform officers (MAROs) to approve conversions of agricultural lands to nonagricultural purposes (Banzuela interview, Feb. 22, 1994; Tumbado et al. interview, Jan. 24, 1992). In the words of one DAR official, landowners are waging a "cold war" against MAROs on this and other reform-related issues (Biadora interview, Feb. 12, 1991). To counter these pressures, Congressman Bonifacio Gillego and others introduced a series of bills in 1993 to prohibit the conversion of irrigated and irrigable agricultural lands to nonagricultural uses (Cariño 1993e).

Leadership Problems at the Department of Agrarian Reform

From the outset of Aquino's presidency, the position of secretary of the DAR has been problematic—the nominees have typically been inexperienced in agrarian reform, and their nominations have often been delayed, if not derailed.[17] Heherson Alvarez was the last appointee to Aquino's original cabinet, named almost two months after she took office in late February 1986. A long-time opponent of Ferdinand Marcos, Alvarez had little direct experience in agriculture or agrarian reform. After a tenure marked by modest accomplishments, Alvarez resigned his post in February 1987 to run for the Philippine Senate. The secretarial post remained vacant during the critical final months of executive deliberations on the scope and nature of the reform program. Philip Juico was appointed to the post in July 1987 following Aquino's announcement of Executive Order 229. Juico at least had the benefit of participating as a Department of Agriculture undersecretary in the cabinet action committee deliberations and came from an agribusiness background. The latter qualification was of little solace to proreform peasants, as was Juico's reputation as one who would not confront the president in defense of the reform. Juico was forced from office in June 1989 following the Garchitorena land-valuation scandal. He attributed his downfall to undue deference to DAR underlings, notably undersecretaries Jose Medina, Jr., and Salvador Pejo, both of whom were holdovers from the Marcos era (as was much of the DAR staff).

Miriam Defensor-Santiago, Juico's successor, was initially welcomed by members of Congress and newspaper editorials, but she soon found her nomination in trouble. Some members of the House-Senate Commission on Appointments cited Defensor-Santiago's combative personality in explaining their opposition to her nomination. Others

cited her lack of experience with agrarian reform. The latter objection had not surfaced in the cases of Alvarez or Juico, neither of whom had notably more experience than Defensor-Santiago. Her abrasive personality appeared to be a problem primarily in terms of her lack of deference to Congress, raising the possibility that she might not heed the bidding of members who were hostile to the reform program. Indeed, in mid July 1989, Defensor-Santiago announced a potentially significant change in DAR policy, calling for expedited compulsory acquisition of farms over 50 hectares (Ferriols 1989). Although fully consistent with the provisions of the reform law, this thrust was at considerable odds with her predecessors' focus on the less controversial elements of the reform—completion of Marcos's reform of rice and corn tenancy (PD 27), distribution of public lands, and solicitation of voluntary offers of sale. In adopting this new posture, Defensor-Santiago threatened the interests of the landed elite, and their henchmen in Congress quickly set about derailing her appointment (see McBeth 1989b). Although President Aquino made clear her desire that Defensor-Santiago be confirmed, Congress continued to balk until the nomination was withdrawn in December 1989.[18]

In the aftermath of the nearly successful military coup attempt of early December 1989, Aquino substantially revamped her cabinet, including naming Congressman Florencio B. Abad as the new secretary-designate of the DAR. As a member of the nationalist bloc that had introduced the most radical reform bill in the House, Abad was expected to be very sympathetic to the reform cause, and he moved quickly to improve relations between the DAR and peasant organizations. His most controversial act, however, was to contest the conversion of the government-owned Langkaan estate to nonagricultural uses. Landowners' opposition to Abad's nomination resulted in another protracted confirmation battle, and he eventually withdrew in the face of stiff congressional opposition led by Aquino's brother, Jose Cojuangco, Jr. Equally important to Abad's withdrawal was the declining evidence of support from the president. In a significant blow to the agrarian reform, Aquino sided with Secretary of Justice Franklin Drilon and Secretary of Trade and Industry Jose Concepcion, Jr., in upholding the reclassification of the Langkaan estate (Anda and Pastor 1990; *Asian Wall Street Journal* 1990; de Guzman 1990; Jara 1990).

Aquino's repeated inability to win the necessary congressional support for approval of her nominees to the DAR secretariat in part re-

flected her continuing refusal to institutionalize her public support or participate in party politics. The dominant party in the House of Representatives at the time, the Laban ng Demokratikong Pilipino (LDP), claimed to support the president and her reform agenda, but it led the fight against the nominations of both Defensor-Santiago and Abad. Some observers suggested a different explanation for the failed nominations. In this view, Aquino desired the popular goodwill attendant on naming tough, proreform DAR secretaries, but was unwilling to see such nominations through to approval because of her underlying ambivalence, if not hostility, toward agrarian reform (Abad interview, Mar. 25, 1994).

In April 1990, Aquino named Benjamin T. Leong acting secretary and indicated that Leong would serve in that capacity for the remainder of her administration so as to avoid another congressional showdown (Anda 1990). Leong's nomination was in fact later submitted to, and confirmed by, the congressional Commission on Appointments. Legislators cited Leong's previous experience in the DAR—he was appointed undersecretary for policy and planning under Juico—and his noncombative, uncontroversial personality in explaining their support for his nomination. Congressman Edcel Lagman, then chair of the House Committee on Agrarian Reform, was less enthusiastic, characterizing Leong as neither pro-landlord nor pro-peasant. In Lagman's view, the DAR secretary must be pro-peasant to be an effective advocate for reform (CPAR 1991: 9). Leong served as DAR secretary through the end of the Aquino administration in June 1992.

President Fidel Ramos, elected in May 1992 to succeed Aquino, appointed Ernesto D. Garilao as DAR secretary. Garilao had 21 years of experience with Philippine Business for Social Progress (PBSP), one of the most prominent—if elite-based—NGOs in the Philippines.[19] He had also worked on agrarian reform in Negros Occidental, utilizing DAR resources and PBSP personnel to conduct "social preparation" activities on haciendas offered for voluntary sale to DAR (Bulatao interview, Feb. 16, 1994), and he brought with him a number of senior staff with extensive NGO experience.[20] Garilao has given greater emphasis than his predecessors to the reform's impact on its beneficiaries, devoting considerable energy to consolidating the economic gains of existing beneficiaries (Garilao 1992; Mejorada 1993). Although it is understandable and consistent with the development thrust of NGOs such as the PBSP, a DAR secretary not fully committed to redistributive reform

could use such an approach to redefine agrarian reform and slow land redistribution, but in Garilao's case, land transfers have not suffered as a consequence.

Legal Challenges to the Reform Law

Despite the modest scope of the new reform law, disgruntled land-owners have repeatedly challenged its constitutionality. The Philippine Supreme Court initially rebuffed these efforts, but over time it has appreciably narrowed the scope of the reform. In its first ruling, the court upheld the law by distinguishing the taking of property under the agrarian-reform program from the traditional exercise of the government power of eminent domain, deeming the former "revolutionary" expropriation and thus exempt from the standard of payment entirely in cash. At the same time, the court ruled that compensation, whatever its form, must be paid in full to the affected landowner before the DAR could transfer title to the reform beneficiaries.[21] This portion of the decision promised to slow the reform process dramatically. The vast majority—80 percent by one estimate—of affected landowners were contesting their land valuations, potentially delaying issuance of compensation and completion of the reform (Vistan interview, Feb. 20, 1991). The DAR sidestepped the problem by exercising its authority, under Section 16(e) of the reform law, to deposit compensation awards—in cash and bonds—in trust accounts pending resolution of valuation disputes. In early 1994, a case that would prevent the DAR from depositing compensation payments in this fashion until the landowner had exhausted all valuation challenges was pending before the Supreme Court. Were the court to rule in favor of the landowner-complainants, it would severely hamper, if not halt, implementation of the reform on private agricultural lands, as landowners spent years litigating land valuations.

In late 1990, the Supreme Court restricted the scope of the reform by exempting commercial livestock, poultry, and swine operations on the grounds that these enterprises were capital-dependent industries rather than land-based agricultural enterprises.[22] The ruling exempted an estimated 400,000 hectares of rural land from the reform process. The ruling also created incentives for landowners illegally to shift from crop production to livestock, poultry, or swine. In 1991, there were news accounts of Mindanao coconut producers felling their trees and switching to poultry raising (Cruz 1991b).

Finally, in a case involving Central Mindanao University, the court adopted an expansive reading of the law's exemption of school lands from the reform process. The court overturned the DAR's redistribution of university-owned lands to those who farmed them.[23] On the positive side, this ruling is unlikely to increase the scope for private landowner evasion of the reform law.

Congressional Challenges to the Reform Law

Opponents of the reform law have repeatedly introduced bills to amend it. Among the various bills have been proposals for decentralization of the reform program; exemption of all commercial farms; exemption of aquaculture and prawn farms; exemption of livestock, poultry, and swine raising operations (eventually achieved through a court ruling); suspension of land reform in Mindanao until the year 2020 to facilitate industrialization; exemption of lands in the Calabarzon region for the same reason; extension of the filing deadline for corporations to avail themselves of the stock-distribution option; and exemption of industrial tree plantations from the reform.[24] During the second half of the Aquino administration, the House Agrarian Reform Committee chair, Edcel Lagman, a strong proponent of reform, kept many of these bills tied up in his committee. Following the 1992 elections, similar bills were filed in the new Congress. The new committee chair, Roger Mercado, is reputed to be less fervent in his support of agrarian reform.

That few of these amendments have made any headway may simply reflect inaction on the part of the current House and Senate committees. Alternatively, landowners and their supporters in Congress may find that the *threat* posed by these amendments is sufficient to derail or slow the reform process. Or landowners may be enjoying such success evading application of the reform law, that passage of the amendments is unnecessary. Finally, legislators may be concerned about the political fallout of being identified as antireform were they to pass some of these amendments (Gillego interview, Feb. 17, 1994; Serrano interview, Feb. 21, 1994; Soliman interview, Feb. 22, 1994).

The Retention Limit Revisited

The new Philippine agrarian reform law left open the possibility that the Presidential Agrarian Reform Council (PARC) could set a retention

limit under five hectares, were it to determine that smaller holdings constituted "viable family-sized" farms.[25] Section 25 of the law limited reform beneficiaries to a maximum of three hectares, suggesting three hectares might be taken as an appropriate measure of the viable family-sized farm under Philippine conditions. The PARC could set landowner retention limits at the same 3-hectare maximum and appreciably expand the land area available for reform.[26] The retention limit for children was also couched in terms allowing for PARC action setting a lower limit.

This administrative discretion heightened the importance of strong, proreform leadership from the Philippine president and the secretary of the DAR. With strong executive support, the scope of the reform could be significantly expanded within the framework of the 1988 law (Abad interview, Jan. 15, 1992; Bulatao interview, Feb. 16, 1994; Gillego interview, Feb. 6, 1991). This flexibility explained part of the landowner opposition to the appointment of Florencio Abad as DAR secretary. Abad understood the opportunity afforded by the law and made clear his intention to pursue the reform to its fullest extent (Abad interviews, June 21, 1989, and Jan. 15, 1992; Resurreccion 1990). Antireform forces in the Philippine legislature stonewalled Abad's nomination, eventually forcing his withdrawal.

There is no evidence that the PARC, as currently configured, will establish lower limits for either the owners' retention areas or those of their children. Reducing the landowners' right of retention from five to three hectares more than doubles the number of landowners potentially affected by the reform, considerably increasing the prospect of political backlash.[27] In strict numerical terms, the political trade-off involved in reducing landowners' retention rights from five hectares to three hectares would appear favorable. The ratio of additional beneficiaries served by the reform to additional landowners affected by the reform is, by my rough calculations, more than 2:1. In the cases of Japan and Taiwan, where many petty landlords with holdings of five hectares or less were subject to postwar reform programs, the ratios of beneficiaries to affected landowners were roughly 2:1 and 1.8:1 respectively.[28] However, political calculations are made of more than sheer numbers; the continued support of the (more socially and economically influential) affected landowners weighs much more heavily on the minds of most Philippine politicians than the potential electoral support of the additional reform beneficiaries.

Peasant Initiatives

Responding to the flawed reform law, the Congress for a People's Agrarian Reform launched a nationwide signature campaign for a national referendum on its alternative People's Agrarian Reform Code (PARCode) in July 1988.[29] This reform proposal set a single 5-hectare retention limit, eliminated the deferment for commercial estates, established a program of selective and progressive compensation, and credited beneficiaries with the value of land rentals and uncompensated labor from the outset of their tenancy relations, reducing their repayment obligations accordingly. The PARCode initiative was supported by important elements of the Catholic Church (see Bishops-Grassroots Dialogue 1988). Over 500,000 of the estimated 2.5–3.0 million signatures needed were gathered before the campaign was effectively abandoned in the early 1990s.

The campaign's greatest achievement may have been its role as a vehicle for education and democratic mobilization of the peasantry (Juliano-Soliman and Ramiro interview, June 30, 1989; Modina interview, Oct. 17, 1988). Democratic grassroots organizational activities had been limited by years of martial law, human rights abuses, and exclusionary political practices. At the same time, a substantial violent left— the NPA—continued to opt out of the political process. In consequence, CPAR's leaders acknowledged their continuing political weakness even before they disbanded in late 1993, holding out little hope that they would be able to pressure the Philippine Congress into adopting progressive amendments to the reform.

Within the framework of the existing law, some peasant organizations have begun direct negotiations with the DAR for the purchase of lands foreclosed by government banking institutions. The DAR is perceived by peasant organizations to be favorably disposed to such land acquisitions and willing to make concessions on land valuation. Organizations such as National Federation of Sugar Workers (NFSW) provide legal and other assistance to erstwhile sugar workers contemplating land purchases, in the process attracting new adherents.[30] With or without government sanction, NFSW members occupied over 8,700 hectares of foreclosed lands between 1986 and 1990. Members of the KMP were similarly active in occupying foreclosed properties. All together, peasants claimed to have occupied roughly 49,000 hectares in Negros, out of

an estimated 208,000 hectares of foreclosed farms.[31] The NFSW was also enjoying modest success effectuating land transfers in the case of "idle and abandoned" properties—that is, properties on which the land-owner had abandoned cultivation, often for reasons of its marginality and the threat posed by communist insurgents.

One of the most promising peasant initiatives involves cooperation between people's (peasant) organizations (POs), nongovernmental organizations (NGOs), and government organizations (GOs) in the implementation of the reform program. This program is supported and advised at the national level by NGO representatives, rural development scholars, and former DAR officials affiliated with Kaisahan Tungo sa Kaunlaran ng Kanayunan at Repormang Pansakahan (KAISAHAN = Solidarity Toward Countryside Development and Agrarian Reform). The Tripartite Partnership for Agrarian Reform and Rural Development (TriPARRD) was launched in 1989 in the provinces of Antique (Visayas), Bukidnon (Mindanao), and Camarines Sur (Luzon).[32] TriPARRD was initiated by the Philippine Partnership for the Development of Human Resources in Rural Areas (PhilDHRRA) with modest support from the Ford Foundation's Manila office.[33] With little "push" for implementation of the reform coming from the DAR, PhilDHRRA concluded that NGOs and POs would have to provide the "pull" (demand) for implementation (Korten interview, Feb. 6, 1991). This reflected a strategic decision to work with the DAR within the framework of the new law, however flawed, rather than denounce the government and obstruct implementation of the law.

The TriPARRD program involves land redistribution, community organizing, productivity enhancement utilizing local and foreign resources, and partnership between the community, NGOs, and a variety of government line agencies.[34] By mid 1990, the program had begun trial application of this tripartite approach in 28 communities. By early 1992, TriPARRD personnel were expecting to expand the program to Davao, Leyte, and Quezon provinces.

For its part, the DAR identified roughly 20 provinces with the greatest potential scope of coverage under the new law as priority areas in 1990 (Amio 1989; Juico interview, Oct. 14, 1988). However, the practical effect of this designation was not readily apparent at the time, as there was little evident acceleration of the reform process in these areas. Three years later, the DAR increased the number of strategic operating provinces to 28 (DAR 1993c: 4). At year-end 1993, the DAR had launched 256 agrarian reform communities (ARCs) and anticipated ini-

tiating another 264 in 1994. The aim is to establish 1,000 ARCs by the year 2000 in a massive replication of the TriPARRD model (Cariño 1993d; ROP, DAR 1993a: 6, 11).

The program's principal success has been in expediting local implementation of agrarian reform. Land valuation has been the most controversial issue in the reform process on the project estates. Nonetheless, project participants report that agrarian reform claims folders that had been "sleeping" at the municipal level for two to five years had been forwarded to, and in many cases approved by, the regional and national DAR offices (San Antonio interview, Jan. 24, 1992). A more complex problem confronted the TriPARRD program on three estates in Camarines Sur—namely, the occupation of the estates by persons other than the rightful farmer-beneficiaries.[35]

The TriPARRD model appears particularly effective in settings where peasants are well organized and assertive, local NGOs are capable and committed to agrarian reform, and the local government and line agency officials are supportive of the reform process. The success of the TriPARRD program explains part of the cautious optimism expressed by some proponents of agrarian reform when they are discussing the decentralization of government activities under the new Local Government Code.

Where they do not exist, POs have been established with the assistance of NGO community organizers and then registered with the government. The POs, whether new or preexisting, meet regularly with PhilDHRRA or cooperating national peasant organizations, several of which are CPAR members. One aim of the program is for POs to establish their own voice, to assert themselves vis-à-vis the NGOs and government agencies and to monitor the project's community organizers. At several sites, project NGOs have been replaced at the request of POs dissatisfied with their performance. Eventually, it is expected that the POs will contract directly for NGO services.

For all its success, the TriPARRD model is not without problems. There is continuing distrust between some local DAR officials and the project NGOs.[36] There is also a considerable disjuncture between the locations the DAR has selected to be accelerated agrarian reform communities and the communities in which NGOs are presently working. NGO flexibility is constrained by existing commitments to donor-funded projects and a lack of resources. Philippine NGOs are experiencing problems in "scaling up." At issue is their absorptive capacity in terms of skilled management and technical personnel. As NGOs take on

larger projects, their original project staff must assume managerial responsibilities. Crucial community organizing work falls to less experienced staff, often at a significant cost in effectiveness. The TriPARRD program now requires that all participating NGOs undergo a process of organizational development. Even this is frustrated by high turnover in NGO personnel. Of the twenty-four community organizers trained in 1990, only six were still with the program in early 1994 (Banzuela interview, Feb. 22, 1994).

Peasant-Sector Unity and Disunity

The years since the promulgation of the reform law have been marked by episodes of remarkable unity within the peasant sector and, more recently, notable disunity. One of Florencio Abad's first acts as DAR secretary-designate was to foster unity among the peasant organizations and give them a greater voice in DAR policy deliberations. Abad's actions provided the impetus for the creation of the Peasants Forum, a loose alliance of the three peasant sector organizations— CPAR, the FFF, and SANDUGUAN (the National Farmers Supreme Council, a government-sponsored confederation of Marcos-era reform beneficiaries and cooperative members). Officially founded at the February 10, 1990, All-Leaders Peasant conference, the Peasants Forum grew out of a multisectoral effort to address the National Food Authority's low support price—the government-guaranteed floor price—for rice.[37] As the member organizations represented divergent political perspectives, the Peasants Forum functioned primarily as a medium for exploring issues of common concern. There were considerable differences of opinion on the critical issues of agrarian reform, forms of land ownership, and relations with the Aquino government. Nonetheless, the Peasants Forum reached a series of agreements, including the Magna Carta of Peasants.[38] On March 31 and May 8–9, 1990, the Peasants Forum conducted workshops to promote understanding of and support for CPAR's PARCode. Peasants Forum members began building cross-sectoral support for their Peasants Agenda for National Unity and Survival at a May 22–23, 1990, Conference on Agrarian Reform and Rural Development Towards National Development.

Despite these agreements and coordinated actions, the tensions within the Peasants Forum eventually led to its dissolution. During the Abad nomination controversy, SANDUGUAN broke ranks with the other member organizations that had refused invitations to meet with

the president in protest of her mishandling of the Abad appointment. However, the forum continued to function formally until mid December 1990, when the FFF withdrew, complaining that the formation of local chapters of the Peasants Forum in Mindanao undermined the FFF's national organization. The FFF agreed to continue meeting with the other organizations outside of the Peasants Forum framework (Juliano-Soliman 1993: 301–2; Mariano interview, Feb. 8, 1991).

The history of the CPAR exhibits a similar pattern of surprising unity ultimately giving way to the ideological differences among the member organizations. The most prominent and effective alliance supporting genuine agrarian reform within a democratic context, the CPAR functioned from May 1987 until October 1993. The most divisive issues among CPAR members concerned the appropriate posture toward the new reform law and the regionalization of the organization. At issue in the first instance was the choice between promoting the PARCode versus promoting local action within the framework of the reform law. The KMP consistently adopted a public posture of "total rejection" of the reform law, although in private it was willing to "use the [law's] provisions wisely" (Mariano interviews, Jan. 21, 1992, and Nov. 24, 1992; also Soliman interview, Feb. 22, 1994). The KMP also rejected the policies of the Aquino and Ramos governments with respect to foreign debt, U.S. military basing rights, and various sectoral issues. Less militant CPAR members—among them KASAMA and LAKAS—preferred a posture of "critical support" for the Aquino and Ramos governments, pressing both governments to improve the reform law while working to maximize its implementation.

The second issue of contention within the CPAR concerned the decision to establish regional CPAR offices in Mindanao, the Visayas, and Luzon. This initiative, launched in 1989–90, was intended to build local coalitions in support of the PARCode and the cause of genuine agrarian reform, as well as to enhance the CPAR's ability to assist farmers at the local level in their struggles for land and support services. The KMP in particular challenged the regionalization initiative out of concern that the process undermined the national member organizations, that the CPAR national secretariat could not effectively direct the activities of local CPAR personnel, and that such regional bodies reflected an unnecessary proliferation of CPAR staff (Mariano interview, Nov. 24, 1992).

The demise of the Peasants Forum and CPAR has meant a substantial weakening of the peasant "voice" in current policy debates on agrarian reform. Individual peasant organizations continue to press

their causes. Missing, however, is the relative unity over strategies and aims that was critical, for example, to CPAR's ability to influence congressional deliberations and local implementation. The factional infighting in the CPP/NPA has similarly undermined its influence, removing a "check" on the militant right and reducing the urgency accorded to social reform on the part of Philippine elites.

The Current Status of the Agrarian Reform Program

Assessing the performance of the Aquino and Ramos administrations in implementing agrarian reform is complicated by changes in the baseline (cumulative performance through the end of the Marcos regime), changing reporting practices and reporting periods, and over-reporting.[39] By my reading of DAR data, a total of somewhat under 315,000 hectares had been acquired for distribution to roughly 168,000 families as of the end of 1985. By another accounting, which credits the Marcos government with far less redistribution of tenanted rice and corn lands, the DAR and its predecessor organizations had transferred 125,955 hectares of agricultural land to 46,384 beneficiaries as of the end of 1985.[40] DAR Secretary Garilao's office credits pre-Aquino administrations with distributing less than 64,000 hectares (ROP, DAR 1993e: 1). These less charitable interpretations of pre-1986 performance serve to inflate the accomplishments of the Aquino and Ramos governments.[41] Such data as are available on the reform accomplishments of the Aquino and Ramos administrations are presented in Table 8.

Land-Redistribution Achievements

Operation Land Transfer is the Marcos-era program to redistribute land to rice and corn tenants whose landlords held more than seven hectares. Renewed commitment to completing the Operation Land Transfer program, and several administrative changes in the titling process, have resulted in substantial progress in distributing Emancipation Patents (EPs) under the Aquino and Ramos governments. Expedited issuance of EPs has also been facilitated by the preparatory activities of the Marcos administration, notably the cumulated land surveys and previously generated EPs (Bulatao 1992: 7; ROP, DAR 1987b: 9). In the period July 1, 1987–December 31, 1993, EPs covering 420,848 hectares were distributed. Between them the Aquino and Ramos governments had completed 57.9 percent of the planned reform of rice and corn lands

by year-end 1993 (see Table 7). This element of the reform accounted for 20.3 percent of the land area for which ownership has been distributed (public lands) or redistributed (private lands) in this period.

The new reform law provides both voluntary and compulsory mechanisms for redistribution of private agricultural lands. All together 259,312 hectares of private agricultural lands were redistributed in the period July 1, 1987 to December 31, 1993. This represents 11.3 percent of the target set by the DAR for that element of the reform program. Private agricultural lands accounted for 12.5 percent of the total land area distributed in this period. The most recent year for which disaggregated data are available is 1992. In that year, 15,619 hectares (18.2 percent) were acquired by compulsory acquisition, 49,576 hectares (57.8 percent) were acquired through voluntary offers to sell, and 20,597 hectares (24 percent) were acquired through voluntary land transfers. If these ratios hold true for the cumulative accomplishments, then compulsory acquisition has accounted for a little over 2 percent of the reform program as implemented through year-end 1993.[42]

DAR officials offer a variety of justifications for the slow pace of the compulsory acquisition program. By some accounts, the agency is overwhelmed with the administrative demands of distributing lands owned by government financial institutions (GFIs) and processing voluntary offers of sale (Adversario interview, Jan. 29, 1992). Others blame the complex valuation and compensation requirements or the difficulties of coordinating the DAR's actions with those of the LBP (Bueno interview, Feb. 4, 1992; Miranda and Yongque interview, Feb. 12, 1991). Certainly this is the most controversial element of the reform program.

Whatever the explanations for the almost complete avoidance of compulsory acquisition to date, the DAR will have to devote almost all of its energy to this component of the reform program during 1994–98. To achieve the reform target of redistributing 1.89 million hectares through compulsory acquisition, the DAR will have to distribute roughly 365,000–370,000 hectares per year. Put differently, during 1994–98, the DAR must redistribute more land each year for this single component of the reform program than it distributed annually for all elements of the reform program during 1987–92.[43] Instead, DAR Secretary Garilao has chosen to emphasize the reform of rice and corn lands, the Resettlement and Landed Estates programs, and voluntarily offered lands, in the hope of completing these programs by 1995 (ROP, DAR 1993a: 11).

The Landed Estates Program involves government acquisition of

TABLE 8

Summary of Accomplishments Under Philippine Land-Reform Programs July 1, 1987 to December 31, 1993

Program	1987	1988	1989	1990	1991	1992	1993	Total
PD 27 (1972)								
Operation Land Transfer[a]								
(a) EPs[b] distributed	35,027	106,254	221,736	103,644	48,028	—	—	—
(b) Area (ha)	25,554	100,941	201,261	83,697	34,798	31,747	33,958	420,848
(c) Beneficiaries	—	75,559	138,904	70,787	32,534	—	—	—
CA 539 (1940; as amended)								
Landed Estates / Resettlement								
(a) HPs[d] distributed	439	10,764	9,564	35,038	—	—	—	—
(b) Area (ha)	1,193	11,345	37,153	148,655	85,877	65,224	77,866	370,500
(c) Beneficiaries	234	5,809	5,745	75,073	30,105	—	—	—
RA 3844 (1963; as amended)								
Operation Leasehold[e]								
(a) Lease Contracts	6,037	—	—	—	77,225	58,165	—	—
(b) Area (ha)	3,459	—	43,439	28,726	85,282	57,514	—	—
(c) Beneficiaries	4,864	—	18,720	24,389	76,851	51,519	—	—
RA 6657 (1988)								
Leasehold Program								
(a) Lease Contracts	—	—	—	—	102,490	68,548	—	—
(b) Area (ha)	—	—	—	43,439	181,878	131,577	122,302	683,491
(c) Beneficiaries	—	—	—	18,720	94,053	62,228	72,447	428,075

Government-owned Lands								
(a) CLOAs[f] distributed	297	243	2,196	8,857	16,423	–	191,312	–
(b) Area (ha)	136	21,787	10,187	61,075	126,995	89,173	–	431,440
(c) Beneficiaries	–	–	–	–	54,691	–	–	–
Private Lands:								
Compulsory Acquisition								
(a) CLOAs distributed	–	–	–	–	1,801	15,619	–	–
(b) Area (ha)	–	–	–	–	10,904	–	–	–
(c) Beneficiaries	–	–	–	–	4,620	–	–	–
Voluntary Offers of Sale								
(a) CLOAs[f] distributed	–	–	–	–	6,381	49,516	109,082	259,312
(b) Area (ha)	–	–	–	–	27,083	–	–	–
(c) Beneficiaries	–	–	–	–	13,805	–	–	–
Voluntary Land Transfer								
(a) CLOAs[f] distributed	–	–	–	–	4,909	–	–	–
(b) Area (ha)	–	–	–	–	14,444	20,597	–	–
(c) Beneficiaries	–	–	–	–	9,300	–	–	–
Public Alienable & Disposable Lands								
(a) FPs[g] Issued	61,354	62,233	16,521	43,503	–	–	–	–
(b) Area (ha)	163,815	166,162	42,459	111,803	–	–	39,082	595,442
(c) Beneficiaries	61,354	62,233	16,521	43,503	–	–	–	–

SOURCES: Department of Agrarian Reform, *Accomplishment Report CY-1987* (Manila, n.d.); id., *Accomplishment Report, 1988,* (Manila, n.d.); id., *1989 CARP Accomplishment Report* (Manila, n.d.); id., *Comprehensive Agrarian Reform Program, 1990 Year-End Accomplishment Report* (Manila, n.d.); id., *1991 Accomplishment Report* (Manila, n.d.); id., *1992 Accomplishment Report* (Manila, n.d.); id., *1993 Accomplishment Report* (Manila, n.d.).

NOTES: Entries do *not* add to total; total reflects cumulative performance as presented in Department of Agrarian Reform, *1993 Accomplishment Report* (Manila, n.d.). In the many cases of discrepancies in the data, the revised data found in later DAR reports have been used. The many missing values reflect DAR's changing reporting practices and reporting periods, and DAR's failure to consistently present the same types of data in each report.

[a] Operation Land Transfer redistributed tenanted rice and corn holdings to landless tenant cultivators.

[b] Emancipating patents (equivalent to final title).

[c] Certificate of land transfer.

[d] Certificate of land ownership award.

[e] Operation Leasehold provided for the transformation of share tenancy to leasehold (fixed rent) tenancy.

[f] Homestead patents.

[g] Fee patents.

large private estates for redistribution to the tenant cultivators. The Resettlement Program involves relocating farm families from areas of acute landlessness and near-landlessness to public lands. Both programs were introduced in 1940. Together these programs distributed 370,500 hectares between July 1, 1987 and December 31, 1993. This achievement is 77.4 percent of the goal for 1987–97. These programs accounted for 17.8 percent of all lands distributed since July 1987. The most recent year for which disaggregated data are available is 1992. In that year, 49,487 hectares (75.9 percent) were distributed under the Resettlement Program, 15,737 hectares (24.1 percent) under the Landed Estates Program.

Three types of land are included under the rubric of government-owned lands: idle and abandoned, sequestered (those acquired by the Philippine Commission on Good Government from Marcos cronies), and lands owned by government corporations or financial institutions. In aggregate, 431,440 hectares of such government-owned lands were distributed in the period July 1987–December 1993. This represented an achievement of 131.9 percent of the program goal for 1987–97. These government-owned lands accounted for 20.8 percent of the land area distributed for this period.

Considerable controversy has surrounded "lease-back" arrangements on some of the redistributed government-owned lands. On government-owned lands leased to transnational corporations (TNCs), employee-beneficiaries of the reform program were encouraged to form corporations and then lease their farms back to the TNCs. In theory, this arrangement enabled the employee-beneficiaries to retain stable employment while securing additional income in the form of rental payments. It was also expected that rent levels would increase relative to the modest rents previously paid to the Philippine government. As a practical matter, lease-back arrangements enabled TNCs to skirt the reform program's limitations on landownership and leasing of government-owned lands.[44]

Lease-back arrangements by Del Monte Philippines and Dole Philippines gained particular notoriety early in the reform program. Both TNCs operated substantial pineapple plantations—8,700 hectares and 8,964 hectares respectively—in Mindanao on lands leased from the Philippine government. Shortly after the reform law was passed, the DAR targeted these plantations for rapid implementation of the reform—they were to be showcases of President Aquino's commitment to the reform and, it would appear, Philippine nationalism (*Business World* 1988; Flo-

resca 1988). Under pressure from the DAR to expedite the process, leaders of the resident unions on the Del Monte plantation selected— rather than putting to a vote of the members—a group of incorporators, who promptly approved DAR-drafted articles of incorporation on December 1, 1988. Union leaders were barred from leadership positions in the new cooperative, a stricture that did not apply to management personnel. In the event, the Del Monte plantation cooperative was heavily influenced, if not controlled by, management (Putzel 1992: 339–40).

On February 21, 1989, the cooperative board entered into a 25-year growers' contract with Del Monte at an initial rent of P1,500 per hectare, with a guaranteed production bonus equivalent to P200 per hectare and an agreement that Del Monte would pay all property taxes, bringing the total payment per hectare to just under P1,800. The rent was to increase by 7 percent each year. Del Monte and the cooperative board defended this rent level by comparing it to the P776 rent Del Monte previously paid to the government's National Development Corporation per hectare (CPAR 1989: 68). Nonetheless, DAR Secretary Juico rejected the leaseback agreement on the grounds that the rent was too low and the term of the contract was too long.

In the case of the Dole plantation, the employee union, the National Federation of Labour, was an affiliate of the militant Kilusang Mayo Uno (KMU = May First Movement). Vehemently objecting to the first DAR-sponsored election of incorporators, which had heavily favored management, the union obtained a second election, in which management was to be all but excluded from the board. In contrast to the experience at the Del Monte plantation, the union-dominated cooperative board on the Dole plantation rejected management's rental offers, insisting on a 3-year contract, an initial rent of P7,000 per hectare, a share of the net profits, employment security, and an allocation of 300 hectares (Putzel 1992: 344). Dole refused to meet these terms, and the matter went unresolved for several years, as did the Del Monte plantation case, which the DAR had linked to the Dole case.

In late 1990 and early 1991 respectively, Del Monte and Dole Philippines settled their disputes with the reform beneficiaries and the DAR. The terms of the 10-year leases included initial rental payments of P3,000 per hectare, annual rent increases of 7 percent, a guaranteed minimum annual production bonus of P200 per hectare, and payment of property taxes by the lessee (Bancod 1990; id. 1991a).

The Department of Environment and Natural Resources (DENR) is responsible for administering the distribution of alienable and dispos-

able public lands under the new reform law. From July 1987 to December 1993, the DENR distributed 595,442 hectares of public lands, or 28.7 percent of the cumulative land area, public and private, redistributed during that period. This achievement represents 13 percent of the program goal for 1987–97. In late 1993, the DENR indicated that another 1.2 million hectares of alienable and disposable public lands had been surveyed and were ready for distribution (Cariño 1993h).

Non–Land Distribution Programs

Operation Leasehold—which dates from 1963, with revisions in 1971—was designed to convert share tenancies to fixed-rent leaseholds. On paper Operation Leasehold had exceeded its goals by 1985. Even so, Operation Leasehold and a leasehold program introduced under the new reform law reached an additional 428,075 beneficiaries, with 683,491 hectares, in the period July 1987 to year-end 1993. The most recent year for which disaggregated data are available is 1992. In that year, 51,519 beneficiaries (45.3 percent) and 57,514 hectares (30.4 percent) were covered by Operation Leasehold. The new leasehold program reached 62,228 beneficiaries (54.7 percent) and 131,577 hectares (69.6 percent). There is a dramatic difference between the two programs in terms of average parcel size: 1.12 hectares under Operation Leasehold, 2.11 hectares under the new leasehold program. The average parcel size for Operation Leasehold beneficiaries appears to have remained relatively constant over the years, at least judging from cumulative program accomplishments as of 1985 (1.07 hectares) and calendar-year accomplishments for 1992 (1.12 hectares).

The Integrated Social Forestry Program does not involve the redistribution of title to land. Instead, beneficiaries are awarded usufruct rights in the form of 25-year Certificates of Stewardship Contracts (CSCs). These rights are renewable once, for an additional 25 years, conditional on proper care for the forest area. As of year-end 1993, the DENR had issued CSCs for a total of 580,116 hectares, or 30.9 percent of the program goal for 1987–97.

Through the end of 1993, the stock-distribution program had elicited applications from 88 corporations. Eight of these corporations were subsequently exempted from the reform program by virtue of the Supreme Court's ruling in *Luz Farms* v. *Secretary of the Department of Agrarian Reform*. Of the remaining 80 applications, 13—affecting 8,946 farmworker-beneficiaries (FWBs) and 8,288 hectares—had been approved

by the Presidential Agrarian Reform Council. Another 19 applications—affecting 1,811 FWBs and 2,624 hectares—were either pending PARC executive committee consideration or had received committee approval. Twelve applications—affecting 3,603 FWBs and 5,701 hectares—had been disapproved, and another 17 applications—affecting 789 FWBs and 2,851 hectares—were disallowed for late filing. Sixteen applications affecting 9,330 FWBs and 5,315 hectares were withdrawn (ROP, DAR 1993b: Summary of SDO).

Production and profit-sharing arrangements had been adopted by 57 corporations as of year-end 1993. A total of 56,326 FWBs and 52,739 hectares were covered by these arrangements. For the period July 1987–December 1993, these FWBs received P321.3 million in profit and production distributions. In 1993, they were to receive over P58.7 million in profit distributions, but in practice, only 44 of the 57 corporations (77 percent) were in compliance with their statutory obligations. The FWBs had received just under P49.4 million (84 percent) of the amount owed them (ROP, DAR 1993b: Status on Production and Profit Sharing).

Reform Implementation in Negros Occidental

By 1994, Negros Occidental had come to be regarded as one of the leading provinces in terms of the DAR's performance in implementing the reform program. In 1993, a total of 24,261 hectares of public and private land were distributed in Negros, second only to the distribution of 25,349 hectares in Cagayan (ROP, DAR 1993b: Top 10 Performing Provinces). In 1992, the most recent year for which disaggregated data are available, the DAR distributed 6,858 hectares.[45] Voluntary offers of sale accounted for 4,052 hectares, or well over half (59.1 percent) of the total redistributed land area. Compulsory acquisition, a distant third as a source of redistributed land in Negros Occidental in 1992, encompassed 795 hectares (11.6 percent). Reflecting the dominance of sugar production in the province, only 359 hectares (5.2 percent) were distributed under Operation Land Transfer. Government-owned lands accounted for another 1,503 hectares (21.9 percent) of the total. The Resettlement Program distributed 149 hectares (2.2 percent).

Apparently favorable compensation arrangements, coupled in some cases with the difficulties of farming marginal lands in conflicted areas, have prompted a number of Negros landowners to offer their farms for voluntary acquisition. As of year-end 1993, compulsory acquisition had played a larger role in Negros than nationally, a reflection in part of the

large landholdings in the province. This progress represents a break, however modest to date, with the province's history of avoiding redistributive reform. It is too early, however, to write off the sugar bloc. The DAR still confronts considerable obstacles to completion of the reform process in Negros.

The Reform Agenda for 1994–1998

In the final five years (1994–98) of scheduled implementation of the reform program, the DAR and the DENR will have to distribute titles or CSCs to roughly 7.64 million hectares if the various program goals are to be attained. Of this total, the DAR will be responsible for redistributing 2.34 million hectares of private agricultural lands, and the DENR will be responsible for distributing 5.3 million hectares of public lands. By the DAR's calculation, the leasehold program must also be extended to more than 213,160 beneficiaries on nearly 404,550 hectares (ROP, DAR 1993c: 6). The Ramos government and the DAR have sent conflicting signals concerning their intention to complete the reform by 1998. Ramos has expressed his hope that the reform will be completed by that date (Reuters News Service 1993). Senior DAR officials, on the other hand, have expressed skepticism that the goal can be met (Cariño 1993a; id. 1993c).

The Politics of Agrarian Reform Revisited

The Aquino and Ramos governments have made notable progress in implementing the Marcos-era reform of tenanted rice and corn lands and in distributing public lands. Compulsory acquisition of other croplands has lagged badly, even by the standards of the circumscribed land-reform law. The Aquino and Ramos governments felt it necessary to undertake some measure of agrarian reform in response to the political pressures generated by the insurgency and by peasant organizations who took advantage of the opening of democratic political space, however modest. Not surprisingly, both governments elected to implement the least contentious and least costly elements of the reform program. Most of the reform, as it has been implemented, could have been accomplished by a combination of previous legislation, bank foreclosures, and voluntary transfers.

The emphasis on government-owned and public lands requires little explanation. That still leaves the question of why the reform of tenanted

rice and corn lands entailed so little controversy, apart from land-owners' complaints concerning compensation. Part of the explanation, particularly in the early years of the Aquino regime, could be found in the predilections of the Marcos-era holdovers in the DAR bureaucracy (Bulatao interview, Feb. 16, 1994). The more important explanation, however, appears to be the political marginalization of landlords in the rice and corn sectors (ibid.; Gillego interview, Feb. 17, 1994). In the mid 1950s, these landlords were extremely prominent in the legislative debates over Magsaysay's agrarian-reform proposals. They largely derailed efforts to redistribute their properties, although even then they had less success in limiting the reform than did corporate landowners producing export crops. Rice and corn growers were conspicuously absent from the agrarian-reform debates of 1986–88. After decades of contesting redistribution of their holdings, these landlords had lost much of their political force.[46] The foreign exchange crisis of the 1980s afforded export-crop producers at least a partial defense against reform, on the argument that redistributive reform would eliminate economies of scale and threaten foreign exchange earnings.[47] No such argument was available for landlords in the food-crop sector. They concentrated their energies instead on securing a new valuation formula that would reward them for the increases in land values attendant on the expansion of the nation's irrigation network and the widespread adoption of high-yielding rice varieties in the years since Marcos announced his reform. In 1994, DAR responded, raising remaining valuations by 300 percent.

International Assistance

Sustained political and financial commitment on the part of the international donor community is indispensable to establishing an environment conducive to reform in developing countries still afflicted with acute land-tenure problems. The Philippine case presented an opportunity for foreign donors to support a democratizing country preferentially as it tackled the controversial, but vital, process of agrarian reform. Although significant assistance was made available, little of it was targeted on agrarian reform. The funds that have been made available for the reform have typically been earmarked for support services rather than land transfer and compensation (see ROP, DAR 1991: Table 9; ROP, DAR 1992: Table 13).

By the end of 1990, the DAR had firm commitments for foreign funding in the amount of $95.8 million, a fraction of the projected $6.6–

8.4 billion in foreign funding that would be needed over the life of the program (Putzel 1992: 347, 349; USAID 1989: 21). The principal donors were the United States ($50 million), the Netherlands ($31.72 million), Japan ($13.54 million), and the United Nations Food and Agricultural Organization (UNFAO; $6.17 million) (Putzel 1992: 349). The U.S. appropriation was initiated by Congressman Stephen Solarz, with little support from the executive branch. USAID used the appropriation for general budgetary support for land reform exclusive of compensation. Disbursement of funds was, however, conditional on progress in land surveying and in generating and distributing titles (ROP and USAID 1989). The Japanese expressed willingness to similarly tie releases of their cash transfers, but were slow to commit funds to the program.[48] By 1993, however, Japan had become the largest foreign contributor to the reform program. Of the P828 million ($31.1 million) in ongoing funding made available to the DAR in 1993, Japan contributed P467.7 million ($17.6 million). Sweden and the UNFAO were the other leading donors, contributing P138.7 million and P136.7 million respectively. Reflecting USAID's disinterest and the general decline in U.S. aid to the Philippines, the United States committed a mere P1.4 million to the Philippine reform program in 1993.

The anticipated program costs for 1994–98 total P103.78 billion. Foreign donors are expected to finance the bulk of the anticipated P77 billion ($2.9 billion) shortfall in funding (ROP, DAR 1993c: 8–10), but based on past performance, there is no reason to expect that foreign donors will meet even a significant portion of this. DAR Secretary Garilao attributes the reluctance of foreign donors to the controversial nature of the reform program, particularly as it applies to smaller holdings (Garilao interview, Nov. 25, 1992). Apart from the Marcos-era reform (PD 27), however, the reform had involved very little compulsory acquisition of holdings, small or otherwise, as of early 1994. The reluctance of the donor community to contribute in recent years more likely reflects concerns that the program is troubled and lacks the wholehearted support of the Philippine government (see Bancod 1991c; Cariño 1993g; cf. *Business World* 1993).

Repression of Peasant Organizations

During her campaign and presidency, Aquino touted agrarian reform as one measure, among several, that would help consolidate Philippine democracy. Despite the restoration of democratic institutions in

1986–87, Philippine peasant organizations continue to confront a variety of human rights abuses that belie images of democratic transition. Members of militant organizations such as the KMP and the NFSW have been particularly targeted and have been subjected to harassment, torture, and, in some cases, execution (Amnesty International 1991). In January 1987, following the Mendiola Massacre, Jaime Tadeo, chairman of the KMP, was charged with sedition. At the height of the Garchitorena land-valuation scandal, the offices of the KMP and the Forum for Rural Concerns were raided by Philippine soldiers and policemen searching for firearms and subversive documents.[49] On May 10, 1990, three days before the KMP's third national congress, Tadeo was arrested on the 1987 sedition charge. The government then dropped that charge and held Tadeo on a 1987 conviction for misappropriation of funds (*estafa*). The *estafa* charge was originally lodged in 1982 following Tadeo's involvement in a major anti-Marcos rally.[50] The charge was widely regarded at the time as politically motivated. The timing of Tadeo's criminal conviction and the role of an outspokenly antireform Supreme Court justice in denying Tadeo's appeal suggested that the Aquino government's pursuit of the criminal trial was also politically motivated (Putzel 1992: 327). Tadeo was sentenced to four to eighteen years imprisonment in the national penitentiary at Muntinlupa. Peasant organizations across the political spectrum denounced the imprisonment, as did domestic and international human rights organizations.

At least in its public statements, the KMP believed that Tadeo's imprisonment would backfire on the government, renewing the commitment of the KMP's mass membership to reform. The intense militarization in the countryside following Aquino's declaration of "total war" against the communist insurgents had reduced the KMP's mass base in 1987–89.[51] By early 1992, KMP leaders believed they had recovered that base by organizing a variety of province-level, crop-specific alliances (Mariano interview, Jan. 21, 1992).

Tadeo remained imprisoned for three years. Upon his release, he found himself embroiled in an internal debate over the appropriate orientation and strategy for the KMP.[52] Tadeo assumed leadership of the more moderate faction of the KMP, the Demokratikong Kilusang Magbubukid ng Pilipinas, taking with him much of the KMP's old guard. Rafael Mariano heads up the more militant KMP faction and appears to have drawn more of the rank-and-file membership with him (Bulatao interview, Feb. 16, 1994; Gillego interview, Feb. 17, 1994).

Labor relations on Negros remain tense. In the case of the NFSW, a

successful Negros-wide strike in 1990 was countered by increasing repression from the *hacenderos* and Philippine military. Utilizing a divide-and-rule strategy, the military deployed Special Operations Teams to individual sugar haciendas. In exchange for "surrendering"—that is, renouncing communism and the NFSW—farmworkers were granted safe-conduct passes for use in areas of military activity.[53] In some cases, torture was used to extract the "surrender" agreement (farmworker interviews, Hacienda Mandayo, Feb. 11, 1991). In a dispute involving the peasant organization Lakas ng Magsasaka, Manggagawa at Mangingisda ng Pilipinas (LAKAS), the Negros Occidental Congressman Romeo Guanzon used military and CAFGU forces to destroy the rice crop of the farmworkers on his Hacienda Sta. Rosa (CPAR 1990: 6). A leading opponent of the agrarian reform program, Guanzon stepped up the harassment of farmworkers when the DAR failed to act on his voluntary offer of sale of the hacienda. The democratic space implicit in the transition from Marcos's authoritarian rule has frequently been encroached upon by Negros elites, their private armies, and the Philippine military (McCoy 1991).

Barriers to Democratic Participation

The accountability and competition in politics ordinarily associated with democratic governance are limited by other significant, albeit largely informal, barriers to entry in the Philippines. The House's single-member districts advantage local socioeconomic elites, who are better financed and better able to mobilize local clientelist networks and prevent the mobilization of opposition. Not surprisingly, all but 16 of the 199 members elected to the House in 1992 were (peso) millionaires. By putting a premium on the fund-raising capabilities of would-be candidates, the at-large (i.e., nationwide) elections for the Philippine Senate similarly limit entry to members of wealthy families or their agents. In a setting of well-financed political parties, the high cost of campaigning would enhance party discipline: candidates who failed to adhere to the party platform would run the risk of losing party funding. In the Philippines, however, political parties qua parties have limited funds. For the most part, candidates must arrange their own funding. They thus have little incentive to respect calls for party discipline. Party weakness persists, and particularism supplants uniformity in tailoring responses to the challenges of economic development.

Responsiveness and accountability are further frustrated by the leg-

islature's failure to create a system of popular initiative and referendum, despite a mandate to do so in the 1987 Constitution (Art. 6, Sec. 32). The 1987 Constitution provided at least partial representation, in the form of a "party list" system of proportional representation for 20 percent of 250 House seats, for smaller political parties and other groups previously excluded from politics (Art. 6, Sec. 5[2]). However, the Aquino administration ignored this provision. The House was limited to 200 members, all of them elected from single-member districts.

The May 1992 Elections: Change and Continuity

The results of the May 1992 elections, in which local, provincial, and national offices were contested, both suggest important elements of continuity in Philippine politics and provide evidence that traditional political practices have lost some of their efficacy. Election spending remained high, and congressional, provincial, and local results reflected the continuing importance of political patronage and political dynasties. More encouraging was the success of the ban on the display of guns by politicians and their bodyguards, which appeared to reduce election-related violence and coercion sharply. A generational shift was increasingly evident in the national legislature, as well as in provincial and local offices, although in a number of cases the victorious candidates were simply younger members of political dynasties.

The presidential contest afforded some evidence that traditional politics was on the wane, although the message was mixed. A record number of candidates (eight) contested the presidency, suggesting an opening of political competition. The poor showing of Ramon Mitra, former Speaker of the House, was widely viewed as a rebuff for traditional politicians (*trapos*). At the same time, Miriam Defensor-Santiago's second-place finish, despite limited resources and a near-absence of party organization, pointed to the popularity of her anticorruption campaign theme and the reduced importance of the traditional political parties. Another positive sign was the growing visibility in the electoral process of nongovernmental organizations and cause-oriented groups, hundreds of which aligned themselves with both the Ramos and Salonga presidential campaigns.

Despite the positive features, the presidential election also revealed disquieting continuities in Philippine politics. Eduardo "Danding" Cojuangco finished a close third in the campaign, notwithstanding his identification with the crony capitalism of the Marcos regime and wide-

spread opposition among the business community to his candidacy. Even Ramos's victory carried a mixed message. Ramos benefited enormously from the endorsement of Corazon Aquino. Moreover, Ramos switched party identification in the pre-election period, as Magsaysay and Marcos had before him. Ramos's switch was eloquent testimony to the weakness of political party discipline, and his victory was testimony to the continuing importance of personalities in Philippine politics.

The role of personalities (and patronage) has been similarly evident in the party-switching in Congress following the May 1992 elections. Between the elections and June 1993, 71 members of the House switched parties to join Ramos's Lakas–National Union of Christian Democrats (Lakas-NUCD) party. Sixty-four of the 89 members of Aquino's Laban ng Demokratikong Pilipino (LDP) party defected to the pro-administration "Rainbow Coalition." On paper, the 159-member coalition afforded Ramos a solid legislative majority. In practice, weak party discipline continued to make executive-legislative cooperation extremely problematic. At mid-year 1993, only 18 of 74 administration bills had been passed by the legislature.

The May 1992 election results for the House of Representatives also epitomized the continuing importance of political dynasties and elites in Philippine politics, and the economic diversification of leading Philippine families. According to one study, 130 of the 197 members had other relatives in public office. The House membership included 117 medium and large landowners and 109 directors of manufacturing or commercial business firms. Members also had interests in banking or investment firms (72), real estate (51), agribusiness (40), commercial fishing (27), construction (22), commercial poultry (21), mining (16), logging (15), hotels and restaurants (12), and overseas employment agencies (6).[54] Elite domination of sectoral politics was reinforced by the failure to enforce conflict-of-interest laws with respect to legislators. Nineteen of the 40 members of the Committee on Banks and Financial Intermediaries have past or present interests in the banking industry. Twelve of the 29 members of the Committee on Agrarian Reform have substantial agricultural interests. Peasant representation, by contrast, was negligible both on the committee and in Congress.

Agrarian Reform and the 1992 Elections

Following the passage of the agrarian-reform law, opponents of the law had pointed to the 1992 elections as a referendum on the program

and hoped to unseat proreform legislators. These threats were taken seriously by reformist politicians, some of whom sought to distance themselves from the reform law or emphasize their other legislative accomplishments (Alvarez interview, Feb. 20, 1991). Others stood firm, recognizing that the reform law would likely be attacked as radical or communist, and that reform proponents would be blacklisted by the leading parties (Gillego interview, Feb. 6, 1991). Representatives of the peasant movements had mixed expectations. Some expected land-owners to be even more dominant in the next congress (Montemayor interview, Feb. 18, 1991). Others hoped for a more progressive outcome, citing the large number of first-time voters and the growing participa-tion of peasants and nongovernmental organizations in the electoral process.[55] This cautious optimism was tempered by the memory of pre-vious elections and by a recognition of the splits within the peasant and NGO community, with some groups supporting Ramos's candidacy and others backing Jovito R. Salonga, and the reluctance of some leftists, notably national democrats, to participate in the electoral process.

In the event, the new Congress is by most accounts more conserva-tive than its predecessor, but the agrarian-reform issue appears to have played a minor role in the outcome. The National Coalition, consisting of the Liberal Party and the Pilipino Democratic Party–Lakas ng Bansa (PDP-LABAN), campaigned on the most reformist platform, calling for full implementation of the new reform law and improvement of the law to achieve "genuine" agrarian reform (Montiel 1992). The coalition did miserably at the polls, however.[56] By contrast, the victorious Fidel Ramos had pledged during the campaign to exempt farms under 50 hectares in size from the reform program permanently.[57] Following his election, however, Ramos abandoned the pledge at the urging of his nominee for DAR Secretary, Ernesto Garilao. Ramos thereafter ex-pressed support for a "realistic and implementable" agrarian reform, one based on a determination of viable farm size for each crop (Garilao interview, Nov. 25, 1992).

Peace Negotiations

Democratic practices have received a boost from several initiatives of the Ramos government. In 1993, the National Unification Commis-sion (NUC) began negotiations with all three seditious elements—communist insurgents, Muslim separatists, and military rebels. Under his amnesty program, Ramos released several hundred communist and

military rebels beginning in September 1992. The NUC held exploratory talks with the National Democratic Front (NDF), the united front of the Communist Party of the Philippines (CPP). Further talks, slated to be held in Manila, have been repeatedly delayed. Negotiations with the communists have been complicated by a major factional split within the rebel movement. The Manila Rizal Regional Committee and regional committees in the Visayas and Mindanao, together representing as much as 60 percent of the CPP membership, broke from the Maoist line of the CPP's founder, Jose Maria Sison, who remained in exile. Sison loyalists remained committed to a protracted people's war based in the countryside; the breakaway groups gave greater emphasis to an urban struggle. These divisions have reduced the threat posed by the CPP/ NPA. Still, the grievances upon which they built a popular following persist. Following nationwide public consultations, the NUC identified the government's dilatory implementation of the agrarian-reform program as a primary cause of civil unrest (Reyes 1993).

There have been no ongoing formal negotiations with the military rebels—the Reform the Armed Forces Movement (RAM) and the Young Officers Union (YOU). Since December 1989, the rebels have not engaged in military action against the government. Indeed, under the auspices of the Warriors for Peace, some of the military rebels joined with elements of the CPP to tour the Philippines in 1993 promoting public awareness of and dialogue about the nation's social problems. Fundamental disagreements remain, however. The CPP group remained disposed toward armed struggle. The military rebels focused on electoral reform and broadening political participation, yet they too viewed rebellion as appropriate should the government waver in its commitment to political and economic reform.

Complementing the peace negotiations, Ramos launched "Operation Paglalansag" in early July 1993. His aim was to abolish all private armies within 60 days. Although they were prohibited by the 1987 Constitution (Art. 18, Sec. 24), little effort had previously been made to disband these armies. The deadline was subsequently extended from September 9 to November 30, 1993. As of September 16, 1993, the government claimed to have disbanded 283 of an estimated 558 armed groups and to have accepted the surrender of over 3,600 weapons (out of an estimated total of 11,200). There was continuing skepticism, however, regarding the government's commitment to this initiative. Most of the surrendered weapons were of World War II vintage, and the major-

ity of the disbanded groups were small. Critics claim the government was ignoring the large armies of prominent Filipinos.

Local Government Code

Philippine political history has been marked by a tension between centralized and decentralized governance, reflecting the contest for control between the central state and local and provincial elites. Centralization of the formal institutions of government reached a peak under Marcos; even then local elites retained considerable authority and autonomy. The balance swung back toward decentralization under Aquino, a function of her passive leadership style and popular reaction—orchestrated in part by provincial and local elites—to the abuses of martial law. Acting pursuant to Article 10, Section 3, of the 1987 Constitution, the Philippine legislature enacted Republic Act 7160, the Local Government Code of 1991.[58] The law provides for the transfer of functions from the central government to its field agencies (deconcentration) and also for the transfer of functions of the central government to local government (devolution). The aim of this code (and constitutional provision) is to provide for a more responsive and accountable local government structure and mobilize local resources for development through a system of decentralization.

Decentralization is likely to have a mixed impact on economic and political development in the Philippines. To its supporters, decentralization means a curtailing of bureaucratic control at the national center and a development process more oriented to the countryside, with initiatives flowing from the bottom up. Efficiency considerations are also cited, with an emphasis on mobilizing local resources, improving service delivery, and overcoming bottlenecks that stem from overcentralization. It is possible, however, that in a country as geographically fragmented as the Philippines, decentralization will lead to many inconsistencies in the ways that administrative patterns develop from locality to locality with respect to budgeting, planning, and taxation. Moreover, decentralization is likely to enhance the already considerable power of local and provincial elites, who may use local administrative and political structures in antidemocratic and inegalitarian ways, to the detriment of redistributive agrarian reform and the rural poor.

Philippine reaction to the Local Government Code has been mixed. Some observers expressed concern that local politicians would use their

enhanced authority to slow the reform program (Alvarez interview, Feb. 20, 1991; Lara interview, Feb. 19, 1991). The efforts of Congressman Jose Cojuangco, Jr., to decentralize implementation of the reform program were widely viewed in this light (*Business World* 1991; Tadem 1993: 95–96). The most troublesome portion of the code was Section 20, which devolved the power of land-use determination to local government authorities. Peasant organizations expressed considerable concern that local officials would exempt agricultural lands from the reform by reclassifying them as residential or commercial (Mariano interviews, Jan. 21 and Nov. 24, 1992; Ramiro interview, Jan. 21, 1992). They offered substantial, albeit anecdotal, evidence by way of confirmation.

Some prominent proponents of agrarian reform viewed the code as the most significant accomplishment of the Aquino administration, however (Abad interview, Feb. 7, 1991; Aquino interview, Jan. 14, 1992). Recognizing the risks attendant on it, they argued that the code could facilitate significant progress on the reform in roughly one-third of the Philippine provinces. In those provinces with supportive governors, mayors, and local DAR officials, peasant and nongovernmental organizations could more effectively press their demands for expedited implementation of the reform, as evidenced in the TriPARRD experience. In this view, supportive local politicians are critical to success; peasant and nongovernmental organizations cannot generate the requisite pressure for reform by themselves (Abad interviews, Feb. 7, 1991, and Jan. 15, 1992; Lara interview, Feb. 19, 1991).

Summary

The first five years (1988–93) of implementation of the new reform law have been marked by scandal, continuing landowner resistance, continuing abuses of peasants' rights, and some notable progress in certain areas and for certain components of the reform program. The Philippine government has been implicated in land-valuation and land-conversion controversies. During the Aquino presidency, the Department of Agrarian Reform suffered from recurrent leadership changes. Under both the Aquino and Ramos administrations, the DAR has met with continuing and concerted congressional and landowner resistance. After a period of unity, the frustrations of the reform process and ideological differences have riven the Philippine peasant movement, significantly hindering its ability to press for accelerated implementa-

tion of the reform or for more progressive reform legislation. Politics continues to be dominated by Philippine elites, although the 1992 elections afforded a glimpse of positive change.

Yet for all these problems, Aquino and her successor, Fidel Ramos, have made substantial progress in implementing the Marcos-era reform of tenanted rice and corn lands and distributing public lands. Between them, the Aquino and Ramos governments have redistributed more private agricultural land than had all previous Philippine governments combined. Particularly striking is the difference between the performance of the Aquino and Ramos governments and that of Marcos's authoritarian regime. In thirteen years (1972–85) of implementation, Marcos transferred no more than 259,000 hectares under Operation Land Transfer, his principal reform program. Under the most pessimistic reading of his accomplishments, Marcos transferred final title to less than 12,000 hectares (see Table 5). By contrast, the Aquino and Ramos governments redistributed over 431,000 hectares in five years (1987–93) of implementation of Operation Land Transfer (see Table 8).

The Aquino and Ramos governments have concentrated their energies on the least contentious and least costly elements of the reform program, however. In the five years remaining for implementation of the new reform program, the Ramos government must confront the most politically volatile component of the reform: compulsory acquisition of private agricultural holdings down to five hectares. The capacity and commitment of the Ramos government to complete this segment of the reform program remain in doubt.

8

State-Society Relations, Democratic Transitions, and Redistributive Reform

In recent years, through the medium of television, the global community has witnessed a series of transitions in which authoritarian regimes in Africa, Asia, eastern Europe, and Latin America have given way to the forces of political liberalization. One of the earliest of these dramas, with unarmed civilians facing down columns of tanks, was the Philippine "People Power Revolution" of February 22–25, 1986, which brought to an end President Ferdinand Marcos's 20-year history of economic, human rights, and political abuses. A nonviolent popular movement headed by Corazon Cojuangco Aquino, the widow of Marcos's political archrival, ousted the Marcos regime, restored a semblance of democracy, and ushered in a regime publicly committed to social and economic reform.

Such transitions provide new cases with which to address age-old questions concerning the links, if any, between political liberalization and the reduction of socioeconomic inequalities. The transition imagery ought not, however, to mask the persistence of important structural and cultural features. Of particular concern are the authoritarian features that persist in nominally democratic polities. To further our understanding of the processes of political liberalization and attendant social and economic reform, this study has examined the Philippine experience with redistributive agrarian reform under the governments of Corazon Aquino and Fidel Ramos. The central question of my inquiry concerns the prospects for significant redistributive agrarian reform under the auspices of a new democracy. Conventional political science wisdom suggests a fundamental incompatibility between democratic institutions and such reform.

Yet if authoritarian regimes were presumed to have a comparative

advantage in effectuating major economic and social reform, the short-comings of Marcos's land-reform program (and his broader economic legacy) suggest that authoritarian rule was not a *sufficient* condition for effecting significant agrarian reform in the Philippines. The question of whether authoritarian rule was nonetheless a *necessary* condition for such reform remains.

Marcos had justified his declaration of martial law in September 1972 as necessary to overcome the constraints of Philippine democracy in order to restore law and order, initiate an export-oriented strategy of economic growth, and enhance social justice through redistributive re-form. After some initial improvements, the promise of martial law—such as it was—gave way to human rights abuses, corruption, and eco-nomic mismanagement. Rather than reducing inequalities, Marcos and his cronies established themselves as a new privileged elite. Even judged against the modest goals of his reform program, Marcos's per-formance was dismal. In the most pessimistic reading, only 3 percent of the targeted beneficiaries of land redistribution actually received final titles (emancipation patents) in Marcos's 14-year implementation of Operation Land Transfer. Meanwhile, the provisions of Operation Leasehold, designed to convert share tenants to fixed-rent leaseholds, were often ignored. Share-tenancy continued to be practiced, and rent levels, whether determined on a share or leasehold basis, often ex-ceeded the rent ceiling.

In addition to its limited scope and the glacial pace of land redistri-bution, agrarian reform under the Marcos government was seriously flawed in several regards: a poorly conceived program of beneficiary "pre-cooperatives" was moribund; a program of agricultural credit had failed due to inadequate technical assistance, corruption, and poor re-payment experience; the process of compensating affected landowners was subject to long delays, in many cases lasting more than a decade; and a substantial element of "reverse land reform" had occurred in connection with the promotion of corporate and export agriculture.

Ultimately, Marcos's failure to effect significant reform, coupled with his repressive tactics and mismanagement of the Philippine econ-omy, spelled his political demise. Politics and religion fused in Aquino's campaign. In challenging Marcos for the presidency, Aquino con-demned his reform program as wholly inadequate and pledged to un-dertake a program of "genuine" agrarian reform. Aquino's call for agrarian reform was a response to a series of related factors: a highly skewed pattern of Philippine landownership, characterized by wide-

spread rural poverty, low agricultural productivity, and a history of tenure-related peasant unrest; concerns about political legitimacy and a related desire to incorporate the rural poor into political life (motivated both by rural unrest and a commitment to participatory democracy); and the influence of Philippine and international development strategists, who pushed reform as an economic and political corrective.

Aquino's Construction of Democracy

Aquino came to office pledging to correct the shortcomings of past reform initiatives and address the tenure-related grievances of the Philippine peasantry. Reform experiences in other democratic settings strongly suggested the importance of a disciplined, reform-oriented, mass-based political party in seeing redistributive reform through to completion. For reasons of personal disposition and in reaction to the abuses of the Marcos political machine, President Aquino was unwilling to consolidate her grassroots support in a reform-oriented political organization. She appeared determined to curtail the powers of the presidency relative, not only to those exercised by Marcos, but to those exercised by earlier Philippine presidents under the 1935 Constitution. At the same time, her commitment to the restoration of democratic institutions and democratic decision making predisposed her to leave major social policy decisions to a constitutionally elected body. Philippine experience suggested that any legislative body would be strongly influenced by landed interests. Aquino's support appeared such that it was within her power to change this script—to lead a reform-minded populist party to legislative victory. She chose to do otherwise.

Although Aquino used her executive powers to appoint all of the members of the Constitutional Commission, once it began its deliberations, she adopted a hands-off policy, refusing to use it to push through a specific economic, political, or social agenda. The May 1987 congressional elections presented the best opportunity for Aquino to democratically institutionalize "People Power." Aquino used the elections to repay old favors, however, backing candidates with little regard to their loyalty or ideology. She neither formed nor joined a political party for these elections. Instead the President's brother, Jose "Peping" Cojuangco, Jr., fashioned the PDP-LABAN political alliance from the premartial law network of provincial bosses, including many Marcos loyalists. Quite apart from Peping's machinations, regional and provincial strongmen enjoyed considerable power and influence. Marcos's efforts

to break the traditional elite had been largely unsuccessful. When negotiations with the communist insurgents broke down, the Aquino government turned to vigilante groups and to local bosses to establish stability in the countryside.

Over time, elements of the Philippine military increasingly threatened the survival of the Aquino regime.[1] Not coincidentally, the Aquino government's concerns about the insurgent CPP/NPA and militant peasant organizations and Aquino's enthusiasm for agrarian reform appeared to wane. Political interest in reform has long been linked to the threat of insurgency in the Philippines, as it often has been in other developing nations plagued by acute landlessness. This dynamic of response to violence has important implications for the nature of the reform adopted and implemented. Ronald Herring attributes the frequent failure of reforms to their genesis as responses to legitimation crises. "Regimes persist in believing that symbolic responses will produce almost as much quiescence as real ones."[2] The Aquino and Ramos regimes, by their actions, appeared to reach just such a conclusion. Theirs were not the first regimes to act upon this belief. That agrarian reform pledges have remained a staple of Philippine politics says much about the failure of successive regimes to enact or implement more than symbolic reforms. Yet the explosive growth of the CPP/NPA during the Marcos years and the increasing militancy of Philippine peasants, mirroring growing dissatisfaction with the reform programs of the Marcos, Aquino, and Ramos regimes, suggest that the political limits of token reform are being reached (Lara and Morales 1990).

Shortcomings of the New Reform Law

Although only one of its members was a true representative of the Philippine peasant sector, the Constitutional Commission adopted—and the Philippine populace overwhelmingly ratified—a new Constitution containing unprecedented provisions on land reform, albeit with important qualifications. The Comprehensive Agrarian Reform Law that subsequently emerged from protracted cabinet and congressional deliberations is, unfortunately, the latest installment in the Philippine legacy of inadequate reform measures. Aquino's reform promises far more than it is likely to deliver. The decade-long implementation schedule invites both landowner evasion of the law as written and further debilitating legislative amendments. Exemption of commercial farms from the law for ten years or more only exacerbates these problems.

Corporate farms are effectively insulated against redistribution of their land, being permitted to distribute corporate stock instead. This provision appears to violate the constitutional right of farmers and farmworkers to own the land they are tilling. Nonetheless, Aquino's relatives have availed themselves of this provision, providing leadership by example to those resisting land redistribution. The contradictory provisions of the new law afford little protection against anticipatory and fraudulent land transfers. Even apart from the issues of land transfers, landowner retention rights severely constrain the reform's potential impact. The maximum retention areas are set well above those of the successful Asian land reforms and will exempt some seven-eighths or more of the land in farms.

The complex provisions regarding land valuation seem to invite landowner abuse, a finding amply corroborated by a series of scandals marking the first anniversary of the new reform program. Moreover, the valuation provisions seem likely to embroil the program in protracted administrative and judicial proceedings. In the event of efforts by landowners to sabotage the reform program, the provisions for legal sanctions are at present either weak or not credible.

A Broader Legacy of Failure

The shortcomings of the reform program evidence a larger failure of the Aquino and Ramos presidencies: refusal or failure to institutionalize their political support and failure to address important constraints to democratic political mobilization. The events of February 1986 ushered in a return to a brand of democratic governance characterized by weak parties, factionalism based primarily on personalities rather than ideology, and the dominance of traditional regional elites. Meanwhile, the milieu in which the CPP/NPA so successfully expanded its operations in the late 1970s and early 1980s remains largely unaltered: land-tenure grievances and rural poverty remain acute, significant human rights abuses have (after an initial decline) resumed, and, despite the termination of U.S. military basing rights in the Philippines, nationalist sensitivity to dependent relations with foreign powers and markets continues.

Philippine Culture and State-Society Relations

The modest nature of the new reform and the dismal record of earlier agrarian-reform initiatives can only be explained by persisting fea-

tures of Philippine society. Philippine culture has been shaped by the interplay between the traditions of Philippine villages and regions and a variety of foreign influences (Islam, Catholicism, and Spanish, American, and Japanese rule). The transformation of Philippine society occasioned by colonial policies and the penetration of the world market economy in the late nineteenth and early twentieth centuries institutionalized patterns of substantial inequality in landownership and fragmented social control. The Spanish, and later the American, colonial regime paved the way for massive land grabbing by socioeconomic elites. Not only did the various land-registration laws not protect the interests of native cultivators, these laws worked against more secure state control of the nation, promoting further growth of the power of local and regional (landed) elites. The resulting concentration of landownership, and the often-illegal means by which land was acquired, repeatedly made land tenure–related grievances a focal point for agrarian unrest.

Part of the difficulty in establishing a national identity and effective national control is explained by Philippine geography: the country encompasses roughly 7,100 islands. Reflecting this archipelagic landbase, linguistic diversity in the Philippines is extreme, and linguistic identity remains an important part of Philippine political life. Spanish colonialism in the Philippines was based in considerable part on indirect rule through collaborating local elites. American introduction of political parties and periodic elections strengthened local elites, whose clientelist networks became the foundation for national political alliances. The persisting power of the provincial landowning elite frustrated the development of an effective, centralized state organization capable of effecting nationwide redistributive agrarian reform.

Democracy and Agrarian Reform

Quite apart from the specifics of the Philippine context, political scientists have singled out several factors characteristic of democratic or parliamentary politics as obstacles to redistributive reform: (1) democratic political forms institutionalize the possibility of regular transfer of political power between competing parties, thereby undermining public confidence that policy measures initiated by one party will survive the next election; and (2) democratic institutions in developing-country settings are frequently dominated by socioeconomic elites.

The significance of democratic institutions cannot, however, be un-

derstood divorced from the context in which they have emerged. As this study evidences, what is needed is a political process–oriented approach, not a models or ideal-type approach.

Democracy: An Institutionalized "Change of Sky"

There is an inherent tension in democratic political forms: democracy requires the possibility of regular transfers of power, yet such transfers threaten continuity in government policy. By institutionalizing the "change of sky" phenomenon—the possibility that parties of privilege will return to power and reverse reforms—democracy undermines peasant confidence that promised reform initiatives will be seen through to completion and strengthens landowners' resolve to work to achieve the reversal of reform policies.[3] The legacies of broken promises and failed programs that characterize the history of agrarian reform in many countries reinforce peasant skepticism of reform pledges.[4]

If there has been one constant in Philippine politics with respect to agrarian reform, it has been the considerable gap between promises and performance. In the postwar era, successive Philippine presidential aspirants have sounded the theme of agrarian reform. Successful candidates have introduced a variety of reform initiatives. Yet in the end, few landless Filipinos have benefited from these programs. Peasant skepticism about the prospects for reform was surely warranted, yet the religious dimension of the Aquino crusade against Marcos tapped a deep millenarian undercurrent. Aquino's evident religiosity, the staging of some of her campaign appearances before local Catholic churches, the support her campaign enjoyed from prominent elements of the Catholic hierarchy, and from many priests, nuns, and layworkers, all suggested the possibility of a fundamental shift in the nature of Philippine politics, one marked by a genuine commitment to social justice.[5]

The Political Influence of the Landed Elite

Democratic politics in the pre–martial law Philippines were of an exclusionary nature, with traditional regional and local elites exerting substantial political influence, while effectively limiting the independent participation of Philippine peasants. From independence in 1946 until 1972, Philippine political life was dominated by two parties, the Nacionalista Party (NP) and the Liberal Party (LP). Reflecting their common origin, there was little of substance, composition, or constituencies to distinguish the two parties. The parties were noted more for their personalities than for ideological or issue orientation. Party-

switching was frequent as national, provincial, and local leaders (and their coteries) sought advantage in access to government resources. Elections were typically marred by violence and fraud.[6] To the extent that there were any evolutionary tendencies toward stronger, ideologically oriented party politics in the Philippines, these tendencies had been halted by martial law.

Yet, for all of his constitutional power, Marcos found it necessary to create the trappings of popular legitimacy, scheduling a series of plebiscites and referenda to approve his 1973 constitution and the continuation of martial law (Hernandez 1985). As they had in earlier eras, regional and local politicos demonstrated their ability to survive the vicissitudes of political dominance in Manila. Many provincial and municipal functionaries of Marcos's political apparatus, the Kilusang Bagong Lipunan (KBL = New Society Movement), were traditional politicians—members of the very class vilified by Marcos when he established his "New Society."[7]

The autonomy of the Aquino and Ramos regimes in executing agrarian reform was similarly conditioned by the political power of the landed elite and the economic significance of agriculture. As in other countries, the Philippine agricultural sector is expected to provide cheap food for the urban, industrial sector and generate foreign exchange earnings. Faced with acute foreign indebtedness, senior government officials put a considerable premium on avoiding any disruption in existing sources of foreign exchange. Landowners in commercial agriculture played on this concern, repeatedly arguing that land redistribution would cause sizable losses in foreign exchange.

As landowners would have it, farmworkers and tenants had little cause to complain or agitate for reform. Nor, by landowners' accounts, did many peasants aspire to landownership, preferring instead the security of employment as tenants or farm laborers. Elite paternalism appears central to the dominant elite ethos. Political and economic elites repeatedly evoke this disempowering imagery for political and strategic advantage. Many self-styled patrons are unwilling to bear the costs associated with the paternal role, however. It appears that each new generation of the elite places decreasing emphasis on social solidarity, increasingly resisting the social responsibilities traditionally attendant on positions of wealth.

The paternal ethos is also costly for peasants, as it calls for peasant deference and passivity in relationships of interdependence. The dominant discourse mutes the sense of peasants as thinking individuals.

Elites view peasant violence as irrational and expect that a combination of token concessions and forceful reprisals will alleviate each crisis. The paternalistic discourse is belied, however, by structural and behavioral features of Philippine society.

Another factor in the local and regional influence of landed elites in the Philippines is the absence of a state monopoly on coercion. Private armies constrain both peasant activism in support of agrarian reform and government implementation of such reform measures as might be adopted. In settings such as El Salvador, such groups have seriously impeded reform efforts through intimidation and assassination of farmer-beneficiaries, peasant organizers, and government land-reform officials (Prosterman and Riedinger 1987: 158; Union Communal Salvadoreña 1981). Private armies and vigilante groups have functioned in ways similarly antithetical to agrarian reform in the Philippines.[8]

The Cultural Dimensions of Peasant Activism

Peasant activism is not only limited by threats of repression; Philippine cultural values have constrained class-based action among the peasantry by directing feelings of affinity along other axes, including personal and group identifications along regional and ethnolinguistic lines, the principle of *utang na loób* (debt of gratitude), bilateral kinship and fictive-kinship relations, and patterns of rural dependency embodied in patron-client relations. However, some of the cultural traditions and norms that otherwise foster quiescence have potentially revolutionary connotations. In the Philippines, folk Catholicism has nurtured a millennial undercurrent that has repeatedly facilitated the organization of peasant protest movements and rebellions. Catholic proselytization provided Philippine peasants with a powerful idiom capable of cutting across regional and linguistic differences. Although the historical impact of the Catholic Church is often (correctly) seen as conservative, the story of Christ has had potentially radical implications. In times of acute economic or social crises, the *pasyones*, epic poems detailing the suffering, death, and resurrection of Christ, provided a language for criticism both of wealth and status disparities and of economic and political oppression. Moreover, the *pasyones* provided a vision of liberation from the oppression of peasant life (Ileto 1979; see also Nash 1967–68).

Philippine peasants have responded to the varying impacts of commercialization and Spanish, American, and Japanese rule with episodic rebellions despite the appreciable constraints on peasant activism. Nationalism has been a prominent theme in the most significant Philippine

rebellions, from the fight for independence from Spain and resistance to American intervention and conquest at the turn of the century to the current armed struggle of the CPP/NPA. Japanese occupation of the Philippines during World War II brought the issue of elite alliances with foreign powers and interests into particularly sharp relief. The legacy of peasant rebellion and its cultural underpinnings are important to our understanding of present-day peasant activism and the role peasant-based organizations have played, and can play, in advancing redistributive reform in the Philippines.

Obstacles to Peasant Political Influence

At least initially, the transition to the Aquino government meant a reopening of political space for peasant activism. Sensitivity to agrarian relations was heightened by the knowledge that land-related griev-ances were fueling the nationwide insurgency of the CPP/NPA. The convergence of these forces suggested the possibility that this time, the interests of the landless might acquire enough political urgency to result in some significant measure of redistributive reform. Still, the obstacles confronting attempts to convert majority interests into political organi-zations and, in turn, political power and redistributive policies, are con-siderable.[9] For one, there are both objective and subjective constraints on the emergence of a perception of shared interests among the lower classes. Yet models of democratic class struggle (as well as Marxist analysis) presuppose that class is the most politically salient identity. Where it is not, strong, class-based political parties are unlikely to emerge to pursue fundamental redistributive reform.

The existence (and persistence) of powerful, crosscutting class and group cleavages in Philippine society has been a recurrent theme of the present study. These cleavages make national control and nationwide reform problematic. Class is but one dimension by which individuals identify themselves; ethnicity, kinship, region, and religion are only some of the other multiple and crosscutting identities that are operative. Even where class is the operative identity, we must bear in mind the differing interests of Philippine peasants. The agrarian reform–related interests of landless agricultural laborers and tenant farmers are not syn-onymous, as reform outcomes in other settings have demonstrated.[10] In the Philippines, the diversity in peasant interests is evidenced, for exam-ple, in the decisions of the NFSW and NACUSIP to concentrate their organizational efforts on permanent laborers resident on sugar ha-ciendas and on mill workers. The *sacadas*, migratory laborers who have

historically harvested the sugarcane, are ignored as too transient and individualistic.[11]

Peasant mobilization and political activism appear to be essential in pressing for adoption and implementation of significant programs of agrarian reform. Yet even where peasants perceive themselves to have common interests, they may well abstain from costly (in terms of money, time, and the risk of reprisals) union or party membership in the belief that individual contributions will have no perceptible impact on the reform process. Collective action puts a premium on effective leadership and the provision of incentives sufficient to bring individual and collective interests into alignment (Migdal 1974; Popkin 1981). However well institutionalized, the myriad farmer organizations in the Philippines are all headed by articulate, charismatic personalities. The pool of potential union or party organizers is limited by minimal economic rewards, scarce organizational resources, and threats of physical harm to leaders. Landowners' private armies have long been an instrument of oppression in rural Philippine society. The recent proliferation of vigilante organizations has increased the risks of repression for peasant activists even further.

Illustrative of the problems facing peasant organizers in the Philippines, even those of moderate-to-conservative political persuasion, is the experience of the First Farmers Human Development Foundation, Inc. (FFHDF), an offshoot of the First Farmers (sugar) milling cooperative (a landowner cooperative). Members of organizations such as the NFSW typically use the sobriquet "yellow"—that is, company—organization when referring to the FFHDF. Notwithstanding the apparent political moderation of their organization, FFHDF personnel recounted the atmosphere of suspicion that greeted their efforts to organize sugar-plantation workers. Landowners suspected them of being recruiting agents for the (communist) NPA, while the farmworkers were concerned that they might be spies for the Philippine military, sent to ferret out activists (Belarmino et al. interview, June 17, 1986).

Dependency relations and fears of reprisals also influence the behavior of potential members.[12] In settings of multiple dependency relations, tenants must generally avoid alienating powerful people.[13] Institutionalization of the FFHDF's organizational work, and that of peasant organizations such as the KMP or NFSW, is ultimately dependent on community volunteers. Enjoying neither the guarantee of external employment nor the relative physical security attendant on institutional affiliation, these unpaid volunteers face many of the same

suspicions and are subject to greater threat of punishment than those who organize them. FFHDF organizers can always flee hostile landowners. Farmworker activists, by contrast, must generally live—or, in the case of numerous NFSW organizers and Basic Christian Community leaders, die—with the consequences of their activities.

The conversion of an organizational base into effective political power is also hampered by the limited resources of the peasant membership. The level and nature of membership resources are important considerations in union organization. For example, by law and in practice sugar-mill workers, as industrial employees, enjoy considerably higher daily wages than do permanent or migratory farmworkers.[14] Equally important, from the standpoint of the NACUSIP (the dominant union among mill workers), sugar-mill payrolls lend themselves to regular payroll deductions. Union dues can be directly deducted from mill workers' earnings, a much more reliable source of union finances than voluntary contributions from farmworkers.[15]

As latecomers to Philippine politics, organizations such as the KMP and NFSW must challenge established patterns of political behavior and state action. In so doing, these and other self-described "people's organizations" have found themselves regularly branded "leftist," "subversive," or "communist" by antireform rural and national elites.[16] By manipulating the terms of public discourse, opponents of agrarian reform worked to portray reformists as extremists threatening the wellbeing of the nation.

Meanwhile, the legislative process afforded landed interests ample opportunity to defuse reform initiatives. Such was the perceived political urgency of agrarian reform that few went on record as being against it; for the most part, resistance was couched instead in terms of support for the concept of reform, but opposition to program specifics. Practicing a landowner version of "everyday forms of resistance," Philippine landowners manipulated language to mask their antipathy to reform and their efforts to subvert the reform process.

At a more general level, proponents of agrarian reform were hampered by the peasants' limited access to mass media and national political fora.[17] Although there has been considerable grassroots demand for agrarian reform, variously defined, it would appear that only the more politicized landless farmers were aware either of the proreform campaign pledges of Aquino (or the later pledges of various congressional candidates) or of the terms of the subsequent reform debates. Even after some eighteen months of often-heated political debate, and the atten-

dant, near-daily media coverage, fewer than half the Filipinos surveyed
nationally were aware of the Comprehensive Agrarian Reform Law of
June 1988. Public awareness was even lower in rural areas (Mangahas
1989: 3). These findings denote both a notable ignorance concerning one
of the most important political initiatives dealing with rural life and a
profound failure to incorporate rural inhabitants into the reform debate.

Even where Philippine peasants were aware of the various proreform campaign promises, there remains the question of how these
pledges were understood. There has been no universally accepted definition of agrarian reform in the Philippine context. Indeed, the very
vagueness of the agrarian-reform concept made it attractive as a campaign slogan, for it encompassed a wide range of agendas, from free-
market pricing and termination of Marcos-era marketing monopolies to
subsidized credit and agricultural inputs, from voluntary land sales to
confiscatory land redistribution. Landowner candidates could promise
reform, then seek refuge in these ambiguities. Agrarian reform has
often been discussed in Philippine political life and is embodied in
numerous legislative enactments, but these do not a consensus definition make.

Peasant Initiatives Promoting Agrarian Reform

Despite the myriad obstacles to peasant political activism, several
national peasant organizations did play a role in the reform deliberations. As the Aquino government initially deferred action on agrarian
reform, peasant organizations attempted to shape agrarian-reform deliberations by setting the policy agenda. The KMP submitted a six-point
proposal for agricultural and rural development to the government in
April 1986, supplementing it in June 1986 with several documents
aimed at giving definition to the government's promise of "genuine
agrarian reform" (KMP 1986a–c, e). Among the organization's demands were confiscation of lands owned by Marcos and his cronies and
free distribution to the actual tillers; expansion of free distribution to all
croplands, with selective compensation to former landowners; and nationalization of transnational agribusiness plantations and the abolition
of feudalism (KMP 1986c–d).

Joining the call for genuine agrarian reform were the Congress for a
People's Agrarian Reform, a unique and ideologically diverse coalition
of peasant and nongovernment development organizations and the
Bukluran sa Ikauunlad ng Sosyalistang Isip at Gawa (BISIG = Union for
the Advancement of Socialist Thought and Action), an alliance of aca-

demics, community activists, trade unionists, and former communists committed to a democratic transition to socialism.

The center-right Federation of Free Farmers (FFF) identified its agrarian reform priorities in early May (Montemayor 1986a). The FFF directive was in substantial agreement with the reform agenda of more militant peasant groups. Among the FFF demands were calls for the immediate completion of the Marcos-era Operation Land Transfer (PD 27) program; reform of all remaining tenanted rice and corn lands; changes in credit and pricing policies to increase the incomes of reform beneficiaries; expansion of agrarian reform to include idle and abandoned lands, as well as sugar, coconut, and other crop lands; and recovery of all lands unfairly taken over by domestic and multinational corporations.

These organizations, and others like them, suggested the potential for democratic mass mobilization of the Philippine poor, the possibility of giving voice to the disadvantaged in a society where they had long been ignored. In the event, the capacity of the new social organizations to influence the national politics of agrarian reform proved to be greater than in any previous era of Philippine politics. Yet most of these groups were still in their infancy when the Marcos regime collapsed. Even as these organizations succeeded in mobilizing significant blocks of Philippine peasants, there remained vast parts of the country that were not articulated with national organizations, the national media, or national politics. In these areas, the peasants' reality remained local, largely shaped by local strongmen. The full promise of social organization and mobilization in democratic society has yet to be realized in the Philippines.

The Church and Peasant Activism

Beginning with Vatican II, the Catholic Church in the Philippines moved toward a more activist role in the struggle for social justice. The Church provided both a new idiom for, and institutional guidance to, peasant organizational activities. Church functionaries and concerned lay members were instrumental, for example, in the organization and expansion of the FFF and the NFSW. In borrowing the concept of Basic Christian Communities from the liberation theologists of Latin America, the Philippine Catholic Church has also worked to redefine community, stressing the biblical importance of social justice and the necessity of united action among the disadvantaged.

The hierarchy of the Catholic Church and Church-affiliated organi-

zations such as the Institute on Church and Social Issues (ICSI) and the Bishops-Businessmen's Conference for Human Development provided important support to peasant organizations promoting agrarian reform. The ICSI kept the Church community and other concerned observers up-to-date on developments concerning agrarian reform. The reporting was avowedly proreform and detailed the deficiencies of various legislative proposals.

The senior body of the Church, the Catholic Bishops' Conference of the Philippines, issued a pastoral letter that lent the Church's official, albeit qualified, support to agrarian reform (CBCP 1987). The CBCP's National Secretariat of Social Action, Justice and Peace organized a "Campaign for a Genuine Agrarian Reform Program" within the Church community.

Given President Aquino's evident religiosity and the dominance of Catholicism in the Philippines, one might have expected the Church's efforts to influence the reform debate to have borne greater fruit. However, even when combined with the political resources of a variety of peasant organizations, the Church's influence proved inadequate in the face of the resistance of landowners and their representatives in Congress. Aquino's sweeping promise of genuine agrarian reform was reduced in practice to little more than completion of earlier reform programs and distribution of public lands.

Lessons from the Philippine Experience

Aquino saw her principal duty as president of the Philippines to be reestablishing democratic institutions. Her concern with agrarian reform, it would appear, related chiefly to that objective; agrarian reform was to be a vehicle for countering the rural insurgency and incorporating the rural poor into a new democratic political and social order. At the same time, reform would both shift the resources of noncultivator landowners from land to industry and rationalize and increase agricultural production.

The urgency Aquino and later Ramos attached to the communist insurgency and the social problems on which it was built—notably land-tenure relations, poverty, and human rights abuses—noticeably waned over time. This diminished commitment appears to be a function of the exclusionary nature of Philippine democracy, of disarray within the CPP/NPA, and of the considerable threat posed by rebellious elements of the Philippine military. In Aquino's case, she may

have mistaken the great antipathy toward Marcos, and her own early popularity, as suggesting that little more than the ouster of Marcos and the revival of democratic trappings was necessary to entice most of the rebels to renounce violence and simultaneously keep the military at bay.

The result, in the case of agrarian reform, is a program that includes important improvements in scope and process over previous Philippine initiatives, yet ultimately fails to meet peasant demands for social justice, supply the requisites for economic and political empowerment of the peasantry, or create economic efficiency and development. Unless the shortcomings of the law are redressed through administrative or legislative action, and this seems unlikely, the problem of landlessness (exacerbated by rapid population growth) will remain acute, agricultural productivity will remain low by Asian and world standards, and civil unrest will continue to be fueled by tenure-related peasant grievances. The shortcomings of the reform reflect the political and rhetorical strategies that landowning elites, their representatives in Congress, and President Aquino shared in working to limit the scope and direction of the reform. They concentrated on certain critical, and contested, issues as they sought to legitimize the abandonment of important elements of reform. In the effort to shape reform policy, elites and peasants alike advanced and debated images of landowners and laborers, of connections to land, economies of scale in agricultural productivity, peasant capacities and aspirations, and the contractions of paternalism.

At the same time, large landowners have expanded their private armies, while "anticommunist" vigilante organizations have proliferated through the assistance of landowners and the Philippine armed forces. After a brief hiatus in the early months of the Aquino government, human rights abuses have increased. The targeted "subversives" include members of the Church community and union activists. In some instances, militarization of the countryside has increased under the "democratic" Aquino and Ramos regimes, as military units previously posted in the greater Manila area for purposes of protecting the Marcos regime have been reassigned to the countryside.

The respective roles of state and society are still being contested in the Philippines. Agrarian and industrial elites have extensively penetrated the Philippine state. The landowning elite retains considerable local and national influence, stymieing the development of a strong central state. At the same time, the NPA and the autonomy struggle of the Muslims of Mindanao and Sulu pose direct, armed challenges to state authority and control.

The Philippine case suggests that there is little likelihood that the rhetoric of reform will translate into substantive reform in a democratic polity where parties are weak, patronage-oriented, and have only tenuous ties to the peasantry. Philippine political parties are undisciplined, and patronage concerns rather than programs drive party behavior. Traditionally, Philippine political parties have relied on patron-client networks to mobilize the rural poor, and then only for elections. Permanent organization and mobilization of the peasantry has been discouraged, often forcibly, notwithstanding nominally democratic rule for much of this century. The needs and aspirations of the rural poor rarely command national attention; attention is paid peasant demands only when they are expressed in militant or military terms.

Experience elsewhere points to a number of situational conditions conducive to the organizational success of redistribution-oriented, mass-based political parties: widespread disruption of existing agrarian patterns, resulting radicalism, and the absence of political alternatives (Herring 1990: 54). These conditions were in fact present to varying degrees in the Philippines when Aquino became president. Increasing population and the declining availability of new land had exacerbated agrarian relations, turning the "terms of trade" further against tenants and laborers. Sharp downturns in sugar and coconut prices, coupled with the abuses of "crony" marketing monopolies, devastated these segments of Philippine agriculture in the late 1970s and early 1980s. Tenant and landless laborer cultivators bore the brunt of this economic decline as unemployment soared and wages plummeted.

A high incidence of landlessness, extreme inequality in landownership, underemployment, and poverty set the stage for agrarian unrest. When the Marcos regime failed to act upon these grievances, a political niche was created for the CPP/NPA, as well as various left-of-center peasant organizations, to make credible reform-based appeals to voters. The rapid expansion of the CPP/NPA in the late 1970s and early 1980s demonstrated that geographic and cultural barriers to collective action among a differentiated Philippine peasantry could be surmounted. The success of the CPP/NPA also gave new impetus to the democratic opposition and heightened the urgency accorded to the ouster of the Marcos regime and the introduction of meaningful agrarian reform.

The situation appeared opportune for the emergence of a redistribution-oriented, left-of-center political party in the Philippines. Still lacking, however, were essential institutional and social conditions. The

1987 Constitution set important boundaries on redistributive reform. Many of the same social conditions that had long limited the development of effective parties—dependency relations embodied in patron-client networks, powerful regional elites, private landlord armies, and crosscutting social cleavages that constrain solidarity along class lines—similarly hindered the emergence of mass-based, democratic social organizations.

Contrasting the experience in Kerala state (India) with the Philippine experience highlights the critical role played by a disciplined, reform-oriented political party in effecting redistributive reform (Herring 1983: 153–216). In Kerala, the impetus for agrarian reform was supplied primarily by the Communist Party of India (Marxist), a party with relatively bottom-up organizational origins. In particular, the cadres and local leadership of the CPI(M) were drawn largely from a radical stratum of landless cultivators. Even here, the party cadres were drawn predominately from one segment of landless cultivators—namely, tenants. The ensuing reform, not surprisingly, served primarily to benefit that segment of the landless population, at the expense of rentiers and other landless cultivators, notably laborers.[18]

"Operation *barga*" in West Bengal is another example of agrarian reform pursued under democratic auspices. Again, the CPI(M) was instrumental in effectuating the reform. However, the CPI(M) of West Bengal was of a relatively elite origin, with professionals, middle peasants, and schoolteachers prominent in its cadres and local leadership (Kohli 1987: 103–5). In this case, the top-down reform program—regulation of sharecropping relationships—stopped considerably short of the redistribution of property carried out in Kerala, suggesting the exceptionalism of the Kerala case. Similarly, in Sri Lanka, the urban orientation of the otherwise well-organized leftist parties, their lack of class-based rural networks, and the conflicting objectives and perceived interests of the various sectors of the peasantry stymied redistributive reform in that country.[19]

The experiences in these countries would seem to support the view that democratic political structures place important limits on the scope of reform. The agrarian reform experience under the Aquino and Ramos governments in particular suggests that nonrevolutionary processes of regime transition and political liberalization are unlikely, in and of themselves, to foster significant redistributive economic reform. The introduction of democratic institutions can afford the disadvan-

taged a greater political and policy "voice," and thereby amplify the pressures for redistributive reform. Where the regime transition does not materially alter the political influence of national or regional economic elites, however, democratizing the electoral process holds little promise of concurrent redistribution of wealth within the society. Some analysts have gone further, raising the possibility that democratic political transitions may be inherently incompatible with income redistribution.[20] The obstacles confronting proponents of agrarian reform are particularly acute in settings such as the Philippines, where democratic institutions are superimposed on historic and continuing patterns of fragmented social control and substantial economic inequality.

The Philippine experience suggests caution in interpreting political liberalization in eastern Europe and elsewhere entirely through the imagery of transition. Although it represents an important break with the past, such liberalization should not be seen as ridding societies of every vestige of past regimes and societal forms. In the Philippine case, there is considerable continuity between the old authoritarian order (and even the preauthoritarian order) and the new "democratic" society. Important segments of the traditional economic and political elite weathered the turmoil of transition to the new regime with marked success. If anything, they were strengthened in their resolve to assure that any new political order would protect their interests.

Nonetheless, the transition afforded greater political space for more segments of civil society to contest the institutional arrangements governing the polity. Assisted by progressive elements of the Catholic Church, Philippine peasants developed a policy "voice" and adopted a more militant stance in pressing for social reform. At the same time the posttransition period saw the expression of divergent interests within the new regime. The unity of the struggle against authoritarian rule gave way to factional infighting. The contest over who would determine the "rules of the game" included efforts to establish hegemony and a hegemonic ideology; images and symbols were contested in rhetoric and action. Although the new reform law suggests the continuing dominance of the paradigm of agrarian relations purveyed by the commercial landowners, that paradigm has been widely challenged.

The new reform law has serious shortcomings, and the Aquino and Ramos governments have so far failed to implement the more controversial and costly elements of the reform. Yet they have proven more responsive to reformist pressures than all previous Philippine regimes and have substantially exceeded the reform accomplishments of Mar-

cos's authoritarian regime. The Philippine case suggests that authoritarian rule is neither sufficient nor necessary to effectuate an appreciable measure of redistributive reform. However flawed and incomplete, the new Philippine democracy has proven more conducive to redistributive reform than its authoritarian predecessor.

Reference Matter

Notes

Chapter 1

1. Peru and Guatemala, for example, evidenced extensive grassroots mobilization, albeit in social organizations other than political parties, under authoritarian conditions that included episodes of extreme violence and repression. In neither country has political liberalization meant an end to the violence. See Bourque and Warren 1989; Carmack 1988; Stern 1987.

2. Migdal 1988: 28. Taking my cue from Alfred Stepan, the state may best be defined as "the continuous administrative, legal, bureaucratic, and coercive system that attempts not only to manage the state apparatus but to structure relations *between* civil and public power and to structure many crucial relationships *within* civil and political society" (Stepan 1988: 4; emphasis in original). Civil society is defined as that "arena where manifold social movements (such as neighborhood associations, women's groups, religious groupings, and intellectual currents) and civic organizations from all classes (such as lawyers, journalists, trade unions, and entrepreneurs) attempt to constitute themselves in an ensemble of arrangements so that they can express themselves and advance their interests" (ibid.: 3–4).

3. See Migdal 1974; Popkin 1979; Scott 1976. Moral economists such as James Scott (1976) argue that peasants were risk-averse, acting on a "safety first" principle. In this view, precolonial, precapitalist villages were marked by a variety of social institutions that reflected a normative concern for the right of subsistence of even the poorest members of the community. Where the demands of the colonial state or of landlords were perceived to violate the moral order—the subsistence ethic—and threaten peasant survival strategies, peasants engaged in acts of rebellion with the aim of restoring protective communal arrangements.

Political economists such as Samuel Popkin (1979) challenge both the extent and effectiveness of traditional communalism. They characterize peasant behavior in terms of a rational (economic) actor model; peasants were seen as profit-maximizing, risk-taking individuals. In this analysis, peasant uprisings

were of a revolutionary nature, taking hold, not in areas of destitution, but in regions marked by relatively prosperous, politically conscious, competent peasants.

4. See Bates 1981; Evans 1992; Evans et al. 1985; Nettl 1968; Stepan 1978. This state-oriented literature follows in the tradition of classic works on the role of the state in facilitating economic development, among them Gerschenkron 1962; Polanyi 1944; and Weber 1978.

5. The state-building process is an ongoing one, with state authority continually contested, if more directly in much of the Second and Third worlds these days than in the First. Still, the politically charged issues of abortion rights and gun control in the United States provide evidence that no matter how "complete" the state-building process, the boundaries of state authority continue to be debated and redefined.

6. Tribal groups in the Cordillera mountain region of Luzon are also waging an autonomy campaign, which has overlapped with NPA activities in the region.

7. The excessive process of surplus extraction from the rural sector in Africa is detailed by Bates 1981. The classic formulation of the "urban bias" thesis is Lipton 1977.

8. This paradox is not unique to the Philippines. See Huntington 1968: 381; Prosterman and Riedinger 1987: 25.

9. Aside from the obvious external influence of the Vatican, the Catholic Church in the Philippines has been influenced by, and borrowed from, a variety of foreign doctrinal and organizational models. Most notable has been the influence of liberation theology as it has developed in Latin America. See O'Brien 1987; Giordano 1988.

10. The term "fragmented" social control is taken from Migdal 1988: 39.

11. Implementation of agrarian reform is necessarily decentralized, entailing myriad interactions between agents of the state and local interests groups and individuals. For discussions of the problems of implementation of such programs, see Grindle 1980.

12. Merilee Grindle argues that land reform has frequently been undertaken in Latin America in the absence of significant direct pressure from peasants. Yet her discussion makes clear that in the wake of the Cuban revolution, the *perception* among political elites, and within the U.S. government, that land-related peasant grievances might precipitate rural unrest or political agitation was instrumental in the announcement of numerous reform programs. Thus the threat of political action may be as important in some circumstances as the fact of political pressure (Grindle 1986: 136–43).

13. See Migdal 1988: 35–36; Nelson 1987: 111–12. On the conflict between primordial attachments and civil sentiments, see Geertz 1973: 255–310. For a discussion emphasizing the fluid and intermittent character of ethnic-based political participation, see Kasfir 1979.

14. For a cogent argument on the importance of the politics of implementation in the Third World, see Grindle 1980.

15. As events demonstrated in countries such as Peru, authoritarian states could encounter the same problems of elite and peasant opposition facing democratic regimes, and in the process lose the momentum for implementation of policy reform (McClintock 1980).

16. Huntington (1968: 288). The subsequent experience of the Peruvian military with agrarian reform, with all its complexities and traumas, and the counterreform measures of the Chilean military, suggest little reason to alter Huntington's assessment. See Lowenthal 1975; McClintock and Lowenthal 1983; North 1976; Valenzuela 1978.

17. Remmer 1985–86: 81. Remmer makes a persuasive case for categorizing many past and present Latin American democracies as exclusionary: political leaders are drawn from a narrow social elite, and few channels exist for popular political participation.

18. The political considerations involved in agrarian reform generally are described in Grindle 1986: 139–43; Herring 1983: 217–38; and Prosterman and Riedinger 1987.

19. Data on landlessness and rural employment are presented in detail in Chapter 3.

20. On the need for ideological unity, see Stepan 1978. The importance of bureaucratic capacity is emphasized in Callaghy 1989; and Kaufman 1985: 477.

21. See Prosterman and Hanstad 1988a; id. 1988b; Putzel 1988; Riedinger 1990b. In early 1988, Secretary of Agrarian Reform Philip Juico claimed that "75 percent" of the reform program could be implemented without new legislation (Sicam 1988). Agrarian reforms based on voluntary land transfers are of a willing-seller, willing-buyer nature. Widespread landowner offers to transfer their lands voluntarily typically arise only in circumstances where the terms of compensation are extremely favorable, where civil unrest has rendered the landowner's use of the land impractical or impossible, or where there is a substantial threat of direct confiscation by revolutionary forces. All three elements have been present to varying degrees in the Philippines in recent years, the former reflecting fraudulent overstatement of land values.

22. Interview with Congressman Bonifacio H. Gillego, June 17, 1989. See also Shaplen, 1987: 73 (quoting Armando Doronila); Wurfel 1988: 323; Karnow 1989: 423.

Chapter 2

1. The term "everyday forms of peasant resistance" is taken from Scott 1985: xvi. See also Kerkvliet 1990; Scott and Kerkvliet 1986.

2. As is described more fully below, pre-Hispanic Philippine society was typified by village communities that were "more or less politically self-contained and economically self-sufficient" (Corpuz 1957: 2). Subsistence agriculture and fisheries activities dominated economic life. The archipelago was marked (then as now) by considerable ethnolinguistic diversity.

3. The search for a Philippine identity is explicit in the 1987 Constitution,

Article 16, Section 2 of which provides: "The Congress may, by law, adopt a new name for the country, a national anthem, or a national seal, which shall all be truly reflective and symbolic of the ideals, history, and traditions of the people."

4. See, e.g., Agoncillo 1975; Agoncillo and Guerrero 1977; Constantino 1975; Constantino and Constantino 1978. For a telling critique of this scholarship, see May 1987.

5. For an extended discussion of public administration under the Spanish, see Corpuz 1957.

6. By contrast, in Mesoamerica and the Andes, the Incan and Aztec languages—Quechua and Nahuatl respectively—united diverse Indian populations and served the Spanish as the medium of Christian conversion and governance (Rafael 1988: 20).

7. Description and classification of pre-Hispanic Philippine society are problematic. Spanish accounts from the sixteenth and early seventeenth centuries are the principal bases for reconstructing the indigenous social order. Yet these accounts are ambiguous. As William Henry Scott notes, "They do not . . . even indicate whether *datu* is a social class or a political order" (1982: 96–97). Vicente Rafael attributes the ambiguities to the inadequacy of Spanish political terminology and the incongruence between Spanish descriptions and native reality (1988: 138).

8. The available literature provides relatively little information on the process by which independent *datus* were transformed into local extensions of the colonial elite. See de Jesus 1982: 24–26.

9. Rafael 1988: 146. The policy of assimilation was formally embodied in law: "It is not just that the members of the former ruling class among the Indios [natives] in Filipinas should be in a worse state after having been converted; on the contrary, they should be accorded such treatment as will make them happy, or incline them to loyalty, in order that, to the spiritual blessings which God has extended to them . . . shall be added temporal benefits, and so that they will live agreeably and conveniently. To this end we order the governors of those islands to treat them well, and entrust them in our name with the government of the Indios of whom they were formerly lords.

"In all else the governors shall see that their services are availed of justly, giving them the same recognition according to the form that prevailed in the days of their heathenism, *provided that this shall be without prejudice to the tributes which they owe to us, nor to those which belong to the encomenderos*" (Act 16, art. 7, sec. vii, quoted in Corpuz 1957: 107; emphasis added).

10. The ideology of Spanish colonialism was the subject of considerable contention. Lewis Hanke (1949) demonstrates that the Spanish conquest of America entailed extensive debate over whether the native Indians should properly be considered human beings. Definition of the other assumes importance because of its use in defining whether conquest or war is "just" or "unjust." Witness the terms used by armed forces throughout history to characterize (and dehumanize) their adversaries.

11. In his analysis of class relations in a Malaysian village, James Scott makes

this point—hegemonic ideologies create contradictions that permit them to be criticized in their own terms—as part of a general critique of the concepts of hegemony, false-consciousness, and ideological state apparatuses elaborated by Marxist theorists following in the tradition of Antonio Gramsci (1985: 315–50).

12. The principal export crops by region were: tobacco—northeastern Luzon; rice and sugar—Central Luzon; *abaca* (a hemp substitute)—Bicol Peninsula; sugar—Western Visayas; and Chinese foodstuffs—Sulu. The dominant labor systems by region were: tenancy—Central Luzon; tenancy, then wage labor and debt bondage—Negros (Western Visayas); sharecropping—Bicol; and slavery—Sulu (McCoy 1982a: 8–9).

13. As elaborated in Chapter 3, there were recurrent episodes of rebellion in the colonial era. These were, however, typically confined to a particular locality or region. Not until 1896 did the semblance of a nationwide rebellion against colonial rule emerge.

14. This is not to suggest that centralization of political authority is for all purposes preferable to decentralization. Rather, it is a reflection of the historical record. Nationwide agrarian reform has only been accomplished by centralized polities.

15. For discussions of Philippine political parties, see Abueva 1988: 41–42; Landé 1969; Milne 1969; Tancangco 1988.

16. The Socialist Party was founded in 1929 by Pedro Abad Santos, a wealthy landowner. The party's principal organizing themes were land reform for landless peasants and improved pay for urban laborers.

17. Steinberg 1967: 62–64, 84; Anderson 1988. José Laurel, Sr., was president of the Japanese-sponsored republic, and father of Corazon Aquino's vice president, Salvador H. Laurel. Benigno Aquino, Sr., was Speaker of the Occupation Assembly, director-general of the pro-Japanese party Kalibapi (Kapisanan Sa Paglilingkod Sa Bagong Pilipinas = Association for Service in the New Philippines), and Corazon Aquino's father-in-law.

18. While Sergio Osmeña, Sr., served as vice president in exile, Sergio Osmeña, Jr., built a considerable fortune by supplying scrap iron to the Japanese occupation regime (Mojares 1986: 10–15; Wurfel 1962: 32–33).

19. For a discussion of the role of elites in "legitimizing" grievances of the poor and related social protest, and in weakening the legitimacy of oppressive institutions, see Piven and Cloward 1977: 13.

20. Wurfel 1988: 75 n. 1. For discussion of the concept of democracy and distinctions between inclusionary and exclusionary forms of democracy, see Remmer 1985–86; Dahl 1971.

21. On the similarities in the class composition and ideologies of the two parties, see Corpuz 1958; Milne 1969; Wurfel 1962. On patron-client dyads, see Landé 1977.

22. The martial law decree was backdated to Sept. 21, 1972, to make the date divisible by seven, Marcos's lucky number (Karnow 1989: 359).

23. Richard Kessler argues persuasively that the pre–martial law military exhibited neither the professionalism, commitment to civilian authority, nor

concern for the preservation of the state typically ascribed to it (1989: 106–15). Yet whether deemed a difference in kind or a significant difference in degree, the militarization of Philippine society and politicization of the Philippine military were considerable under the martial law regime.

24. General Fabian Ver, the Marcos-loyalist par excellence, concurrently commanded the Presidential Security Unit, the National Intelligence and Security Authority, and the National Intelligence Board. Ver's chief rival within the military was General Fidel Ramos, head of the Philippine Constabulary (and a cousin of Marcos's).

25. On local government appointments, see Abueva 1988: 56; de Guzman et al. 1988. On judicial appointments, see de Guzman 1988: 275.

26. Hernandez 1985. Marcos's insistence on constitutional forms reflects much the same elite preoccupation with legalisms that David Wurfel (1988: 75 n.1) notes in characterizing the period 1946–72 as "constitutional" rather than "democratic."

27. Discussions of politics in the martial law era can be found in de Guzman et al. 1977; Hernandez 1985; Noble 1986; Tancangco 1988; Villacorta 1983.

28. Among the families so punished by Marcos was the Lopez clan, then regarded as the nation's wealthiest family (Wurfel 1979: 240; Karnow 1989: 382–83). At the time of martial law, the Lopez family was one of the most prominent backers of Benigno "Ninoy" Aquino, Jr., in his candidacy for the presidency. Ironically, Fernando Lopez was vice president under Marcos and the Lopez family had helped finance Marcos's presidential campaigns in 1965 and 1969. Unlike Marcos, Lopez stepped down from office at the Dec. 30, 1973, expiration of his elected term.

29. A variety of government initiatives in the early martial law years benefited non-crony businessmen and landowners. The government devoted significant resources to infrastructural improvements, including roads and irrigation networks. Government incentives and programs facilitated a marked expansion of production and export of nontraditional products, including electronic components, textiles, finished wood products, leather goods, footwear, housewear, giftware, and fresh and processed foodstuffs (Villegas 1986: 159). Labor policies assured that wages remained low and labor organizing and strikes were curtailed. Tax, profit repatriation, and other policies bolstered foreign investment, much of it in partnerships with Filipino business concerns (Wurfel 1988: 190–93).

30. The sugar sector is illustrative. After the 1974 collapse in world sugar prices, the Marcos government increased the domestic sugar price, halted lending to marginal producers, and exempted sugar land temporarily planted to rice and corn from the agrarian-reform process. These measures cushioned the losses of large sugar *hacenderos* and mill owners. Farmworkers, small (marginal) landowners, and consumers bore the brunt of the crisis and the government response thereto (Noble 1986: 93).

31. In this regard the parallel to the anti-Somoza (Anastacio Somoza, Jr.) political fallout in Nicaragua stemming from the assassination of Pedro J.

Chamorro, the leading opposition figure, is striking; all the more so with the election of Chamorro's widow as president of Nicaragua.

32. Steinberg 1986: 31. Stanley Karnow (1989) captures the religious imagery of Ninoy's assassination and Cory's political ascendancy in his chapter 14 title, "Martyr and Madonna."

33. The ensuing discussion is drawn from Landé 1986: 122–26; Tancangco 1988: 95–104; Villacorta 1983; Wurfel 1988: 131–33, 208–11, 278–87.

34. Best known among the clergy that joined the underground were Fathers Edicio de la Torre, Luis Jalandoni, and Conrado Balweg. De la Torre became a leading figure in the Christians for National Liberation movement, an organization of national democrats within the Church. By the late 1970s, CNL was openly affiliated with the NDF. De la Torre was imprisoned by the Marcos regime from 1974 to 1980 and 1982 to 1986. Jalandoni is from a prominent landowning family in Negros Occidental. Jalandoni was captured in 1973 and imprisoned for a number of years by the Marcos regime. He now works in exile in the Netherlands as an international liaison for the NDF. Balweg broke away from the NPA to form the CPLA, an armed force representing tribal populations in the Cordillera mountain region of Luzon. In September 1986, Balweg signed a cease-fire agreement with President Aquino. He later campaigned on behalf of the new Constitution, with its provision for an autonomous Cordillera region (Art. 10, Sec. 1).

35. The members of the local defense forces (formally named Civilian Home Defense Forces in 1976) formed and armed on Mindanao were typically Christian, reinforcing the religious dimension of the secessionist conflict.

36. For a discussion of the Civilian Guards, see Kerkvliet [1977] 1979a: 147–62. The Barrio Self-Defense units are briefly described in Kessler 1989: 142, and information on the relative costs of maintaining CHDF units versus regular military forces can be found in ibid.: 120.

37. An example of this process can be found in Kay Warren's discussion of attempts by Guatemalan Indians to reformulate their ethnic identity and resist continuing Ladino (Hispanic) domination ([1978] 1989).

38. See Cariño 1988: 10; Steinberg 1982: 19; Wurfel 1988: 27. English receives much greater emphasis as the medium of instruction in the private school system. The gap in English competence between private and public school graduates is seen as exacerbating class differences, given the importance of English in the higher echelons of business and government.

39. See the remarks of Antonio de Leon in Collins 1989: 125–27. Several farmworker unionists and Catholic social activists regard the introduction of the conservative Mormon faith as part of the low-intensity conflict (counterinsurgency campaign) conducted by the Philippine government with the guidance and assistance of the United States.

40. The term "imagined community" is taken from Anderson 1983.

41. See Ileto 1979. Similarly, through the ritual reenactment of the Passion, Maya Indians "reveal a sense of their oppression, a definition of the dominant

group as oppressors and an imagined victory over their masters" (Nash 1967–68).

42. For an extensive discussion of this cultural trait and empirical studies of its role in Philippine life, see Lynch [1961] 1973. This remains the seminal work on Philippine cultural values.

43. *Utang na loób* is variously translated as debt of gratitude, debt inside one's self, reciprocity, and debt without end (Green 1987: 269, 275). The seminal work on the various cultural notions of reciprocity and *utang na loób* is Hollnsteiner [1961] 1973.

44. See Doronila 1985; Nowak and Snyder 1974. For an argument that Philippine political relations as of the 1960s and 1970s—being short in duration, impersonal, and instrumental—differed from the multifaceted, dyadic relationships normally connoted "patron-client," see Wolters 1983. The patron-client or "factional" model of politics is also challenged in Kerkvliet and Mojares 1991: 8–11. Traditional patron-clientelism does appear to be on the decline. Still, many peasants explain their support for particular congressional and local candidates by describing the local health clinic, school, or road "built" by the candidate or members of the candidate's family who had previously held public office (author's interviews, 1986–92). Almost invariably the facilities the peasants describe have been financed out of the public treasury. Filipino politicians have developed the process of garnering private credit for public expenditures to an art form.

45. Wurfel 1988: 35–36. The importance of political entrepreneurs in organizing collective action in any society is stressed in Popkin 1981.

46. Lacson 1987. Lacson's use of pejorative terms—"bondage," "backward"—to describe the prospective relationship between reform beneficiaries and their land is instructive. There is nothing inherent in agrarian reform that would make either term apt. Indeed, the terms are more appropriately used in reference to the debt-bondage conditions and cultivation practices on many existing large farm operations.

47. Alunan interview, June 16, 1986. At the time of the interview, the prevailing agricultural minimum wage was P32.

48. Starke interview, June 16, 1986. Intercropping rights refer to the opportunity to plant rapid-maturing vegetables between the rows of newly planted sugarcane, the vegetables to be harvested before the cane reaches a height that blocks the sunlight. While intercropped legumes should improve the soil and boost sugarcane yields, farmworkers noted that landowners frequently viewed intercropping as deleterious to the main crop, refusing farmworkers the right to intercrop or charging them for the extra fertilizer deemed necessary to offset the negative impact of the intercropping.

49. See del Rosario 1989; NFSP n.d.: 7. In describing the difficulties faced in expanding participation in Partners in Land Ownership with Workers (PLOW), a program of voluntary land transfer on Negros Occidental, government and development foundation officials agreed that "the planters are reluctant to part

with 10 percent of their land and the workers are reluctant to assume responsibility for the land" (Dumankas et al. interview, June 17, 1986).

50. Interviews with tenant farmers in Batangas, Bulacan, Laguna, Nueva Ecija, and Pangasinan, March and June–July 1986, and in Camarines Sur, Cebu, and Negros Occidental, Feb. 1991. Also Bercaro interview, Mar. 2, 1989; Lara interviews, Feb. 19, 1991, and Feb. 24, 1994. For similar findings in another developing country, see Sri Lanka, ARTI 1974: 37–38, cited in Herring 1983: 258. This 1974 study in Kandy district, Sri Lanka, found that among traditional share tenants, all of whom paid rent at more than double the legal maximum, 50 percent received *no* assistance from their landlords. By contrast, a survey of sharecropping in four states in India found that cost sharing emerged on a widespread basis with the diffusion of high-yielding varieties (Bardhan and Rudra 1980).

Chapter 3

1. McLennan 1969: 654. Renato Constantino implies that farming, though in transition, was communal rather than individual in all but the more advanced communities when the Spanish first arrived (1975: 38).

2. Some 120 Spaniards received land grants in the late sixteenth and early seventeenth centuries. The grants, all within a 100-kilometer radius of Manila, typically involved several hundred to several thousand hectares. These grants were rapidly consolidated: by 1612, the grants had been merged into thirty-four *estancias*, which became the core of the friar estates, although eleven *estancias*, as such, vanished altogether. The apparent Spanish lack of interest in landownership in the Philippines is to be attributed primarily to the much greater profits to be realized from the galleon trade (Roth 1982; see also Cushner 1976). Nicholas Cushner gives (apparently incorrect) area equivalencies, which are 20 percent higher than those of Dennis Roth. Cushner also calculates the number of land grants as over 200.

3. These legal prohibitions date from a royal decree of Philip II's in 1596, although this specific enactment was later revoked at the insistence of the Spanish friars (Constantino 1975: 70; Cushner 1976: 26; Roth 1977: 40).

4. In its present usage, the Spanish term *pacto de retroventa* encompasses a variety of credit schemes in which land serves as collateral (Bauzon 1975: 4 n. 5).

5. Wickberg 1964: 77. The 1768 legislation was specifically aimed at ending the use of the *pacto de retroventa* by the Chinese and part-Chinese mestizos.

6. Wickberg 1964: 87 nn. 81–84. Wickberg indicates that the "*indio* attitude toward the *mestizo* was not one of unmixed admiration. In many areas the *mestizo* was, after all, the *indio*'s landlord and moneylender . . . no doubt there was some basis for hostility in this kind of relationship" (1964: 87).

7. Haciendas are to be distinguished from *encomiendas*, which in the Philippines were grants of administrative jurisdiction for purposes of collecting tribute from the natives, who retained ownership of their landholdings, while all

uninhabited land was reserved for the Crown. Inheritance of *encomienda* grants was limited to two, at most three, generations, after which it was to revert to the Crown. The *encomienda* system was in rapid decline by 1755.

The hacienda system, which was based on landownership, became prominent in the Philippines after 1780 when the Spanish began to encourage export-crop production. The nineteenth century was marked by the emergence of significant rice and sugar haciendas in Central Luzon and, from midcentury onward, sugar haciendas in Negros. See Bauzon 1967; Constantino 1975: 43–49.

8. Many of the friar landholdings were acquired from Spanish land grantees through donations or mortgage foreclosures—the early Spanish *hacenderos* frequently borrowed from religiously endowed loan funds called *capellanías*. Donations and sales were also made by *datus*. Although the *datus'* traditional authority over land remains ill-defined, scholars suspect that these transactions were often made "without a scrupulous regard for legal niceties" (Roth 1977: 43; see also Roth 1982: 135; Cushner 1976: 18–20). At the end of the Spanish colonial era, the holdings of the various religious orders in the Philippines totaled some 215,000 hectares (Roth 1977: 2).

9. Although some of the friar estates initially employed sharecroppers, the system was completely phased out in the nineteenth century. The *inquilinato* system became the dominant mode of production on friar estates quite early. On some estates, *inquilinos* paid rent in kind; on others, payment was denominated in cash but paid in kind commensurate with prevailing rice prices.

10. Filipino peasants were ordinarily required to perform one month of labor per year for the Crown. The principal labor requirements were for logging and shipyard activities related to the galleon trade and maintenance of the Spanish navy. Although laborers were supposed to be paid for their service, the government frequently failed to do so. Monasteries and landowners (primarily religious orders) could petition the government for exemption of households—known as *casas de reservas*—that would work full-time on their haciendas. The prospect of exemption from the onerous forced labor requirement of the Crown apparently attracted considerable numbers of peasants to the friar estates (Cushner 1976: 50–53; Roth 1977: 67, 71–82).

11. The revolution of 1896 broke out in the Tagalog provinces with the greatest concentrations of friar landholdings (Hayami et al. 1990: 47). Located close to Manila, the friar landholdings were situated in those provinces most exposed to Western liberalism and the revolutionary ideologies of Filipino nationalists. Moreover, José Rizal and Marcelo del Pilar, two of the most prominent leaders of the Propaganda (or Reform) movement of the late 1800s, had grown up on or near friar estates (Roth 1977: 2).

Under Commonwealth Act 1120 (1903), some 166,000 hectares of friar lands were purchased at a price of roughly $7 million. More than half the area thus acquired was sold or leased to American and Filipino business concerns. As to the remainder, distribution favored villagers over existing tenants. In the absence of credit and extension or other support services, many of the tenants and villagers who received land eventually lost their parcels to local *hacenderos*.

12. Roth 1977: 79. Discussion of this revolt and the ensuing general uprising is extremely limited in the secondary literature. A 1725 account describes similar large-scale defections of exempted laborers from the same hacienda of Calamba, whereupon the government ordered the landowner to adopt the more humane labor practices of a neighboring hacienda (ibid.: 78–79).

13. In one case in 1603 part of a Jesuit hacienda was apparently returned to the residents of Quiapo with the assistance of the archbishop; the controversy appears to have been principally between Spaniards, with the benefits derived by the natives being somewhat incidental to the conflict's resolution (Cushner 1976: 57–58).

14. Well-defined property rights are generally regarded as essential to capitalist development. For example, cadastral surveys are seen as laying a "foundation for modern agricultural development" in Japan, Taiwan, and Korea (Kikuchi and Hayami 1978: 841).

15. Hayami and Kikuchi 1982: 74; Douglas 1970 (suggesting that at least 400,000 farmers lost their lands by this process); McLennan 1969: 673.

16. The *pasyon* is relived with extraordinary intensity each year in various villages of Luzon; one measure of its abiding influence in Philippine culture.

17. Initiation rites, pilgrimages, Holy Week retreats into the mountains, narratives describing revolutionary leaders in Christ-like terms, and *awits* (metrical romances) describing the Filipino-American war all reflect and borrow from the form, imagery or substance of the *pasyones*. See Ileto 1979.

18. We should not, however, mistake this for a vacillation between irrational and rational discourse. The term "supernaturalism" often connotes belief systems that are but quaint relics of the premodern era. Yet in our "modern," "secular" world, we too imbue inanimate objects with supernatural powers. For a broader discussion of the process of animating commodities in "modern" market economies and the attendant disruptions in precapitalist belief systems, see Taussig 1980.

19. The term "cult" is widely used in the Philippine media. An elite construction, the term tends to trivialize religious groupings that villagers see as expressions of local beliefs and as a means of revitalizing local culture. Having trivialized these social groupings, elites, be they traditional or revolutionary, are surprised when these groups rise up in rebellion or resistance. The term and the phenomenon—revival of local religions at a time of political strife—point up the continuing interplay between religiosity and politics. The often-successful attempts of the Philippine military to co-opt these groups or otherwise involve them in counterinsurgency campaigns makes this interplay all the more evident. For accounts of religious-based vigilante organizations and the military's role in promoting such groups, see LCHR 1988; van der Kroef 1988. Not all vigilante organizations are religion-based. For example, the Alsa Masa, one of the most prominent vigilante groups, was initiated by disgruntled former members of the NPA. The organization grew rapidly, with substantial assistance from the Philippine military.

20. The emphasis given the 1745 revolt reflects both the availability of Span-

ish archival materials describing it and the significance of the threat posed to Spanish rule by the revolt, which also provided the first evidence of widespread hostility toward the religious orders.

Rebellion was not the first course of action pursued by the disgruntled peasants. The 1745 revolt was preceded by a lawsuit begun in 1740 contesting land usurpation by a Dominican-owned hacienda. Gifts, bribes, and procedural injustices served to assure outcomes favorable to the religious orders in such cases. A resurvey fraudulently increased the already contested area of the hacienda by some 60 percent. This fraud, and the Dominicans' celebrations attendant on their legal victory, ultimately precipitated a revolt by aggrieved villagers (Roth 1977: 105–6).

21. Roth 1977: 100–116. In the case of one hacienda, the usurped lands were turned over to Chinese and mestizo tenants, adding an ethnic dimension to the grievances of those displaced. In the initial stages of the revolt, there was also an element of interclerical rivalry, with the Jesuits siding with the aggrieved villagers against the Dominicans. As the revolt spread, Jesuit haciendas were subject to attacks like those on the other religious orders, evidence of the general antipathy toward the religious orders as landowners.

22. See Scott 1976. For examination of rebellion in the Philippines using this analytical framework, see Kerkvliet [1977] 1979a; Scott and Kerkvliet 1973. Although intervening factors—alliances with other classes, the repressive capacity of landlords and the state, and the social organization of the peasantry—condition peasant activism and rebellion, the literature on moral economy concerns itself with peasant perceptions of exploitation that set the stage for such activism (Scott 1976: 4). "Moral economy" is a term coined by E. P. Thompson (1966). The literature on moral economy also owes much to anthropological work on closed corporate communities. See, e.g., Wolf 1957.

23. Many of the groups are listed in Kerkvliet [1977] 1979a: 37. For a discussion of the links between the KPMP and urban labor organizations, as well as with the Partido Komunista ng Pilipinas (PKP = Communist Party of the Philippines), see Pomeroy 1978: 501–3.

24. Lachica 1971: 14 (quoting a landowner); Kerkvliet [1977] 1979a; Kessler 1989: 18–19. William Pomeroy argues that in areas outside of Central Luzon, the Huk appeal was based primarily on the issues of corruption, repression, nonrepresentative government, and the betrayal of Philippine independence (1978: 512).

25. Theda Skocpol (1979), has identified this type of "revolutionary crisis"—defeat in war or the threat of invasion—as so undermining existing political authorities and state controls as to pave the way for the social revolution, but she overemphasizes the structural preconditions for successful social revolution, denying ideology, perceptions of exploitation, and volition any real role. By contrast, Eric Hobsbawm (1963) has emphasized the breakdowns in the structures and routines of everyday life—much as occurred in the Philippines when landlords fled to the cities or found themselves unable to continue advancing

rice and credit—in explaining the undermining of social control and the resultant unleashing of peasant discontent. See also Hobsbawm and Rudé 1968.

26. For a more inclusive listing of the organizations represented at the founding meetings of the United Front, of which the Huks were the military wing, see Kerkvliet [1977] 1979a: 98.

27. Ibid.: 66–67. Kerkvliet's analysis of the Huk movement during and after the war is widely treated as the authoritative work on the subject.

28. Pomeroy 1978: 504–5. Although the PKP "posed socialism as the ultimate goal, it was essentially the Philippine party of revolutionary nationalism," according to Pomeroy, an American Communist Party member who participated in the postwar Huk rebellion (ibid.: 502).

29. On the wartime activities of the Huks, see Kerkvliet [1977] 1979a: 78–104. See also Lachica 1971: 103–17.

30. In the context of social protest in the United States, Francis Piven and Richard Cloward note the importance of extreme social distress—in their case during the 1930s and 1960s—in fostering a "transvaluation" whereby social arrangements ordinarily perceived to be just and immutable come to be seen as both unjust and mutable (1977: 12).

31. For extensive discussion of the repression aimed at Huk veterans and their sympathizers, see Kerkvliet [1977] 1979a, chs. 4 and 5. Interestingly, the campaign of government repression was nearly two years old before the PKP and the Huk organization were declared illegal in March 1948.

32. Ibid.: 128–29 cites a PKM document claiming a membership of 500,000, which by his calculation was "nearly four times the combined membership of the two largest prewar peasant associations, the KPMP and AMT."

33. With the disqualification of these members, the "parity" amendment passed by one vote (ibid.: 150–51). Eduardo Lachica argues that the DA candidates won under "highly doubtful circumstances," suggesting that the former Huks had engaged in fraud and violence, yet the Philippine Supreme Court, which heard the case protesting the DA candidates' ouster, viewed the disqualifications as reflecting, not electoral irregularities, but the candidates common opposition to the parity amendment and the Bell Trade Agreement (Lachica 1971: 120–21).

34. Kerkvliet [1977] 1979a: 168. "Peasants who rebelled in Central Luzon, therefore, did so in desperation. They felt they had no other choice. Rebellion was not a step they had planned to take in order to get what they wanted. It was instead a reaction to an impossible situation" (ibid.: 262).

35. Letter from Luis Taruc, Huk commander, to President Roxas, quoted in ibid.: 154–55.

36. Ibid.: 171, quoting an interview with Luis Taruc in the *Manila Chronicle*, Feb. 7, 1947. In explaining the "mailed fist" policies of Presidents Roxas and Quirino, Lachica characterizes the various Huk demands as "near-impossible conditions" and "virtually dictatorial" (1971: 121, 122). Yet the demands were hardly revolutionary. Given the animosities involved, the Huks' call for dis-

missal of charges against Huk and Philippine military personnel alike is strikingly balanced. Nor were the agrarian reform demands extraordinary. The Agricultural Tenancy Act of 1954 (RA 1199) limited rent to 30 percent of the crop. Although limited to rice tenancy and largely unenforced, the passage of this provision suggests the moderate nature of at least part of the Huks' agrarian demands.

37. Pomeroy takes issue with this characterization, asserting that HMB expansion reached 27 provinces, including northern and southern Luzon and the Visayas (1978: 512).

38. For an extensive discussion of the Hardie Report and U.S. policy on land reform in the Philippines, see Monk 1990.

39. By Robert Hardie's account (1952), rural interest rates ranged from 30 to 400 percent per annum, with rates in the range of 100 to 200 percent per annum common for tenants.

40. This accusation was embodied in House Special Committee on Un-Filipino Activities, "A Preliminary Study and Analysis of the M.S.A. Hardie Report" (Manila, 1953). Filipino reaction to the report was mixed. President Quirino, House Speaker Eugenio Perez, Representative (later President) Diosdado Macapagal, Representative Jose O. Corpus, chairman of the Committee on Agrarian and Social Welfare, and Representative Tito V. Tizon, chairman of the House Committee on Un-Filipino Activities were among the most prominent critics of the Hardie Report. Nationalist Party leaders such as Senate President Eulogio Rodriguez, and Senators Gil Puyat and Cipriano Primicias defended the report, in part as a means of capitalizing on the embarrassment it caused the governing Liberal Party. A number of prominent Philippine journalists and newspapers also endorsed the report (Monk 1990: 42–51).

41. Dean Acheson, confidential cable to U.S. embassy, Manila, Apr. 18, 1952, DFB 5710, quoted in Monk 1990: 20 (emphasis added).

42. John Foster Dulles, to U.S. embassy, Manila, 2865, May 6, 1954, DFB 5710, quoted in Monk 1990: 71–72.

43. In language reminiscent of that used by critics to tar Hardie and his report, U.S. Secretary of Agriculture Ezra Taft Benson branded Ladejinsky a "socialist" and a "national security risk" and dismissed him from the Department of Agriculture. Although Benson subsequently had to withdraw and publicly apologize for his remarks (*New York Times* 1955) and Ladejinsky was reinstated in U.S. government employment, the die was cast. Ladejinsky was forced to resign permanently on obscure grounds, unrelated to security, in 1956 (Egan 1956; see also Prosterman and Riedinger 1987: 122 n. 25).

44. The United States delivered some $383 million in economic assistance and $117 million in military assistance between 1951 and 1956. Another $700 million in economic and military assistance had been provided between 1946 and 1950. The United States supplied "nearly all" of the tanks, firearms, ammunition, transportation, and communication equipment used by the Philippine military in combating the Huks (Kerkvliet [1977] 1979a: 244).

45. Robert Hardie argued with considerable prescience that the financial

costs of resettlement and the effects of rapid population growth would undermine any anticipated benefits of such resettlement. More important, he observed: "If not corrected, pernicious land tenure practices which have led to violent rebellion in Luzon will continue being transported to the newly developed area, thus spreading misery and unrest. Land tenure reform is needed quite as much for Mindanao as for Luzon" (1952: vi; see also 9–10). To Hardie's concerns should be added the ethnoreligious overlay that resettlement of Christians from Central Luzon in Muslim Mindanao would introduce to conflicts over land rights.

46. U.S. interest in agrarian reform appears to have waned even earlier, by mid 1953, prior to the election of Ramon Magsaysay as Philippine president (Monk 1990: 68).

47. The CPP was officially established on Dec. 26, 1968, the seventy-fifth anniversary of Mao Ze-dong's birth. By Gregg Jones's account, the CPP organizing group did not convene until Jan. 3, 1969 (1989: 17).

48. The principal party documents, all authored by "Amado Guerrero" (a pseudonym generally attributed to Jose Maria Sison, writing in collaboration with other colleagues), are Sison 1968a, a scathing critique of the PKP and justification for a new communist party; Sison 1970, the party bible, a workbook for party organizers; and Sison 1974, a reformulation of the military struggle in the light of martial law.

49. In addition to the earlier-noted significance of the CPP's founding date, Sison's penchant for establishing historical linkages by choice of organizational founding dates is illustrated by the case of the Kabataang Makabayan (KM = Nationalist Youth, or Patriotic Youth), which was created to unite militant trade unionists, students, and the children of the PKP's farmers' organization MASAKA (Malayang Samahan ng Magsasaka = Democratic Union of Peasants). Sison and colleagues established the KM on Nov. 30, 1964, the 101st anniversary of the birth of Andres Bonifacio, the plebeian founder of Katipunan (Kataastaasan Kagalanggalang Katipunan ng mga Anak ng Bayan = Highest and Most Honorable Society of the Sons of the Country). Katipunan is credited with initiating the Philippine fight for independence from Spain. The Nationalist historian Teodoro Agoncillo first popularized the view that Bonifacio should be seen as the true hero of the independence struggle, rather than the *ilustrados* José Rizal and Emilio Aguinaldo. For further discussion of Bonifacio's role, his use of the *pasyon* form in communicating Katipunan's message, and the revolutionary impulse Katipunan supplied "from below," see Ileto 1979: 93–139.

50. Kessler 1989: 61. The CPP/NPA has operated on the principle of self-reliance, receiving almost no foreign military assistance. The only exceptions appear to be token early assistance from the People's Republic of China (much of which was intercepted), alleged assistance from the Soviet Union via the Palestine Liberation Organization in the early 1980s, and alleged Soviet assistance in 1988. For a discussion of the Chinese assistance, see Jones 1989: 71–83. For discussions of the alleged assistance from the PLO and the USSR, see Kessler 1989: 100. Gareth Porter characterizes accounts of earlier Soviet assistance

as "very dubious" (1987b: 17). On the issue of foreign arms support, see also Chapman 1987: 21–22, 261.

As part of its international solidarity work, the Philippine insurgent movement kept abreast of, and expressed support for, the armed struggles of Palestinian nationalists and the Salvadoran insurgents. See *Liberation* 1988a; id. 1988b; id. 1988e. In 1992, the latter signed a peace accord with the Salvadoran government and are now pursuing elective office. In 1993, the former, at least as represented by the PLO, signed an agreement with the Israeli government establishing limited Palestinian rule in the West Bank and Gaza. These decisions have doubtless fueled the internal debates now raging within the CPP/NPA over the appropriateness and viability of prolonged armed struggle as a strategy.

51. While Pomeroy (1978: 512) takes exception to suggestions that Huk operations were limited to Central Luzon, the principal military engagements were confined to Central Luzon.

52. ROP, President, Office of the Press Secretary 1989: 6. At the time, the National Democratic Front (NDF), the CPP/NPA's popular front, placed the number of armed combatants at 12,500 (Babst-Vokey 1988). Note that the 1987 estimates of CPP/NPA armed forces by the AFP and NDF respectively represent almost exact reversals of the estimates they issued in 1986. At that time the NPA was claiming 20,000 full- and part-time guerrillas, while the government was insisting that NPA armed forces did not exceed 10,000 (Mediansky 1986).

53. Formally the CPP and the NPA are member organizations of the NDF. Satur Ocampo, an early NDF leader and NDF representative in the cease-fire and peace negotiations convened in late 1986—early 1987, insisted that "the NDF is *not* a Communist organization. Although the Communist Party is part of it, the NDF is not a total communist organization nor its program, communist. Communism is not on the agenda of the national democratic revolutionary movement" (interview printed in *Liberation* [the NDF publication] 1986b; emphasis in original). The NDF appears to be dominated by the CPP/NPA; it is frequently treated as essentially synonymous with the CPP/NPA. However, William Chapman, for one, argues that the NDF is not merely an arm of the party; the NDF pursues an independent course on occasion (1987: 215; see also Kessler 1989: 70).

54. All three were eventually arrested by the Marcos regime; they were among the political prisoners released by President Aquino. Zumel and Ocampo thereafter resumed their NDF activities. Morales assumed the leadership of the Philippine Rural Reconstruction Movement (PRRM).

55. Although the 1985 platform remained committed to genuine land reform and agricultural improvement, national industrialization was characterized as the "leading factor in economic development" (Kessler 1989: 83; see also *Liberation* 1986d). NDF publications make it clear, however, that industrialization is envisioned as a long-term process complementing agrarian reform and rural development. Implementation of a "genuine and comprehensive land reform aimed at eradicating the excessive monopoly of land ownership by a few and

the fair redistribution of lands to peasants and farm workers" was a fundamental element in NDF demands in the peace negotiations with the Aquino government in 1986 (*Liberation* 1986e).

56. Quoted in Jones 1989: 21. Nemenzo is referring to one of two widely protested incidents in which Filipinos were killed for innocently trespassing into U.S. military base areas in late 1964.

57. Jones 1989: 23–24. The influence of Mao and the Cultural Revolution is explicit in the earliest CPP document: "[The People's Republic of China] has consolidated itself as an iron bastion of socialism and the world proletarian revolution by carrying out the epochal and great proletarian cultural revolution and by holding aloft Mao Tsetung's Thought to illumine the road of armed revolution throughout the world. . . . The most significant development in the entire history of the Filipino people so far is the re-establishment and rebuilding of the Communist Party of the Philippines as a party of Mao Tsetung's Thought" (Sison 1968b: 45).

58. Corpus 1989: 183. Corpus's career is rather extraordinary. On Dec. 29, 1970, then a young lieutenant and instructor at the Philippine Military Academy, he defected to the New People's Army after leading a rebel raid on the PMA armory. Corpus played an instrumental role in honing the military skills and tactics of the NPA until his capture/surrender in January 1976. Imprisoned for ten years, Corpus was released as part of President Aquino's general release of rebel detainees. In October 1986, Corpus was reinstated into the Philippine armed forces as a lieutenant colonel.

59. NPA agrarian reforms are described in Chapman 1987: 126–28; Jones 1989: 176–82; *Liberation* 1986a; id. 1987a.

60. *Ang Bayan* 1987; Alag 1988; Jones 1989: 99, 176–82; *Liberation* 1988c; id. 1988d; Paredes-Japa 1988. Although they have encouraged CPP/NPA–mediated rent reductions, the insurgents have discouraged "silent" rent reductions— that is, individual acts of rent withholding or understatement of crop production, which promote individualism, undermining collective action and CPP/NPA authority (Lara interview, Feb. 19, 1991).

61. Although Marxist analysis is implicit in the social critiques and educational programs of the CPP/NPA, there are suggestions that peasants and workers are exposed only to a basic course in Marxist doctrine. More detailed instruction is reserved for educated cadres and party members. One scholar describes this decision in terms implying something of a condescending attitude toward the masses (Chapman 1987: 141). Although most of his remarks refer to NPA combatants, Gregg Jones's discussion suggests that the doctrinal portion of the mass educational process is more extensive (1989: 35, 49, 88, 225, 230–31). Yet Jones quotes a university-educated rebel who asserts that "peasants get bored with political sessions" (1989: 230).

62. Hawes 1990: 269–70; Hayami and Kikuchi 1982: 99–123. For discussion of tactical considerations in location of NPA base areas, see also Corpus 1989: 33–36.

63. Some landowners acknowledged the widespread nature of human

rights abuses. Hortensia Starke asserted that "the military and the CHDF are twice as guilty, if not more, than the NPA for the violence [in the countryside]" (interview, June 16, 1986).

64. Autonomy for the Muslims of Mindanao and the tribal populations throughout the Philippines—there are more than one hundred recognized tribal groups in the archipelago—has long been an element of the CPP/NPA plat-form. The CPP/NPA has enjoyed considerable success among tribal groups in the Cordillera mountain region of north-central Luzon. The most notable early success was the CPP/NPA's 1976 support of the Kalinga tribe in its resistance to government plans to construct a series of four dams on the Chico River with substantial foreign assistance, which would have flooded tribal villages, farms, and sacred ritual sites. After several years of conflict, the government aban-doned the project. See Chapman 1987: 127–28; *Diliman Review* 1987: 16–17.

65. In most instances, references to Marcos as the most effective recruiter for the NPA are figurative, reflecting the human rights abuses, destruction of demo-cratic political institutions, corruption, and economic mismanagement that characterized his rule. In one case, however, the allegation of a Marcos-NPA link was quite literal: Emilio N. Benedicto, Jr., a prominent conservative sugar planter, thought Marcos had promoted, indeed financed, the NPA insurgency as a means of securing greater military aid—with the attendant opportunities for graft—from the United States (interview, June 18, 1986).

66. So great was the student exodus that the CPP/NPA found itself un-prepared to accommodate all the potential revolutionaries (Chapman 1987: 101–3).

67. Jones 1989: 125. An account of revolutionary justice, involving the trial and reeducation of Civilian Home Defense Force members, is found in *Libera-tion* 1986c. While acknowledging the continuing human rights abuses under the Aquino government, Gregg Jones argues that "by 1989, land issues and rural poverty were the twin engines driving the revolution" (1989: 182). Rather than engage in the fruitless task of determining a dominant motivation, the analysis of Jones and other commentators should be seen as pointing to a variety of motivations underlying participation in the insurrection, all of which call for fundamental societal reforms.

68. See Chapman 1987; Jones 1989: 186–87; Kessler 1989: 78. Efforts to curb wife-beating, a practice evidently widespread in the Philippines, are mentioned in several accounts of CPP/NPA justice. CPP/NPA concern with this practice is ascribed to the prominent role of women in the movement (although there are suggestions that there is less gender equality within the movement in practice than in theory). See Chapman 1987: 120, 151 (see the latter page for an interview suggesting that repeat wife-beaters might be executed). For a discussion of women's involvement in the current insurgency, as well as the historical role of women in the Philippines, see Davis 1989: 119–55. For general discussions of the role of selective incentives—in the form of basic social services, rent reductions, and the like—as recruitment tools for institutionalizing revolutionary move-ments, see Migdal 1974: 241–49; Popkin 1979.

69. Kessler 1989: 152–53. Kessler approvingly cites Jeffrey Race's (1972) similar analysis of Vietnam.

70. For discussions of the Catholic Church and its relations to the CPP/NPA, see Chapman 1987: 199–213; Jones 1989: 201–13; Kessler 1989: 45–48; Porter 1986; Youngblood 1987: 1251–54.

71. Five days after the Sept. 21, 1972, declaration of martial law, the entire country was declared subject to land reform in Presidential Decree No. 2. On Oct. 21, 1972, Marcos announced the "emancipation of tenants from the bondage of the soil" in Presidential Decree No. 27, providing for the transfer of landownership to erstwhile rice and corn tenants. "Mr. Marcos is building the new Filipino society on the bedrock of land reform" (ROP 1973).

72. The notion of political space, specifically "democratic space," gained considerable currency in the early period of the Aquino government. The term referred to the enhanced opportunities for legal political action by the National Democratic Front and its constituent organizations, including the CPP/NPA. This space was most evident in the release of Sison and other CPP/NPA notables and the participation of NDF members and NPA rebels in public demonstrations and public news conferences at the outset of the government-NPA ceasefire. See Chapman 1987: 251–53; Jones 1989: 161–62.

73. Transcript of news conference by Antonio Zumel in *Liberation*, Feb.–Mar. 1986, 6, cited in Porter 1987b: 19.

74. For discussion of the CPP/NPA's 1986 election boycott decision and the resulting political fallout, see Jones 1989: 155–63; Porter 1987b; Third World Studies Center 1988. Party acknowledgment of a "tactical" error in the boycott policy appears in Communist Party of the Philippines 1986. See also *Ang Bayan* 1986a; Villalobos n.d.; id. 1986.

75. The CPP/NPA adopted Mao's "Three Main Rules of Discipline" and "Eight Points of Attention." The latter deals primarily with public relations, providing that rebels speak politely; pay a fair price for everything purchased; return everything they have borrowed; refrain from hitting or swearing at people; avoid damaging crops; abstain from taking liberties with women; and eschew ill-treatment of prisoners. Constitution of the Communist Party of the Philippines, reprinted in ROP 1970, quoted in Jones 1989: 33–34.

76. NDF tax policy is outlined in *Liberation* 1986f.

77. For discussions of the Mindanao purges, see Chapman 1987: 185–89; Jones 1989: 265–68, 274; and LCHR 1988: 19–20. The massacre of the cult members is described in Arguillas 1989; *Manila Chronicle* 1989c. Reflecting the Philippine practice, I use the terms "cult" and "cultists," although again I advert to the pejorative connotations often attendant to those terms.

78. NOPA and AABT 1987: 4 (emphasis in original). The position articulated above is echoed in congressional testimony of Nelson Oquendo: "The social problem that exists in Negros is not caused by the rift of the hacenderos as well as the workers. This is caused and aggravated by the presence of radical people whose approach to our economic problems are radical. They are trying to promote anger and hatred among our people. They divide our people and

that is not the cure of the present crisis that we are having now" (Oquendo 1987: 83).

79. In some contexts, landowners' references to external "communist" agents mean CPP / NPA cadres from other provinces or villages; in other cases, the external agents are foreigners, often priests, working in the Philippines. Emilio N. Benedicto, Jr., a prominent conservative sugar planter, decried the civil unrest in Negros Occidental, attributing it in part to Fr. Hector Mauri, an outspoken proponent of agrarian reform and a harsh critic of multinationals. Benedicto branded Mauri a "communist from Milan," commenting that there are "few who are not communist in Milan." Benedicto also suggested that foreign donors were witting or unwitting supporters of the NPA, accusing local priests of financing the NPA by inflating expenses for foreign-funded humanitarian work. Interview, June 18, 1986.

80. There is, however, some scholarly support for the notion articulated in the passage quoted in text. Kerkvliet emphasizes the moderate nature of the Huk agrarian demands—restoration of equilibrated tenancy relations—and attributes calls for land reform to the PKP ([1977] 1979a: 227–28, 254).

81. "Many guerrillas live in the city. They go to the hills periodically to collect taxes, to make money the easy way" (Benedicto interview, June 18, 1986).

82. Montemayor is a law graduate and former dean of the Law School of the Jesuit-operated Ateneo de Manila University. A descendant of landowners, Montemayor was reportedly related to some three-quarters of the landowning class in Pangasinan at the time of the FFF's founding. Cater 1959: 5, cited in Po and Montiel 1980: 39.

83. The 1971 legislation was RA 6389, the Code of Agrarian Reforms of the Philippines, approved Sept. 21, 1971. This law was effectively superseded by PD 2 and PD 27, dated Sept. 26 and Oct. 21, 1972, respectively.

84. Among those purged were Fr. Luis Jalandoni, later prominent in the National Democratic Front (NDF), and Gerardo Bulatao, later assistant secretary for support services at the Department of Agrarian Reform. See Monk 1990: 161 n. 115. See also Po and Montiel 1980; USAID 1975; Rocamora and Conti-Panganiban 1975.

85. The farmworkers were entitled to a production bonus under RA 809 (the Sugar Act of 1952), a reward for their support of landowners' efforts to increase the landowners' share of processed sugar relative to that paid to the mill.

86. Sa Maria seminars involved four days of intensive Christian training and dialogue. Originated by a sugarcane grower as a means of promoting passivity among farmworkers, the movement, under the leadership of Fr. Niall O'Brien, set the stage for the establishment of Basic Christian Communities and the attendant process of social analysis and criticism (O'Brien 1987; McCoy 1984b: 112–14).

O'Brien and others admit to considerable disappointment with the Sa Maria experience because of its emphasis on spiritual growth and the traditional liturgy. The grassroots impact was found to be "really domesticating, it simply reinforced the values of the landlords. Workers felt it was unchristian to join

unions because of the affront to landlords" (interview with Fr. Romeo Empestan, director, Diocesan Pastoral Center, Bacolod, July 5, 1989). As the lessons of Vatican II took hold, and the experiences of the Church in Latin America became better known, elements of the Philippine Church adopted a more activist social posture. BCCs became a vehicle for people to address local problems from a Christian perspective. "Religious teachings and faith were made concrete in real life" (ibid.).

87. Interviews, Mar. 3, 1989; July 5, 1989. See also *Ang Kristianong Katilingban* 1988; remarks of Serge Cherniguin in Collins 1989: 69–79.

88. As quoted by Serge Cherniguin, interview July 5, 1989. To illustrate the exploitative behavior of Negros landowners, Cherniguin stated that "in the past not more than 5 percent of the sugar planters observed the minimum wage [laws]. Now the planters claim that 29 percent are doing so." Unconvinced that compliance was this high, Cherniguin found it unsurprising that the planters should cite this woeful level of enforcement and compliance with basic social legislation as evidence of their commitment to the well-being of their farmworkers. Interview, July 5, 1989.

89. Letter from Zoilo de la Cruz to secretary of defense, quoted in McCoy 1984b: 144. The NACUSIP has consistently fared better than the NFSW in organizing sugar-mill workers; the NFSW claims greater success in organizing farmworkers. NFSW leaders attribute the NACUSIP's mill-related successes to the tight management control of the mills and management's preference for a nonmilitant "company" union. One consequence of the varying membership compositions of the two unions is the NACUSIP's considerable concern that agrarian reform not disrupt the production of sugarcane, lest it lead to unemployment among its mill-worker members. The NFSW, by contrast, emphasizes the importance of land redistribution and generally urges beneficiaries to attend first to food crops.

90. Association of Major Religious Superiors 1975, quoted in McCoy 1984b: 146. When I contacted the AMRS in 1988 to obtain a copy of this study, I was informed that all copies in their possession had been confiscated during a raid on their offices by the Marcos government years earlier, one measure of the controversial nature of the exposé.

91. Cherniguin interview, July 5, 1989. The remarks may involve some poetic license; Alfred McCoy indicates that only 60 complaints had been filed as of early 1975 (1984b: 143).

92. Again Cherniguin appears to have exercised some poetic license. Reliably determining union membership is well-nigh impossible, but McCoy puts NFSW membership at 8,000 in 1974, with chapters on 82 haciendas (1984b: 143). Another source states the 1974 membership figure as 6,400 (Jagan and Cunnington 1987: 18).

93. NFSW field offices—often little more than a room in a private residence—typically have a chalkboard inscribed with the details of numerous ongoing court proceedings, as well as pending union certification elections. The specifics of the various cases sound a common refrain: hearings on cases filed to contest

labor-code violations or land grabbing have been postponed time and again. The costs to the farmworker-complainants—in time away from work, travel costs, and the like—are not inconsiderable. Yet failure to appear at any one hearing may result in the rendering of a default judgment against the complainant. Judicial proceedings are often a war of attrition, with *hacenderos* much better equipped to go the distance (Hanisch 1978: 15–19). McCoy notes that of the 60 complaints filed by early 1975, 2 had been settled "amicably," but the remainder had been dismissed or were "hopelessly mired in procedural delays" (1984b: 143).

94. Cherniguin interview, Mar. 3, 1989. Increasing harassment, torture, and assassinations of union officials and members have somewhat dampened overt union participation in recent years, making any effort to determine union membership systematically impractical. For documentation of abuses directed against NFSW, see Amnesty International 1991.

95. Landowners may be justified in their concern. Judging from their actions in defense of farm-lot cultivators, the NPA (and, to a lesser extent, the NFSW) view this process of direct cultivation as establishing a basis for more permanent claims to the land on the part of landless cultivators. At least one NFSW official interprets the 1988 agrarian-reform law as prohibiting landowners from reclaiming farm lots (interview with NFSW program coordinator for land conflicts, Mar. 6, 1989). The law does provide that idle, abandoned, foreclosed, and sequestered properties be distributed as home lots and family-size farm lots (RA 6657, Sec. 40(5)). In the context of corporate farm stock-distribution and production-sharing arrangements, the law provides that such benefits are to be over and above the compensation currently received by farmworkers (RA 6657, Secs. 31–32). If farm lots are deemed a form of current compensation, the legislative language prohibits landowners who opt for stock distribution or production sharing from reclaiming farm lots.

Chapter 4

1. The process of ideological domination was first termed "hegemony" by Antonio Gramsci (1971). The concept is anticipated in the work of Marx and Engels (1965: 61; see also Tucker 1978: 172–73).

2. Rojas et al. interview, June 17, 1986. Accord, Benedicto interview, June 18, 1986.

3. One study of the sugar economy of Negros Occidental found 11 percent of the landowners surveyed to have operational holdings in excess of 200 hectares; 21 percent of the owners surveyed had holdings of 100 hectares and above (Lopez-Gonzaga n.d.: 1). A subsequent, comprehensive survey of landholding patterns in Negros Occidental by the same author revealed that fewer than 2 percent of all landowners in the province had holdings in excess of 100 hectares. However, these holdings averaged nearly 278 hectares each and accounted for over 35 percent of the province's total farm area (1988b: table 2).

4. Illustrative are the remarks of Eduardo M. Alunan, vice president, Rafael Alunan Agro-Development, Inc.: "Eighty percent of the [Negros Occidental]

landowners have under 10 hectares, 86 percent have under 25 hectares. Only 2 percent have holdings of 100 hectares or more. [The reform should] leave alone all farms below 100 hectares. No one is getting rich on 50 hectares unless they are growing herbs or prawns" (interview, June 16, 1986). Other Negros Occidental landowners asserted that only 2 percent of their brethren owned more than 50 hectares (Rojas et al. interview, June 17, 1986).

5. Although forestry and fishery activities are denominated as agricultural for census purposes, families engaged in these activities (as many as 0.65 million households in 1985) are not of immediate concern to our discussion of *redistributive* agrarian reform. Such families have thus been excluded from the agricultural population figures throughout this study. I do not intend thereby to minimize the economic or social plight of households engaged in forestry or fisheries. Nor should this choice be interpreted as prejudicing the claims of households engaged in forestry activities as squatters on public lands to have their status regularized through formal title or some form of long-term usufruct right.

6. Figures for physical area of farms, both total and by crop, appear in some cases to have been mistaken by Philippine government agencies and Filipino and foreign scholars as data for land under cultivation.

7. ROP, NEDA 1986b: 10, 25–26; World Bank 1985: 26. The higher estimate is from the World Bank study, which also defines underemployment differently—less than 60 days of employment annually. If this estimate, using this definition, is correct, then underemployment had reached alarming dimensions.

8. Data for the 1970s were conflicting; some studies showed wage levels declining, others indicated some recovery during 1970–78 (Hayami and Kikuchi 1982: 47–49; Lal 1983: 8; Quisumbing and Cruz 1986; World Bank 1985: 28–29). Meanwhile, wages in the manufacturing sector fell 3.0 percent per annum in 1970–80, then plummeted at an annual rate of 11.5 percent in 1980–85 (World Bank 1987c: 216; id. 1989: 176).

9. Some of this increase may reflect more inclusive census work in 1980.

10. The census reports data by operational farmholding—that is, by integrated farm operation—rather than by ownership. It thus *understates* concentration of landownership where, for example, a landowner leases out multiple operational holdings.

11. Shifting crops and eviction of tenants were prohibited by PD 815, dated Oct. 21, 1975. See also ROP, DAR 1974. However, the Marcos regime made no provision for effective enforcement of the ban. Interviews with evicted tenants, Nueva Ecija province, Mar. 22, 1986. Accord, Cornista et al. interview, Mar. 24, 1986. That evictions remained a continuing problem is acknowledged in a series of presidential directives. See PD 316, Oct. 22, 1973; PD 583, Nov. 16, 1974; and Letter of Instruction 226, Nov. 16, 1974. The reform also caused some landlords to terminate tenant cultivation rights between the rows of coconut trees for fear that the tenants might thereby establish a claim under the reform law. Cornista et al. interview, Mar. 24, 1986. Accord, remarks of Minister of Agrarian Reform Heherson Alvarez reported in Sandoval 1986: 121.

12. The estimate assumes rough equivalence between the number of hold-

ings under owner or ownerlike possession (nearly 2 million) and the number of landowning agricultural families. This procedure likely *overstates* the dispersion of landownership. The figures for landless agricultural laborers and total land-less families are commensurately *understated*. On the other hand, this procedure includes as "landless" those peasants with steady rural jobs and those who work on their parents' land. To the extent that peasants in either category have no desire to possess and operate their own farms, the estimate *overstates* the number of landless peasants who must be served by land reform (Seligson 1993: 4).

13. James Putzel (1992: 25) uses a smaller figure for agricultural families (3.9 million), based on NCSO 1985e. This figure reflects a lower estimate (39.8 percent) of the proportion of Philippine households engaged in agriculture in 1985 than is found in NCSO 1988 (49.6 percent) or FAO 1987 (49.2 percent). Putzel estimates that at least 2.2 million agricultural families, 56 percent, were landless or near-landless in 1985. Including farm families whose primary income was nonagricultural, Putzel argues that the landless and near-landless constituted 72 percent of all *rural* households in 1985 (1992: 25–27). These figures serve to confirm the pervasiveness of landlessness (and near-landlessness), even as their variance from the data in the text substantiates the need for more accurate data on land tenure and landlessness in the Philippines.

14. Institute of Agrarian Studies 1987b: 4. FAO figures for 1986 place the economically active population in agriculture at 9.92 million. The DAR uses a comparable figure (9.95 million).

15. By the calculations of two sugar-planters' organizations in Negros Ori-ental, parcelization of their farms would result in each farmworker receiving 0.6 hectares of land. The divisor—farmworkers—was not defined, so it cannot be determined whether both regular and temporary farmworkers were included. Nor are there data on the number of farmworkers per family (NOPA and AABT 1987: 3). Others put the ratio of farmworker families to hectares of sugar lands at 1:1 (Villarosa interview, June 19, 1986). Some peasant organization officials were similarly concerned that land redistribution would result in parcels of under one hectare (de la Cruz et al. interview, June 13, 1986). NACUSIP union mem-bers from Haciendas San Miguel, LabiLabi, and Aurora cited a ratio of two farmworker families per hectare of sugar land on the haciendas they worked (interview, June 18, 1986).

16. This argument was raised, for example, in interviews with Hortensia L. Starke, June 16, 1986, and Tadeo Villarosa, June 19, 1986.

17. Multiple cropping explains the apparent anomaly between land-use data—4.37 million hectares planted to all temporary crops—and data on ef-fective area harvested—6.42 million hectares for rice, corn, and sugarcane alone.

18. For the period 1950–80, Romeo Bautista found evidence of a "persistent and significant bias in relative incentives against agricultural export production in favor of non-traditional (mainly industrial) exports and, most strongly, of import-competing industrial consumer goods" (Bautista 1987: 9). Rice enjoyed a relatively favorable trade regime in the 1960s, but an unfavorable one in the 1970s.

19. The Bureau of Lands estimated, perhaps optimistically, that as of 1951, some 16.4 percent of the total Philippine land area was still arable and uncultivated. ROP, Director of Lands 1951: 90; id. 1956: table 9, both cited in Wurfel 1988: 60.

20. Villegas 1986: 153. The transfer of fertilizer-responsive high-yielding varieties from Japan to Taiwan and Korea is described in Barker et al. 1985: 56–57; Hayami and Ruttan 1985: 280–94. Japan also underwrote a significant expansion of irrigation infrastructure in Korea in the 1920s (Kikuchi and Hayami 1978: 850).

21. For a review of various formulations of the classic (and misnamed) "Marshallian" view concerning the relative efficiency of owner-operators, see Jaynes 1984. In the now-voluminous theoretical economic literature on share tenancy, challenges to the Marshallian position date largely from Cheung 1969. For reviews of the empirical studies of tenure and productivity, see Binswanger and Rosenzweig 1984; Herring 1983: 239–67; Otsuka and Hayami 1988 (this article also provides a review of the theoretical literature); Prosterman and Riedinger 1987: 35–71. In reviewing the literature, some scholars have concluded that share tenancy is not inefficient. See Johnston and Clark 1982: 87–88; Newbery 1975. Other scholars acknowledge inefficiencies attendant on share tenancy but argue that they are not significant. See Otsuka and Hayami 1988; Otsuka et al. 1990.

22. Depletion of soil fertility ("mining" the soil) by tenants is an established hazard in tenancy contracts. See Wallace and Beneke 1956; and studies by John F. Timmons and Wade Hauser of Iowa State University, cited in Stokes 1978.

23. Proper cross-national comparison should control for, among other variables, pricing policies for agricultural commodities and related inputs, infrastructural investment, trade policies, and the physical environment, all of which play a role in explaining differential productivity. Such analysis is beyond the scope of the present work. Although the comparison made here thus includes the effects of nontenure variables, the relation between dominant tenurial forms and average national crop yields remains striking.

24. For a discussion of China's effective decollectivization of agriculture, beginning in the late 1970s, and the attendant early productivity increases, see Prosterman and Hanstad 1990. As the name implies, the household responsibility system devolved farm decision making to individual households. It did not, however, confer the long-term security of ownership. Prosterman and Hanstad point to this shortcoming in explaining Chinese farmers' refusal to make long-term capital investments in the land, such as irrigation wells, land leveling, terracing, or tree planting. In consequence, Chinese agriculture has stagnated since the mid 1980s.

25. Data for Maharashtra state, India, were collected by the author during 1985 fieldwork.

26. Thailand assesses an export tax on rice, depressing the farm-gate price and with it the incentives for farmers to intensify production.

27. Collectivized agricultural systems were intermediate; they typically performed better than tenant/laborer systems, but rarely achieved the productivity levels of owner-operator systems (Prosterman and Riedinger 1987: 40–71).

28. See Powelson and Stock 1987; Prosterman and Riedinger 1987: 40–55, 213. Robert Bates (1981) has pointed to an alliance between the state and urban elites in explaining the adoption of policies that discourage small-farmer production in Africa.

29. Although the relative desirability of owner-operated farms versus tenant-operated farms might have been settled in the Philippines, there were some who questioned the appropriateness of a reform policy that called for the abolition of tenancy yet permitted the continuation of farm operations based on hired labor. See, e.g., Padilla 1986: 11–12.

30. Banana and pineapple producers made similar—if less vociferous—arguments. See, e.g., Sebastian 1987: 37–59.

31. Alunan interview, June 16, 1986. In support of the contention that farm-workers' incomes would decline with the fragmentation of large holdings, Alunan cited the prevalence of below-minimum wages on small farms. Despite the alleged inefficiency and low yields of these farms, the small planters "want to live as well as the big planters." Unable to afford the more luxurious lifestyle of the large landowners and simultaneously meet minimum-wage requirements, by Alunan's account, these small landowners choose the more privileged lifestyle at the expense of the legal entitlements and well-being of their farmworkers.

Whatever the relative greed of small versus large landowners, a 1976 ROP Department of Labor survey found that, with one exception, the differences between average daily farm wages on large (100 hectares and above), medium (40–99 hectares), and small (under 40 hectares) sugarcane farms in either the milling or nonmilling seasons were not statistically significant. Only during milling season were average daily earnings on small farms significantly lower than those on medium farms. Despite the general absence of statistically significant differences in average daily earnings, the percentages of workers earning less than the minimum daily wage were consistently and significantly higher on small farms than on large farms (Inocentes et al. n.d.: 42–47).

32. For a brief account of LUPA's founding convention, see Anda and Pastor 1990.

33. Remarks of Jeremias U. Montemayor, longtime president of the Federation of Free Farmers and former dean of the College of Law, Ateneo de Manila University, reported in *Solidarity* 1986: 23. Montemayor goes on to qualify his remarks by noting that in operational terms, coconut holdings are already fragmented; it is only ownership that is consolidated. While not contradicting his economies-of-scale argument, the implication of these further remarks is that reform of the coconut sector, to the extent it involved transfer of ownership to current operators, would entail no *decrease* in output.

34. For discussions of empirical studies of the relative efficiency of small-scale agriculture, see Berry and Cline 1979; Dorner and Kanel 1971; Herring

1983: 240–52; Lau and Yotopoulos 1971; Prosterman and Riedinger 1987: 58–65; World Bank 1987a: 79–83.

35. On the positive correlation between adoption of high-yielding varieties and farm size, see Frankel 1971; Lockwood et al. 1971; Schluter 1971. The last two studies confirm that smaller farmers adopted high-yielding varieties shortly after the larger farmers. Moreover, small farmers planted a greater proportion of their rice area to high-yielding varieties. See, generally, Barker et al. 1985: 146–50; Ruttan 1977.

36. See India, NCAER 1978; Barker and Herdt 1978: 91, 94, both discussed in Barker et al. 1985: 147–49. The IRRI study is also discussed in Hayami and Kikuchi 1982: 53–54.

37. Note that the history of Philippine cooperatives, most notably production cooperatives, is marked by frequent failures, a function of the political environment and government regulations as much as of the oft-cited individualism of Philippine peasants (Lopez-Gonzaga interview, June 17, 1986).

38. The ineffectiveness of efforts to diffuse innovations through progressive farmers has been attributed to a number of factors: progressive farmers have limited time and limited incentives to school others in the new techniques; and being socially distant from them, other cultivators are often reluctant to approach those identified as "progressive" by government bureaucrats and foreign aid personnel, who are frequently members of the local elite (Schönherr and Mbugua 1974, cited in Johnston and Clark 1982: 101). For discussions of successful credit and extension programs utilizing "blocks" of small farmers, see Johnston and Clark 1982: 101–2; Prosterman and Riedinger 1987: 209–10.

39. In production co-operatives, output is sensitive to the labor input—in time and effort—of each member. Where proceeds are divided equally or where proceeds are imperfectly tied to labor input—because supervision, particularly of effort, is difficult and costly—each member has an incentive to shirk, "free riding" on the labor of other members (Dorner 1972: 54–62).

40. The data presented are aggregate, with no control for land quality, access to infrastructure, and the like.

41. One picul equals 63.25 kilograms of raw sugar. For the period 1974–83, Philippine sugar producers averaged roughly 1.6 piculs of raw sugar per metric ton of harvested sugarcane (Aguilar 1984: 52, table 3.4).

42. Sabino 1987: 18; Nasol 1987: 19. See also Hayami et al. 1987: 15. A survey of Manapla district in northern Negros Occidental revealed an average of one tractor for every 44 hectares planted to sugarcane (McCoy 1984b: 62). For tractor specifications and depth of plowing, see McCoy 1984b: 60–63. See also Hernandez 1987: 28.

43. Recent data on the relative efficiency of small sugarcane farms in Batangas and Bukidnon are not available. The development of the custom-plowing markets largely antedates the 1980 agricultural census, which still suggested economies of scale in sugarcane production in these provinces. ROP, NCSO 1985c: 6, table 1.8; id. 1985d: 6, table 1.8.

44. In 1986, it was the consensus of 32 union officials from eleven Negros

Occidental sugar haciendas that the laborers they represented would grow corn, rice, and vegetables if given individual parcels under the reform program (interview with NACUSIP officials, June 15, 1986). It is less appropriate to generalize, as some landowners do, from the crop choices of farmworker-participants in various land-sharing schemes. While virtually all of these parcels are devoted to basic staples and vegetables, such planting choices reflect the immediate scarcity of such items in farmworkers' diets, the commercial potential of vegetables and herbs, and the limited possibilities for commercial production of sugar on parcels of a few hundred or a thousand square meters.

45. Those arguing for maintenance of sugar production included Bernardo Villegas, Center for Research & Communication (viewpoint attributed to him by Violeta Lopez-Gonzaga, interview, June 17, 1986), and the National Congress of Unions in the Sugar Industry of the Philippines (Jimenea and Gison interview, Mar. 1, 1989). Those stressing the need for diversification or food security included Violeta Lopez-Gonzaga (interview, June 17, 1986), the National Federation of Sugar Workers (Espallardo interview, Mar. 6, 1989); and Asian Development Bank 1988.

46. Dago-ob interview, Oct. 25, 1988; also Fortich interview, Oct. 22, 1988. Bishop Fortich put the contribution at P5 per picul, for a total of P50 million per year. Dago-ob described the contribution as P7 per picul, and the total as P100 million annually. See also Amnesty International 1991.

47. See also National Federation of Sugarcane Planters n.d.: 9. Focusing on milling, Hans Binswanger and Mark Rosenzweig describe sugarcane growing as "a classic case of economies of scale, combined with the co-ordination problem" (1986: 529). They note, however, that the requisite coordination of harvesting and processing has been accomplished in settings of smallholder agriculture such as India and Thailand.

48. This logic is accepted, e.g., in Bautista et al. 1983: 76. As a member of a 1987 World Bank mission, William C. Thiesenhusen of the University of Wisconsin's Land Tenure Center subsequently repudiated the idea of economies of scale (World Bank 1987a: 83).

49. Author's interviews or observations of operations at Victorias Milling Company, Negros Occidental; Central Danao, Negros Occidental; Central Azucarera de Don Pedro, Batangas; Southern Negros Development Company (SONEDCO); and the Hawaiian-Philippine Company, Negros Occidental. See also Asian Development Bank 1988; Hayami et al. 1987: 15–16.

50. For a discussion of the CADP experience, see Hayami et al. 1987: 15–16, citing Picornell et al. 1984; Picornell 1985. Similar processing issues have arisen and been successfully addressed in Africa in connection with small-farmer production of tea, long regarded as a plantation crop par excellence (Johnston and Clark 1982: 100–101).

51. That political considerations should drive political decisions is hardly surprising. As understood by economists, "rational" decision making—that is, decision making based purely on considerations of Pareto efficiency—is a mythical situation. What I mean to emphasize is that such decision making is even less likely where views on how best to promote economic efficiency differ.

52. These are the principal pieces of reform legislation. They are by no means the only legislative enactments aimed at regulating landlord-tenant relationships or effecting land redistribution. Texts of several early enactments, or summaries thereof, can be found in Hardie 1952. Citations to the early enactments can also be found in Tai 1974: 145.

53. For discussions of the Friar Lands Act, see Connolly 1992: 3–4; Constantino 1975: 303–4; IBON Databank Philippines 1988: 28–29; Sturtevant 1976: 54–56.

54. The text of the Rice Tenancy Act, and related amendatory legislation, can be found in Hardie 1952: G24–G37. See also Bauzon 1975: 16; Hayami et al. 1990: 54; Murray 1973: 154–55.

55. The Magsaysay campaign, including the CIA's prominent role in promoting Magsaysay's candidacy, is described in Karnow 1989: 352–53, and Thompson 1989: 2–4. See also Abueva 1971; Starner 1961.

56. The distinction between share-tenancy and leasehold blurs when leases are short-term, as is generally the case in the Philippines. Where the landlord can annually adjust the rent level to take account of any increases in production, the notion of "fixed" rents becomes essentially meaningless—at least to landlords; since they bear all risks of crop failure under the leasehold, leasehold tenants are likely to be disadvantaged relative to their share-tenant status.

57. The debates are detailed in Starner 1961; excerpted in id. 1969, and Tai 1974: 144–71 (which draws heavily on Starner's work).

58. Starner 1961: 273, quoting Manuel V. Gallego, "Communism Under the Guise of Democracy."

59. Reflecting the importance of sugar as an export crop, prominent members of the sugar bloc held senior positions in the executive and legislative branches and the Philippine Chamber of Agriculture. The sugar bloc thus had an opportunity to influence the reform deliberations without attracting the kind of public attention given NRPA (Starner 1969: 232–33).

60. For the calculations, based on the 1948 agricultural census, see Tai 1974: 170. Tai also provides an excerpted version of the 1955 law (1974: 513–14).

61. Hayami et al. 1990: 56. Tai cites somewhat higher figures, indicating that 50,000 hectares were acquired between 1954 and 1958 (1974: 537). This would still represent less than 1 percent of Philippine farm area.

62. PD 27, Oct. 21, 1972. So great was the landless pressure on the available land resources at the time PD 27 was announced that distribution of 3- or 5-hectare parcels to beneficiaries would have required the displacement of at least two tenant families for every family benefited. In the event, the average parcel distributed under the program was, as of year-end 1988, 1.38 hectares (ROP, DAR 1988: 4).

63. Specifically, the valuation formula was "two and one half times the average harvest of three normal crop years immediately preceding the promulgation of [PD 27]" (PD 27, Oct. 21, 1972).

64. The dates listed represent the principal years of land redistribution; in both South Korea and Taiwan, redistribution continued on a very modest scale in subsequent years. These land reforms and others were well known in the

Philippines. See, e.g., Golez and Gayo 1987; Ledesma 1980; Mao 1987; Wang 1987. The classic analyses of the Japanese land reform are Hewes 1955 and Dore 1959. For Taiwan, see Cheng 1961; Koo 1970; Kuo et al. 1981. For South Korea, see Harrison 1968; Morrow and Sherper 1970.

65. PD 816, Oct. 21, 1975, provided that tenants who refused to make such rent payments for two years would lose their rights under the reform program. In practice "many" leasehold tenants discontinued their rent payments (Kerkvliet 1983: 47).

66. Later, the government established Barangay committees on land production—made up of the barrio leader, a cooperative representative, four tenant representatives, two landlord representatives, and a DAR official—to determine land values, with little evident improvement in the pace of valuation determinations. Guidelines and procedures for the organization and operation of the Barangay committees on land production can be found in ROP, DAR 1977.

67. Bautista 1978: 27–28, cited in Wurfel 1983: 9. Kerkvliet indicates that DAR officials and researchers had expected valuations to run in the P4,500–5,000 per hectare range; in practice the average price paid as of late 1975 was P6,500 per hectare (Kerkvliet 1979b: 140). By these figures, the average price paid was 30–44 percent higher than the expected valuations.

68. Some 1,000 hectares of the Cojuangco family holdings in Central Luzon were also taken, but in this instance Marcos reportedly rewarded Eduardo Cojuangco, a top "crony," with 10,000 hectares on Bugsuk Island and additional holdings elsewhere (Mangahas 1987b: 148).

David Wurfel argues that Marcos pushed the reform until the holdings of owners with more than 100 hectares had been expropriated (1983: 8). DAR had prioritized—to little effect—the redistribution of "large" estates, those with 100 hectares or more, even before PD 27 was decreed. See ROP, DAR 1972. Formally at least, Marcos ordered the reform be implemented on landholdings down to 7 hectares (1974). To facilitate this process, Marcos increased the cash portion of the compensation to 20 percent (30 percent in some cases) for landowners with holdings of 7–24 hectares (1975). However, small landowners continued to evidence considerable opposition to the reform, apparently dampening Marcos's interest in pursuing the reform process (Richter 1982: 68–69). In explaining the poor implementation record, Linda Richter also cites the reform's disappointing impact on productivity, its administrative complexity, and the limited offers of foreign assistance for land transfers.

I have been unable to locate national data on the patterns of implementation of PD 27. It is my impression that implementation was not applied as uniformly by farm size as Marcos's public instructions to the DAR would suggest. Political enemies appear to have been subjected to expropriation regardless of farm size, although the prominence of some political opponents was related to the size of their holdings. At the same time, many large landowners were well positioned to influence local DAR officials and avoid application of the law.

69. To inflate their own relative accomplishments, both the Aquino and Ramos governments adopted this most negative reading of Marcos's reform

performance. Other observers have contested the reform accomplishments of the Aquino government, arguing that the Marcos administration had implemented much of its reform program, save only for the formalities of surveying and titling (Bulatao 1992: 7; Bulatao interview, Feb. 16, 1994).

70. See, e.g., press release of government-owned Philippine News Agency, quoted in Wurfel 1983: 9 (Minister of Agrarian Reform Conrado F.) Estrella 1976: 36.

71. At every administrative step in the reform process, there was a significant fall-off in performance. Figures compiled in late 1977 illustrate the problem. CLTs had been printed in Manila for 247,862 tenants. The CLTs of 130,000 tenants (52 percent of those for whom CLTs had been printed) had been delivered to the villages; perhaps one-fifth of these had not been given to tenant-beneficiaries because of legal challenges to their land claims. The Department of Agrarian Reform had received property valuations for the parcels of only 80,865 tenant-beneficiaries. Of these, valuations for the parcels of 68,072 tenant-beneficiaries had been transmitted from the DAR to the Land Bank, the agency responsible for payment of compensation. Finally, the Land Bank had paid compensation for the properties of only 41,614 tenant-beneficiaries. The process of delivering CLTs and transforming tenant-beneficiaries into "amortizing owners" had thus reached fewer than 17 percent of the tenant-beneficiaries for whom CLTs had been printed, and only 4.6 percent of the government-estimated 914,000 rice and corn tenants, or 8 percent of the 514,000 tenants the government then estimated to be eligible under the redistribution program (Hickey and Wilkinson 1977: table 1).

72. Talatala interview, Mar. 20, 1986; F. Lara, Jr. interview, Feb. 21, 1989. See also ROP, DAR 1986a; IBON Databank Philippines 1988: 37.

73. ROP, DAR 1987b: 9; id. 1988: 5. The latter report cites a number of other administrative simplifications designed to facilitate issuance of Emancipation Patents.

74. In theory, fixed-rent tenants have greater incentives to make production-enhancing investments—such as land improvements or increased use of labor, fertilizer or pesticides—since they receive the full return on such investments. Share tenants, by contrast, receive only a portion of the return on such investments. In practice, many fixed-lease contracts are negotiated anew each year (affording landlords ample opportunity to increase rent levels in order to capture much of any increase in production) and thus differ from share-tenancies only in the leasehold tenant's assumption of more of the risks of production.

There is, however, evidence from one Philippine village that leasehold contracts there were fairly stable and rarely renegotiated, at least in the years preceding the introduction of high-yielding rice varieties. The study also indicates that as a consequence of Operation Leasehold, leasehold tenants captured a greater portion of the economic returns on land as yields increased than did share tenants; in turn, leasehold tenants increasingly, and illegally, captured this return by subrenting their parcels (Hayami and Kikuchi 1982: 110–13). Nonetheless, the study found that leasehold tenants made lower investments in cur-

rent inputs than did share tenants or subtenants. Leasehold tenants committed more capital and labor per hectare than did share tenants, but still trailed subtenants. Rice output followed the same pattern: leasehold tenants outperformed share tenants (2.89 mt/ha versus 2.75), and both were surpassed by subtenants (3.45 mt/ha). These results evidence a more complex relationship between the various forms of tenancy and investment incentives than is suggested by classical economic theory.

75. The maximum allowable rent is "the equivalent of 25 percent of the average normal harvest for the three agricultural years immediately preceding the date the leasehold was established after deducting the amount used for seeds and the cost of harvesting, threshing, loading, hauling and processing, whichever are applicable" (RA 3844 [1963]).

76. Interviews of share and leasehold rice tenants in Bulacan, Nueva Ecija, and Pangasinan, Mar. 1986. Also Adriano interview, Mar. 20, 1986. See also Bautista et al. 1983: 76; ROP, ITFAR, 1987b: 23 (which assumes rice and corn share rents of 33.3 percent of the gross crop); Panganiban 1983: 111; Samson 1991: 347, 351.

77. DAR personnel were variously threatened, shot, or transferred (Cornista et al. interview, Mar. 24, 1986).

78. See Herring 1983: 26–31; Lipton 1974; Prosterman and Riedinger 1987: 179–82. Bruce Johnston and William Clark view regulation of tenancy relations as promising illusory benefits and, because of problems of enforcement, often resulting in a deterioration in the status of tenants through increased use of short-term, verbal tenancy agreements or eviction. Interestingly, they cite the Philippines as an exception to this rule (1982: 87 n.18). In my experience, tenancy regulations are generally unenforceable, but even so they can be harmful to the status of tenants. Contrary to the implication of Johnston and Clark, most tenants in developing countries are already operating under short-term, typically verbal leases. Where they exist, written leases are often supplemented by verbal "understandings" (Prosterman and Riedinger 1987: 36–40, 179–81).

79. As amended or supplemented by RA 1400 (1955), RA 1266 (1956), and RA 3844 (1963).

80. "After generations of population pressure, *the amount of unoccupied public land available for distribution is no longer significant*," Mahar Mangahas concluded in 1986 (1987b: 146; emphasis in original). Other Philippine scholars had reached much the same conclusion.

81. This figure reflects the area approved for payment of compensation under Operation Land Transfer (258,638 ha) and the area covered by Certificates of Land Transfer under the Landed Estates program (54,986 ha).

82. This is the number of families associated with land approved for payment of compensation under Operation Land Transfer (134,371), plus those families who have received CLTs under the Landed Estates Program (33,503).

83. IBON Databank Philippines 1988: 39; ROP, ITFAR 1987b: 14. Minister of Agrarian Reform Heherson Alvarez put the amortization payment rate at 9 percent (Sandoval 1986: 123).

84. By the account of a representative of sugarcane landowners, 33 percent of the PD 27 reform beneficiaries had sold their lands or subleased them (Hernandez 1987: 26). One grower claimed that landowners affected by PD 27 had been paid the "very low price of P5,000 to P6,000 per hectare," while reform beneficiaries sold cultivation rights for "P50,000 to P52,000" per hectare (Dizon 1987: 92–93). Philippine scholars believed that members of the Philippine military and wealthy landowners were buying up land covered by CLTs. In other cases, cultivation rights (*puesto*) to redistributed parcels were allegedly sold to nonbeneficiary tenants for more than the cost of the land (Adriano et al. interview, Mar. 20, 1986; Beebe interview, Mar. 21, 1986 (citing personal observations from dissertation-related research during 1976 in a village in Bulacan province); Guanzon interview, June 19, 1986; Villarosa interview, June 19, 1986).

85. Villarosa interview, June 19, 1986. The "dead season" is the nonmilling season in the sugar industry, when employment opportunities are few for landless laborers and hunger-related infant and child deaths are relatively high.

86. For a description both of mechanisms by which to simplify reform administration and the consequences of failure to adopt these procedures, see Prosterman and Riedinger 1987: 136–39, 165–68, 179– 89. Local politics and the relative ignorance of *barangay*-level adjudicatory groups concerning the formal provisions of the reform law in part explain the frequent recourse to agrarian relations courts (Cornista et al. interview, Mar. 24, 1986). Landowners, with their superior resources, could better afford protracted litigation and, given their political influence, were more likely to prevail in such litigation. In what was described as "the most common practice," landowners would file spurious criminal charges against tenants; once imprisoned, these tenants could lose their rights under the reform program, being unable to demonstrate that they currently cultivated the parcels for which they had applied. See Takigawa 1974: 71, cited in Kerkvliet 1979b: 126.

87. Hernandez 1987: 26. See also Billig 1992; id. 1991. In attributing the slow pace of compensation to "bureaucratic obstacles," Michael Billig (1992) appears uncritically to adopt the landowners' viewpoint. He largely ignores—although he does cite—DAR estimates that landowners have rejected "over 90 percent" of the valuations established by the Land Bank of the Philippines (Billig 1991). In this view, the "bureaucratic obstacles" appear to consist primarily of bureaucratic unwillingness to abdicate responsibility and accede to landowners' valuation demands.

88. Typical of the complaints was that of Eduardo Alunan, who reported that his family's 600-hectare farm in northern Luzon, taken under PD 27 in 1972, was not paid for until 1982 (interview, June 16, 1986).

89. ROP, General Order 47 (May 27, 1974). This order reflected the same 1973 shortfall in basic food-crop production that prompted the introduction of the Masagana 99 credit program. The order expected that corporations would either open new land to rice and corn production, increase productivity on existing parcels by applying corporate "profit-making" know-how, or directly import the required foodstuffs. When announced, the corporate food-crop pro-

duction program was to last a minimum of three years; it remained in force through the Marcos era.

90. Wurfel 1988: 173. Rene Ofreneo cites figures suggesting that corporations were directly cultivating almost 27,000 hectares of rice, corn, and other grains as of December 1978 (1987: 79). Mari Tiongson et al. indicate that by 1979, the corporate farming program had extended to a total of 487 corporations operating 60,424 hectares (1988: 29–30). Without citation, Steven Hick indicates that the corporate farming program encompassed 487 corporations and 66,424 hectares (1987: 33). There would appear to be a typographical error in one or other of these sources, but I have been unable to determine which figure is correct. Eduardo Tadem states elsewhere that the corporate farming program resulted in the transfer of 47,801 hectares to 70 corporate farms (1980: 2, cited in Feder 1983: 128–29).

91. Cf. Asian Development Bank 1988: 17; and ROP, NCSO 1985a. The area planted to sugarcane in 1958–59—before Cuba's share of the U.S. sugar import quota was reallocated to the Philippines—was 195,851 hectares (NFSP 1960).

92. PD 1066, Dec. 31, 1976, exempted from land reform all untenanted sugar land converted to priority crops (rice and corn) and livestock production. To the extent that landowners substituted rice and corn for sugarcane, the permanent plantation labor force was afforded some continuing employment opportunities. Generally, the decline in sugar prices and the resulting sharp reductions in the area planted to sugarcane were accompanied by wage freezes and significant cutbacks in benefits for the *duma-ans* ("permanent" or "regular" plantation laborers). In response, laborers backed a campaign of demonstrations and strikes by the NFSW. Hacienda workers began planting food crops on idle sugar land. Under the guidance of Roberto Benedicto, the chairman of the Philippine Sugar Commission (Philsucom) and a Marcos crony, the Philippine Constabulary harassed, arrested, and tortured union organizers and sympathizers. See McCoy 1984b: 149–58. On Negros, the retrenchment in sugarcane production also occasioned a marked decrease in employment opportunities for migratory laborers from other islands, the traditional harvest labor force.

93. Data on areas planted to bananas, coconuts, and pineapples are from Feder 1983: table 20, p. 164. For further discussions of the expansion of banana and pineapple production in the 1970s, see David 1982; Ofreneo 1987: 97– 122.

94. The areas devoted to banana, coconut, and pineapple production in Mindanao increased 160 percent (82,400 ha), 108 percent (819,470 ha), and 205 percent (38,970 ha) respectively between 1970 and 1980 (Feder 1983: tables 23 and 24, p. 167). Note that during the same period the area devoted to rice and corn production in Mindanao also increased, by 32 percent (209,670 ha) and 30 percent (360,520 ha) respectively.

95. On the earlier studies—Sandoval and Gaon 1972, and Takahashi 1969— see Ledesma 1980: 326; on the 1978 studies—Angsico et al. 1978, and San Andres and Illo 1978—see ROP, ITFAR 1987b: 4.

96. The term "weapons of the weak" is taken from Scott 1985.

97. The theoretical literature posits the existence of share-tenancy to be a

function of tenants' aversion to risk—providing a mechanism for sharing of the risk between landlord and tenant—and the high costs to landlords of monitoring tenants' work. See, e.g., Braverman and Stiglitz 1982; Stiglitz 1974. For classic discussions of the risk aversion of peasants near subsistence and the willingness of those with small surpluses to incur certain investment risks, see, respectively, Scott 1976 and Popkin 1979.

98. One notably distressing finding in the Plaridel study was the apparent decline in real terms of the net value of rice production per hectare; this despite a marked increase in rice production and in household labor devoted to the farm. While the study attributes this to rapidly rising input costs, the findings seem inconsistent with other data in the survey indicating improved living conditions and real increases in both farm and household income. John Carroll (1983) suggests that the results may be reconciled if the increased farm income came from production other than rice. Alternatively, weaknesses in the baseline income data may explain the discrepancies.

99. The remaining 114 respondents fit none of these categories, often working multiple parcels under a mixture of tenure statuses.

Chapter 5

1. Speech to the Management Association of the Philippines, Makati Business Club, and Bishops-Businessmen's Conference for Human Development, Jan. 6, 1986, reprinted in Aquino 1986a.

2. Aquino identified "restoring democracy" as her primary objective (*Philippine Daily Inquirer*, Mar. 1, 1986). This commitment can also be seen in the agenda Aquino outlined for her first 100 days in office during a campaign speech on Feb. 3, 1986. She promised a constitutional convention, an end to presidential decree-making authority, and restoration of the writ of habeas corpus. She further pledged to end the media's progovernment bias and repeal legal prohibitions on the right to strike (*New York Times* 1986b). Aquino's second presidential proclamation restored the writ of habeas corpus (Proclamation No. 2, Mar. 2, 1986).

3. A spokesperson testified to Congress that "75%" of the lands of sugarcane growers on Negros had already been foreclosed (Hernandez 1987: 31). A publication of the provincial government estimated that 75 percent of sugar land was mortgaged, of which 70 percent was foreclosable. See *Negros Development Digest* 1987: 13. At the time, Negros landowners regularly estimated that 80 percent of the sugar planters were in serious financial difficulty (Locsin interview, June 16, 1986; Starke et al. interview, June 16, 1986; Guanzon interview, June 19, 1986). Romeo Guanzon estimated that without financial relief "at least 80 percent of the sugarcane farms in Negros will be foreclosed" (letter to President Corazon C. Aquino, May 5, 1986). In recounting the sugar crisis, an official of the National Federation of Sugar Workers gave an even higher estimate—86 percent (Cherniguin interview, Mar. 3, 1989). It appears that more accurate estimates for Negros Occidental would be as follows: 70 percent (140,175 ha) of

the *mortgaged* sugar land (199,067 ha) and 53 percent of *all* sugar land in the province (267,000 ha) was foreclosable; of the 7,145 sugar planters with mortgaged property, 75 percent (5,383) held property that was foreclosable (ROP, ITFAR 1987c: table 1). Another source put the total mortgaged sugar land at 203,705 hectares (David n.d.: 2).

4. Guanzon interview, June 19, 1986. In his successful campaign for a seat in the Philippine House of Representatives, Guanzon also purported to support agrarian reform. See *Viewpoints* 1987: 5 (criticizing Guanzon's abandonment of his campaign promise). Congressman Guanzon subsequently asserted his opposition to the Comprehensive Agrarian Reform Law, while claiming to favor land reform in principle (interview, July 1, 1989).

5. Private armies were explicitly banned by the 1987 Constitution, and the CHDF was to be dissolved or, where appropriate, integrated into the regular armed forces. 1987 Constitution of the ROP, Art. 18, Sec. 24.

6. This is not to say that the Catholic hierarchy was united behind a program of liberal reform. Many bishops remained quite conservative in outlook. For discussions of the Catholic Church in the Philippines, see Giordano 1988; Ofreneo 1987; Shoesmith 1985; Youngblood 1990.

7. Aquino's natal (Cojuangco) family owns Hacienda Luisita, a 6,000-hectare sugar plantation in Tarlac province, Central Luzon. Her first minister of agriculture, Ramon Mitra, had extensive cattle holdings in Palawan. He had also served previously as "one of the [sugar] planters' most outstanding lawyers" (Wurfel 1969: 215). By contrast, a prominent sugar planter argued that Mitra was a coconut grower who did not understand the sugar business (Benedicto interview, June 18, 1986). Aquino's first minister of defense, Juan Ponce Enrile, had profited handsomely in the coconut business during the martial-law years, serving as director of the Philippine Coconut Authority, chairman of the United Coconut Planters Bank, and chairman of the Philippine National Bank, all concurrently with his service as defense minister. Enrile also had important interests in the timber industry (Bonner 1988: 264, 329; Butterfield 1978). With one exception, all of Aquino's cabinet appointees were peso millionaires or multimillionaires.

8. The most notable of the late-defecting members of the Aquino regime were Defense Minister Enrile and General Fidel V. Ramos, the two leaders responsible for launching the military rebellion that ousted Marcos. Concerns were expressed over the depth of the pro-Aquino commitment of former Marcos supporters in Estacio interview, June 16, 1986. See also Bello 1986. For a discussion of prominent political defections from Marcos's KBL party to the opposition in the final weeks before the February 1986 presidential election, see Crisostomo 1987: 171–72.

9. This interpretation is widely, although not universally, accepted. By contrast, Jose Maria Sison, founder of the CPP, emphasized the role of BAYAN (see n. 26 below) and cause-oriented organizations of the left, the "hard core," in sustaining the revolutionary demonstrations at EDSA and in pressuring Malacañang. Remarks of Jose Maria Sison in Mercado 1986: 243. See also *New York Times* 1986d.

10. An account of the political involvement of President Aquino's extended family—the Cojuangcos, Sumulongs, and Aquinos—and of her upbringing can be found in Crisostomo 1987.

11. See Doronila 1986. In a remark apparently intended to suggest Aquino's affinity with peasants, Lewis Simons in fact conveys a sense of considerable distance between Aquino and peasants: "Coming from a background in which she was naturally treated with deference by thousands of plantation workers, she was completely at ease in the midst of masses of poor Filipinos" (1987: 224).

12. Doeppers 1987: 280. One longtime observer of Philippine politics characterized Aquino's following as a "genuine populist movement," but attributed her popularity to the "affection and love that people have for her as a kind of Joan of Arc figure" (Shaplen 1986: 69; id. 1987: 57). Jaime Cardinal Sin used the same Joan of Arc imagery in his conversation with Aquino when she first announced her intention to run for the presidency to him (Crisostomo 1987: 157). Aquino attributed her electoral following jointly to her role as the widow of "Ninoy" Aquino and her own personality (Mydans 1986c).

13. General Fidel V. Ramos was constantly cautioning Aquino about a possible backlash within the military in the event she initiated prosecutions for human rights abuses (Abad interview, June 21, 1989; see also Wise 1987: 441).

14. This sentiment was shared by many participants at a dinner hosted by Enrique D. Rojas (interview, June 17, 1986). Although personal sentiments were not directly offered, several of those in attendance commented that "some [people] favor a coup d'état" and "some predict [a military] revolution by October."

15. For a discussion of dependency relations and their impact on peasant political behavior, see Herring 1981. Gary Hawes cites the differentiation of peasants in Central Luzon as one factor explaining the absence of peasant rebellion in the region since the 1950s (1990: 269–70). What Hawes fails to clarify is why differentiation among the peasantry should preclude peasant rebellion in Central Luzon, but not in the peripheral regions of the Philippines.

16. See, e.g., Kohli 1987: 43. Political scientists have tended to invoke socialization as a black box explanation of political behavior. Ideological domination by elites—hegemony—or processes of socialization may script the "on-stage" behavior of peasants, but their "off-stage" behavior bespeaks a reality of competing cleavages and identities, and challenges to the seemingly dominant social norms. See Colburn 1989; Scott 1985; Scott and Kerkvliet 1986.

17. In Karen Remmer's schema, the degree of political inclusiveness is determined by formal rates of electoral participation—inclusive democracies are those in which 30 percent or more of the total population participates in elections (1985–86).

18. In the first Aquino cabinet, these men became deputy executive secretary for energy, minister of public works and highways, minister of trade and industry, and minister of finance respectively.

19. The nucleus-estate program links numerous small landholdings to central plantations for purposes of standardizing and improving production. The plantation serves as a demonstration farm, disseminates new agricultural technologies to the smallholders, and provides processing, storage, and marketing

facilities for the united enterprise. Ongpin's interest in the Malaysian nucleus-estate program is noted in an interview early in the Aquino presidency (Gigot 1986). Ongpin's views were also related to the author in Schieck, interview Mar. 17, 1986. Similar views were attributed to Carlos G. Dominguez, deputy minister of agriculture, in Adriano et al. interview, Mar. 20, 1986.

20. As of early 1986, the Philippine economy was experiencing considerable difficulty: foreign debt exceeded $26 billion; the government budgetary shortfall was projected at nearly $1.4 billion (equivalent to 4.5 percent of GNP); inflation had jumped from 10 percent to over 50 percent per annum in 1984, declining to 23 percent in 1985; real gross national product had fallen 6.8 and 3.8 percent respectively in 1984 and 1985; world prices for the principal Philippine agricultural exports (coconut products and sugar) were depressed; and an estimated 11.8 percent of the labor force was unemployed, while 35.2 percent was underemployed (defined as working less than 40 hours per week) (ROP, NEDA 1986a). Scholars of Philippine agrarian reform foresaw little immediate prospect of radical redistribution under the Aquino regime, citing the government's lack of resources (Cornista interview, June 13, 1986).

21. See FFF 1986b; id. 1986c. See also *Malaya* 1986; *Manila Bulletin* 1986; *Philippine Daily Express* 1986. On May 16, 1986, Minister of Agrarian Reform Heherson T. Alvarez issued a memorandum to all DAR officers informing them that "the present government has no intention to discontinue the agrarian reform program but rather would strengthen and accelerate its implementation. It is, therefore, necessary that both farmer-beneficiaries and landowners be properly informed about the commitment of the government of President Corazon C. Aquino to implement a genuine agrarian reform program."

22. See, e.g., the remarks of Dr. Patricia Licuanan, Ateneo de Manila University, reported in Shaplen 1987: 56–57.

23. Among others, Blas Ople, member of the 1986 Constitutional Commission and former minister of labor under the Marcos regime, predicted in advance that most members of the House of Representatives would represent landed interests and would seek to circumvent the Constitution's agrarian reform mandate (ROP 1986a: 3: 25. See also Sionil 1986).

24. For a discussion of (unsuccessful) efforts by the papal nuncio to limit the Catholic Bishops' Conference of the Philippines' criticism of the Marcos regime and Marcos's manipulation of the February 1986 election results, see Youngblood 1987: 1247. On the issue of Church involvement in Philippine politics with the advent of the Aquino administration, note that Vatican instructions to curtail political activity were not limited to the Philippines. The Vatican had, for example, earlier proscribed active participation of clergy in the Sandinista regime in Nicaragua. Fathers Miguel D'Escoto (foreign minister), Ernesto Cardenal (minister of culture), and Alvaro Arguello (clergy representative to the Council of State) were stripped of their religious duties for their participation in the Sandinista government. See, e.g., Dionne 1986.

In any event, the Vatican evidenced little interest in directly promoting social reforms, its rhetoric describing "service of the poor as a preferential op-

tion" notwithstanding. Cf. Pope John Paul II's "To Priests and Seminarians" (Cebu City, Feb. 19, 1981) with his "Homily at the Mass for Men Religious" (Manila, Feb. 17, 1981), both in de Achutegui 1981: 100, quoted in Giordano 1988: 83, 184. Institutionally, the Philippine Catholic Church may have been prepared to accept a reduced role, having secured Aquino's presidency and constitutional provisions banning abortion, exempting the Church and its institutions from taxation, permitting religious instruction in public schools, and banning divorce (1987 Constitution of the ROP, Art. 2, Sec. 12; Art. 6, Sec. 28 (3); Art. 14, Sec. 3 (3); Art. 15, Sec. 2 respectively).

25. Gillego interview, June 17, 1989. The *balimbing* is a five-sided fruit that looks the same whichever way it is viewed.

26. In mounting her presidential campaign, for instance, Aquino rejected the overtures of the leftist political alliance BAYAN (Bagong Alyansang Makabayan = New Nationalist Alliance), dominated by the National Democratic Front. Her decision apparently reflected reaction both to CPP criticism of her campaign and to Marcos's accusations that she harbored communist sympathies. See, e.g., Jones 1989: 158; *New York Times* 1986a.

27. Blackton interviews, July 27, 1987, Oct. 7, 1988, Mar. 17, 1989; Bosworth interview, Mar. 19, 1986; Moore interview, June 26, 1986; Schieck interviews, Mar. 17 and June 11, 1986. Putzel (1992: 283–308) extensively documents the division—between what he terms "conservative" and "liberal" reformers—within the U.S. government and among American scholars and development consultants concerning the desirability and appropriate scope of agrarian reform in the Philippines. "Conservative" reformers, more accurately described as opponents of redistributive reform, held sway in official policy circles, but they were not without quite vocal critics. Leading American proponents of redistributive reform included Congressman Stephen Solarz, chairman of the House Foreign Affairs Subcommittee on Asian and Pacific Affairs, Roy L. Prosterman, professor of law at the University of Washington, and William C. Thiesenhusen of the University of Wisconsin's Land Tenure Center.

28. Thompson 1989: 5. RAM members expressed concerns about corruption within the military and the Marcos government and the ineffectiveness of the military as a fighting force, which they attributed primarily to leadership that rewarded loyalty rather than merit. Not coincidentally, the "overstaying" generals—those kept on by Marcos beyond retirement age—were blocking career advancement for the younger officers associated with RAM.

29. The military was thus particularly suspicious of two of Aquino's closest advisers, Executive Secretary Joker Arroyo and Presidential Spokesman Rene Saguisag. Both had been leading human rights lawyers in the Marcos years, and within the Aquino government, both supported amnesty for erstwhile insurgents and punishment of military officers for human rights abuses. See, e.g., Sacerdoti 1986c: 45.

30. The closest Aquino came to promoting unity through her appointments was the prominence she accorded the so-called "Jesuit Mafia"—Jesuit-trained advisers. Yet even among this group there existed significant ideological differ-

ences. The most notable of the Jesuit advisers were Jaime V. Ongpin, the minister of finance, and Joaquin G. Bernas, president of Ateneo de Manila University. In addition to Ongpin, government appointees with strong Catholic ties included Alfredo R. A. Bengzon, minister of health; Jose S. Concepcion, Jr., minister of trade and industry (and head of the Laity Commission of the Catholic Church); Jose B. Fernandez, governor of the Central Bank; Jose Antonio Gonzalez, minister of tourism; Vicente Jayme, president of Philippine National Bank; Teodoro L. Locsin, Jr., minister of public information; Solita Collás-Monsod, minister of economic planning; Aquilino Q. Pimentel, minister of local government; and Lourdes R. Quisumbing, minister of education (and former president of Maryknoll University). Bernardo Villegas of the Center for Research and Communications, an organization with close links to the conservative Opus Dei, was a key presidential economic adviser. See Henares 1986; Ofreneo 1987: 331; Youngblood 1987: 1248–49.

31. Among the social democrats appointed were Jose Diokno (human affairs commissioner), Joker P. Arroyo (presidential executive secretary), Augusto S. Sanchez (minister of labor), Rene Saguisag (presidential spokesman), Aquilino Pimentel (minister of local government), Alfredo R. A. Bengzon (minister of health), Mamita Pardo de Tavera (minister of social services and development), Joey Lina (acting governor of Metro Manila), Jun Simon (acting mayor of Quezon City), Linggoy Alcuaz (chairperson, National Telecommunications Commission), and Mar Canonigo (chairperson, Urban Poor Commission). Thompson 1990: 4.

32. Human rights investigations were also downgraded and a variety of military prerogatives restored and demands met, including restoration of the privilege of buying certain tax-free consumer items; provision of combat clothing for officers assigned to combat operations; and two measures relating to reserve officers. See Davis 1989: 207; Thompson 1990: 5.

33. In June 1986, a senior U.S. State Department official was quoted as urging that Sanchez be "reined in." Sanchez's pro-labor policies were seen as harming the investment climate (Chanda 1986: 46).

34. See Brillantes 1988: 127–28. Under the influence of Manuel Quezon, the 1935 Constitution provided Philippine presidents with an array of powers—among them explicit emergency powers, wide discretion in the issuance of executive orders, and general control of local government—not found in the United States. See Wurfel 1988: 76. Alex B. Brillantes, Jr., defines the role of the president under the 1935 Constitution as being that of chief executive, chief administrator, chief legislator, and diplomatic chief (1988: 116).

35. Despite the broad range of viewpoints represented in Aquino's selections, the appointment process drew criticism from Marcos loyalists and others. The critics urged election of the constitutional commissioners. In support of the selection process, the Catholic Bishops' Conference of the Philippines issued a "Pastoral Exhortation on the Constitutional Commission and Its Work" on May 18, 1986. Church officials and organizations, Catholic and Protestant, were

also instrumental in facilitating public hearings on the new Constitution. Youngblood 1987: 1249–50.

36. Sacerdoti 1986b. Progressives included Jaime Tadeo, head of the KMP; Sister Christine Tan, a leading figure working with Manila's poor; Chito Gascon, student council president at the University of the Philippines; and Minda Luz Quesada, leader of the Health Workers Association. Leading figures from the pre-Marcos era included Jose Laurel, Jr., former minority leader of the lower house; Ambrosio Padilla, a former senator; Celia Muñoz Palma, a retired Supreme Court justice; Napoleon Rama, former vice president of the 1971 Constitutional Convention (until his arrest under martial law); and Francisco Rodrigo, another former senator. The Catholic Church was represented to varying degrees by Bishop Teodoro C. Bacani, Jr.; Joaquin G. Bernas, S.J., president of (the Jesuit) Ateneo de Manila University; and Bernardo Villegas, a free-market economist. The KBL party members were Blas Ople, a former labor minister, and four former members of Congress: Alejandro Almendres, Teodulo Natividad, Regalado Maambong, and Restituto de los Reyes.

37. A Constitutional Commission had been elected in 1970, but was still meeting in late 1972. The drafting process was extremely slow, reflecting weak leadership and the enormous number of resolutions under consideration. The deliberations suggested widespread hostility to any changes (including shifting to a parliamentary system) that might facilitate continuation of Marcos's rule; this despite Marcos's sizable cash contributions to ConCom delegates regarded as pliable. With martial law came the arrest of more than a dozen ConCom delegates. Thereafter, a new constitutional draft was prepared in close consultation with the president and was quickly approved. Marcos thereupon decreed new "citizens' assemblies," convened them, and obtained ratification of the new Constitution. Although the Supreme Court held that this procedure did not comply with applicable constitutional provisions, it dismissed legal challenges to the Constitution in acknowledgement of Marcos's dominance through force (Wurfel 1988: 106–17).

38. Of the 200 members elected to the House of Representatives in 1987, at least 108, and as many as 145, owned agricultural lands (Gilding 1993: 17, 49–64).

39. IPD 1987: 4–5. The relevant part of the study concerns the political affiliation of candidates from "political clans," defined as those with an electoral track record dating back at least to 1980.

40. Peterman 1988: 20. By John Peterman's calculation (communication to the author, Sept. 1988), 31 percent of the members had previously served in Congress, and 36 percent were from political dynasties. Peterson characterized an additional 20 percent of the House membership as new and conservative, deeming only 11 percent to be "progressive." On the Senate side, 39 percent of the members had previously held national office, and 26 percent were from political dynasties. By another calculation (Mojares 1988, cited in Rosenberg 1990: 184), 130 of the 200 elected members of the House of Representatives were

from traditional political families. Another 39 members were related to such families. Of these 167 representatives, 67 were identified as being from pro-Marcos families.

41. Notable families in Central Luzon include the Sumulongs (President Aquino's maternal grandparents), Salongas, Nepomucenos, Mercados, and Josons. In the Ilocos region, the Singsons and Crisologs enjoy considerable power. The Barberos and Paredes clans are similarly influential in the mountain provinces of Luzon. Panay is dominated by the Roxas family, Cebu by the Osmeñas, and Lanao, Mindanao, by the Dimaporos (Clad 1987: 72).

42. Identified with the LDP were 186 of the 204 members of the Philippine House of Representatives and 7 of the 24 senators.

43. A 1967 article recommending corporate farm ownership with worker-stockholders in lieu of subdividing large estates (Aquino 1967) shows "Ninoy" Aquino's commitment to reform. For a description of his redistribution of portions of the Aquino family holdings to the tenant cultivators, see Joaquin 1983.

44. Between 1960 and 1964, fourteen countries adopted significant new reform legislation: Brazil, Chile, Colombia, Costa Rica, the Dominican Republic, Ecuador, El Salvador, Guatemala, Honduras, Nicaragua, Panama, Paraguay, Peru, and Venezuela. See Grindle 1986: 140.

45. ROP, NEDA 1986b: 2. NEDA was headed by Solita Monsod, a progressive economist frequently at odds with the more conservative members of the Aquino cabinet over payment and rescheduling of the foreign debt, and the terms of economic structural adjustment. Monsod resigned over these continuing differences in June 1989.

46. Quoted in Montemayor 1987: 1; also quoted, with slight modifications, in IBON Databank Philippines 1988: 59.

47. Bulatao 1987: 9. The terms "farmers" and "farm workers" refer, in this context, to tenants and agricultural laborers respectively.

48. Doronila 1985: 101; Tancangco 1988: 81–82. Benedict Anderson rejects the notion of a much-expanded franchise, asserting that "even on the eve of World War II, only about 14 per cent of the potential electorate was permitted to vote" (1988: n. 26). However, this figure appears to be at considerable odds with population and voter-registration figures for that period. Cf. Huke 1963: 140 (total population of 16 million) and Liang 1970: 232 (3 million registered voters).

49. Quoted in Simons 1987: 224. Aquino made the comment by way of explaining her decision after her husband's assassination to remain in the Philippines and go into politics.

50. Medina 1987: 27–28. NEDA similarly concluded that increased rural incomes would "stimulate investment and change consumption patterns towards products and industries that are more labor-intensive and enterprises that are small and medium scale" (ROP, NEDA 1986b: 4–5).

51. Fortich interview, June 16, 1986; Locsin interview, June 16, 1986. See also Bascog 1987: 50. For a discussion of the importance of the *threat* of insurgency in shaping landowners' views on reform in Latin America, see Grindle 1986: 141.

52. Herring 1983: 231. In congressional testimony, Carlos G. Dominguez, the

secretary of agriculture, sounded just such a note of apology, although in this case tying the reform to a constitutional mandate rather than to violence (1987: 30).

53. Huntington 1968: 385, 393. The theme of violence as impetus for political action is echoed in Theda Skocpol's analysis of the crises preceding the social revolutions of France, Russia, and China (1979). My focus is primarily on *intra*-national violence, whereas Skocpol's analysis emphasizes violence of an *inter*-national nature: defeats in wars or threats of invasion and struggles with colonial powers. See also Migdal 1988: 269.

54. MacArthur's and Ladejinsky's influence on the Japanese reform is best evidenced in Supreme Commander for the Allied Powers, Directive 411, Dec. 9, 1945, reprinted in Walinsky 1977: 579–80.

55. See Prosterman and Riedinger 1987: 143–73. Notwithstanding these efforts, antireform elements of Salvadoran society have effectively blocked—frequently through violence—much of the promised reform program. See also Seligson 1993.

56. Bosworth interview, Mar. 19, 1986. One U.S. Agency for International Development official posited that Ambassador Stephen Bosworth's personal caution on the reform issue was reflective of the trauma Bosworth and other State Department officials had experienced in connection with U.S. support of agrarian reform in El Salvador in the early 1980s. State Department and USAID institutional disinterest in agrarian reform also reflected the pernicious impact of Senator Jesse Helms (R–North Carolina). Taking advantage of Senate protocol, Helms repeatedly held up senior State Department and USAID nominations and promotions where the nominee's views, or U.S. policy in a given country, suggested sympathy for agrarian reform. Interview with USAID personnel, Washington, D.C., Apr. 15, 1986.

U.S. disinterest in agrarian reform had earlier been expressed in USAID's research funding priorities. Members of the Institute of Agrarian Studies at the University of the Philippines, Los Baños, indicated in March 1986 that agrarian reform was "number 7" on the list of research priorities, a ranking reflective of USAID disinterest. Cornista et al. interview, Mar. 24, 1986.

57. Fermin Adriano noted Filipino sensitivity to foreign involvement in the reform process, remarking that "formulation of the agrarian-reform program is properly a Philippine decision." Where appropriate, outside expert advice would be sought. Interview, Mar. 20, 1986.

58. For an extended discussion of the Philippine state's relative weakness vis-à-vis external actors such as the World Bank and International Monetary Fund, see Broad 1988. While taking issue with important elements of Broad's analysis, Paul Hutchcroft (1991) also characterizes the Philippine state as relatively weak with regard to external actors.

59. This may be a case in which the standard caveat accompanying World Bank publications—that the views expressed therein should not be attributed to the World Bank, nor do they necessarily represent official policy—takes on greater force. The World Bank mission that authored the report was composed

equally of World Bank staff (Martin Karcher, Mohan Gopal, and David Jarvis) and outside consultants (John H. Duloy, Sein Lin, and William C. Thiesenhusen). The World Bank is not known, as an institution, for a strong pro–agrarian reform posture. Constantino and Karganilla 1987: 11–12, observed, e.g., that the World Bank, "an institution that could hardly be expected to be sympathetic to the people's plight," had adopted "a 'radical reformist' and critical stance toward Aquino's land reform program," and Wurfel 1988: 322 terms the World Bank report on Philippine agrarian reform "surprising."

60. "The land transfer component poses some specific problems for foreign agencies: the World Bank, itself, for instance, by its Articles of Association, is not able to finance compensation payments for the transfer of existing assets," the World Bank mission noted (World Bank 1987a: 74). In a May 1987 interview, Finance Secretary Jaime V. Ongpin indicated that no international institution could be interested in financing land transfers, because the money would benefit erstwhile landowners (*Business Day* 1987).

61. "The only thing I can really offer the Filipino people is my sincerity," Aquino remarked early in the campaign (Mydans 1985). Aquino's campaign literature and television advertisements focused largely on her husband's assassination (see Mydans 1986c). Some discussions of the Aquino campaign suggest that her more forceful attacks on Marcos and her series of policy speeches were prompted by disquiet in the United States as to her suitability for the presidency. These concerns were fueled by an interview for the *New York Times*, Dec. 16, 1985, in which Aquino remarked, "What on earth do I know about being President?" See *New York Times* 1986c; Bonner 1988: 399–408.

62. Aquino 1986a: 6–8. The most prominent members of Aquino's economic policy and speech-writing team during the campaign were Jaime V. Ongpin (president, Benguet Corporation) and Romulo del Rosario (IBM-Philippines). Other speechwriters included Teodoro L. Locsin, Jr. (a journalist), and Joaquin G. Bernas, S.J. (president, Ateneo de Manila University).

63. Aquino 1986b. Taking some liberties with Aquino's Ateneo de Davao speech—at least as written—Jaime Tadeo publicly characterized her pledge as again being one of "genuine land reform." See Tadeo 1986: 16 (text of a speech Tadeo delivered Mar. 19, 1986).

64. Bernas interview, July 10, 1989. Fr. Bernas was a key Aquino adviser during and immediately after the campaign period. He authored Aquino's Jan. 16, 1986 speech at Ateneo de Davao. The absence of specifics in the campaign consideration of agrarian reform was confirmed by the late Gaston Ortigas, dean of the Asian Institute of Management (interview, June 22, 1989). One Filipino observed at the time, "There is a recognition of rural problems, but the Aquino regime lacks clear ideas on what to do and how to do it" (Adriano et al. interview, Mar. 20, 1986).

65. The KMP defined "genuine agrarian reform" as encompassing: (1) confiscation and free distribution of lands owned by Marcos and his cronies to the actual tillers; (2) expansion of free distribution to all croplands; and (3) nationalization of transnational agribusiness plantations and the abolition of feudalism

(KMP 1986a). Similarly, Jose Maria Sison, founder of the CPP, characterized free land distribution as the key measure in genuine land reform (1986).

66. E.g., Bercaro et al. interview, Mar. 2, 1989; Dago-ob interview, Oct. 25, 1988; Potente interview, Feb. 27, 1989; Tadeo et al. interview, Feb. 22, 1989.

67. Arthur Bercaro of SFAN insisted that prior to the 1987 congressional elections, all of the Negros Occidental candidates favored "genuine" agrarian reform and mocked the Marcos-era reform program; he attributed the various electoral victories to these reform promises (interview, Mar. 2, 1989). Bishop Antonio Fortich of Bacolod, Negros Occidental, similarly noted that all seven members of the province's congressional delegation had been "singing the tune of land reform" during their campaigns, only to "change their tune" once in office (interview, Oct. 22, 1988).

A 1969 survey of farmer awareness of the 1963 Philippine Agricultural Land Reform Code revealed that a little more than 11 percent of the respondents knew the year the reform law was enacted. Nearly 20 percent offered incorrect answers, while roughly 69 percent said they did not know or offered no answer. See Tai 1974: 376. Interestingly, although nearly 90 percent of the survey respondents failed to give a correct response to the question above, fewer than 40 percent indicated that they didn't know or gave no answer to a question concerning their perceptions of the success of the reform program. Of those with opinions, nearly 11 percent of the respondents considered the program very successful; another 36 percent thought it successful (Tai 1974: 377).

68. Speaking more generally, Isagani Serrano of the Philippine Rural Reconstruction Movement noted: "As for the ordinary peasants that somehow have not had access to propaganda or political education, either by the government or the NPA, they would of course be in a haze as to what democratic revolution means or should mean. And their perceptions would differ as to the concept of freedom, the changes it would bring about in their livelihood and in their life itself. So that is quite a difficult question—what exactly democratic revolution signifies to an ordinary peasant" (remarks reported in Sandoval 1986: 100).

69. Interviews with tenant farmers and landless laborers, Bulacan, Nueva Ecija, and Pangasinan provinces, Mar. 1986, and Negros Occidental, June–July 1986.

70. The legal implications of the phrase "genuine agrarian reform" were explored in a colloquy between Constitutional Commissioners Aquino, Sarmiento, Tadeo, and Tingson. This phrase was included in early drafts of the 1987 Constitution as a means of distinguishing the type of reform envisioned by Tadeo and other commissioners from previous Philippine land-reform programs, which were criticized as too narrow in scope, poorly implemented, the source of economic difficulties for beneficiaries, and lacking farmer involvement in planning and implementation. The colloquy included explicit reference to the KMP's definition of "genuine agrarian reform." ROP 1986a: 2: 651–54. The word "genuine" was subsequently dropped from the constitutional draft by the Committee on Social Justice. See remarks of Commissioner Nieva in ibid.: 3: 5.

71. There is evidence that "genuine" agrarian reform was ill-defined at the outset of the Aquino administration. Faculty at the Institute of Agrarian Studies (formerly the Agrarian Reform Institute) at the University of the Philippines, Los Baños, were calling for a conference involving the major farmers' organizations, the ministries of Agrarian Reform, Agriculture, Natural Resources, and Local Government, and the Land Bank of the Philippines for the specific purpose of conceptualizing a "genuine" agrarian reform program. Cornista interview, June 13, 1986.

Several months after Aquino became president, a number of scholars and peasant organization representatives indicated that they believed the Aquino regime might expand agrarian reform to include lands sequestered from Marcos "cronies," idle and abandoned lands, foreclosed properties, public lands, and lands offered for voluntary sale. Only in the event these initiatives proved successful did they expect the program to be broadened further. There were some who foresaw no possibility that the reform would be extended to sugar and coconut lands. Cornista interview, June 13, 1986; de la Cruz et al. interview, June 13, 1986.

72. Morales 1986: 79. In dialogues with Bishop Antonio Fortich (Bacolod diocese, Negros Occidental) in June 1986, the NPA defined its reform demand as one of "realistic land reform." Such reform would be based, in the case of private lands, on "reasonable" compensation and repayment by beneficiaries on easy terms. Public lands were to be distributed gratis to true cultivators. In the meantime, the NPA demanded usufruct rights to idle farmlands (Fortich interview, June 16, 1986).

73. In April 1986, the Aquino government had not yet developed a model of agrarian reform. Aquino and her minister of agriculture, Ramon Mitra, were careful to avoid specifics in their public statements on reform, for fear that they would later have to retreat from such pronouncements (Adriano et al. interview, Mar. 20, 1986). Members of the UPLB faculty were "working overtime" to draft these broad statements.

74. To his considerable credit, Alvarez had during his years of exile been a leader of the anti–martial law, anti-Marcos movement (eventually known as the Ninoy Aquino Movement) in the United States and a close associate of Benigno Aquino's. As for his substantive qualifications, his "bio" cites his work on issues of rural poverty while a member of the 1971 Constitution Convention and his studies of rural poverty and rural development while a master's degree candidate (and later Fellow in Government) at the Kennedy School of Government, Harvard University. See ROP, DAR 1986b. Prior to his appointment as minister of agrarian reform, Alvarez served as ambassador extraordinary plenipotentiary, acting as a roving goodwill ambassador to Europe and North America in search of foreign assistance for the Aquino government.

75. Montemayor 1987: 2. Other observers suggested that President Aquino had not so much sided with Mitra as remained silent in the face of this important policy dispute (Cornista interview, June 13, 1986).

76. Among the provisions that thus remained in effect were those of Article

14 of the 1973 Constitution, which provided: "Sec. 12. The State shall formulate and implement an agrarian reform program aimed at emancipating the tenant from the bondage of the soil and achieving the goals enunciated in this Constitution. . . . Sec. 13. The Batasang Pambansa may authorize, upon payment of just compensation, the expropriation of private lands to be subdivided into small lots and conveyed at cost to deserving citizens." Despite the preservation of such provisions under the "Freedom Constitution," some uncertainty persisted, at least among local DAR officials, resulting in continuing threats to the rights of beneficiaries of the Marcos-era reform. See FFF 1986d.

77. "At the earliest possible time, the Government shall expropriate idle or abandoned agricultural land as may defined by law, for distribution to the beneficiaries of the agrarian reform program," Section 22 of Article 17 of the 1987 Philippine Constitution later provided.

78. In a campaign-related move in early January 1986, Ferdinand Marcos had ordered the gradual expansion of his agrarian-reform program to include private lands other than those planted to rice and corn, beginning with idle, abandoned, and foreclosed farmholdings. The order is described in FFF 1986a. The press release also contains the farmer organizations' position paper on which the order was based: "Position Statement of the National Congress of Farmers' Organizations," Jan. 8, 1986.

79. Abad interview, June 21, 1989; Jones interview, Oct. 10, 1988. See also *Christian Science Monitor* 1983 (Q: "What about yourself being the [president]?" A: "No, thank you." Q: "You wouldn't be prepared to?" A: "I know my limitations and I never liked politics. I was only involved because of my husband"). To similar effect, see "In Our Image," a PBS television special produced by Stanley Karnow in 1989 (Aquino: "I just didn't want to be a politician. I didn't want to be a candidate. . . . I felt I had already done my share as far as the restoration of democracy was concerned. . . . So it was a very sad decision for me. In fact, I was in tears when I was telling my children that I had to be the candidate"). For some, Aquino's reluctance was instrumental in their decision to back her, preferring her to discredited traditional politicians. See the remarks of Vicente T. Paterno in Mercado 1986: 44.

80. See the remarks of Maria Serena Diokno, executive director, Trend Researchers and Analysts, Inc., in Peterman 1988: 21.

81. Mananzan interview, Feb. 22, 1989; Modina interview, Oct. 17, 1988. See also *Ang Bayan* 1986b; *Liberation* 1987b; and the remarks of Virginia A. Miralao, Ramon Magsaysay Award Foundation, in Mydans 1987c.

82. At a time when peasant groups were criticizing the Aquino government for its inactivity on reform, and some U.S. officials were criticizing the slow pace of economic policy reform, U.S. Assistant Secretary of State for East Asia and the Pacific Gaston Sigur argued: "The new government has been in power only 13 weeks and enjoyed no transition period. This is a short time to organize and launch new directions of policy of far-reaching consequence to the future of the country" (Chanda 1986: 47).

83. Abad interview, June 21, 1989; Gillego interview, June 17, 1989. Gaston

Ortigas ascribed the concern with the fragility of the Aquino coalition to her advisers rather than to Aquino personally (interview, June 22, 1989). Ultimately, Aquino was responsible for the policy decisions of her government; she chose the path of concessions to the military and the go-slow approach to agrarian reform.

84. See the position of the Council of Agricultural Producers of the Philippines as described in Guevarra 1987. This characterization of the public posturing of the antireform forces was endorsed by Edcel C. Lagman, chairman of the Committee on Agrarian Reform of the Philippine House of Representatives, who went on to note that landowners would "concede to something cosmetic" (interview, Mar. 15, 1989). For a general discussion of the "I-am-for-land-reform-but" phenomenon, see Ledesma 1980.

85. Starke interview, June 23, 1989. In other settings, Starke evidenced much greater antipathy to agrarian reform. She is quoted as saying, e.g., "We're not afraid of anything more than land reform" (Simons 1987: 166).

86. Wurfel 1969: 222. Antonio Ledesma used different gender-based imagery to describe this process of legislative evisceration, saying the proponents of land reform had become "its most effective opponents—by presiding over its legislative abortion" (1980: 341).

87. "We most vigorously register our opposition to this Agrarian Reform Law . . . which is unjust, confiscatory, oppressive, and which is at best, of doubtful efficacy" (CAP n.d.).

88. See Miller 1988a; *Newsweek* 1987; Palacios 1987; Sa-Onoy 1987. Other organizations made veiled threats of violence against the state and the reform program. See, e.g., PLADAR and DATU-Panay 1987: 2.

89. Business associate quoted in Gallardo 1987. Gallardo's parentheticals have been deleted and punctuation marks inserted.

90. Starke et al. interview, June 16, 1986. Starke's use of the phrasing "emancipate from the soil" was quite deliberate, it echoed the subtitle of Marcos's Presidential Decree 27: "Decreeing the Emancipation of Tenants from the Bondage of the Soil." As a number of Filipino tenants and peasant representatives remarked to me, the notion of "emancipating" tenants from the "bondage of the soil" is a peculiar one. Strictly interpreted, the phrase would suggest that tenants are to be freed of their ties to the land—that is, freed from farming. What was intended, of course, was that they be freed of the burden of tenancy by becoming owner-cultivators.

91. Villarosa interview, June 19, 1986. Where land was necessary to the livelihood project, Villarosa suggested it should be leased or the subject of a voluntary sale.

92. "There was no hunger, no insurgency [in Negros Occidental] before Marcos" (Alunan interview, June 16, 1986). See also the remarks of Congresswoman Hortensia L. Starke reported in Gob 1988 and Simons 1987: 164. See also Hernandez 1987: 32.

93. Guanzon interview, June 19, 1986; Locsin et al. interview, June 14, 1986; Nolan interview, July 8, 1989; Pelaez interview, July 16, 1986; Rojas et al. interview, June 17, 1986; Starke interview, June 16, 1986.

94. Gallardo interview, Feb. 11, 1991. The most prominent exposition of the supposed benefits provided by sugar *hacenderos* is found in NFSP and PSA 1960. According to this publication, sugar mills and farms provided "cradle to old age" benefits, including medical, housing, educational, and recreational services. At "modern hospitals and clinics," it was possible for the "humblest farm or central worker and members of his family [to] get personal attention from physicians maintained by centrals and farms" (12). An "extensive medical field service" was also available (13). Sugar mills and farms provided "homes for everyone, executives and laborers alike, free of charge" (14–15). "Community services are regular features in haciendas and centrals" (photos depict labor halls, cooperative stores, and flower and vegetable gardens) (16–17). The sugar industry "constructs school buildings at no cost to the government and maintains them throughout the year." (Several photos are captioned: "These are the children of sugarcane planters and workers in mills growing up to be good citizens") (18–19). The industry also "encourages and promotes sports to ensure a healthy body" (20–21). "The Sugar Industry takes care of the spiritual needs of its people" (22–23). Social welfare funds are raised for "the disabled, for the sick and ailing, for playgrounds, recreation facilities, for the old and retired, for funeral services" (26–27).

95. Acuña 1987: 58–59. "The landowner never allows [the farmworkers] to go hungry," Acuña went on to assert. Landowners also, by Acuña's account, provided their farmworkers with funds for marriages, schooling, and funerals (1987: 73).

96. In 1969, Arsenio Jesena, a Jesuit priest, spent several months living as a *sacada* on sugar haciendas in Negros Occidental. His account of this experience exploded many of the myths about life on sugar haciendas, calling attention to the misery and degradation that was the lot of many *sacadas*.

97. CAP n.d.: 6. The NFSP similarly pushed for a 24-hectare retention limit, citing a congressional proposal (eventually adopted) to exempt homesteads of up to 24 hectares from the reform as evidence that farmers with less than 24 hectares were "small landowners" within the meaning of the Constitution, and were thus to be excluded from the reform process. See Acuña 1988.

98. Existing publicly available data do not permit testing of Osmeña's claim concerning the backgrounds of owners of medium-sized holdings. The image of teachers, professionals, and merchants constituting the core of middle-class landowners enjoys some currency in Manila, if only by virtue of its repetition by Osmeña and others in an environment otherwise marked by ignorance.

99. Landowners involved in sugarcane, prawn, and livestock production all sought exemptions from the reform process in toto or alternatives to land redistribution. Illustrative are the remarks of a sugarcane grower: "We think that the sugar industry, more than any other of the crops under the Agrarian Reform program, will require perhaps greater examination of alternative options or schemes for agrarian reform especially over and above the individual land transfer. We can mention corporate schemes, stock dispersal and such other types of schemes" (Sabino 1987: 19).

100. Barcelona 1987: 16–17. In defining the coconut workforce as something

other than tenants, Barcelona is at odds with the conventional designation. By one account, some 40 percent of the coconut-farm operators in the Philippines are tenants, and are defined as such (Nasol 1987: 5). Other data suggest that tenants make up 28–39 percent of coconut farmers (IAS 1987b: 24). However, scholars at IAS's institutional predecessor—the Agrarian Reform Institute—had previously noted a trend toward use of hired laborers for coconut harvesting. Although there was considerable regional variation, tenant-operators were increasingly confined to "watching over the coconut trees and cleaning the farm" (Cornista and Escueta 1983: 3).

101. Acuña 1987: 65. "We do not have people actually tilling the land. Some of them really do not even go off their tractors. They just operate the tractors with the farm implements behind."

102. Simons 1987: 169. In June 1986, the author and a colleague drove out to Gustillo's seaside hacienda in northern Negros Occidental. At the end of a long, circuitous driveway marked at regular intervals by heavily armed men in guard towers, we were denied admission to a well-fortified compound. After extended consultations in the house, a guard returned to inform us that Gustillo was away at an offshore island retreat.

103. As with other incidents of mass violence, the exact number of fatalities is difficult to determine. The death toll from the "Escalante massacre" is variously estimated at 27, 29, and over 30. See Simons 1987: 169; O'Brien 1987: 305; Jagan and Cunnington 1987: 23.

104. For discussions of the status and abuses of vigilante groups, private armies, civilian armed forces, and the military, see LCHR 1988; id. 1990; van der Kroef 1988.

105. The most notable occasion being a speech made in praise of the vigilante group "Alsa Masa" (variously translated as "Risen Masses," "Masses Uprising," or "Masses Arise") on Oct. 23, 1987, in Davao City, Mindanao (*Manila Chronicle* 1987). Earlier Aquino had praised a "supposedly unarmed" vigilante group, NAKASAKA (Nagkahiusang Katawhan alang sa Kalinaw = People Unite for Peace) (Mar. 26, 1987, speech, Davao, Mindanao, reported by Agence France Presse, Davao, Mar. 29, 1987, in Foreign Broadcast Information Service, *Daily Report, East Asia*, Mar. 30, 1987). In October 1987, government guidelines on anticommunist citizens' groups were released, which provided among other things that membership be voluntary, that members be "thoroughly screened," and that such groups operate "exclusively for self-defense." See LCHR 1988: xvi.

106. ROP, Executive Order No. 264, July 25, 1987, "Providing for Citizen Armed Force." In June 1986, a prominent conservative sugar planter had argued for precisely this continuation of a CHDF-like force, suitably renamed (Benedicto interview, June 18, 1986). For a discussion of the overlap between CHDF and CAFGU personnel, see Asia Watch 1990: 41–44.

107. The founding dates of many of the organizations interviewed by the author bespeak this organizational proliferation in the late Marcos–early Aquino years. See also Landé and Hooley 1986: 1093; Tancangco 1988: 101–2.

108. Tadeo et al. interview, Feb. 22, 1989. While noting that a decade of rural organizational efforts by the "underground" (the CPP / NPA)—as well as by the Church, nongovernmental organizations, and the government—preceded the founding of the KMP in 1985, the leaders of the KMP deny ties to the CPP / NPA, but they do not hide their sympathy with the CPP / NPA's nationalist and reform agendas. Gregg Jones characterizes the KMP and the urban labor organization Kilusang Mayo Uno (May First Movement = KMU) as the "revolutionary movement's most successful legal mass organizations" (1989: 301). In the view of a prominent functionary of the Philippine Social Democratic party, the size of KMP rallies was directly proportional to the approval or nonapproval of the same by the National Democratic Front (NDF), the CPP's popular front organization (interview, July 13, 1989; accord, Alvarez interview, Feb. 24, 1989).

109. This has been a repeated theme in interviews with landless and near-landless peasant cultivators during 1986–94. See, generally, Doronila 1985; Landé 1977; Nowak and Snyder 1974; Wolters 1984.

Chapter 6

1. Tadeo 1986: 17. In June 1986, this list was expanded to include expropriation and distribution of all foreclosed private agricultural holdings, confiscation and distribution of all idle and abandoned agricultural lands, and allocation of 20 percent of plantation lands to farmworkers for use as food lots (KMP 1986b).

2. KMP 1986c. The proposal was delivered to Minister of Agriculture Ramon Mitra, because no minister of agrarian reform had then been appointed. The KMP demanded that the government: (1) carry out a genuine land-reform program; (2) work for a nationalist, self-reliant, and progressive economy, dismantling foreign and local monopoly control of agriculture; (3) lower agricultural production costs to within the reach of the peasants and ensure just prices for their produce; (4) ensure appropriate support programs for agriculture that manifest the central role of the peasantry in their determination and planning; (5) uphold the democratic rights of peasants to free and collective actions and self-organization; and (6) stop militarization in the countryside.

3. The remaining FFF demands included expedited issuance of homestead patents, upland stewardship contracts, and fishpond leases, construction of farm-to-market roads, remedial action for "overly small farms," and elimination of the abuses of the government resettlement programs, including reclaiming land allocated to unqualified persons (Montemayor 1986a: 13–14).

4. *Agrarian Reform Monitor* 1988: 1; CPAR 1987b; Ramiro interview, Oct. 14, 1988. The CPAR founding conference had the blessing of the Church Bishops' Conference of the Philippines and the National Economic Development Authority (Putzel 1992: 228).

5. Report of the PCGR Task Force on Agrarian Reform, quoted in Tadem 1987: 24–25. The PCGR was established in March 1986. Task forces were formed to conduct a two-month analysis of the operations of each government organization (Bulatao interview, Mar. 15, 1989).

6. ROP, NEDA 1986a. The principles set forth in this document and much of the text were subsequently incorporated into id. 1986b.

7. NEDA's trade policy recommendations did not have the benefit of wide-spread public support. Groups that stood to benefit from export-oriented policies—landless laborers, small farmers, the informal sector, and nontraditional exporters—were, for the most part, poorly organized and faced significant collective action problems in promoting appropriate policy reform. Some organized peasant groups rejected export-oriented policies as foreign-inspired and antithetical to Philippine interests; instead they emphasized a "food first" approach to agriculture.

8. Prominent among the land-reform proponents in the Constitutional Commission were Jaime Tadeo, Fr. Joaquin Bernas, Sister Christine Tan, and Rene V. Sarmiento.

9. The committee decision was reported, without elaboration, in ROP 1986a: 3: 5.

10. Constitutional Commission President Cecilia Muñoz Palma, summarizing remarks of Commissioner Bacani (ROP 1986a: 3: 8).

11. The Constitution was adopted by the commission on Oct. 15, 1986 and ratified by national plebiscite on Feb. 2, 1987.

12. NEDA shared this viewpoint, terming agrarian reform "the centerpiece of the effort towards distributive justice to ensure that the gains from agricultural growth are fully transmitted to small farmers" (1986b: 43).

13. ROP 1986a: 3: 16–17. The discussion suggests considerable confusion as to what was intended by "progressive" compensation. The textual description comports with author's interview of aides to the Constitutional Commission's Jaime Tadeo, June 25, 1986.

14. The Constitutional Commission's failure to reach agreement on the definition of "just compensation" was confirmed by the Philippine Supreme Court in *Association of Small Landowners* v. *Secretary of Agrarian Reform* (July 14, 1989), a case consolidating four separate lawsuits challenging the constitutionality of the Comprehensive Agrarian Reform Law.

15. Montemayor n.d.: 28. Under PD 27, land was valued at "two and one-half times the average harvest of the three normal crop years immediately preceding the promulgation of [the] decree." The basis for the FFF estimate is not given, but it may not be excessive. Wurfel presents data suggesting that, properly determined, average PD 27 land values should have been roughly P4,860 per hectare. Even this figure seems high; at the 1972 government support price for rice—P35 per 50 kilograms—the estimate implies average yields of 2.78 mt/ha. National average rice yields ranged from 1.4 to 1.7 mt/ha in 1970–72. The average price actually paid by PD 27 beneficiaries was P7,000 per hectare as of 1977 (Wurfel 1983: 9). In 1987, ITFAR estimated average fair-market land values at P25,000 per hectare. If this were the average market value of rice lands, it would represent an increase of at least 500 percent relative to (correctly determined) PD 27 valuations. This market value would also represent a 250 percent

increase over valuations based on application of the PD 27 formula to rice yields and prices for 1987, which gives an average value of roughly P10,000 per hectare (ITFAR 1987b: 19).

16. Remarks of Commissioner Tadeo, ROP 1986a: 2: 637; Remarks of Commissioner Aquino, ibid.: 3: 10, 243. Minister of Agrarian Reform Heherson Alvarez was among those on record as supportive of a zero retention limit for absentee landowners (Icamina 1986).

17. Remarks of Commissioner Sarmiento, made in objection to language subjecting agrarian reform to such "priorities . . . and other conditions as Congress may prescribe" (ibid.: 3: 23). Jeremias Montemayor of the FFF raised similar objections to this provision, arguing that it could be used to "limit, obstruct, delay or emasculate agrarian reform" (n.d.).

18. Among the assurances received, according to the FFF, was a pledge by Minister Alvarez that the repayment obligations of reform beneficiaries would be no more than they could afford (Montemayor 1987: 6). Alvarez also pledged to expand the area covered by reform to eleven million hectares following ratification of the constitution (Gilding 1993: 6). In Ministry Order 210, dated Oct. 15, 1986, Alvarez stated that the reform program would eventually cover "all arable public and private lands, regardless of size of landholding, crop and tenurial arrangements."

19. Executive Order 229 accompanied Presidential Proclamation No. 131, which was little more than a recitation of reasons for carrying out an agrarian reform, including the constitutional mandate. The Executive Order contained the substantive provisions.

20. Policy guidelines for a "Genuine Agrarian Reform Program" had been published by the Department of Agrarian Reform on Oct. 15, 1986. They provided few substantive details, however. The KMP land invasions encompassed roughly 70,000 hectares and involved 50,000 families as of early 1989 (Tadeo et al. interview, Feb. 22, 1989). See also Francia and Capistrano 1988: 12. For further discussion of land invasions, see CPAR 1989; id. 1991; *Farm News & Views* 1988b.

21. These land occupations encompassed over 20,000 hectares by 1990. The Small Farmers Association of Negros (SFAN), a KMP affiliate, began occupying idle farmland in Negros Occidental in September 1986 (Gilding 1993: 7). For descriptions of land occupations and other forms of peasant activism and resistance, see CPAR 1989; id. 1991; Lara 1988: 132–33.

22. The cabinet action committee was created on Jan. 28, 1987; it first convened on Feb. 4, 1987.

23. An Inter-Agency Task Force on Agrarian Reform (ITFAR), consisting of representatives of concerned ministries and the academic and research community, had been established in December 1986. It was this body that prepared the various drafts considered by the CAC. All told the draft decree went through over 20 revisions (Bulatao 1987: 4). Member institutions of the task force eventually included the departments of Agrarian Reform, Agriculture and Food, Budget and Management, Finance, Justice, and Natural Resources; the Land

Bank of the Philippines; the Institute of Agrarian Studies; the National Economic and Development Authority; and Social Weather Stations, Inc., a private research organization.

24. Ongpin and Vistan 1987. Note the first passage in Ongpin and Vistan's proposed Executive Order: "Whereas, the people have long clamored for *genuine* and comprehensive agrarian reform . . ." (emphasis added). As issued, Proclamation 131 read: "Whereas, the essential element in any policy of agricultural revival and development is a comprehensive and *realistic* agrarian reform program . . ." (emphasis added).

25. See Acuña 1987: 69; Berenguer 1987: 70; Miller 1988a. Other organizations made veiled threats of violence against the state and the reform program. See, e.g., PLADAR and DATU-Panay 1987: 2.

26. The authors of the final text apparently were Executive Secretary Joker P. Arroyo; Presidential Special Counsel Teodoro Locsin, Jr.; Deputy Executive Secretary Catalino Macaraig, Jr.; Natural Resources Secretary Fulgencio Factoran, Jr., of the CAC; Land Bank President Deogracias N. Vistan; Justice Secretary Sedfrey Ordonez; and Constitutional Commissioner Adolfo Azcuna. See Mangahas 1987.

27. This interpretation was implicitly confirmed in a conversation with Evelyn Lim, then serving in a media consultant/television production role for the Office of the President, shortly after EO 229 was announced. "We [the Aquino government] have done it; we have done all we promised" (interview, July 28, 1987).

28. The "nationalist" bloc consisted of Florencio B. Abad, Gregorio A. Andolana, Juanito G. Camasura, William F. Claver, Venancio T. Garduce, and Oscar S. Rodriguez.

29. See BBCHD 1988; id. n.d. Among the signatories to the latter were the Archdiocese of Manila, Jaime Cardinal L. Sin; Association of Foundations; Association of Major Religious Superiors for Men; Bishops-Businessmen's Conference for Human Development; Chamber of Filipino Retailers; Integrated Bar of the Philippines; Manila Jaycees, Philippine Science Foundation; Philippine Social Science Council; Philippine Institute of Certified Public Accountants; and Trade Union Congress of the Philippines.

30. Sin 1988 (emphasis in original). EDSA is the acronym for the major highway (Epifanio de los Santos Avenue) around the perimeter of Metropolitan Manila. It was the site of many of the key events of the February 1986 revolt against Marcos.

31. The nationalist bloc introduced the first agrarian reform bill, HB 65 (Aug. 4, 1987). Congressman Gillego's original HB 400 was filed on Aug. 17, 1987. Senator Aquino filed SB 123 on Oct. 1, 1987. Other proreform members of the House Committee on Agrarian Reform included Romeo Angeles, Edcel C. Lagman, and Raul Roco (Gillego 1988: 10).

32. Guanzon introduced HB 941 on Sept. 3, 1987. The measure was endorsed by 116 additional House members.

33. Gillego and the other original co-sponsors withdrew their sponsorship

of HB 400 on Mar. 22, 1988, arguing that the bill was now "morally unacceptable and incompatible with the democratic and libertarian ideals" of land reform (*Farm News & Views* 1988a: 5).

34. Alvarez filed SB 16, SB 133, and SB 249 (a consolidation of SB 16 and SB 133).

35. Variants on this theme were mentioned so frequently that it appeared to be the "conventional wisdom" (Alvarez interview, Feb. 24, 1989; Bulatao interview, Mar. 15, 1989; Illo interview, Oct. 11, 1988; Morales interview, Oct. 14, 1988; Starke interview, June 23, 1989; Valenzuela interview, Oct. 21, 1988; See also Gilding 1993: 25–26; Miller 1988b). Taking exception to this view, on the grounds that there was little to meaningfully distinguish the Senate and House drafts, was Edcel C. Lagman, chairman of the House Committee on Agrarian Reform, who did note, however, that "directly or indirectly the majority [of House members] must have received support from landowners . . . many [members] are beholding [*sic*] to the landowning families" (interview, Mar. 15, 1989). The view that little distinguished the bills of the two chambers is also expressed in Guieb 1988.

36. "The members of the Philippine House of Representatives, chosen from single-member districts, are amenable to the pressures of local politics, where landed interests are influential. They tend to be conservative with regard to economic and social policies and often show strong opposition to land-reform legislation. The senators, elected by the entire national electorate, usually take a relatively moderate to liberal stand on major domestic policies. Though some senators who come from families with large land possessions may strongly oppose reform measures, the Senate as a whole tends to show less reluctance than the House to support these measures" (Tai 1974: 152).

37. In asserting the enormity of the task involved in completing Programs A, B, and D, Secretary of Finance Ongpin and Land Bank President Vistan estimated the public lands to be redistributed at 2.988 million hectares (1987: 2).

38. On the Japanese land reform, see Hewes 1955; Dore 1959. For Taiwan and South Korea, see Cheng 1961; Harrison 1968; Koo 1970; Kuo et al. 1981; Morrow and Sherper 1970.

39. The CAC draft Ongpin and Vistan were criticizing contained a uniform retention limit of seven hectares. In a remark recalling Ferdinand Marcos's well-known superstitious attachment to the number, they commented, "We do not know what is so magic about the number seven" (Ongpin and Vistan 1987: 2).

40. Ibid.: 3. On the issue of the administrative burden placed on the DAR, Jeremias Montemayor of the FFF was in agreement with Vistan and Ongpin: "Full implementation of PD 27 will tax DAR's administrative capacity" (interview, June 13, 1986).

41. Ongpin and Vistan 1987: 3. In my experience, credit-starved and moneylender-dependent landless peasants are only too aware of the cost of money. Village notables and presidential cronies, with their preferential access to subsidized credit, often have the more distorted view of the cost of money. Implicit in Ongpin and Vistan's remarks is an image of peasants as conniving,

dissembling, financial shirkers. Yet large landowners and big business operators frequently have poorer repayment records than landless and near-landless borrowers, a reflection of the relative impunity with which the former can default. (This is not to argue, of course, that borrowers, large or small, should be exempt from repayment.)

42. This change would in turn enable the Aquino government to include the distribution of these generated-but-not-distributed Emancipation Patents among its reform accomplishments.

43. See NOPA and AABT 1987: 5–6; PLADAR and DATU-Panay 1988: 4. See also Barcelona 1987: 23–24. Daniel L. Lacson, Jr., then governor of Negros Occidental and a prominent landowner, maintained that tenanted rice and corn lands, alienable public lands, and foreclosed properties held by government financial institutions amounted to 75 percent of all agricultural lands in the country. He argued that the reform program should begin with these lands and only in the event that this reform proved "successful and redound[ed] to the upliftment of all sectors of society involved" should the government consider imposing reform on the "small minority of lands considered as estates, plantations, or medium scale farms" (Lacson 1987: 3).

44. Alunan interview, June 16, 1986 (alleging the existence of thousands of hectares of undeveloped public lands on the islands of Leyte and Samar); Guanzon interview, June 19, 1986 (reporting the availability of 30,000 hectares of alienable public land in southern Negros). See also Baliao 1987 (Congresswoman Starke quoted as against redistributive reform, favoring the development of the "millions of hectares of undeveloped land"); Barcelona 1987: 24 (estimating the land area of government-owned, idle, sequestered, and foreclosed properties at 4 million hectares).

45. Remarks of Jeremias U. Montemayor, president, Federation of Free Farmers, reported in "Agrarian Reform Now!" 1986: 30. In agreement that extensive public lands were available for distribution, if not explicitly championing the notion of initiating the reform process with these lands, was Zoilo V. de la Cruz, president, NACUSIP (interview, June 13, 1986).

46. See BBCHD 1988; id. n.d. Among the signatories to the latter was the Trade Union Congress of the Philippines. Jerry Montemayor's Federation of Free Farmers is a principal member of the TUCP, suggesting an institutional position at odds with Montemayor's remarks cited earlier. See also Cuizon 1987: 7.

47. Lopez-Gonzaga n.d.: 5. In a subsequent monograph, the percentage of public land is revised slightly downward, to 8.54 percent (Lopez-Gonzaga et al. 1988: table 5, p. 27). The provincial assessors' data cited in this monograph show the total farm area of Negros Occidental, inclusive of pasture and forests, to be some 668,000 hectares. These data are in very marked contrast to the 1980 agricultural census figure of just under 296,000 hectares (and 325,000 hectares in 1971). No explanation for this extraordinary discrepancy is provided in the monograph. On the general issue of the insufficiency of public lands, even in combination with idle, abandoned or voluntarily offered lands, to meet the country's reform needs, see Dominguez 1987: 29.

48. See, e.g., Cainglet 1987: 56. Cainglet argued for a 3-year deferral of this portion of the reform for the sake of landowners' children who might reach the age of majority in that period and, presumably, thereby become entitled to a share of the property.

49. RA 6657, Sec. 31. The notion of distributing corporate stock in lieu of land transfers is not new in the Philippines. It had been previously advocated by President Aquino's late husband, among others. See Aquino 1967.

50. This question has not been addressed by the Philippine Supreme Court.

51. RA 6657, Sec. 3, defines a "farmer" as "a natural person whose primary livelihood is cultivation of land or production of agricultural crops, either by himself, or primarily with the assistance of his immediate farm household, whether the land is owned by him, or by another person under a leasehold or share tenancy agreement or arrangement with the owner thereof." A "farm-worker" is "a natural person who renders service for value as an employee or laborer in an agricultural enterprise or farm regardless of whether his compensation is paid on a daily, weekly, monthly, or *'pakyaw'* [piece rate] basis. The term includes an individual whose work has ceased as a consequence of, or in connection with, a pending agrarian dispute and who has not obtained a substantially equivalent and regular farm employment." A "regular farmworker" is "a natural person who is employed on a permanent basis by an agricultural enterprise or farm."

52. For the landowners' views, see NOPA and AABT 1987.

53. See del Rosario 1989. Lopez-Gonzaga echoed this concern that efficient haciendas, specifically the president's Hacienda Luisita, not be fragmented (interview, June 17, 1986).

54. The term "heir" normally connotes "a person who inherits or is legally entitled to inherit another's property or title upon the other's death" (*Webster's New Universal Unabridged Dictionary*). What the Philippine agrarian reform law, RA 6657, in effect provides is an *inter vivos* transfer of property to qualified offspring of existing landowners.

55. I first encountered this line of argument—the "widow with children" hypothetical—in a meeting with senior government officials in El Salvador in April 1980. President Napoleon Duarte, publicly a champion of agrarian reform, argued that the reform should exempt all small landlords, otherwise the reform would deprive widows with small children of their only means of support. The response to this line of reasoning, then as now, is presented in the text.

In the event, landholdings of less than seven hectares were administratively exempted from the Salvadoran reform process when one of five additional criteria applied: the landlord was a widow with children; the land was the owner's only fixed asset (no home or business); rents from the land were the sole means of support for a family with minor children; the landlord had been officially declared mentally incompetent; or a physical handicap of the landlord precluded his or her direct cultivation of the land. FINATA n.d.

56. Another situation in which this is likely to be true is a landlord-tenant relationship involving close kinship.

57. In Taiwan, special arrangements were made for widows, orphans, and the disabled affected by the land reform. See "Relief Measures Applicable to Old and Infirm, Orphaned, Widowed, or Physically Disabled Joint Owners of Land Compulsorily Purchased by the Government in 1954," promulgated by the Taiwan Provincial Government, Feb. 25, 1954, reprinted in full in Cheng 1961: 261–68.

58. See Acuña 1987: 62; NOPA and AABT 1987: 3; NFSP n.d.; PLADAR and DATU-Panay n.d.: 1–2. Prawn producers also argued that the land fragmentation attendant on agrarian reform would adversely affect prawn production because of the need to coordinate water supply and other operations (Marasigan 1987a: 24). Note that though the largest prawn operations might involve as much as 100 hectares of ponds, individual ponds rarely exceeded 10,000 square meters (1 ha).

59. See Dominguez 1987: 64–66. Secretary of Agriculture Carlos Dominguez emphasized that for stock sharing to be constitutionally acceptable, the tiller must receive "*effective* ownership of the land" on terms that were financially comparable to or better than those which would apply in the case of actual land transfer (1987: 67; emphasis added).

60. Locsin et al. interview, June 14, 1986; Rojas et al. interview, June 17, 1986. In September 1986, Negros Occidental Governor Daniel Lacson formally proposed a "60•30•10" program that would have reduced the area planted to sugar by 40 percent. Lacson described the proposal to the author in a Mar. 10, 1986 interview. See also Jones 1986. An Asian Development Bank study suggests that to be viable in the future, the Philippine sugar industry will have to devote 35 percent less land to sugar than was true in the mid 1970s (1988: cf. pp. xii and 17).

61. Nasol 1987: 21. On the positive side, Ramon Nasol noted that fragmentation would result in small farms, which would be "more efficient users of existing resources," maximizing their use of abundant resources and minimizing their use of scarce resources. See also Hernandez 1987: 33; Sawit 1987: 40.

62. NOPA and AABT 1987: 4. Accord, Alunan interview, June 16, 1986: "The island [of Negros] was developed by entrepreneurs. Now they are being told to give the land to the workers."

63. Baliao 1987. Starke's claim that she "started from zero," although hardly atypical of wealthy Filipinos, is pure mythology, as she has indicated elsewhere. "My grandfather was a sugar baron. Sugar made our family and some other families fabulously rich," she told Lewis Simons (Simons 1987: 163). By birth, Starke (née Lopez) is a member of one of the richest families in the Philippines (see McCoy 1992: 114–15).

64. Bautista n.d.: 5 (as much as 82 percent of production costs borne by sugar tenant), citing Revilleza 1976.

65. See Bascog 1987: 48–49. The term "sweat equity" is mine, not Bascog's (Prosterman and Riedinger 1987: 38).

66. SB 16, Sec. 2, provided for a 7-hectare retention limit effective July 1, 1997. SB 133, Sec. 6, provided for retention limits of fifteen hectares for sugar lands,

seven hectares for rice and corn lands, and twelve hectares for all other private agricultural lands. For academic support of crop-specific retention limits, see remarks of Eduardo Tadem, Research Fellow, Third World Studies Center, University of the Philippines, reported in *Solidarity* 1986: 33. Fermin Adriano and Luzviminda Cornista each stressed the need for flexibility to accommodate regional diversity, arguing that no one model of agrarian reform was appropriate for the entire country (Adriano et al. interview, Mar. 20, 1986). Prominent among the landowner organizations urging variable retention limits were the Panay Landowners Alliance for Democratic Agrarian Reform (PLADAR) and the Democratic Alliance for a Truly Unified Panay (DATU-Panay). See PLADAR and DATU-Panay 1988: 9–10. Within the government, Deogracias N. Vistan, president of the Land Bank of the Philippines, was outspoken in favoring a crop-specific retention limit. See *Malaya* 1987.

67. Variable retention limits provide strong incentives for crop shifting in favor of crops entitled to larger retention areas. The results are particularly perverse where "viable" farm size is the basis for retention rights: the less suited a locale is for a given crop, the greater the retention area allowed. For a discussion of the administrability of retention limits, and an argument for *zero* retention in the case of tenanted holdings, see Prosterman and Riedinger 1987: 182–87.

68. RA 6657, Sec. 6, providing in pertinent part: "No person may own or retain, directly or indirectly, any public or private agricultural land, the size of which shall vary according to factors governing a viable family-sized farm, such as commodity produced, terrain, infrastructure, and soil fertility as determined by the Presidential Agrarian Reform Council (PARC) created hereunder, but in no case shall retention by the landowner exceed five (5) hectares."

69. RA 6657, Sec. 6, providing: "Three (3) hectares *may* be awarded to each child of the landowner, subject to the following qualifications: (1) that he is at least fifteen (15) years of age; and (2) that he is actually tilling the land or directly managing the farm" (emphasis added). This provision creates powerful incentives for landlords to evict tenants on lands devoted to crops other than rice and corn. Only by doing so can the claim be made that the landowner's heirs are "tilling the land or directly managing the farm." Sections 6 and 22 make such evictions illegal, but enforcement of tenant protections is extremely problematic. See Prosterman and Hanstad 1988a: 6–7.

70. See, in particular, Senator Neptali Gonzalez's request for information on the number of coconut landowners by farm size "so we will be able to know just how many really would be affected by whatever retention limits that the Congress may decide to provide" (Gonzalez 1987: 65). Early in the legislative process, the Institute of Agrarian Studies of the University of the Philippines at Los Baños provided members of Congress with land-tenure data and a graph depicting the effect of various retention limits in terms of the number of farmers and the land area covered by the reform (IAS 1987b: 11–14).

71. Abad interview, June 21, 1989. The Philippine demographic profile is inconsistent with Abad's assumption that, on average, three of four children per

family would be fifteen years of age or older and thereby meet the age criteria for retention rights. On the other hand, the law is not explicit as to the date by which heirs must be fifteen years old. Thus many presently underaged children might become "eligible" during the program's decade-plus period of implementation. To forestall this possibility, the DAR issued Administrative Order 4 in 1994, requiring that children be at least 15 years old as of June 15, 1988, the date RA 6657 became effective.

72. The extreme concentration of landownership in Negros Occidental means that proportionately more land will be available for reform than is suggested by national figures. A 5-hectare retention limit would exempt around 46 percent of total farm area in the province from reform. A retention limit of 8 to 11 hectares would exempt 50–56 percent of farm area.

73. A "unimodal" pattern of farmholdings is characterized by narrow distributions of farm units and farm area around the median farm size. A "bimodal" pattern is typified by skewed distributions; farm units are concentrated in the smaller size categories and farm area is concentrated in the relatively few large holdings. For discussions of the merits of unimodal patterns of agricultural development and the drawbacks of bimodal patterns of development, see de Janvry 1981; Johnston and Clark 1982; Johnston and Kilby 1975.

74. Powelson and Stock 1987: 191, table 13.1. Note the text accompanying this table contains erroneous and contradictory equivalencies for the Taiwanese measurement of land. One *chia* is equivalent to 0.97 hectares.

75. Hernandez 1987: 26 described the infrastructural advantages of the East Asian countries as including their systems of irrigation, farm credit, and farmers' associations, as well as import controls, farm price supports, and population control.

76. "We feel that if we are going to own a land of 3 hectares that would be enough for a family. . . . We feel, Mr. Senator, that 3 hectares is more than enough. Our position is that, for irrigated land planted to rice 2 hectares is enough" (Dimagiba 1987: 11–12). Accord Oquendo 1987: 14. Attorney Leonardo Garcia, administrator, Philippine Coconut Authority, estimated that a coconut farm of 2–3 hectares, properly intercropped, constituted a family-sized farm (Garcia 1987: 62).

77. In the event, the average parcel distributed under PD 27 was, as of year-end 1988, 1.38 hectares (ROP, DAR 1988). In the case of El Salvador, distribution of the theoretical minimum farm size of nine hectares per beneficiary (Simon and Stephens 1981: 2) would have required approximately twice the land area of the entire country, and if cultivable hectares were meant, five times the total amount of land in cultivation (Prosterman and Riedinger 1987: 283 n. 45).

78. These higher figures are not themselves estimates of fair market value. They are the estimated fair market values inflated by 50 percent to account for anticipated overstatements of land values by landowners, a rather telling acknowledgement of probable landowner misconduct and the government's inability to control the same.

79. HB 400, Sec. 11, as originally introduced. "Fair market value" was de-

fined as the value "declared by the owner in his latest tax declaration," subject to PARC controls. "Small landholdings"—defined as 7 hectares or less—would be compensated at fair market value. "Lower medium sized landholdings"—defined as 7–24 hectares—were to receive 75 percent of the fair market value. "Upper medium sized landholdings"—24–50 hectares—were to receive 50 percent of fair market value.

80. HB 941, Sec. 8. In lieu of cash, compensation could be made in shares of stock in corporations, owned or controlled by the government, an exchange of assets administered by the government, or, where acceptable to the landowner, in bonds guaranteed by the Land Bank of the Philippines.

81. SB 16 was silent on the valuation issue, leaving the criteria set forth in Executive Order 229 operative. SB 133, Sec. 18, SB 123, Sec. 11, and the first draft of SB 249, Sec. 11, all provided for compensation based on the owner's tax declaration of current fair market value.

82. Chapter 5, "Land Acquisition," Sec. 16, of RA 6657. Landowners are afforded fifteen days to submit evidence as to just compensation after receipt of notice concerning the pending administrative proceedings.

83. Pursuant to her decree authority under the so-called Freedom Constitution, President Aquino had effectively frozen—sequestered—many of the assets of former President Marcos and his cronies, alleging that these properties were ill-gotten gains.

84. In September 1988, the Presidential Agrarian Reform Council estimated that foreign sources would need to provide P176.3 billion ($8.4 billion) of the projected P402.7 billion ($19.2 billion) in total program costs during 1987–97 (USAID 1989: 21). By March 1989, PARC's estimate of the total program costs—net of amortization and loan repayments—was P221.1 billion ($10.4 billion), of which P140.5 billion ($6.6 billion) would need to be provided by foreign donors (Putzel 1992: 347). The former figures cannot be reconciled with the latter by netting out the amortization and loan repayments.

85. Merrill and Muncy interview, Apr. 15, 1986; Blackton interview, Oct. 7, 1988; Cornista interview, Feb. 23, 1989. See also Ebro 1988. Although unwilling to fund compensation, Italy and the Netherlands pledged $6.2 million and $10 million respectively to the reform program in 1988. See Research Conference Board 1988. The Asian Development Bank was similarly unwilling to finance compensation, expressing significant interest in funding additional agricultural credit instead (Martokoesoemo and Tacke interview, Mar. 25, 1986). The ADB was reinforced in this view by the then U.S. representative to the bank, a person characterized by one USAID employee as "very hostile to land reform."

86. Among the proposed amendments are SB 740 and HB 918 (excluding fishponds and prawn farms from the coverage of RA 6657); HB 9612 (exempting farms of 24 hectares or less from the coverage of RA 6657); HB 10817 and HB 13875 (redirecting the thrust of the agrarian reform program from land redistribution to support services and creating a nationwide community-based framework for agricultural development); HB 2941 (exempting lands cultivated by religious associations or denominations living and working together in com-

munities from the coverage of RA 6657); HB 360 (exempting lands intended for retirees and tourism development from the coverage of RA 6657).

87. See *Business World* 1990b. The notion of province- or region-specific reform initiatives is popular among Philippine landowners (Locsin interview, June 16, 1986).

88. For a review of the potential problems of decentralization, see Bienen et al. 1990.

89. For discussions of administrative arrangements and protection of the interests of the landless, see Montgomery 1972; Prosterman and Riedinger 1987: 137–39, 165.

90. Starke interview, June 23, 1989. See also Anda and Pastor 1990 (discussion of threatened alignment between LUPA and the block-voting, conservative religious organization Iglesia ni Kristo for the 1992 elections, to promote candidates sympathetic to landowners' objections to the reform law).

Chapter 7

1. The Garchitorena scandal and similar "land scams" were front-page news in all of the Manila newspapers for most of June–July 1989. See Estella 1989; *Manila Chronicle* 1989b; Tangbawan and Narito 1989. For international coverage, see *Asiaweek* 1989; Miller 1989; Tiglao 1989. One of the overvaluations involved the 327-hectare Villasor estate in Negros Occidental. Purportedly planted to upland rice and coconuts, the land was deemed "unproductive" by the DAR, which nonetheless, with LBP approval, purchased the estate for P9.22 million in August 1988. Following public disclosure of the overvaluation, the DAR rescinded the transaction.

2. There was a history of tension between Vistan and DAR Secretary Philip Juico and thus an element of personal animosity as well as a battle for agency "turf" in Vistan's disclosure of the valuation scandal (de la Cruz 1989; Reuyan interview, Jan. 29, 1992). Vistan attributed some of the tension to their differing perspectives on the reform process. In his view, the DAR emphasized the hectares acquired and distributed, whereas the LBP stressed the economics of reform and the viability of the affected farms (interview, Feb. 20, 1991).

3. Biadora interview, Feb. 12, 1991. Following the Garchitorena scandal, the DAR and the LBP became more insistent that lands be cultivated before they would approve them for acquisition under the VOS program (Reuyan interview, Jan. 29, 1992).

4. The UCPB defended its actions by arguing that the reform guidelines were unclear, that the buyer bore responsibility for complying with the reform law, and that the DAR was charged with scrutinizing land transactions and voiding those that violated the reform law (Narisma 1989).

5. Sharp's purchase was financed by loans from Romeo Santos to Sharp's president, Alex Lina, on Dec. 2, 1988. Santos concurrently financed Sharp's attempted purchase of the 1,187-hectare Liboro estate, also in Camarines Sur, from the UCPB. Santos had close ties to Aquino's brother, Jose Cojuangco, Jr.,

and had played an important role in Aquino's presidential campaign in the Bicol (southern Luzon) region. Aquino appointed Santos to manage Manila's international airport and later backed his disputed, but ultimately successful, candidacy for congressional office. Santos had a long history of speculation in agricultural land and of land sales to the DAR (Gillego interview, Feb. 6, 1991; Narisma 1989; Putzel 1992: 315–16).

6. Lagman interview, Mar. 15, 1989; Riedinger 1990b. In particular, reliance on pre-1986 tax declarations coupled with generous determinations of the previous social and economic contributions of the farmers, farmworkers, and government would likely result in compensation payments well below current "fair market value." Farmers' organizations have repeatedly urged that they be credited for their contributions to the land. Similarly, these organizations have argued that government contributions (infrastructural investments, etc.) be excluded from the determination of landowner compensation (KMP 1986d: 7–8; Montemayor 1988; Tadeo 1986: 14).

7. Administrative Order No. 6, 1988 series. Total land value was defined as the mean of the market value as determined by comparable sales, the market value as determined by government assessors, and the landowner's declared value. The latter could not exceed 200 percent of the average of the two "market" values. The regulations provided that in the absence of an owner declaration, the declared value "shall be based on this upper limit." The practical effect was to value the land for compensation purposes at four-thirds of market value (ROP, DAR 1989a).

8. Bancod 1991b. Prior to 1987, average land values under PD 27 ranged from P6,000 per hectare for unirrigated corn lands to P12,000 per hectare for irrigated rice lands (David 1987b: 12). Affected landowners have repeatedly objected to the PD 27 valuations, often obstructing the valuation process (Adversario interview, Jan. 29, 1992; ROP, DAR 1993a: 10). Landowner rejection rates of land valuations for all components of the reform program have apparently declined from 80 percent (Vistan interview, Feb. 20, 1991) to 43 percent (Cabezon interview, Feb. 11, 1992), a reflection perhaps of the use of more lucrative valuation formulas.

9. These values are typically 12–16 times the value previously declared by the owners for tax purposes (Juico interview, Oct. 14, 1988). The average expected compensation of P37,000 per hectare was based on estimated land values, which were then inflated by *50 percent* to account for landowner overstatement. For sugar the uninflated per-hectare estimates were P50,000 for first-class lands, P30,000 for second-class lands, and P20,000 for third-class lands. For plantation crops (defined to include fishponds), the per-hectare estimates were P150,000 for first-class lands, P100,000 for second-class lands, and P75,000 for third-class lands. See Dominguez 1987: 31. Market values for sugar lands in Negros Occidental were estimated to range from P20,000 to P100,000 per hectare, averaging P50,000 per hectare (Lopez-Gonzaga interview, June 17, 1986).

10. Strictly speaking, Aquino was not an owner of Hacienda Luisita, having sold her stock upon assuming the presidency. However, members of her mater-

nal family retain ownership of the hacienda. The distinction between the president's interest in Hacienda Luisita and that of her family was unimportant symbolically.

Aquino's family was not alone in applying for the stock-distribution option. Eduardo Cojuangco and Roberto Benedicto, two of Marcos's closest cronies, sought to avail themselves of this option on properties they had acquired during the Marcos era that had subsequently been sequestered by the Aquino government (Lopez-Gonzaga interview, Feb. 12, 1991). The Acuña family, prominent in the antireform movement, similarly sought to avoid land redistribution by distributing stock (*Philippine Daily Inquirer* 1991).

11. See, e.g., interview with President Aquino in *Veritas*, June 27, 1986: "Sugar workers in Luisita are among the highest paid, if not the highest paid in the [country] and at a time when sugar workers are being laid off none of our sugar workers were laid off."

12. This valuation reflected dramatic increases in the value of various non-land assets—including residential land and land improvements—over corporate asset declarations filed six months earlier (Putzel 1992: 333–35). The Hacienda Luisita case thus confirmed concerns that corporate owners would dilute peasant stock holdings by undervaluing the agricultural land or overvaluing the non-land assets. The case also suggested fraud on the part of Aquino's family, to which she then gave her imprimatur.

13. In Drilon's view, the DAR's authority to authorize or refuse conversions dated from June 15, 1988, the date the reform law became effective.

14. In so arguing, Drilon misconstrued the plain meaning of key passages of several enactments. Illustrative is his reading of Section 5 (1) of Executive Order 129-A of July 26, 1987, which provides that the DAR shall "have exclusive authority to approve or disapprove conversion of agricultural lands for residential, commercial, industrial and other uses as may be provided by law." Drilon interprets the phrase "as may be provided by law" as modifying the DAR's "exclusive authority." He concludes that the executive order was not a source of exclusive authority for the DAR, but merely reaffirmed the existence of such powers as were granted under previous laws. The proper interpretation of the phrase, from both a grammatical and legal standpoint, is that it modifies "uses." The phrase is intended to leave open the possibility that the legislature might by law identify other uses for which conversion of agricultural lands was appropriate. Thus interpreted the phrase places no limit on the exclusivity of the DAR's authority to approve or disapprove conversions of agricultural lands.

15. There is some suggestion that payment was made before the vote (Putzel 1992: 326). Many of the critics of this conversion directly or indirectly suggest that the farmers who approved the conversion were bought off (see *Business World* 1990a). If the farmers' choices were freely made, there can be no grounds for complaint about their decision. Similarly, one cannot condemn the members of the KMP and other militant peasant organizations who have sold lands received under the reform program when they were offered generous prices by would-be industrial developers. To condemn these farmers for what the critic

perceives to be improvident behavior is to embrace the same ethos of paternalism attributed to Philippine elites. Peasant choices, freely made, ought to be respected. However, objection is appropriately made when extra-economic coercion shapes the peasants' decision.

16. The Langkaan farmers agreed among themselves not to press claims for the Ramos estate lands, but to seek additional land on the Langkaan estate or comparable nearby property.

17. In the view of some, the negative impact of the turnover in DAR secretaries was exacerbated by the turnover in senior DAR staff accompanying all secretarial changes beginning with Juico's ouster (Cabezon interview, Feb. 11, 1992). Others welcomed the removal of longtime senior DAR staff, arguing that they must bear part of the blame for the DAR's many years of poor performance.

18. Subsequent to her failed nomination, it was discovered that Defensor-Santiago had inflated the figures on land distribution during her tenure, further tarnishing the DAR's poor public image (Bulatao interview, Feb. 16, 1994; Gillego interview, Feb. 17, 1994; Leong interview, Feb. 22, 1991).

19. The more militant peasant and nongovernmental organizations often condemn elite-based NGOs such as the PBSP and the Negros Economic Development Foundation (NEDF) as unable or unwilling to challenge the privileges and power of Philippine elites upon which they depend for funding.

20. Jose Noel Olano, undersecretary for field operations, had previously served as national coordinator for PhilDHRRA. Hector Soliman, undersecretary for legal affairs, had served both in KAISAHAN and as head of the legal office of the Haribon Foundation, the leading environmental organization in the Philippines. Clifford Burkley, Garilao's chief executive assistant, had served as the top administrator and financial officer for KAISAHAN. Charlito Manlupig, the DAR's top-performing regional director for 1993, had been coordinator for PhilDHRRA Mindanao. Teodorico Peña, the DAR's top-performing provincial reform officer for 1993, had worked for CARE Philippines after leaving an earlier position in the DAR in 1990 (Bulatao interview, Feb. 16, 1994).

21. *Association of Small Landowners* v. *Secretary of Agrarian Reform*, Phil. Sup. Ct. GR 78742 (July 14, 1989).

22. *Luz Farms* v. *Secretary of the Department of Agrarian Reform*, Phil. Sup. Ct. GR 86889 (Dec. 4, 1990). Subsequent to the ruling, the chair of the Senate Committee on Agrarian Reform, Heherson Alvarez, indicated that he had never favored inclusion of these enterprises in the reform program (interview, Feb. 20, 1991).

23. In *Central Mindanao University* v. *Department of Agrarian Reform*, GR 100091 (Oct. 22, 1992), the Supreme Court rejected the DAR's application of the reform law to 400 hectares of the 3,080-hectare land-grant university campus. The DAR had awarded these lands to university faculty and staff and farm laborers—aligned as the Bukidnon Free Farmers and Agricultural Laborers Organization (BUFFALO)—who farmed the university-owned property. The court's ruling was based on Section 10 of RA 6657, which exempts all lands

"actually, directly and exclusively used and found necessary for . . . school sites."

24. CALABARZON refers to a zone marked for industrial development in the provinces of Cavite, Laguna, Batangas, Rizal, and Quezon.

25. Here the legislation explicitly refers to "viable family-sized farm"; consideration of viable size is mandated (RA 6657, Ch. II, Sec. 6).

26. The available data only permit comparison of 3- and 5-hectare landowner retention limits *exclusive* of the retention rights of heirs. A 5-hectare landowner retention right would exempt 75.6 percent of the land in farms, leaving 24.4 percent (2.37 million ha) available for reform, assuming no retention right for heirs. A 3-hectare landowner retention limit would exempt 62.4 percent of the land in farms, leaving 37.4 percent (3.64 million ha) available for redistribution. Were this latter area actually redistributed, the Philippine agrarian reform would be comparable, in terms of the proportion of agricultural land redistributed, to the postwar reforms in Japan, South Korea, and Taiwan. Assuming beneficiary families received on average 1.6 hectares—the current Philippine ratio of cropped hectares to farm families—lowering the retention limit from 5 to 3 hectares would increase the number of beneficiary families potentially reached from 1.48 million to 2.27 million.

27. This assumes that the distribution of landowners is roughly proportional to the distribution of operational farm holdings by size. With a 5-hectare retention limit, 13.9 percent of the operational farm holdings are potentially affected by the reform process. Were the retention limit set at 3 hectares, 31.1 percent of the farm holdings would potentially be subject to reform. With roughly 1.99 million agricultural landowners in the Philippines (see Chapter 4), 5- and 3-hectare retention limits would potentially subject 277,000 and 620,000 landowners respectively to the reform process. On the other hand, lowering the landowner retention limit from 5 hectares to 3 hectares, with a zero retention limit for heirs, would increase the number of beneficiary families potentially reached from 1.48 million to 2.27 million. A landowner retention right of 3 hectares, with no retention right for heirs, might thus increase the number of reform beneficiaries by roughly 800,000 families, while potentially affecting another 343,000 landowner families.

28. The ratios were calculated from data in Dore 1959: 174; Cheng 1961: 76.

29. Article 6, Sec. 32, of the 1987 Constitution provides: "The Congress shall, as early as possible, provide for a system of initiative and referendum, and the exceptions therefrom, whereby the people can directly propose and enact laws or approve or reject any act or law or part thereof passed by the Congress or local legislative body after the registration of a petition therefor signed by at least ten per centum of the total number of registered voters, of which every legislative district must be represented by at least three per centum of the registered voters thereof."

30. Interview with NFSW program coordinator for land conflicts, Mar. 6, 1989.

31. CPAR 1990: 12; Mariano interview, Feb. 8, 1991. For further discussion of land occupations and rent moratoriums, see CPAR 1991: 18–20. A Sugar Res-

titution Law, RA 7202, was passed in the final months of the Aquino administration. It promised to make good the funds withheld from sugar producers by Marcos's sugar-marketing monopoly, although the modalities of payment were not spelled out. KMP leaders expressed concern that the government, in meeting the claims for restitution, might absolve the landowners of their bank debts on foreclosed properties and return the lands to them. Such action would result in the eviction of the peasant occupants (Mariano interview, Nov. 24, 1992).

32. As of early 1994, the TriPARRD program in Antique was being phased out in favor of an integrated area-development project funded by the Netherlands (Banzuela interview, Feb. 22, 1994).

33. PhilDHRRA is a national NGO association. Its antecedents date back to the 1974 Development of Human Resources in Asia conference in Swanganiwas, Thailand. The institutional framework for PhilDHRRA was established in preparation for the 1979 World Conference on Agrarian Reform and Rural Development. In 1983, 20 Philippine NGOs participated in a 20-village study of agrarian reform and rural development. A series of national NGO workshops followed, resulting in the formal launching of PhilDHRRA on Apr. 1, 1984. PhilDHRRA initially concentrated on community organizing before assuming an active advocacy role on behalf of agrarian reform in 1986. PhilDHRRA was a principal sponsor of both the first and the second National Consultation on Agrarian Reform and Rural Development (NCARRD). NCARRD II inaugurated the national peasant federation Pambansang Kilusan ng mga Samahang Magsasaka (PAKISAMA). PhilDHRRA also played an instrumental role in the founding of the Congress for a People's Agrarian Reform (CPAR) (Banzuela interview, Feb. 10, 1992; Flores 1993).

34. The government agencies involved in the TriPARRD program include the departments of Agriculture, Agrarian Reform, Environment and Natural Resources, Public Works and Highways, and Trade and Industry, as well as the National Irrigation Authority and the Register of Deeds.

35. The most intractable case involved the Pecuaria estate in Camarines Sur, which was under voluntary offer of sale to the DAR. Fifty-five members of the FFF, 48 of whom had not previously been associated with the estate, occupied 250 hectares of the estate in 1989. Another 400 relatives and friends joined the FFF members beginning in November 1990. DAR Secretary Leong decided the dispute in favor of the former estate workers, but as of early 1992, FFF members still occupied a significant portion of the estate and were seeking title to that land. The landowners had rejected the government's land valuation in the meantime, lending further uncertainty to the status of the rightful (DAR prequalified) beneficiaries.

36. Obias interview, Jan. 26, 1992. The "distrust" described by some local DAR officials appears to reflect jealousies over bureaucratic "turf" and a prejudice against working through or with NGOs. For his part, DAR Secretary Garilao views the TriPARRD approach as a means of rekindling the partnership with NGOs and correcting the DAR's loss of public support (interview, Nov. 25, 1992).

37. Peasant complaints about the support price were twofold: the price, at

P3.50 per kilo of *palay*, was too low; and the NFA had inadequate resources to purchase more than a small fraction of the crop. The first forum on the topic was held July 22, 1989. A second conference, on Sept. 3, 1989, led to the drafting of a National Rice Policy. Members of the Peasants Forum picketed the Department of Agriculture on several occasions in October 1989, and at the end of the month President Aquino and the NFA agreed to increase the support price to P5.00 per kilo (CPAR 1990: 14–16).

38. This manifesto was eventually embodied in RA 7607, the Magna Carta of small farmers (Cariño and Millar 1993).

39. The DAR has presented the data on reform accomplishments in terms of at least three reporting periods: the calendar year; the period since July 1987, when Proclamation 131 launched the Aquino administration's comprehensive agrarian reform program (CARP); and the CARP-related tenure in office of the Aquino and Ramos administrations (July 1987–May 1992 in the former case, and June 1992–May 1998 in the latter). Further confounding public accountability is the DAR's failure to consistently present the same types of data in each report. Beneficiary data are missing from several annual reports, as are disaggregated data for private agricultural lands and the leasehold programs.

In May 1993, the DAR revealed that its previous reports had overstated cumulative accomplishments for July 1987–Dec. 1992 by *200,000 hectares*. The "validated" figure was 1.97 million hectares rather than the 2.17 million hectares originally reported (Cariño 1993b). Manipulation of performance data and obfuscation are hallmarks of neopatrimonial regimes; government data are tailored to serve the interests of the regime rather than public accountability. Taken together, the DAR's practices serve to perpetuate public distrust of its performance claims and hinder peasant scrutiny of (and participation in) the reform process.

40. Bulatao 1992: 7. Bulatao credits the DAR with distributing 11,187 hectares of tenanted rice and corn lands, 19,651 hectares of landed estates, and 95,117 hectares of resettlements (1992: 8). The first figure corresponds to the Emancipation Patents distributed under Operation Land Transfer (see Table 5, which uses DAR figures that differ slightly from those used by Bulatao).

41. It is difficult to tell how much political benefit the government derives from this manipulation of data. It confronts a public weary of DAR scandals and leadership changes, and the frequent attacks directed at the program by reform proponents and opponents alike. As Philippine presidents are constitutionally limited to a single term, they are apparently playing to historians in their manipulation of the accomplishment data.

42. Compulsory acquisition may account for a slightly higher proportion of the cumulative July 1987–Dec. 1993 redistribution achievements than shown in text. A 1993 year-end review indicates that compulsory acquisitions accounted for 5 percent of the land area, private and public, redistributed during the period Jan. 14–Nov. 30, 1993 (ROP, DAR 1993a: 5).

43. The comparison with DAR's annual performance prior to 1993 excludes the distribution of alienable and disposable public lands. The Department of

Environment and Natural Resources is responsible for that element of the reform program.

44. The reform law permits TNCs to continue to lease up to 1,000 hectares of government-owned lands until 1992. Several TNCs have availed themselves of this privilege, over the considerable objections of Philippine peasants.

45. DAR 1993b: table 1. This figure excludes the DENR's distribution of alienable and disposable public lands.

46. This is not to say that the rice and corn sectors had no political influence. The Philippine government has generally maintained protectionist policies for rice and corn, a reflection not so much of the political influence of rice and corn producers, be they owner-operators or landlords, as of the influence of the rice milling / marketing cartels.

47. Landlords in the coconut sector refused to make common cause with landlords in the rice and corn sectors in defense of tenancy relations in general. Instead, landlords in the coconut sector sought to distinguish their production relations from tenancy, notwithstanding conventional descriptions of their operations. The LBP's president, Deogracias Vistan, indirectly confirmed the importance of economies of scale as a consideration when he noted that rice and corn were crops suited to individual cultivation (interview, Feb. 20, 1991). Aquino similarly accepted the arguments that economies of scale existed in the commercial or export-crop sector (Abad interview, Feb. 7, 1991).

48. Personal communication from Roy L. Prosterman, University of Washington, reporting on an Aug. 15, 1988 conversation with Shuji Shimokoji, Ministry of Foreign Affairs, Japan. At least as early as June 1987, Japanese representatives had indicated their willingness to provide substantial financial support for the reform process writ large, only to be met with indifference from Aquino and her government (Quisumbing interview, June 24, 1989; reporting on conversations with Saburo Okita and Akira Takahashi of the Japanese foreign aid agency).

49. The search warrant was apparently related to the investigation of the Apr. 21, 1989, assassination of U.S. Colonel James Rowe (*Manila Chronicle* 1989a).

50. Tadeo served as manager of the Central Bulacan Area Marketing Cooperative in 1981. He was convicted of converting P126,981 worth (66,000 kilos) of rice to his personal use when his cooperative allegedly failed to deliver the rice consignment to a government agency (*Business World* 1990e; Tiglao 1992).

51. For a description of the "total war" program in Negros Occidental, see Arlen 1990.

52. The debate within the KMP paralleled debates within the CPP / NPA and other leftist organizations. These organizations were reassessing the post-Marcos Philippine situation and changed international conditions, notably the collapse of the communist regimes in eastern Europe and the former Soviet Union.

53. The teams conducted a three-day, live-in seminar, gathering the entire labor force together to view pictures of NPA atrocities and screen films such as

The Killing Fields, which depict communist atrocities in Pol Pot's Cambodia. The military typically described the NFSW as a communist front organization. At the seminar's end, the workers were pressured to "surrender" and pledge allegiance to the Aquino government in a mass "graduation" ceremony. For a description of mass surrenders and how they are experienced by the military and by the peasants, see Rutten 1992.

54. Data are from an unpublished study of the Philippine Center for Investigative Journalism as communicated by Sheila S. Coronel, Nov. 23, 1992. At the time of the study (November 1992), the electoral results for three seats in the lower house were still being contested.

55. Abad interview, Jan. 15, 1992; Gillego interview, Jan. 21, 1992; Ramiro interview, Feb. 19, 1991; Serrano interview, Jan. 13, 1992. In January 1991, the Caucus of Development NGO Networks (CODE-NGO) sponsored a conference to address the issue of NGO involvement in building democracy. CODE-NGO is an alliance of ten NGO networks representing a variety of religious and ideological orientations. These organizations are united around an agenda of people-centered, sustainable, and nationalistic development. In February 1991, a formal electoral movement within the NGO community, "Project 2001," was organized. CODE-NGO initially embraced Project 2001, before distancing itself somewhat over the issue of direct support for candidates. In turn, Project 2001 abstained from formally endorsing candidates as an organization. See Rood 1992. Kaakbay ng Sambayanan (AKBAYAN), which included some disgruntled former members of Project 2001, was the alliance of NGOs and other "cause-oriented" groups that provided formal support for the Salonga-Pimentel ticket (Montiel 1992).

56. Although hampered by limited campaign resources, part of the explanation for the coalition's poor showing may have been the low level of electoral awareness among Philippine peasants. Even on an NFSW-organized cooperative farm, for example, few members knew their congressional representative (interviews at Hacienda Mandayo, Feb. 11, 1991).

57. The implementation timetable for the reform program had deferred compulsory acquisition of farms under 50 hectares in size until 1992. By the KMP's calculation, a 24-hectare retention limit would exempt "88.6 percent" of the potential reform beneficiaries, and a 50-hectare limit would mean "no reform" (Mariano interview, Nov. 24, 1992).

58. This law consolidates, with revisions, the former Local Government Code, the Local Tax Code, the Real Property Tax Code, and the Barangay Justice Law.

Chapter 8

1. Extended discussion of the Philippine military, its internal cleavages, and the dissident elements that promoted recurrent challenges to Aquino's authority and presidency can be found in Kessler 1989.

2. Herring 1988: 579. For an elaboration of the argument that token or ineffectual reforms may mystify disadvantaged groups, thereby averting or at least
postponing more forceful demands for government redress of inequalities, see
Dahl 1971: 89–104.

3. The "change of sky" phenomenon is not strictly limited to parliamentary
systems; indeed the phrase was coined with regard to the shifting politics of the
People's Republic of China under Mao Ze-dong (Herring 1983: 235, citing Hinton 1966 and Belden 1970).

4. The "change of sky" phenomenon and past experience similarly affect
bureaucratic behavior. Bureaucrats seem almost instinctively to err on the side
of caution in implementing reform programs.

5. Many of the Protestant churches in the Philippines shared the commitment to ousting Marcos and working for social justice. Cooperation between the
Protestant churches and the Catholic Church has been particularly evident in
work to curb human rights abuses and serve the needs of the rural and urban
poor and tribal communities. See, e.g., Komisar 1986.

6. On the similarities in the class composition and ideologies of the two
parties, see Corpuz 1958; Milne 1969; Wurfel 1962. On patron-client dyads, see
Landé 1977.

7. Discussions of politics in the martial law era can be found in de Guzman et
al. 1977; Noble 1986; Tancangco 1988: 93–105; Villacorta 1983.

8. Personal communications with the late Serge Cherniguin, National Federation of Sugar Workers. See also LCHR 1988; id. 1990.

9. See, generally, Kohli 1987: 43. Kohli does not intend by his discussion to
rule out the possibility of redistributive reform within a democratic-capitalist
framework.

10. The redistribution of the coastal sugar haciendas in Peru directly benefited the permanent agricultural laborers, while temporary and migratory laborers were largely denied land rights (McClintock 1981: 63, 73). The redistribution of tenanted holdings in Kerala state, India, benefited tenants, frequently at
the expense of the landless laborers who actually cultivated the affected parcels
(Herring 1983: 180–216).

11. In 1969, the bishops of Antique (Panay province) and Bacolod (Negros
Occidental) launched an effort to supplant the *contractistas* (labor contractors)
hired by plantation owners to secure labor from the islands adjacent to Negros
Occidental. The initiative apparently came too late in the harvest season and
then collapsed when those *sacadas* who did participate defaulted on the cash
advances provided them by the Church (Empestan interview, July 5, 1989; see
also McCoy 1984b: 127–28).

12. Illustrative is the remark of a farmworker on a Negros Occidental sugar
hacienda: "The workers would like to own home lots and backyard gardens.
This is a good idea but it is difficult to ask our employer for this. We are only
employees."

13. Concerned about alienating powerful patrons, tenants often acquiesce to

illegal tenurial relations in response to programs of reform (Herring 1981). For a discussion of peasant reluctance to claim reform benefits for these reasons in El Salvador, see Prosterman and Riedinger 1987: 166.

14. In 1989, contractual minimum daily wages for the mill workers ranged from P66.33—the legal minimum—to P89.00 in Negros Occidental, while the legal minimum daily wage for farmworkers, rarely observed in practice, was P48.50.

15. Interviews with mill workers and NACUSIP union representatives, SONEDCO (Southern Negros Development Company) sugar central, Mar. 9, 1989; Julayco interview, Mar. 13, 1989.

16. I have generally chosen to characterize these groups as "militant" in recognition of the often-confrontational nature of their political activism. As the term is used in Philippine discourse, "militant" seems variously to connote the most radical of the legal social organizations or the most "legal" of the underground (that is, insurgent) organizations.

17. The archipelagic nature of the Philippines makes regular physical access to the seats of national power (Manila and Quezon City) quite problematic for most Philippine peasants and their organizational representatives.

18. Landlordism was abolished, and with it rentiers as a class. The reform benefited those farming leased land, a stratum made up predominantly of poor tenants cultivating smallholdings. However, the preponderance of the reform benefits, in terms of land area transferred, went to rich lessees who relied on wage laborers to perform most of their agricultural work. The reform did little for these laborers, although they did benefit modestly from separate labor legislation (Herring 1983: 213).

19. Ronald J. Herring, remarks at Curry Foundation conference, "United States Policy and Third World Agriculture: Landlessness and Tenure Patterns in the 1980s and '90s," Washington, D.C.: Sept. 30, 1989; also Herring 1983: 83. The differing objective interests of tenants and landless laborers are apparent in the land-to-the-tenant reform—versus a land-to-the-tiller (cultivator) reform—experience in Kerala. In Sri Lanka the demands of paddy-cultivating Sinhalese peasants for expansion of village lands threatened the employment prospects of the Tamil laborers on hill country estates. In the case of sugar production in the Philippines, the differing interests of laborers and tenants have a regional dimension, as sugar is produced primarily by tenants in Luzon and primarily by farm laborers in Negros Occidental. A land-to-the-tiller reform program would serve the interests of both groups; a land-to-the-tenant reform would not.

20. See, e.g., Przeworski 1986: 63: "We cannot avoid the possibility that a transition to democracy can be made only at the cost of leaving economic relations intact, not only the structure of production but even the distribution of income."

References

Abaya, Antonio M. 1987. "Transcript of the Meeting of the Committee on Agrarian Reform with the Members of the Cabinet Action Committee re Draft of the Executive Order on Agrarian Reform Program." Remarks of Congressman Antonio M. Abaya. Mimeograph. Manila, July 17.

Abueva, Jose V. 1971. *Ramon Magsaysay: A Political Biography*. Manila: Solidaridad Publishing House.

———. 1988. "Philippine Ideologies and National Development." In Raul P. de Guzman and Mila A. Reforma, eds., *Government and Politics of the Philippines*, pp. 18–73. Singapore: Oxford University Press.

Acuña, Arsenio R. 1987. "Transcript of Hearing of the Senate Committee on Agrarian Reform." Testimony of Arsenio R. Acuña. Mimeograph. Manila, Aug. 14.

———. 1988. "5-hectare CARP Retention Limit Is Unconstitutional." *Manila Bulletin*, June 1.

Adams, Dale W., and Douglas H. Graham. 1981. "A Critique of Traditional Agricultural Credit Projects and Policies." *Journal of Development Economics* 8, no. 3: 347–66.

Adams, Dale W., and J. D. Von Pischke. 1992. "Microenterprise Credit Programs: Déjà Vu." *World Development* 20, no. 10 (Oct.): 1463–70.

Adelman, Irma, and Cynthia Taft Morris. 1973. *Economic Growth and Social Equity in Developing Countries*. Stanford: Stanford University Press.

Agoncillo, Teodoro A. 1975. *A Short History of the Philippines*. New York: New American Library.

Agoncillo, Teodoro A., and Milagros Guerrero. 1977. *History of the Philippine People*. Quezon City: R. P. Garcia.

Agrarian Reform Monitor. 1988. "CPAR's First Year: A Chronicle of Events." 1, no. 1 (Third Quarter): 1–7.

"Agrarian Reform Now!" *Solidarity*, no. 106–7, pp. 3–48.

Agrarian Research and Training Institute (ARTI). 1974. *The Agrarian Situation Relating to Paddy Cultivation in Five Selected Districts of Sri Lanka*, part 2, Kandy District, pp. 37–38. Colombo: ARTI.

Aguilar, Filomeno V., Jr. 1984. *The Making of Cane Sugar: Poverty, Crisis and Change in Negros Occidental*. La Salle Monograph Series, no. 2. Bacolod: La Salle Social Research Center.

Alag, Alden. 1988. "CPP-NPA Carries Out Own Land Reform in Provinces." *Philippine Star*, Sept. 9.

Alvarez, Heherson T. 1986. "Strengthening the Agrarian Reform Program Under the Present Administration." Memorandum. May 16. Reprinted in *Vital Documents on Agrarian Reform*, p. xiv. Quezon City: Ministry of Agrarian Reform, n.d.

———. 1988. "Agrarian Reform: A Historic Opportunity for Economic Transformation and Social Justice." Speech delivered in support of Senate Bill 249. Reprinted in Republic of the Philippines, Senate, *The Senate Speaks: A Collection of Speeches by Senators of the Republic*, pp. 5–18. Manila.

Alvarez-Castillo, Fatima. 1988. "Papa Isio and the Babaylan of Negros: From Inchoate Strivings to Revolution." *Philippine Development Forum* 4, no. 4: 2–15.

Amio, Armin A. 1989. "CARP: Compulsory Acquisition by October." *Business World*, July 27.

Amnesty International. 1991. *Philippines: Human Rights Violations and the Labour Movement*. New York: Amnesty International.

Anda, Redempto. 1990. "Leong Is New DAR Chief." *Manila Chronicle*, Apr. 10.

Anda, Redempto, and Cristina Pastor. 1990. "Can Agrarian Reform Be Saved?" *Manila Chronicle*, Apr. 8.

Anderson, Benedict. 1983. *Imagined Communities: Reflections on the Origin and Spread of Nationalism*. London: Verso Editions.

———. 1988. "Cacique Democracy in the Philippines: Origins and Dreams." *New Left Review* 169 (May–June): 3–31.

Ang Bayan. 1986a. "Party Conducts Assessment, Says Boycott Policy Was Wrong." Editorial, 18, no. 3 (May).

———. 1986b. "Aquino Government Cannot Solve Agrarian Problem." 18, no. 9 (Nov.): 6.

———. 1987. "Land Reform and Economic Projects." 18, no. 11 (Jan.): 10–11.

Ang Kristianong Katilingban. 1988. "Serge Cherniguin: Portrait of a Christian Labor Leader." 2, no. 5 (Dec.): 8–9, 15.

Angsico, Josephine C., with Normando de Leon and Jeanne Francis I. Illo. 1978. "Socioeconomic Changes After Eleven Years of Agrarian Reform: A Resurvey of Plaridel (Bulacan) Farmers." Mimeograph. Quezon City: Institute of Philippine Culture, Ateneo de Manila University.

Apter, David E. 1965. *The Politics of Modernization*. Chicago: University of Chicago Press.

Aquino, Benigno S., Jr. 1967. "A Proposal for Cooperative Ownership." *Solidarity* 2, no. 8 (Aug.): 39–46.

Aquino, Corazon C. 1986a. "Building from the Ruins." *Veritas* 3 (Jan. 12): 6–8.

———. 1986b. "Broken Promises in the Land of Promise." Speech delivered at Ateneo de Davao University. Jan. 16.

Arcellana, Emerenciana Y. 1969. "Indigenous Political Institutions." In Jose V.

Abueva and Raul P. de Guzman, eds., *Foundations and Dynamics of Filipino Government and Politics*, pp. 38–42. Manila: Bookmark.

Arguillas, Carolyn. 1989. "NDF Apologizes for Church Massacre." *Manila Chronicle*, June 28, p. 1.

Arlen, Michael. 1990. "A Reporter at Large: Invisible People." *New Yorker*, Apr. 16, pp. 45–65.

Asian Development Bank. 1988. *Sugar Sector Rationalization Project*, vol. 1: *Executive Summary & Main Report*. Manila: ADB.

Asian Wall Street Journal. 1990. "Nominee for Land Reform Post Resigns, Dealing Major Blow to Aquino Program." Apr. 9.

Asia Watch, 1990. *The Philippines: Violations of the Laws of War by Both Sides*. New York: Human Rights Watch, Aug.

Asiaweek. 1989. "So Shall Ye Reap." June 23, pp. 60–62.

Association of Major Religious Superiors. 1975. *The Sugar Workers of Negros*. Manila: AMRS.

Averch, H. A., F. H. Denton and J. E. Koehler. 1970. *A Crisis of Ambiguity: Political and Economic Development in the Philippines*. Santa Monica, Calif.: RAND Corporation.

Babst-Vokey, Arlene. 1988. " 'Guesstimating' NPA Strength." *Manila Chronicle*, Aug. 12, p. 4.

Bacho, Peter. 1987. "The Muslim Secessionist Movement." *Journal of International Affairs* 41, no. 1 (Summer–Fall): 153–64.

Balana, Cynthia D. 1989. "Cory Names Miriam New DAR Secretary." *Philippine Daily Inquirer*, July 1.

Baliao, Ricarte M. 1987. "A Starke Reality in Agrarian Reform." *Manila Bulletin*, p. 2.

Balingcos, Debbie. 1988. "Cory Signs CARP Law." *Manila Times*, June 11.

Bancod, Edgar R. 1990. "Farmers, Del Monte near Accord over Lease Terms." *Business World*, Nov. 30.

——. 1991a. "In Del Monte's Footsteps: Dole Phils. Gives in to DAR." *Business World*, Jan. 11, p. 9.

——. 1991b. "Leong Nixes Proposed 50% Premium for Land Acquired Under CARP." *Business World*, Mar. 13, p. 2.

——. 1991c. "DAR Unfazed by Donor's Apprehensions on CARP." *Business World*, June 25, p. 2.

Barcelona, Manuel. 1987. "Transcript of Hearing of the Senate Committee on Agrarian Reform." Testimony of Manuel Barcelona, Attorney and Spokesperson for Quezon-Tayabas Coconut Landowners. Mimeograph. Manila, Aug. 12.

Bardhan, P. K., and A. Rudra. 1980. "Terms and Conditions of Sharecropping Contracts: An Analysis of Village Survey Data in India." *Journal of Development Studies* 16, no. 3: 287–302.

Barker, Randolph, and Robert W. Herdt. 1978. "Equity Implications of Technology Changes." In International Rice Research Institute, *Interpretive Analysis of Selected Papers from Changes in Rice Farming in Selected Areas of Asia*, pp. 83–108. Los Baños, Philippines: IRRI.

Barker, Randolph, Robert W. Herdt, and Beth Rose. 1985. *The Rice Economy of Asia*. Washington, D.C.: Resources for the Future.

Bascog, Laurentino. 1987. "Transcript of Hearing of the Senate Committee on Agrarian Reform." Testimony of Laurentino Bascog, Chairman, Congress for a People's Agrarian Reform, President, Lakas ng Magsasaka, Manggagawa at Mangingisda ng Pilipinas, and Member of Agrarian Reform Alliance for Democratic Organizations (ARADO). Mimeograph. Manila, Aug. 14.

Bates, Robert H. 1981. *Markets and States in Tropical Africa: The Political Basis of Agricultural Policies*. Berkeley: University of California Press.

Bauer, Ronald. 1973. "Military Professional Socialization in a Developing Country." Ph.D. diss., University of Michigan.

Bautista, Germelino M. 1978. *Philippine Rural Anti-Poverty Programs*. Quezon City: Institute of Philippine Culture, Ateneo de Manila University.

——. N.d. "Agrarian Reform in Sugarlandia: Some Considerations for Constructing Alternative Models of Land Redistribution." Mimeograph. Quezon City: Department of Economics, Ateneo de Manila University.

Bautista, Germelino M., William C. Thiesenhusen, and David J. King. 1983. "Farm Households on Rice and Sugarlands: Margen's Village Economy in Transition." In Antonio J. Ledesma, Perla Q. Makil, and Virginia A. Miralao, eds., *Second View from the Paddy: More Empirical Studies on Philippine Rice Farming and Tenancy*, pp. 73–92. Quezon City: Institute of Philippine Culture, Ateneo de Manila University.

Bautista, Romeo M. 1987. *Production Incentives in Philippine Agriculture: Effects of Trade and Exchange Rate Policies*. Research Report 59. Washington, D.C.: International Food Policy Research Institute.

Bauzon, Leslie E. 1967. "The Encomienda as a Spanish Colonial Institution in the Philippines, 1571–1604." *Silliman Journal* 14 (Second Quarter): 197–241.

——. 1975. *Philippine Agrarian Reform, 1880–1965: The Revolution That Never Was*. Occasional Paper No. 31. Singapore: Institute of Southeast Asian Studies.

Bedford, Michael, and Polly Parks. 1992. "The Problem of Peace in the Philippines." *Christian Science Monitor*, Apr. 20, p. 19.

Belden, Jack. 1970. *China Shakes the World*. New York: Monthly Review Press.

Bello, Walden. 1985–86. "Edging Toward the Quagmire." *World Policy Journal* 3, no. 1 (Winter): 29–58.

——. 1986. "Aquino's Elite Populism: Initial Reflections." *Third World Quarterly* 8, no. 3 (July): 1020–30. Reprinted in Rodolfo Desuasido, ed., *Sowing the Seed: Proceedings of the International Solidarity Conference for the Filipino Peasantry (ISCFP): October 11–21, 1986*, pp. 58–70. Quezon City: Kilusang Magbubukid ng Pilipinas, 1988.

Berenguer, Silverio J. 1987. "Transcript of Hearing of the Senate Committee on Agrarian Reform." Testimony of Silverio J. Berenguer, Coconut Landowner. Mimeograph. Manila: Aug. 12.

Bermeo, Nancy. 1986. *The Revolution Within the Revolution: Workers' Control in Rural Portugal*. Princeton: Princeton University Press.

——. 1987. "Redemocratization and Transition Elections: A Comparison of Spain and Portugal." *Comparative Politics* 19, no. 2 (Jan): 213–31.

Berry, R. Albert, and William R. Cline. 1979. *Agrarian Structure and Productivity in Developing Countries*. Baltimore: Johns Hopkins University Press.

Bhagwati, Jagdish. 1966. *The Economics of Underdeveloped Countries*. New York: McGraw-Hill.

Bienen, Henry, James Parks, Devesh Kapur, and Jeffrey Riedinger. 1990. "Decentralization in Nepal." *World Development* 18, no. 1 (Jan.): 61–75.

Billig, Michael. 1991. "Stuck in Molasses: The Lack of Economic Diversification in Negros Occidental." *Pilipinas* 16 (Spring): 19–43.

——. 1992. "Syrup in the Wheels of Progress: The Inefficient Organization of the Philippine Sugar Industry." MS. Lancaster, Pa.: Franklin and Marshall College.

Binswanger, Hans P., and Mark R. Rosenzweig. 1984. "Contractual Arrangements, Employment, and Wages in Rural Labor Markets: A Critical Review." In Hans P. Binswanger and Mark R. Rosenzweig, *Contractual Arrangements, Employment, and Wages in Rural Labor Markets in Asia*, pp. 1–40. New Haven: Yale University Press.

——. 1986. "Behavioral and Material Determinants of Production Relations in Agriculture." *Journal of Development Studies* 22, no. 3 (Apr.): 503–39.

Bishops-Businessmen's Conference for Human Development (BBCHD). 1988. "Letter to Members of Congress." Manila: National Executive Council, BBCHD, Feb. 24.

——. N.d. "Solidarity Statement on Agrarian Reform." Manila: National Executive Council, BBCHD.

Bishops-Grassroots Dialogue. 1988. "We Reiterate Our Option for the Poor as an Imperative of Our Faith in Jesus Christ." Bacolod City, Oct. 18.

Blair, Emma, and James Robertson. 1903–9. *The Philippine Islands, 1493–1898*. 55 vols. Cleveland: A. H. Clark.

Boglosa, Reinerio D. 1983. "Concentration of Landholdings and Rural Poverty in Western Visayas, 1970–71." *Philippine Sociological Review* 31, no. 1–2 (Jan.–June): 87–99.

Bonner, Raymond. 1988. *Waltzing with a Dictator: The Marcoses and the Making of American Policy*. New York: Vintage Books.

Bourque, Susan C., and Kay B. Warren. 1989. "Democracy Without Peace: The Cultural Politics of Terror in Peru." *Latin American Research Review* 24, no. 1: 7–34.

Braverman, Avishay, and J. Luis Guasch. 1986. "Rural Credit Markets and Institutions in Developing Countries: Lessons for Policy Analysis from Practice and Modern Theory." *World Development* 14, no. 10/11: 1253–67.

Braverman, Avishay, and Joseph E. Stiglitz. 1982. "Sharecropping and the Interlinking of Agrarian Markets." *American Economic Review* 72, no. 4 (Sept.): 695–715.

Bresnan, John, ed. 1986. *Crisis in the Philippines: The Marcos Era and Beyond*. Princeton: Princeton University Press.

Brillantes, Alex B., Jr. 1988. "The Executive." In Raul P. de Guzman and Mila A. Reforma, eds., *Government and Politics of the Philippines*, pp. 113–31. Singapore: Oxford University Press.

Broad, Robin. 1988. *Unequal Alliance: The World Bank, the International Monetary Fund and the Philippines.* Berkeley: University of California Press.

Brooks, Karen. 1990. "Land Tenure in Collectivized Agriculture: The Soviet Union, Poland, and Hungary." In Roy L. Prosterman, Mary N. Temple, and Timothy M. Hanstad, eds., *Agrarian Reform and Grassroots Development: Ten Case Studies,* pp. 235–61. Boulder, Colo.: Lynne Rienner.

Bulatao, Victor Gerardo. 1987. "Transcript of the Meeting of the Committee on Agrarian Reform with the Members of the Cabinet Action Committee re Draft of the Executive Order on Agrarian Reform Program." Statement of Victor Gerardo Bulatao, Department of Agrarian Reform. Mimeograph. Manila: July 17.

——. 1992. "A Workable Agrarian Reform Agenda: 1992–98." Mimeograph. Quezon City: KAISAHAN, Sept.

Bureau of Agricultural Economics (BAECON). 1972. *Agricultural Economics, Statistics, and Market News Digest* 6, no. 46 (Nov. 15).

Buscayno, Bernabe. 1986. "Reflections on Genuine Land Reform." In Romulo A. Sandoval, ed., *Prospects of Agrarian Reform Under the New Order,* pp. 23–26. Quezon City: Urban Rural Mission-National Council of Churches in the Philippines.

Business Day. 1987. "Paris Club Land Reform Meet in July." May 28.

Business World. 1988. "Gov't to Distribute 26,154 has. Previously Leased to MNCs." Nov. 4.

——. 1990a. "Farmers to Take Case to SC If DAR Okays Conversion." Mar. 8, pp. 1, 6.

——. 1990b. "LDP Seeks Decentralized Implementation of CARP." Apr. 3.

——. 1990c. "Senate Likely to Reject Cojuangco Proposal to Decentralize CARL." Apr. 4, p. 12.

——. 1990d. "Pawning of Farm Land Still Widely Practised." June 13.

——. 1990e. "NBI Arrests KMP's Tadeo for Estafa." May 11.

——. 1991. "Farmers' Groups Opposing Measure Decentralizing CARP Implementation." May 17.

——. 1993. "EC Mission Satisfied with CARP Implementation." Oct. 1, p. 2.

Butterfield, Fox. 1978. "Manila Inner Circle Gains Under Marcos." *New York Times,* Jan. 15.

Cabral, Manuel Villaverde. 1978. "Agrarian Structures and Recent Rural Movements in Portugal." *Journal of Peasant Studies* 5, no. 4 (July): 411–45.

Cainglet, Wilfredo G. 1987. "Transcript of the Meeting of the Committee on Agrarian Reform with the Members of the Cabinet Action Committee re Draft of the Executive Order on Agrarian Reform Program." Remarks of Congressman Wilfredo G. Cainglet. Mimeograph. Manila: July 17.

Callaghy, Thomas M. 1989. "Toward State Capability and Embedded Liberalism in the Third World: Lessons for Adjustment." In Joan M. Nelson, ed., *Fragile Coalitions: The Politics of Economic Adjustment,* pp. 115–38. New Brunswick, N.J.: Transaction Books.

Canlas, Mamerto, Mariano Miranda, Jr., and James Putzel. 1988. *Land, Poverty and Politics in the Philippines.* Quezon City: Claretian Publications.

Caparas, José Leo P. 1987. "Transcript of Hearing of the Senate Committee on Agrarian Reform." Testimony of José Leo P. Caparas, President, Council of Landowners for Orderly Reform (COLOR). Mimeograph. Manila, Aug. 12.

Cariño, Conrad M. 1993a. "1993–1998 Land Distribution Target Is Unrealistic, Claims DAR Chief." *Business World*, May 12, p. 11.

——. 1993b. "DAR, DENR's Land Distribution Targets Likely to Be Scaled Down." *Business World*, May 14, p. 12.

——. 1993c. "Scope of CARP Likely to Be Downscaled." *Business World*, June 22, p. 12.

——. 1993d. "DAR Slated to Launch 264 CARP Communities in '94." *Business World*, Aug. 13.

——. 1993e. "House Bodies Disagree on Carp Amendments." *Business World*, Aug. 19, p. 12.

——. 1993f. "CARP Beneficiaries Selling Lands to Previous Owners?" *Business World*, Sept. 2, p. 16.

——. 1993g. "European Rural Development Mission Raises Questions on CARP's Implementation." *Business World*, Nov. 2, p. 12.

——. 1993h. "1.2 Million Hectares of A & D Lands Ready for Distribution." *Business World*, Nov. 4, p. 12.

Cariño, Conrad M., and Micheline R. Millar. 1993. "DA Open to Amending Farmers' Magna Carta." *Business World*, Oct. 22, p. 1.

Cariño, Ledivina V. 1988. "The Land and People." In Raul P. de Guzman and Mila A. Reforma, eds., *Government and Politics of the Philippines*, pp. 3–17. Singapore: Oxford University Press.

——. 1989. "A Dominated Bureaucracy: An Analysis of the Formulation of, and Reactions to, State Policies on the Philippine Civil Service." Occasional Paper 89-4. Quezon City: College of Public Administration, University of the Philippines.

Carmack, Robert M., ed. 1988. *Harvest of Violence: The Maya Indians and the Guatemala Crisis*. Norman: University of Oklahoma Press.

Carroll, John J. 1983. "Agrarian Reform, Productivity and Equity: Two Studies." In Antonio J. Ledesma, Perla Q. Makil and Virginia A. Miralao, eds., *Second View from the Paddy: More Empirical Studies on Philippine Rice Farming and Tenancy*, pp. 15–23. Quezon City: Institute of Philippine Culture, Ateneo de Manila University.

Carroll, Thomas F. 1970. "Land Reform as an Explosive Force in Latin America." In Rodolfo Stavenhagen, ed., *Agrarian Problems and Peasant Movements in Latin America*, pp. 101–37. Garden City, N.Y.: Anchor Books.

Cater, Sonya Diane. 1959. *The Philippine Federation of Free Farmers: A Case Study in Mass Agrarian Organizations*. Ithaca, N.Y.: Southeast Asia Program, Cornell University.

Catholic Bishops' Conference of the Philippines (CBCP). 1987. *Thirsting for Justice: A Pastoral Exhortation on Agrarian Reform*. Manila: CBCP, July 14.

——. 1988. *CBCP Monitor* 9, nos. 1–4 (Jan.–Feb.; Mar.–Apr.; May–June; July–Aug.).

Center for Research and Communication. 1987. *Agrarian Reform: Experiences and*

Expectations. Papers and Discussions, Agrarian Reform Symposia, Apr. 22–23, 1987, and May 23, 1987. Manila: Southeast Asian Science Foundation.

Chambers, Robert. 1983. *Rural Development: Putting the Last First*. London: Longman.

Chanda, Nayan. 1986. "Some Hope, Some Fear." *Far Eastern Economic Review*, June 12, pp. 46–47.

Chapman, William. 1987. *Inside the Philippine Revolution: The New People's Army and Its Struggle for Power*. New York: Norton.

Chenery, Hollis, John Duloy, and Richard Jolly. 1974. *Redistribution with Growth*. Washington, D.C.: World Bank.

Cheng, Chen. 1961. *Land Reform in Taiwan*. Taipei: China Publishing Co.

Cheung, Steven. 1969. *The Theory of Share Tenancy—with Special Application to Asian Agriculture and the First Phase of Taiwan Land Reform*. Chicago: University of Chicago Press.

Christian Science Monitor. 1983. "Mrs. Aquino Picks Up from Her Husband in Philippines: Interview." Nov. 25, p. 1.

Clad, James. 1986. "The More the Merrier." *Far Eastern Economic Review*, Sept. 25, pp. 44–45.

——. 1987. "Still All in the Family." *Far Eastern Economic Review*, Mar. 26, pp. 70–73.

Colburn, Forrest, ed. 1989. *Everyday Forms of Peasant Resistance*. Armonk, N.Y.: M. E. Sharpe.

Collier, David, ed. 1979. *The New Authoritarianism in Latin America*. Princeton: Princeton University Press.

Collins, Joseph. 1989. *The Philippines: Fire on the Rim*. San Francisco: Institute for Food and Development Policy.

Communist Party of the Philippines (CPP), Executive Committee of the Central Committee. "Resolution on the Party's Tactics Regarding the Snap Election" (May 31).

Congress for a People's Agrarian Reform (CPAR). 1987a. "Agrarian Reform: Today's Imperative." Manila: Philippine Partnership for the Development of Human Resources in Rural Areas (PHILDHRRA), Sept., pp. 2–4.

——. 1987b. "The Making of the People's Congress for Agrarian Reform." Manila: Philippine Partnership for the Development of Human Resources in Rural Areas (PHILDHRRA), Sept., pp. 5–6.

——. 1987c. "CPAR's 8-Point Program: The People's Declaration of Agrarian Reform." Manila: Philippine Partnership for the Development of Human Resources in Rural Areas (PHILDHRRA), Sept., pp. 5–6.

——. 1988. "On with the Fight for a Genuine Agrarian Reform." *Intersect* 2, no. 6 (June).

——. 1989. *Popular Grassroots Initiatives Towards Genuine Agrarian Reform: A Descriptive Report*. Quezon City: CPAR.

——. 1990. *Assessment of the Second Year of Republic Act 6657*. Quezon City: CPAR.

——. 1991. *PAGBIBINHI: Grassroots Initiatives Towards Genuine Agrarian Reform in the CARL's Third Year*. Quezon City: CPAR.

Connolly, Michael J., S.J. 1992. *Church Lands and Peasant Unrest in the Philippines:*

Agrarian Conflict in Twentieth-Century Luzon. Quezon City: Ateneo de Manila University Press.

Constantino, Letizia R., and Bernard Karganilla. 1987. "Agrarian Reform." In *Education Forum Teacher Assistance Program*, 7, no. 126–27: *Supplementary Materials*, pp. 126–27. Quezon City: Association of Major Religious Superiors of the Philippines.

Constantino, Renato. 1975. *The Philippines: A Past Revisited. Pre-Spanish–1941*. Quezon City: Tala.

Constantino, Renato, and Letizia Constantino. 1978. *The Philippines: The Continuing Past*. Quezon City: Foundation for Nationalist Studies.

Coquia, Jorge R. 1955. *The Philippine Presidential Election of 1953*. Manila: University Publishing.

Cornista, Luzviminda B., and Eva F. Escueta. 1983. *The Structure of the Coconut Farming Industry*. Occasional Papers, no. 10. Los Baños: Agrarian Reform Institute, University of the Philippines.

Corpuz, Onofre D. 1957. *The Bureaucracy in the Philippines*. Manila: Institute of Public Administration, University of the Philippines.

——. 1958. "Filipino Political Parties and Politics." *Philippine Social Sciences and Humanities Review* 23, no. 2–4 (June–Dec.): 141–57.

——. 1969. "Cultural Foundations." In Jose V. Abueva and Raul P. de Guzman, eds., *Foundations and Dynamics of Filipino Government and Politics*, pp. 6–18. Manila: Bookmark.

Corpus, Victor N. 1989. *Silent War*. Quezon City: VNC Enterprises.

Council of Agricultural Producers of the Philippines (CAP). N.d. "Position Paper on the Comprehensive Agrarian Reform." Manila.

Crisostomo, Isabelo T. 1987. *Cory: Profile of a President*. Boston: Branden Publishing.

Crone, Donald K. 1988. "State, Social Elites, and Government Capacity in Southeast Asia." *World Politics* 40, no. 2 (Jan.): 252–68.

Cruz, Benjamin B. 1988. "CARP Law Has Loopholes Favoring All Landowners." *Business World*, June 21.

——. 1989. "Change Seen in CARP Compensation Formula." *Business World*, Mar. 16.

Cruz, Marie Antonette Z. 1991a. "Landowners Find Way to Skirt CARL." *Business World*, Apr. 1, pp. 1, 6.

——. 1991b. "New Way to Skirt CARP Arises from SC Decision." *Business World*, May 14, p. 2.

Cuizon, Tony. 1987. "Transcript of Hearing of the Senate Committee on Agrarian Reform." Testimony of Tony Cuizon, Congress for a People's Agrarian Reform. Mimeograph. Manila: Aug. 12.

Cullamar, Evelyn Tan. 1986. *Babaylanism in Negros, 1896–1907*. Quezon City: New Day Publishers.

Cushner, Nicholas P. 1976. *Landed Estates in the Colonial Philippines*. Monograph Series, no. 20. New Haven: Yale University Southeast Asia Studies.

Dahl, Robert A. 1971. *Polyarchy: Participation and Opposition*. New Haven: Yale University Press.

——. 1978. "Pluralism Revisited." *Comparative Politics* 10, no. 2 (Jan.): 191–203.

Dasgupta, Partha. 1990. "Well-Being and the Extent of Its Realisation in Poor Countries." *Economic Journal* 100, no. 4 (Mar.; Royal Economic Society Conference): 1–32.

Datta, Samar K., Donald J. O'Hara, and Jeffrey B. Nugent. 1986. "Choice of Agricultural Tenancy in the Presence of Transaction Costs." *Land Economics* 62, no. 2 (May): 145–58.

David, Randolph S. 1982. "Bananas and Underdevelopment: The Philippine Experience." *Alternatives: A Journal of World Policy* 7, no. 4 (Spring): 451–65.

David, Romeo G. N.d. "A Proposal for Lands Covered Under Program B and C of the 1987 Comprehensive Agrarian Reform Program." Mimeograph. Manila.

——. 1987a. "Accelerated Land Reform Program." Revised draft. Mimeograph.

——. 1987b. "Subject: Philippine Land Reform Program." Issue update. Mimeograph.

Davis, Leonard. 1987. *The Philippines: People, Poverty, and Politics.* London: Macmillan Press.

——. 1989. *Revolutionary Struggle in the Philippines.* New York: St. Martin's Press.

de Achutegui, Pedro S., S.J., ed. 1981. *John Paul II in the Philippines: Addresses and Homilies.* Quezon City: Cardinal Bea Institute.

de Bassilan, Jean Mallat. 1846. *Les Philippines.* 2 vols. Paris.

de Guzman, Raul P. 1988. "Towards Redemocratization of the Political System." In Raul P. de Guzman and Mila A. Reforma, eds., *Government and Politics of the Philippines*, pp. 267–82. Singapore: Oxford University Press.

de Guzman, Raul P., Arturo G. Pacho, Ma. Aurora A. Carbonell, and Vicente D. Mariano. 1977. "Citizen Participation and Decision-Making Under Martial Law Administration: A Search for a Viable Political System." *Philippine Journal of Public Administration* 21, no. 1 (Jan.): 1–19.

de Guzman, Raul P., Mila A. Reforma, and Elena M. Panganiban. 1988. "Local Government." In Raul P. de Guzman and Mila A. Reforma, eds., *Government and Politics of the Philippines*, pp. 213–15. Singapore: Oxford University Press.

de Guzman, Roy S. 1990. "Abad Quits: Cites Loss of Cory's Confidence." *Philippine Daily Inquirer*, Apr. 6.

de Janvry, Alain. 1981. *The Agrarian Question and Reformism in Latin America.* Baltimore: Johns Hopkins University Press.

——. 1984. "The Role of Land Reform in Economic Development: Policies and Politics." In Carl Eicher and John M. Staatz, eds., *Agricultural Development in the Third World*, pp. 263–74. Baltimore: Johns Hopkins University Press.

de Jesus, Ed. C. 1982. "Control and Compromise in the Cagayan Valley." In Alfred W. McCoy and Ed. C. de Jesus, eds., *Philippine Social History: Global Trade and Local Transformations*, pp. 21–37. Quezon City: Ateneo de Manila University Press.

de Klerk, Michael. 1991. *A Harvest of Discontent: The Land Question in South Africa.* Cape Town: Institute for a Democratic Alternative for South Africa.

de la Cruz, Rose. 1989. "DAR, LB at Odds on Land Valuation Issue." *Malaya*, Apr. 6.

del Rosario, Corazon Paredes. 1989. Letter from undersecretary of agrarian reform to the author, December 27. Published in part as "Rejoinder from DAR," *Newsday*, Jan. 19, 1990, p. 10.

Desuasido, Rodolfo, ed. 1988. *Sowing the Seed: Proceedings of the International Solidarity Conference for the Filipino Peasantry (ISCFP), October 11–21, 1986.* Manila: KMP.

de Zuñiga, Joaquin Martinez. 1893. *Estadismo de las Islas Filipinas*, vol. 1. Madrid. Trans. H. de la Costa, S.J., in *Readings in Philippine History*. Manila: Bookmark, 1965.

Diamond, Larry, Juan J. Linz, and Seymour Martin Lipset. 1989. *Democracy in Developing Countries*. Boulder, Colo.: Lynne Rienner.

Diaz, Mr. 1987. "Transcript of Hearing of the Senate Committee on Agrarian Reform." Testimony of Mr. Diaz, FILSYN Corporation. Mimeograph. Manila: Aug. 18.

Dick, G. William. 1974. "Authoritarian Versus Nonauthoritarian Approaches to Economic Development." *Journal of Political Economy* 82, no. 4 (July–Aug.): 817–27.

Diliman Review. 1987. "The Political Movement in the Cordillera." 35, nos. 5 & 6: 15–25.

Dimagiba, Pascual. 1987. "Transcript of Hearing of the Senate Committee on Agrarian Reform." Testimony of Pascual Dimagiba, Executive Vice President, Agrarian Reform Beneficiaries Association (ARBA). Mimeograph. Manila: Aug. 12.

Dionne, E. J. 1986. "Church Activism Raises Questions of Pope's Stand." *New York Times*, Feb. 27.

Dizon, Augustin. 1987. "Transcript of Hearing of the Senate Committee on Agrarian Reform." Testimony of Augustin Dizon. Mimeograph. Manila: Aug. 14.

Doeppers, Daniel F. 1987. "Report on the Discussion: Social Change, Social Needs, and Social Policy." In Carl H. Landé, ed., *Rebuilding a Nation: Philippine Challenges and American Policy*, pp. 279–87. Washington, D.C.: Washington Institute Press.

Dominguez, Benito M. 1986. "Land of Promise, Life for All: Biblico-Theological Reflections on Land." In Romulo A. Sandoval, ed., *Prospects of Agrarian Reform Under the New Order*, pp. 33–39. Quezon City: Urban Rural Mission–National Council of Churches in the Philippines.

Dominguez, Carlos G. 1987. "Transcript of the Meeting of the Committee on Agrarian Reform with the Members of the Cabinet Action Committee re: Draft of the Executive Order on Agrarian Reform Program." Testimony of Carlos G. Dominguez, Secretary of Agriculture. Mimeograph. Manila: July 17.

Dore, R. P. 1959. *Land Reform in Japan*. London: Oxford University Press.

Dorner, Peter. 1972. *Land Reform and Economic Development*. Harmondsworth, U.K.: Penguin Books.

Dorner, Peter, and Donald Kanel. 1971. "The Economic Case for Land Reform:

Employment, Income Distribution, and Productivity." In Peter Dorner, ed., *Land Reform in Latin America: Issues and Cases*, pp. 41–56. Madison: Land Tenure Center, University of Wisconsin.

Doronila, Armando. 1985. "The Transformation of Patron-Client Relations and Its Political Consequences in the Philippines." *Journal of Southeast Asian Studies* 16, no. 1 (Mar.): 99–116.

———. 1986. "Analysis." *Manila Times*, Feb. 26.

Douglas, Donald E. 1970. "A Historical Survey of the Land Tenure Situation in the Philippines." *Solidarity* 5, no. 7 (July): 66–67.

Ebro, José G. 1988. "Potential PAP Donors Won't Fund CARP Land Transfers." *Business World*, Oct. 31.

Echaúz, Robustiano. 1978. *Sketches of the Island of Negros [Apuntes de la Isla de Negros]*. Trans. Donn V. Hart. Athens: Ohio University Center for International Studies.

Economist. 1988. "Cory's Magic." May 7.

Egan, Charles E. 1956. "Ladejinsky Ousted Again. 'Conflict of Interest' Cited." *New York Times*, Feb. 5.

Esguerra, Emmanuel F. 1980a. "Masagana 99." *Diliman Review* (Nov.–Dec.): 25–30.

———. 1980b. "Some Notes on the Masagana 99 Program and Small Farmer Access to Credit." Paper presented at annual meeting of the Philippine Sociological Society. Quezon City, Nov.

Esman, Milton J., and Norman Uphoff. 1984. *Local Organizations: Intermediaries in Rural Development*. Ithaca, N.Y.: Cornell University Press.

Estanislao, J. P. 1965. "A Note on Differential Farm Productivity, by Tenure." *Philippine Economic Journal* 4, no. 1: 120–24.

Estella, Chit. 1989. "Aquino Cancels 2 More Land Deals: Orders Prosecution of DAR Men." *Malaya*, June 17.

Estrella, Conrado F. 1976. "Agrarian Reform: Key to Asia's Development and Freedom." *Solidarity* 10, no. 1 (Jan.–Feb.): 33–41.

Evans, Peter. 1992. "The State as Problem and Solution: Predation, Embedded Autonomy, and Structural Change." In Stephen Haggard and Robert R. Kaufman, eds., *The Politics of Economic Adjustment*, pp. 139–81. Princeton: Princeton University Press.

Evans, Peter, Dietrich Rueschemeyer, and Theda Skocpol. 1985. *Bringing the State Back In*. Cambridge: Cambridge University Press.

Fabros, Wilfredo. 1988. *The Church and Its Social Involvement in the Philippines, 1930–1972*. Quezon City: Ateneo de Manila University Press.

Far Eastern Economic Review. 1989. "The South Says No." Dec. 1, p. 29.

Farm News & Views (Quezon City: Philippine Peasant Institute). 1988a. "The Promise of Land Reform: The Long and Winding Road." 1, no. 2 (June–July).

———. 1988b. "R.A. 6657: Legislative Baloney." 1, no. 2 (June–July): 1.

———. 1988c. "A Land Occupation Report." 1, no. 4 (Oct.–Nov.): 2–6.

Fast, Jonathan, and Jim Richardson. 1979. *Roots of Dependency: Political and Eco-*

nomic Revolution in 19th Century Philippines. Quezon City: Foundation for Nationalist Studies.

Feder, Ernest. 1971. *The Rape of the Peasantry: Latin America's Landholding System.* New York: Anchor Books.

——. 1983. *Perverse Development.* Quezon City: Foundation for Nationalist Studies.

Federation of Free Farmers. 1986a. "FM Hailed for Expanding Land Reform." Press release. Quezon City. Jan. 10.

——. 1986b. "FFF Asks Aquino to Investigate Corporate Takeover of Small Farmers' Lands." Press release. Quezon City. Mar. 18.

——. 1986c. "FFF Warns on Reversal of Agrarian Reform." Press release. Quezon City. Mar. 25.

——. 1986d. "New Flare-up of Agrarian Unrest in Tarlac." Press release. Quezon City. Apr. 26.

——. 1986e. "FFF Hails Expansion of Agrarian Reform." Press release. Quezon City. May 2.

Feeny, David. 1988. "The Development of Property Rights in Land: A Comparative Study." In Robert H. Bates, ed., *Toward a Political Economy of Development*, pp. 272–99. Berkeley: University of California Press.

Fegan, Brian. 1972. "Between the Lord and the Law: Tenants' Dilemmas." In Frank Lynch, ed., *View from the Paddy: Empirical Studies of Philippine Rice Farming and Tenancy*, pp. 113–28. Quezon City: Institute of Philippine Culture, Ateneo de Manila University.

——. 1982. "The Social History of a Central Luzon Barrio." In Alfred W. McCoy and Ed. C. de Jesus, eds., *Philippine Social History: Global Trade and Local Transformations*, pp. 91–129. Quezon City: Ateneo de Manila University Press.

——. 1983. "Land Reform and Technical Change in Central Luzon: The Rice Industry Under Martial Law." *Philippine Sociological Review* 31, nos. 1–2 (Jan.–June): 67–86.

Ferriols, Des. 1989. "DAR Issues Major Shift in Policy." *Philippine Star*, July 12.

Financiera Nacional de Tierras Agricolas (FINATA). N.d. "Decree 207: Statement of Policy." Mimeograph. San Salvador: FINATA.

Flores, Ramon. 1993. "PhilDHRRA at 10." *PhilDHRRA Notes* 9, nos. 1 and 2, p. 2.

Floresca, Roman. 1988. "Prime Lands to Be Given to Workers." *Philippine Star*, Nov. 4.

Food and Agriculture Organization (FAO). 1987. *1986 Production Yearbook.* Vol. 40. Rome: FAO.

Fox, Jonathan. 1989. "Popular Participation and Access to Food: Mexico's Community Food Councils, 1979–1986." In Scott Whiteford and Anne E. Ferguson, eds., *Harvest of Want: Hunger and Food Security in Central America and Mexico*, pp. 209–42. Boulder, Colo.: Westview Press.

Fox, Jonathan, and Gustavo Gordillo. 1988. "Between State and Market: The Campesinos' Quest for Autonomy." In Wayne A. Cornelius, Judith Gentel-

man, and Peter H. Smith, eds., *Mexico's Alternative Political Futures*, pp. 131–72. La Jolla, Calif.: Center for U.S.–Mexican Studies, University of California, San Diego.

Francia, Marlene, and P. W. Capistrano. 1988. "Who's Afraid of KMP?" *Peasant Update International.* Quezon City: KMP.

Francisco, Gregorio A., Jr. 1969. "Career Development of Filipino Higher Civil Servants." In Jose V. Abueva and Raul P. de Guzman, eds., *Foundation and Dynamics of Filipino Government and Politics*, pp. 390–408. Manila: Bookmark.

Francisco, Luzviminda B., and Jonathan S. Fast. 1985. *Conspiracy for Empire: Big Business, Corruption and the Politics of Imperialism in America, 1876–1907.* Quezon City: Foundation for Nationalist Studies.

Frankel, Francine. 1971. *India's Green Revolution: Economic Gains and Political Costs.* Princeton: Princeton University Press.

Friend, Theodore. 1965. *Between Two Empires: The Ordeal of the Philippines, 1929–1946.* New Haven: Yale University Press.

Gallardo, Leonardo "Boygie." 1987. "The Development Eye." *Viewpoints* 2, no. 14 (Aug.): 7.

Garcia, Leonardo. 1987. "Transcript of Hearing of the Senate Committee on Agrarian Reform." Testimony of Attorney Leonardo Garcia, Administrator, Philippine Coconut Authority. Mimeograph. Manila: Aug. 12.

Garilao, Ernesto D. 1992. "CARP Implementation Under the Ramos Administration: Faster, Fairer and More Meaningful." Policy statement distributed at National Conference on Agrarian Reform Partnerships in Strategic Operating Provinces. Imus, Philippines. Aug. 31–Sept. 1.

Geertz, Clifford. 1973. *The Interpretation of Cultures.* New York: Basic Books.

Genova, José. 1988. *The Philippine Archipelago: Brief Notes on the Formation of Agricultural Colonies in the Island of Negros [El Archipielago Filipino].* Trans. Sylvia Montenegro-Moreno. Bacolod: University of St. La Salle Social Research Center.

George, T. J. S. 1980. *Revolt in Mindanao: The Rise of Islam in Philippine Politics.* Kuala Lumpur: Oxford University Press.

German, Milagros. 1987. "Transcript of Hearing of the Senate Committee on Agrarian Reform." Testimony of former Appeals Court Justice Milagros A. German. Mimeograph. Manila: Aug. 14.

Gerschenkron, Alexander. 1962. *Economic Backwardness in Historical Perspective.* Cambridge, Mass.: Harvard University Press, Belknap Press.

Ghatak, Subrata, and Ken Ingersent. 1984. *Agriculture and Economic Development.* Baltimore: Johns Hopkins University Press.

Gigot, Paul. 1986. "Manila's Economic Recovery." *Wall Street Journal*, Mar. 5.

Gilding, Simeon. 1993. "Agrarian Reform and Counter-Reform Under the Aquino Administration: A Case Study of Post-Marcos Politics." Working Paper No. 8. Canberra: Department of Political and Social Change, Research School of Pacific Studies, Australian National University.

Gillego, Bonifacio H. 1988. "The Confessions of Bonifacio Gillego." *Katipunan* 1, no. 7 (May): 9–10, 22.

Giordano, Pasquale T., S.J. 1988. *Awakening to Mission: The Philippine Catholic Church, 1965–1981*. Quezon City: New Day Publishers.

Gleeck, Lewis E., Jr. 1974. "Some Accomplishments and Problems of the Agrarian Reform Project, 1971–1974." July 10 memorandum to Keith W. Sherper. Manila: United States Agency for International Development.

Gob, Fely C. 1988. "Laurel Backs Landowners Opposing CARP." *Philippine Daily Globe*, Sept. 25.

Golez, Ramiro L., Jr., and Jose R. C. Gayo. 1987. "Land Reform: Experiences of Other Countries." In *Agrarian Reform: Experiences and Expectations*, pp. 80–99. Agrarian Reform Symposia, Apr. 22–23 and May 23. Manila: Center for Research and Communication.

Gonzalez, Neptali. 1987. "Transcript of Hearing of the Senate Committee on Agrarian Reform." Remarks of Senator Neptali Gonzalez. Mimeograph. Manila: Aug. 12.

Gonzalez-Vega, Claudio. 1977. "Interest Rate Restrictions and Income Distribution." *American Journal of Agricultural Economics* 59, no. 5, pp. 973–76.

Gramsci, Antonio. 1971. *Selections from the Prison Notebooks*. Ed. and trans. Quintin Hoare and Geoffrey Nowell-Smith. New York: International Publishers.

Green, Justin J. 1987. "Political Socialization, Filipino Values, and Prospects for Democracy." In Carl H. Landé, ed., *Rebuilding a Nation: Philippine Challenges and American Policy*, pp. 261–77. Washington, D.C.: Washington Institute Press.

Griffiths, Stephen L. 1988. *Emigration, Entrepreneurs, and Evil Spirits: Life in a Philippine Village*. Honolulu: University of Hawaii Press.

Grindle, Merilee S., ed. 1980. *Politics and Policy Implementation in the Third World*. Princeton: Princeton University Press.

——. 1986. *State and Countryside: Development Policy and Politics in Latin America*. Baltimore: Johns Hopkins University Press.

Grossholtz, Jean. 1964. *Politics in the Philippines*. Boston: Little, Brown.

Guevarra, Carolina I. 1987. "Agrarian Reform a Daunting Challenge." *Business Star*, Oct. 20, p. 6.

Guieb, Eli R., III. 1988. "Agrarian Reform Bills in the Senate and the Lower House: Not Much of a Choice." Quezon City: Philippine Peasant Institute, Apr. 16.

Haggard, Stephan. 1985. "The Politics of Adjustment: Lessons from the IMF's Extended Fund Facility." *International Organization* 39, no. 3 (Summer): 505–34.

——. 1988. "The Philippines: Picking Up After Marcos." In Ramon Vernon, ed., *The Promise of Privatization: A Challenge for U.S. Policy*, pp. 91–121. New York: Council on Foreign Relations.

Haggard, Stephan, and Robert Kaufman. 1989. "The Politics of Stabilization and Structural Adjustment." In Jeffrey Sachs, ed., *Developing Country Debt and the World Economy*, pp. 263–74. Chicago: University of Chicago Press.

——. 1992a. "Economic Adjustment and the Prospects for Democracy." In id., eds., *The Politics of Economic Adjustment: International Constraints, Distributive Conflicts, and the State*, pp. 319–50. Princeton: Princeton University Press.

——, eds. 1992b. *The Politics of Economic Adjustment: International Constraints, Distributive Conflicts, and the State*. Princeton: Princeton University Press.

Hamilton, Nora. 1982. *The Limits of State Autonomy: Post-Revolutionary Mexico*. Princeton: Princeton University Press.

Handelman, Howard, and Sanders, Thomas G., eds. 1981. *Military Government and the Movement Towards Democracy in South America*. Bloomington: Indiana University Press.

Hanisch, Rolf. 1978. "Decision-Making Process and Problems of Implementation of the Land Reform in the Philippines." *Asia Quarterly*, part 2 (1st Quarter): 3–38; part 1 (4th Quarter 1977): 305–22.

Hanke, Lewis. 1949. *Spanish Struggle for Justice in the Conquest of America*. Philadelphia: University of Pennsylvania Press.

Hanstad, Timothy M. 1988. "Philippine Land Reform: The Just Compensation Issue." *Washington Law Review* 63, no. 2 (Apr.): 417–43.

Hardie, Robert S. 1952. *Philippine Land Tenure Reform: Analysis and Recommendations*. Manila: Special Technical and Economic Mission, U.S. Mutual Security Agency.

Harrison, Gregory. 1968. *Korea: Politics of the Vortex*. Cambridge, Mass.: Harvard University Press.

Hawes, Gary. 1987. *The Philippine State and the Marcos Regime: The Politics of Export*. Ithaca, N.Y.: Cornell University Press.

——. 1989. "Aquino and Her Administration: A View from the Countryside." *Pacific Affairs* 62, no. 1 (Spring): 9–28.

——. 1990. "Theories of Peasant Revolution: A Critique and Contribution from the Philippines." *World Politics* 42, no. 2 (Jan.): 261–98.

Hayami, Yujiro, and Masao Kikuchi. 1982. *Asian Village Economy at the Crossroads*. Baltimore: Johns Hopkins University Press.

Hayami, Yujiro, Ma. Agnes R. Quisumbing, and Lourdes S. Adriano. 1987. *In Search of a Land Reform Design for the Philippines*. University of the Philippines, Los Baños, Agricultural Policy Research Program Monograph Series, no. 1. Los Baños: University of the Philippines, Los Baños.

——. 1990. *Toward an Alternative Land Reform Paradigm: A Philippine Perspective*. Quezon City: Ateneo de Manila University Press.

Hayami, Yujiro, and Vernon W. Ruttan. 1985. *Agricultural Development: An International Perspective*. Rev. ed. Baltimore: Johns Hopkins University Press.

Henares, Hilarion M., Jr. 1986. "Snow White's Seven Dwarfs: The Jesuit Mafia." *Philippine Daily Inquirer*, Mar. 22.

Hernandez, Carolina G. 1985. "Constitutional Authoritarianism and the Prospects of Democracy in the Philippines." *Journal of International Affairs* 38, no. 2 (Winter): 243–58.

Hernandez, Eddie. 1987. "Transcript of Hearing of the Senate Committee on Agrarian Reform." Testimony of Attorney Eddie Hernandez. Mimeograph. Manila: Aug. 14.

Herring, Ronald J. 1981. "Embedded Production Relations and the Rationality of Peasant Quiescence in Tenure Reform." *Journal of Peasant Studies* 8, no. 2 (Jan.): 131–72.

——. 1983. *Land to the Tiller: The Political Economy of Agrarian Reform in South Asia.* New Haven: Yale University Press.

——. 1988. Review of *Land Reform and Democratic Development*, by Roy L. Prosterman and Jeffrey M. Riedinger. *Journal of Asian Studies* 47, no. 3 (Aug.): 578–79.

——. 1990. "Explaining Anomalies in Agrarian Reform: Lessons from South Asia." In Roy L. Prosterman, Mary N. Temple, and Timothy M. Hanstad, eds., *Agrarian Reform and Grassroots Development: Ten Case Studies*, pp. 49–75. Boulder, Colo.: Lynne Rienner.

Hewes, Lawrence I., Jr. 1955. *Japan–Land and Men.* Ames: Iowa State College Press.

Hick, Steven. 1987. *Land Our Life: A Study of the Struggle for Agrarian Reform in the Philippines.* Quezon City: Claretian Publications.

Hickey, Gerald C., and John L. Wilkinson. 1977. *Agrarian Reform in the Philippines.* Report of a seminar at the RAND Corporation, Dec. 16–17. Washington, D.C.: RAND Corporation.

Hill, Hal. 1988. "The Philippine Economy Under Aquino: New Hopes, Old Problems." *Asian Survey* 28, no. 3 (March): 261–85.

Hinton, William. 1966. *Fanshen: A Documentary of Revolution in a Chinese Village.* New York: Monthly Review Press.

Hislop, Stephen K. 1971. "Anitism: A Survey of Religious Beliefs Native to the Philippines." *Asian Studies* 9, no. 2 (Aug.): 126–56.

Hobsbawm, Eric. 1963. *Primitive Rebels: Studies in Archaic Forms of Social Movements in Nineteenth and Twentieth Centuries.* New York: Norton.

Hobsbawm, Eric, and George Rudé. 1968. *Captain Swing.* New York: Pantheon Books.

Hobsbawm, Eric, and Terence Ranger. 1983. *The Invention of Tradition.* Cambridge: Cambridge University Press.

Hodgkinson, Edith. 1988. *The Philippines to 1993: Making Up Lost Ground.* Special Report No. 1145. London: Economist Intelligence Unit.

Hollnsteiner, Mary R. 1963. *The Dynamics of Power in a Philippine Municipality.* Quezon City: Community Development Research Center, University of the Philippines.

——. [1961] 1973. "Reciprocity in the Lowland Philippines." In Frank Lynch and Alfonso de Guzman II, eds., *Four Readings on Philippine Values*, pp. 69–91. IPC Papers, no. 2. 4th ed. Quezon City: Institute of Philippine Culture, Ateneo de Manila University.

Horowitz, Donald L. 1990. "Comparing Democratic Systems." *Journal of Democracy* 1, no. 4 (Fall): 73–79.

Huke, Robert E. 1963. *Shadows on the Land: An Economic Geography of the Philippines.* Manila: Bookmark.

Huntington, Samuel P. 1968. *Political Order in Changing Societies.* New Haven: Yale University Press.

Huntington, Samuel P., and Joan M. Nelson. 1976. *No Easy Choice: Political Participation in Developing Countries.* Cambridge, Mass.: Harvard University Press.

Hutchcroft, Paul. 1991. "Oligarchs and Cronies in the Philippine State: The Politics of Patrimonial Plunder." *World Politics* 43, no. 3 (Apr.): 414–50.

——. 1992. "The Political Foundations of Booty Capitalism." Paper presented at the 88th Annual Meeting of the American Political Science Association, Chicago, Sept. 3–6.

IBON Databank Philippines. 1988. *Land Reform in the Philippines*. Manila: IBON Databank Phils. (Jan.).

Icamina, Paul M. 1986. "This Land Is Ours." *Veritas*, Aug. 14–20.

Ileto, Reynaldo. 1979. *Pasyon and Revolution: Popular Movements in the Philippines 1840–1910*. Quezon City: Ateneo de Manila University Press.

India. National Council of Applied Economic Research (NCAER). 1978. *Fertilizer Demand Study: Interim Report*. New Delhi: NCAER.

Inocentes, Antonio A., Amelita M. King, and Ruben Torres. N.d. "The Living and Working Conditions of Sugar Plantation Workers: Negros and Iloilo." In Republic of the Philippines, Institute of Labor and Manpower Studies, *The Sugar Workers: Two Studies*, pp. 1–164. Manila: Ministry of Labor and Employment.

Institute of Agrarian Studies (IAS). 1987a. *The Sugar Industry: Issues and Directions on Agrarian Reform*. Los Baños: University of the Philippines at Los Baños. Feb.

——. 1987b. *Selected Statistics for the Comprehensive Agrarian Reform*. Los Baños: University of the Philippines at Los Baños. Sept.

Institute on Church and Social Issues (ICSI). 1987. "Major Issues Concerning the Agrarian Reform." Mimeograph. Quezon City: ICSI, Sept. 17.

Institute for Popular Democracy (IPD). 1987. *Encore: Between Honesty and Hope*. Manila: IPD, May 30.

Intersect 1988a. "Seminar-Workshop on Agrarian Reform Models." 2, no. 2 (Feb.).

——. 1988b. "Tripartite Dialogue on Agrarian Reform." 2, no. 2 (Feb.).

Jackman, Robert. 1986. "Elections and the Democratic Class Struggle." *World Politics* 39, no. 1 (Oct.): 123–46.

Jagan, Larry, and John Cunnington. 1987. *Social Volcano: Sugar Workers in the Philippines*. London: War on Want. July.

Jara, Manolo. 1990. "Landlords Deal Fatal Blow to Cory's Land Reform." *Manila Chronicle*, Apr. 8.

Jaynes, Gerald D. 1984. "Economic Theory and Land Tenure." In Hans P. Binswanger and Mark R. Rosenzweig, eds., *Contractual Arrangements, Employment, and Wages in Rural Labor Markets in Asia*, pp. 43–62. New Haven: Yale University Press.

Jenkins, David. 1983. "Insurgency, Not External Threat, Is the Worry." *Far Eastern Economic Review* (Mar. 10): 17–18.

Jesena, Arsenio C. 1969. "The Sacadas of Sugarland." *Action Now* 1, no. 44: 4–11.

Joaquin, Nick. 1983. *The Aquinos of Tarlac: An Essay on History as Three Generations*. Manila: Cacho Hermanos.

Johnston, Bruce F., and William C. Clark. 1982. *Redesigning Rural Development: A Strategic Perspective*. Baltimore: Johns Hopkins University Press.

Johnston, Bruce F., and Peter Kilby. 1975. *Agriculture and Structural Transformation: Economic Strategies in Late-Developing Countries.* New York: Oxford University Press.

Jones, Clayton. 1986. "In Philippines, Sugar Barons Seek Ways to Combat Insurgency." *Christian Science Monitor*, Sept. 24.

Jones, Gregg R. 1989. *Red Revolution: Inside the Philippine Guerrilla Movement.* Boulder, Colo.: Westview Press.

Juliano-Soliman, Corazon. 1993. "The Continuing Struggle for Agrarian Reform." In J. Ibarra A. Angeles, ed., *International Conference on Agrarian Reform: Proceedings and Documentation*, pp. 296–310. Quezon City: Secretariat, International Conference on Agrarian Reform held Jan. 28–Feb. 2, 1991.

Karnow, Stanley. 1989. *In Our Image: America's Empire in the Philippines.* New York: Random House.

Kasfir, Nelson. 1979. "Explaining Ethnic Political Participation." *World Politics* 31, no. 3 (Apr.): 365–88.

Kaufman, Robert R. 1985. "Democratic and Authoritarian Responses to the Debt Issue: Argentina, Brazil, Mexico." *International Organization* 39, no. 3 (Summer): 473–503.

Kerkvliet, Benedict J. 1971. "Peasant Society and Unrest Prior to the Huk Revolution in the Philippines." *Asian Studies* 9, no. 2 (Aug.): 164–213.

———. [1977] 1979a. *The Huk Rebellion: A Study of Peasant Revolt in the Philippines.* Berkeley: University of California Press, 1977. Quezon City: New Day Publishers, 1979.

———. 1979b. "Land Reform: Emancipation or Counterinsurgency?" In David A. Rosenberg, ed., *Marcos and Martial Law in the Philippines*, pp. 113–44. Ithaca, N.Y.: Cornell University Press.

———. 1980. "Classes and Class Relations in a Philippine Village." *Philippine Sociological Review* 28, nos. 1–4 (Jan.–Dec.): 31–50.

———. 1983. "Profiles of Agrarian Reform in a Nueva Ecija Village." In Antonio J. Ledesma, Perla Q. Makil, and Virginia A. Miralao, eds., *Second View from the Paddy: More Empirical Studies on Philippine Rice Farming and Tenancy*, pp. 41–58. Quezon City: Institute of Philippine Culture, Ateneo de Manila University.

———. 1986. "In the Interim: Resistance Between Rebellions in Central Luzon, the Philippines." Paper prepared for Association of Asian Studies meeting, Chicago, Mar. 21–23.

———. 1990. *Everyday Politics in the Philippines: Class and Status Relations in a Central Luzon Village.* Berkeley: University of California Press.

Kerkvliet, Benedict J. Tria, and Resil B. Mojares. 1991. "Themes in the Transition from Marcos to Aquino: An Introduction." In id., eds., *From Marcos to Aquino: Local Perspectives on Political Transition in the Philippines*, pp. 1–12. Quezon City: Ateneo de Manila University Press.

Kerkvliet, Benedict J., and Werasit Sittitrai. 1979. "Differences Among Philippine Peasants: A Provincial Sample." *Philippine Sociological Review* 27, no. 3 (July): 133–59.

Kesselman, Mark. 1973. "Order or Movement: The Literature of Political Development as Ideology." *World Politics* 26, no. 1 (Oct.): 139–54.

Kessler, Richard J. 1989. *Rebellion and Repression in the Philippines*. New Haven: Yale University Press.

Khan, Mahmood H. 1975. *The Economics of the Green Revolution in Pakistan*. New York: Praeger.

——. 1977. "Land Productivity, Farm Size, and Returns to Scale in Pakistan Agriculture." *World Development* 5, no. 4 (Apr.): 317–23.

Kikuchi, Masao. 1983. "Recent Changes in a Laguna Rice Village: A New Generation of Changes?" In Antonio J. Ledesma, Perla Q. Makil, and Virginia A. Miralao, eds., *Second View from the Paddy: More Empirical Studies on Philippine Rice Farming and Tenancy*, pp. 59–72. Quezon City: Institute of Philippine Culture, Ateneo de Manila University Press.

Kikuchi, Masao, and Yujiro Hayami. 1978. "Agricultural Growth Against a Land Resource Constraint: A Comparative History of Japan, Taiwan, Korea, and the Philippines." *Journal of Economic History* 28, no. 4 (Dec.): 839–64.

Kilusang Magbubukid ng Pilipinas (KMP). 1986a. *Program for Genuine Land Reform*. Quezon City: KMP.

——. 1986b. *Proposal for the Immediate Implementation of the Minimum Program for Land Reform of the Kilusang Magbubukid ng Pilipinas*. Quezon City: KMP.

——. 1986c. *Policy Proposal for Countryside Development*. Quezon City: KMP. Edited, revised, and approved by the National Council of KMP as KMP 1986d.

——. 1986d. *Policy Statement on Agriculture and Countryside Development*. Quezon City: KMP.

——. 1986e. *Policy Programs on Agrarian Reform*. Quezon City: KMP.

——. 1988. "KMP Commemorates Mendiola Massacre." *Peasant Update International* 8 (Jan.): 1–2.

Kohli, Atul. 1987. *The State and Poverty in India: The Politics of Reform*. Cambridge: Cambridge University Press.

Komisar, Lucy. 1986. "Protestant Churches in the Philippines." *Christianity and Crisis* 46, no. 9 (June 16): 204–5.

Koo, Anthony Y. C. 1970. *Land Reform in Taiwan*. U.S. Agency for International Development Country Papers. Washington, D.C.: USAID.

Kuo, Shirley W. Y., Gustav Ranis, and John C. H. Fei. 1981. *The Taiwan Success Story: Rapid Growth with Improved Distribution in the Republic of China, 1952–1979*. Boulder, Colo.: Westview Press.

Lachica, Eduardo. 1971. *HUK: Philippine Agrarian Society in Revolt*. Manila: Solidaridad Publishing House.

Lacson, Daniel L., Jr. 1987. "Thoughts on Land Reform." *Negros Development Digest* 1, no. 3 (Second Quarter): 3.

Lal, Deepak. 1983. *Real Wages and Exchange Rates in the Philippines, 1956–78: An Application of the Stolper-Samuelson-Rybczynski Model of Trade*. World Bank Staff Working Paper No. 604. Washington, D.C.: World Bank.

Landé, Carl H. 1959. "Political Attitudes and Behavior in the Philippines." *Philippine Journal of Public Administration* 3, no. 3 (July): 341–65.

——. 1965. *Leaders, Factions and Parties: The Structure of Philippine Politics.* New Haven: Yale Southeast Asia Studies.

——. 1969. "Brief History of Political Parties." In Jose V. Abueva and Raul P. de Guzman, eds., *Foundations and Dynamics of Filipino Government and Politics,* pp. 151–57. Manila: Bookmark.

——. 1977. "Networks and Groups in Southeast Asia: Some Observations on the Group Theory of Politics." In Steffen W. Schmidt, James C. Scott, Carl Landé, and Laura Guasti, *Friends, Followers, and Factions: A Reader in Political Clientelism,* pp. 75–99. Berkeley: University of California.

——. 1986. "The Political Crisis." In John Bresnan, ed., *Crisis in the Philippines: The Marcos Era and Beyond,* pp. 114–44. Princeton: Princeton University Press.

——. 1987a. "Introduction: Retrospect and Prospect." In id., ed., *Rebuilding a Nation: Philippine Challenges and American Policy,* pp. 7–44. Washington, D.C.: Washington Institute Press.

——, ed. 1987b. *Rebuilding a Nation: Philippine Challenges and American Policy.* Washington, D.C.: Washington Institute Press.

Landé, Carl H., and Richard Hooley. 1986. "Aquino Takes Charge." *Foreign Affairs* 64, no. 5 (Summer): 1087–1107.

Lara, Francisco, Jr. 1988. "The Filipino Peasantry: Images of Poverty and Revolt." In Rodolfo Desuasido, ed., *Sowing the Seed, Proceedings of the International Solidarity Conference for the Filipino Peasantry (ISCFP), October 11–21, 1986,* pp. 121–33. Quezon City: KMP.

Lara, Francisco, Jr., and Horacio R. Morales, Jr. 1990. "The Peasant Movement and the Challenge of Rural Democratisation in the Philippines." *Journal of Development Studies* 26, no. 4 (July): 143–62.

Larkin, John A. 1984. "The International Face of the Philippine Sugar Industry, 1836–1920." *Philippine Review of Economics & Business* 21, nos. 1 & 2 (Mar. and June): 39–58.

Lau, Lawrence J., and Pan A. Yotopoulos. 1971. "A Test for Relative Efficiency and Application to Indian Agriculture." *American Economic Review* 61, no. 1 (Mar.): 94–109.

Lawyers Committee for Human Rights (LCHR). 1988. *Vigilantes in the Philippines: A Threat to Democratic Rule.* New York: LCHR.

——. 1990. *Out of Control: Militia Abuses in the Philippines.* New York: LCHR.

Lazaro, D'Jay. 1988. "Farm Drive Against CARP On." *Manila Standard,* June 12.

Ledesma, Antonio J. 1980. "Land Reform Programs in East and Southeast Asia: A Comparative Approach." *Philippine Studies* 28, nos. 3 & 4: 305–43 (no. 3), 451–81 (no. 4).

Ledesma, Antonio J., Perla Q. Makil, and Virginia A. Miralao, eds., 1983. *Second View from the Paddy: More Empirical Studies on Philippine Rice Farming and Tenancy.* Quezon City: Institute of Philippine Culture, Ateneo de Manila University.

Ledesma, Antonio J., and Ma. Lourdes T. Montinola, eds. 1988. *The Implementation of Agrarian Reform in Negros: Issues, Problems, and Experiences.* Research Notes Series, no. 3. Bacolod: La Salle Social Research Center.

Levine, Daniel H. 1988. "Paradigm Lost: Dependence to Democracy." *World Politics* 40, no. 3 (Apr.): 377–94.

Liang, Dapen. 1970. *Philippine Parties and Politics: A Historical Study of National Experience in Democracy.* San Francisco: Gladstone.

Libecap, Gary D. 1989. *Contracting for Property Rights.* Cambridge: Cambridge University Press.

Liberation. 1986a. "A Just Solution to a Just Struggle." 14, no. 5 (July–Aug.): 8–11.

———. 1986b. "No Matter How Small the Chance for Peace, We Will Pursue the Talks." Special issue 1 (Sept.): 1–4.

———. 1986c. "Protecting the Masses." 14, no. 7 (Sept.): 8–10.

———. 1986d. "Christmas & Ceasefire." Editorial. 14, no. 7 (Nov.): 1.

———. 1986e. "Agenda for a Just and Lasting Peace." 14, no. 8 (Dec. 15): 1.

———. 1986f. "Harnessing the People's Support," 14, no. 8 (Dec. 15): 13–15.

———. 1987a. "Rising from the Hard Earth." 15, no. 4 (Aug.): 6–7.

———. 1987b. "An Edict for Those to the Manor Born." 15, no. 4 (Aug.): 3–4.

———. 1988a. "Daybreak in My Homeland." 16, no. 1 (Jan.–Feb.): 10–11.

———. 1988b. "NDF Supports Palestinian Protests." 16, no. 1 (Jan.–Feb.): 10–11.

———. 1988c. "This Land Is Ours to Own and Defend." 16, no. 3 (May–June): 3–5.

———. 1988d. "Peasant Power Rises in the North." 16, no. 3 (May–June): 6.

———. 1988e. "A Declaration of Unity." 16, no. 3 (May–June): 11. Joint communique of the NDF and the Frente Farabundo Marti para la Liberación Nacional (FMLN, or National Liberation Front) of El Salvador.

Linz, Juan J. 1990a. "The Perils of Presidentialism." *Journal of Democracy* 1, no. 1 (Winter): 51–69.

———. 1990b. "The Virtues of Parliamentarianism." *Journal of Democracy* 1, no. 4 (Fall): 84–91.

Linz, Juan, and Alfred Stepan, eds. 1978. *The Breakdown of Democratic Regimes.* Baltimore: Johns Hopkins University Press.

Lipset, Seymour Martin. [1960] 1981. *Political Man: The Social Bases of Politics.* Expanded and updated. Baltimore: Johns Hopkins University Press.

———. 1990. "The Centrality of Political Culture." *Journal of Democracy* 1, no. 4 (Fall): 80–83.

Lipton, Michael. 1974. "Towards a Theory of Land Reform." In David Lehmann, ed., *Peasants, Landlords and Governments: Agrarian Reform in the Third World,* pp. 269–315. New York: Holmes & Meier.

———. 1977. *Why Poor People Stay Poor: Urban Bias in World Development.* Cambridge, Mass.: Harvard University Press.

Lockwood, B., P. K. Mukherjee, and R. T. Shand. 1971. *The High-Yielding Varieties Programme in India.* Part 1. Canberra: Planning Commission, Government of India and the Australian National University.

Lopez-Gonzaga, Violeta. 1983. *Mechanization and Labor Employment: A Study of the Sugarcane Workers' Responses to Technological Change in Sugar Farming in Negros.* La Salle Bacolod Monograph Series, no. 1. Bacolod: Alpha Publishing.

———. 1984. *The Sacadas in Negros: A Poverty Profile.* Research Notes Series, no. 1. Bacolod: La Salle Social Research Center.

——. 1985. *Crisis and Poverty in Sugarlandia: The Case of Bacolod*. Monograph Series, no. 3. Bacolod: La Salle Social Research Center.

——. 1986. *Crisis in Sugarlandia: The Planters' Differential Perceptions and Responses and Their Impact on Sugarcane Workers' Households*. Bacolod: La Salle Social Research Center.

——. 1987a. *Capital Expansion, Frontier Development and the Rise of Monocrop Economy in Negros, 1850–1898*. SRC-Negrense Studies Program Occasional Papers, no. 1. Bacolod: La Salle Social Research Center.

——. 1987b. *Voluntary Land Sharing and Transfer Scheme in Negros*. Research Notes Series, no. 2. Bacolod: La Salle Social Research Center.

——. 1988a. "The Roots of Agrarian Unrest in Negros, 1850–90." *Philippine Studies* 36 (Second Quarter): 151–65.

——. 1988b. "The Context and the Resource Base for Agrarian Reform and Development in Negros Occidental." In Antonio J. Ledesma, S.J., and Ma. Lourdes T. Montinola, *The Implementation of Agrarian Reform in Negros: Issues, Problems, and Experiences*, pp. 5–25. Bacolod: Social Research Center, University of St. La Salle. Sept.

——. 1989. *The Socio-Politics of Sugar: Wealth, Power Formation and Change in Negros (1899–1985)*. Bacolod: Social Research Center, University of St. La Salle.

——. N.d. "The Issue of Agrarian Reform in Sugarlandia: A Research Memo for Congress." Bacolod: Social Research Center, University of St. La Salle. Cover letter to Senator Agapito Aquino dated Aug. 7, 1987.

Lopez-Gonzaga, Violeta, Virgilio R. Aguilar, and Ferris Fe Demegilio. 1988. *The Resource Base for Agrarian Reform and Development in Negros Occidental*. Bacolod: La Salle Social Research Center.

Lopez-Torregrosa, Luisita. 1988. "Philippine Land Reform Measure Called a Hoax." *San Francisco Chronicle*, June 17.

Lowenthal, Abraham F., ed. 1975. *The Peruvian Experiment: Continuity and Change Under Military Rule*. Princeton: Princeton University Press.

Lowenthal, Abraham, and J. Samuel Fitch, eds. 1986. *Armies and Politics in Latin America*. New York: Holmes & Meier.

Lowenthal, Richard. 1976. "The Nature of 'Underdevelopment' and the Role of the State." In Richard Lowenthal, ed., *Model or Ally? The Communist Powers and the Developing Countries*, pp. 11–46. New York: Oxford University Press.

Lynch, Frank, ed. 1972. *View from the Paddy: Empirical Studies of Philippine Rice Farming and Tenancy*. Quezon City: Institute of Philippine Culture, Ateneo de Manila University. Also published as *Philippine Sociological Review* 20, nos. 1 & 2 (Jan. and Apr.).

——. [1961] 1973. "Social Acceptance Reconsidered." In Frank Lynch and Alfonso de Guzman II, *Four Readings on Philippine Values*, pp. 1–68. IPC Papers, no. 2. 4th ed. Quezon City: Institute of Philippine Culture, Ateneo de Manila University.

Lynch, Frank, and Alfonso de Guzman II, eds. [1961] 1973. *Four Readings on Philippine Values*. IPC Papers, no. 2. 4th ed. Quezon City: Institute of Philippine Culture, Ateneo de Manila University.

Maglipon, Jo-Ann Q. 1987. *A Smouldering Land: The Mendiola Tragedy, January 22, 1987*. Quezon City: National Council of Churches of the Philippines.

Magno, José P., and A. James Gregor. 1986. "Insurgency and Counterinsurgency in the Philippines." *Asian Survey* 26, no. 5 (May): 501–17.

Majul, Cesar A. 1973. *Muslims in the Philippines*. Quezon City: University of the Philippines.

Malaya. 1986. "Land Reform Policy Sought." Mar. 26.

——. 1987. "Land Bank Head Bucks 7-ha Retention Limit." June 9.

Mangahas, Mahar. 1986a. *Land and Natural Resources Reform*. Social Weather Stations Occasional Paper. Quezon City: Social Weather Stations.

——. 1986b. *Comments on Land Reform and the Proposed Constitution*. Social Weather Stations Occasional Paper. Quezon City: Social Weather Stations.

——. 1987a. *The Comprehensive Agrarian Reform Program as Drafted by the Cabinet Action Committee*. Social Weather Stations Occasional Paper. Quezon City: Social Weather Stations.

——. 1987b. "The Political Economy of Land Reform and Land Distribution in the Philippines." In *Agrarian Reform: Experiences and Expectations*, pp. 139–59. Agrarian Reform Symposia, Apr. 22–23 and May 23. Manila: Center for Research and Communication.

——. 1987c. *Rural Poverty, Social Surveillance and Democratic Development*. Social Weather Stations Occasional Paper. Quezon City: Social Weather Stations.

——. 1988a. *A Research and Development Agenda for Agrarian Reform*. Social Weather Stations Occasional Paper. Quezon City: Social Weather Stations.

——. 1988b. *Philippine Land Reform: Toward the Next Milestone*. Social Weather Stations Occasional Paper. Quezon City: Social Weather Stations.

——. 1988c. *Wages and Incomes Policy: The Issue of Distributive Justice*. Social Weather Stations Occasional Paper. Quezon City: Social Weather Stations.

——. 1989. *The Progress of Public Opinion on Land Reform, 1986–88*. Social Weather Bulletin 89-2. Quezon City: Social Weather Stations.

Mangahas, Mahar, Virginia A. Miralao, and Romana P. de los Reyes. 1976. *Tenants, Lessees, Owners: Welfare Implications of Tenure Change*. Quezon City: Ateneo de Manila University Institute of Philippine Culture.

Mangahas, Maylou. 1987. "Cory Signs Land Reform Law." *Manila Chronicle*, July 23, p. 1.

Manila Bulletin. 1986. "Agrarian Reform Policy Asked." Mar. 26.

——. 1987. "7-hectare Limit May Be Raised." June 14.

Manila Chronicle. 1987. "Cory Backs Alsa Masa." Oct. 24.

——. 1989a. "Peasant Groups' QC Offices Searched." July 9, p. 4.

——. 1989b. "Juico Offers to Quit." June 27.

——. 1989c. "NPA Leadership is Losing Control." Editorial. June 30.

Mao, Yu-Kang. 1987. "Land Reform Implementation and the Supporting Services for Administration: The Experiences of Taiwan, Republic of China." In *Agrarian Reform: Experiences and Expectations*, pp. 35–54. Agrarian Reform Symposia, Apr. 22–23 and May 23. Manila: Center for Research and Communication.

Marasigan, Horacio V., Jr. 1987a. "Transcript of Hearing of the Senate Committee on Agrarian Reform." Testimony of Horacio V. 'Zaldy' Marasigan, Jr., Land's Utmost Productivity Association (LUPA) and Southern Tagalog Aqua-Agriculture Producers and Marketing Cooperatives. Mimeograph. Manila, Aug. 18.

——. 1987b. "Transcript of Hearing of the Senate Committee on Agrarian Reform." Testimony of Horacio V. 'Zaldy' Marasigan, Jr., Land's Utmost Productivity Association. Mimeograph. Manila, Sept. 4.

Marcos, Ferdinand E. 1971. *Today's Revolution: Democracy*. Manila: National Media Production Center.

——. 1985. *The Filipino Ideology*. Manila: Marcos Foundation.

Marshall, T. H. 1964. *Class, Citizenship and Social Development*. Garden City, N.Y.: Doubleday.

Marsh, Robert. 1979. "Does Democracy Hinder Economic Development in the Latecomer Developing Nations?" *Comparative Social Research* 2, pp. 215–48. Greenwich, Conn.: JAI Press.

Marx, Karl, and Friedrich Engels. [1932] 1965. *The German Ideology*. London: Lawrence & Wishart.

Mason, T. David. 1990. "Land Reform, Repression, and Revolution: A Comparison of El Salvador and Peru." Paper presented at the 86th Annual Meeting of the American Political Science Association, San Francisco, Aug. 30–Sept. 2.

May, Glenn Anthony. 1987. *A Past Recovered*. Quezon City: New Day Publishers.

May, R. J., and Francisco Nemenzo, eds. 1985. *The Philippines After Marcos*. New York: St. Martin's Press.

McBeth, John. 1989a. "The Boss System: Manila's Disarray Leaves Countryside Under Local Barons." *Far Eastern Economic Review*, Sept. 14, pp. 36–43.

——. 1989b. "The Old Boys' Act." *Far Eastern Economic Review*, Nov. 2, p. 32.

——. 1990. "Tough Nut to Crack." *Far Eastern Economic Review*, Feb. 8, p. 9.

——. 1993. "Internal Contradictions: Support for Communists Wanes as Party Splits." *Far Eastern Economic Review*, Aug. 26, pp. 16–18.

McClintock, Cynthia. 1980. "Reform Governments and Policy Implementation: Lessons from Peru." In Merilee S. Grindle, ed., *Politics and Policy Implementation in the Third World*, pp. 64–97. Princeton: Princeton University Press.

——. 1981. *Peasant Cooperatives and Political Change in Peru*. Princeton: Princeton University Press.

——. 1984. "Why Peasants Rebel: The Case of Peru's Sendero Luminoso." *World Politics* 37, no. 1 (Oct.): 48–84.

McClintock, Cynthia, and Abraham F. Lowenthal, eds. 1983. *The Peruvian Experiment Reconsidered*. Princeton: Princeton University Press.

McClintock, Michael. 1985. *The American Connection, vol. 2: State Terror and Popular Resistance in Guatemala*. London: Zed Books.

McCoy, Alfred. 1982a. "Introduction: The Social History of an Archipelago." In Alfred W. McCoy and Ed. C. de Jesus, eds., *Philippine Social History: Global Trade and Local Transformations*, pp. 1–18. Quezon City: Ateneo de Manila University Press.

———. 1982b. "A Queen Dies Slowly: The Rise and Decline of Iloilo City." In Alfred W. McCoy and Ed. C. de Jesus, *Philippine Social History: Global Trade and Local Transformations*, pp. 297–358. Quezon City: Ateneo de Manila University Press.

———. 1984a. "The Iloilo General Strike: Defeat of the Proletariat in a Philippine Colonial City." *Journal of Southeast Asian Studies* 15, no. 2 (Sept.): 330–64.

———. 1984b. *Priests on Trial*. Victoria, Australia. Penguin Books.

———. 1985. "Rural Philippines: Technological Change in the Sugar Industry." In R. J. May and Francisco Nemenzo, eds., *The Philippines After Marcos*, pp. 175–93. New York: St. Martin's Press.

———. 1991. "The Restoration of Planter Power in La Carlota City." In Benedict J. Kerkvliet and Resil B. Mojares, eds., *From Marcos to Aquino: Local Perspectives on Political Transition in the Philippines*, pp. 105–42. Quezon City: Ateneo de Manila University Press.

———. 1992. "Sugar Barons: Formation of a Native Planter Class in the Colonial Philippines." *Journal of Peasant Studies* 19, nos. 3 and 4 (Apr. and July): 106–41.

McCoy, Alfred, and Ed de Jesus, eds. 1982. *Philippine Social History: Global Trade and Local Transformation*. Quezon City: Ateneo de Manila University Press.

McLennan, Marshall S. 1969. "Land and Tenancy in the Central Luzon Plain." *Philippine Studies* 17, no. 4 (Oct.): 651–82.

Mediansky, F. A. 1986. "The New People's Army: A Nationwide Insurgency in the Philippines." *Southeast Asia* 8, no. 1 (June): 4.

Medina, Jose C., Jr. 1987. "Transcript of the Meeting of the Committee on Agrarian Reform with the Members of the Cabinet Action Committee re Draft of the Executive Order on Agrarian Reform Program." Statement of Acting Secretary Jose C. 'Jun' Medina, Jr., DAR. Mimeograph. Manila, July 17.

Mejorada, Manuel P. 1993. "DAR to Shift Focus to Productivity from Land Distribution—Garilao." *Business World*, Jan. 29, p. 11.

Melencio, Helen. 1988. "Farmers Hit CARP Delay in Commercial Farms." *Philippine Daily Globe*, Sept. 23.

Mercado, Monina A. 1986. *People Power: An Eyewitness History of the Philippine Revolution of 1986*. Manila: James B. Reuter, S.J., Foundation.

Migdal, Joel. 1974. *Peasants, Politics, and Revolution: Pressures Toward Political Change in the Third World*. Princeton: Princeton University Press.

———. 1988. *Strong Societies and Weak States: State-Society Relations and State Capabilities in the Third World*. Princeton: Princeton University Press.

Millar, Micheline R. 1993. "75% of Pending LBP Land Value Cases Resolved." *Business World*, Oct. 1, p. 13.

Miller, Matt. 1988a. "Land Reform Polarizes the Philippines." *Asian Wall Street Journal*, Mar. 24.

———. 1988b. "Congress Splits in Philippines on Reform Bill." *Asian Wall Street Journal*, Mar. 28, p. 1.

———. 1989. "Scandal Hobbles Manila's Land Reform." *Asian Wall Street Journal*, July 7–8, p. 1.

Milne, R. S. 1969. "The Filipino Party System." In Jose V. Abueva and Raul P. de

Guzman, eds., *Foundations and Dynamics of Filipino Government and Politics*, pp. 181–87. Manila : Bookmark.

Miranda, Felipe B. 1985. "The Military." In R. J. May and Francisco Nemenzo, eds., *The Philippines After Marcos*, pp. 90–109. New York: St. Martin's Press.

Mojares, Resil B. 1986. *The Man Who Would Be President: Sergio Osmeña and Philippine Politics*. Cebu: Maria Cacao Publishers.

——. 1988. "The Dream Lives On and On." Paper presented at the 40th Annual Meeting of the Association for Asian Studies, San Francisco, Mar. 1988.

Monfort, Narciso D. 1987. "Transcript of the Meeting of the Committee on Agrarian Reform with the Members of the Cabinet Action Committee re Draft of the Executive Order on Agrarian Reform Program." Remarks of Congressman Narciso D. Monfort. Mimeograph. Manila, July 17.

Monk, Paul. 1990. *Truth and Power: Robert S. Hardie and Land Reform Debates in the Philippines, 1950–1987*. Monash Papers, no. 20. Victoria, Australia: Centre of Southeast Asian Studies, Monash University.

Monsod, Solita S. 1987. "Transcript of the Meeting of the Committee on Agrarian Reform with the Members of the Cabinet Action Committee re Draft of the Executive Order on Agrarian Reform Program." Statement of Solita S. Monsod, Secretary, National Economic and Development Authority. Mimeograph. Manila, July 17.

Montemayor, Jeremias U. 1986a. "Another Look at Agrarian Reform." Mimeograph. Quezon City: Federation of Free Farmers, May 9.

——. 1986b. "Time-Bombs in Proposed Charter's Agrarian Provisions." Mimeograph. Quezon City: Federation of Free Farmers, Nov. 12.

——. 1988. "Moral Issues on Compensation for Land." *Philippine Star*, Apr. 12. Also appeared as id., "Moral Issues on Just Compensation for Land." *Business World*, Apr. 13, 1988.

——. N.d. "Observations on the Social Justice, Agrarian and Labor Provisions of the Proposed 1986 Constitution." Mimeograph. Quezon City: n.d.

Montemayor, Leonardo Q. 1987. "Agrarian Reform and Agricultural Development: Promises, Performance, and Prospects Under Aquino Administration." Paper presented at national conference "Agrarian Reform and Agricultural Development: Where Do We Go From Here?" Institute of Industrial Relations, University of the Philippines, Dec. 8–10.

Montiel, Cristina J. 1992. "Organizational Dynamics in a Left-of-Center National Coalition: The Salonga-Pimentel Campaign." Paper presented at the Fourth International Philippine Studies Conference, Canberra, July 1–3.

Montgomery, John D. 1972. "Allocation of Authority in Land Reform Programs: A Comparative Study of Administrative Processes and Outputs." *Administrative Science Quarterly* 17, no. 1 (Mar.): 62–75.

Morais, Robert J. 1980. "Dealing with Scarce Resources: Reciprocity in Alternative Form and Ritual." *Philippine Sociological Review* 28, nos. 1–4 (Jan.–Dec.): 73–80.

——. 1981. *Social Relations in a Philippine Town*. De Kalb: Northern Illinois University Center for Southeast Asian Studies.

Morales, Horacio, Jr. 1986. "Rural Development Strategies: Then and Now." In

Romulo A. Sandoval, ed., *Prospects of Agrarian Reform Under the New Order*, pp. 78–82. Quezon City: Urban Rural Mission, National Council of Churches in the Philippines.

Morrow, Robert B., and Kenneth H. Sherper. 1970. *Land Reform in South Korea*. U.S. Agency for International Development Country Papers. Washington, D.C.: USAID.

Murray, Francis R., Jr. 1973. "Land Reform in the Philippines: An Overview." In Frank Lynch, ed., *View from the Paddy: Empirical Studies of Philippine Rice Farming and Tenancy*, pp. 151–68. Quezon City: Institute of Philippine Culture, Ateneo de Manila University Press.

Mydans, Seth. 1985. "Aquino Says If She Is Elected Marcos Faces a Murder Trial," and "Excerpts from Aquino Interview on Candidacy." *New York Times*, Dec. 16.

——. 1986a. "In Manila Press, It's 'Corazon Who?'" *New York Times*, Jan. 20.

——. 1986b. "Charting Aquino's Course: Portrait of the Inner Circle." *New York Times*, Jan. 28.

——. 1986c. "Aquino Stirs a Crowd." *New York Times*, Jan. 28.

——. 1986d. "Aquino Names 17 to Her Cabinet; Marcos in Hawaii." *New York Times*, Feb. 27.

——. 1987a. "Troops in Manila Kill 12 in Crowd at Leftist Rally." *New York Times*, Jan. 23, p. 1.

——. 1987b. "Right-Wing Vigilantes Spread in Philippines." *New York Times*, Apr. 4.

——. 1987c. "In the Big Manila Land Plan, Steps Are Small." *New York Times*, Oct. 18.

——. 1987d. "For Aquino, a Growing Threat from Extremists." *New York Times*, Dec. 27.

Narisma, Corrie S. 1989. "Santos Deep into Land Deal—Execs." *Manila Chronicle*, June 28.

Nash, June. 1967–68. "The Passion Play in Maya Indian Communities." *Comparative Studies in Society and History* 10, no. 3 (Apr.): 318–27.

Nasol, Ramon. 1987. "Transcript of Hearing of the Senate Committee on Agrarian Reform." Testimony of Dr. Ramon Nasol. Mimeograph. Manila, Aug. 14.

National Federation of Sugarcane Planters (NFSP) and Philippine Sugar Association (PSA). 1960. *The Story of Sugar in the Philippines, 1521–1960*. Manila: NFSP and PSA.

National Federation of Sugarcane Planters (NFSP). N.d. *Land Reform in the Philippine Sugar Industry*. Bacolod: NFSP.

Negros Development Digest. 1987. "60-30-10 First." 1, no. 3 (Second Quarter): 13, 20.

Negros Oriental Planters' Association, Inc. (NOPA), and Asociacion Agricola de Bais y Tanjay, Inc. (AABT). 1987. "Land Reform—A View from the Standpoint of the Sugarcane Planters of Northern Negros Oriental with 23,000

Hectares of Private Land Planted to Sugarcane in Bais, Tanjay, Manjuyod, and Mabinay." Mimeograph. Bais City, Aug. 24.

Nelson, Joan M. 1984. "The Political Economy of Stabilization: Commitment, Capacity, and Public Response." *World Development* 12, no. 10 (Oct.): 983–1006.

———. 1987. "Political Participation." In Myron Weiner and Samuel P. Huntington, eds., *Understanding Political Development*, pp. 103–59. Boston: Little, Brown.

———, ed. 1990. *Economic Crisis and Policy Choice: The Politics of Adjustment in the Third World*. Princeton: Princeton University Press.

Nemenzo, Francisco. 1985. "The Left and the Traditional Opposition." In R. J. May and Francisco Nemenzo, eds., *The Philippines After Marcos*, pp. 45–69. New York: St. Martin's Press.

Nettl, J. P. 1968. "The State as a Conceptual Variable." *World Politics* 22, no. 4 (July): 559–92.

Newbery, David M. G. 1975. "The Choice of Rental Contracts in Peasant Agriculture." In Lloyd G. Reynolds, ed., *Agriculture in Development Theory*, pp. 109–37. New Haven: Yale University Press.

New York Times, 1955. "Benson Reverses Ladejinsky Stand." July 3.

———. 1985. "Excerpts from Aquino Interview on Candidacy." Dec. 16.

———. 1986a. "Aquino Says Communists Wouldn't Join the Cabinet." Jan. 7.

———. 1986b. "Aquino Gives New Policy Details and Labels Marcos a 'Pharaoh.'" Feb. 4.

———. 1986c. "From a Symbol to a Leader: The Rise of Corazon Aquino." Feb. 26.

———. 1986d. "Rebels to Fight On, a Communist Says." Feb. 27.

Newsweek. 1987. "Resistance on the Right." Aug. 10, p. 9.

Noble, Lela Garner. 1986. "Politics in the Marcos Era." In John Bresnan, ed., *Crisis in the Philippines: The Marcos Era and Beyond*, pp. 70–113. Princeton: Princeton University Press.

North, Douglass C. 1990. *Institutions, Institutional Change and Economic Performance*. Cambridge: Cambridge University Press.

North, Liisa. 1976. "The Military in Chilean Politics." *Studies in Comparative International Development* 11, no. 2 (Summer): 73–106.

Nowak, Thomas C., and Kay A. Snyder. 1974. "Clientelist Politics in the Philippines: Integration or Instability?" *American Political Science Review* 68, no. 3 (Sept.): 1147–70.

O'Brien, Niall. 1987. *Revolution from the Heart*. New York: Oxford University Press.

O'Donnell, Guillermo. [1973] 1979. *Modernization and Bureaucratic-Authoritarianism: Studies in South American Politics*. Berkeley: University of California.

O'Donnell, Guillermo, Philippe C. Schmitter, and Laurence Whitehead. 1986. *Transitions from Authoritarian Rule*. Baltimore: Johns Hopkins University Press.

Ofreneo, Rene E. 1987. *Capitalism in Philippine Agriculture*. Updated ed. Quezon City: Foundation for Nationalist Studies.

Ofreneo, Rosalinda. 1987. "The Catholic Church in Philippine Politics." *Journal of Contemporary Asia* 17, no. 3: 320–38.

Ongpin, Jaime V. "Memorandum to President Corazon C. Aquino." Mimeograph. Manila, May 4, 1987.

Ongpin, Jaime V., and Deogracias N. Vistan. 1987. "Letter to President Corazon C. Aquino." June 5. Accompanied by draft Executive Order.

Oquendo, Nelson. 1987. "Transcript of Hearing of the Senate Committee on Agrarian Reform." Testimony of Nelson Oquendo, Regional President, Agrarian Reform Beneficiaries Association (ARBA). Mimeograph. Manila, Aug. 12.

Otsuka, Keijiro. 1991. "Determinants and Consequences of Land Reform Implementation in the Philippines." *Journal of Development Economics* 35, no. 2, pp. 339–55.

Otsuka, Keijiro, and Yujiro Hayami. 1988. "Theories of Share Tenancy: A Critical Survey." *Economic Development and Cultural Change* 37 (Oct.): 31–68.

Otsuka, Keijiro, Hiroyuki Chuma, and Yujiro Hayami. 1990. "Land and Labor Contracts in Agrarian Economies: Theories and Facts." MS. 6th draft. Tokyo Metropolitan University.

Overholt, William H. 1986. "The Rise and Fall of Ferdinand Marcos." *Asian Survey* 26, no. 11 (Nov.): 1137–63.

———. 1987. "Pressures and Policies: Prospects for Cory Aquino's Philippines." In Carl H. Landé, ed., *Rebuilding a Nation: Philippine Challenges and American Policy*, pp. 89–110. Washington, D.C.: Washington Institute Press.

Owen, Norman G. 1982. "Abaca in Kabikolan: Prosperity Without Progress." In Alfred W. McCoy and Ed. C. de Jesus, eds., *Philippine Social History: Global Trade and Local Transformations*, pp. 191–216. Quezon City: Ateneo de Manila University Press.

Padilla, Ambrosio B. 1986. "Remarks of Commissioner Ambrosio B. Padilla." *Record of the Constitutional Commission: Proceedings and Debates*, vol. 3. Quezon City: Constitutional Commission of 1986.

Paige, Jeffery M. 1975. *Agrarian Revolution: Social Movements and Export Agriculture in the Underdeveloped World*. New York: Free Press.

Palacios, Joel. 1987. "Negros Landlords Prepare for Battle." *Manila Chronicle*, June 29, p. 1.

Panay Landowners Alliance for Democratic Agrarian Reform (PLADAR) and the Democratic Alliance for a Truly Unified Panay (DATU-Panay). N.d. "Position Paper on the Comprehensive Agrarian Reform Program." Mimeograph. Iloilo City: PLADAR and DATU-Panay.

———. 1987. "Joint Petition of Landowners of Panay Island." Mimeograph. Iloilo City: PLADAR and DATU-Panay.

———. 1988. "Memorandum for the Bicameral Conference Committee on CARP." Mimeograph. Iloilo City: PLADAR and DATU-Panay.

Panganiban, Corazon C. 1983. "A Case Study of the Implementation and Impact of Operation Land Transfer in a Farming Village, 1972–1979." In Antonio J. Ledesma, Perla Q. Makil, and Virginia A. Miralao, eds., *Second View from the*

Paddy: More Empirical Studies on Philippine Rice Farming and Tenancy, pp. 110–17. Quezon City: Institute of Philippine Culture, Ateneo de Manila University.

Paredes-Japa, Divina. 1988. "NPA Land Reform Faster than CARP." *Philippine Daily Globe*, Dec. 2.

Patnaik, Utsa. 1972. "Economics of Farm Size and Farm Scale: Some Assumptions Re-examined." *Economic and Political Weekly*, 7, nos. 31–33 (Aug.): 1613–24.

Peterman, John. 1988. "Democracy and the Dynasties." *Far Eastern Economic Review*, Jan. 14, pp. 19–21.

Petitjean, Paul. 1986a. "After the Election: Reassessment in the Revolutionary Left." *International Viewpoint* 100 (June 2): 5–10.

——. 1986b. "The Trajectory of the Left Forces That Supported Cory Aquino's Campaign." *International Viewpoint* 103 (July 14): 16–18.

Philippine Daily Express. 1973. Sept. 22, p. 6.

——. 1986. "Define Land Reform Policy, FFF Asks." Mar. 26.

Philippine Daily Inquirer. 1989. "Miriam's New Post Welcomed." July 2.

——. 1991. "Six Aggie Firms Adopt Luisita Stock Scheme." Feb. 16.

Philippines, Republic of the (ROP). 1970. *So the People Will Know*. Quezon City: Department of National Defense.

——. 1986a. *Record of the Constitutional Commission: Proceedings and Debates*, vols. 2 and 3. Quezon City: Constitutional Commission of 1986.

——. 1986b. *1986 Agenda for Action for the Philippine Rural Sector*. Quezon City: Agricultural Policy and Strategy Team.

——. Department of Agrarian Reform (DAR). 1972. Department Memorandum D-505. Quezon City: DAR. Jan. 2.

——. ——. 1973. Department Memorandum Circular No. 5. 1973 series. Quezon City: DAR. Mar. 6.

——. ——. 1974. Department Memorandum No. 8. 1974 series. Quezon City: DAR. Apr. 1.

——. ——. 1977. Department Memorandum Circular No. 5. 1977 series. Quezon City: DAR. Mar. 28.

——. ——. 1986a. Ministry Memorandum Circular No. 5. ("Subject: Authority to issue/distribute Emancipation Patents to Farmer-Beneficiaries regardless of amortization payments"). 1986 series. Quezon City: DAR. May 7.

——. ——. 1986b. "A Profile: Minister Heherson T. Alvarez." In *The Philippine Agrarian Reform Program: A Handbook*, pp. 23–25. Quezon City: DAR.

——. ——. 1987a. "Policies, Priority Concerns and External Assistance Needs." Quezon City: Planning and Project Management Office, Department of Agrarian Reform.

——. ——. N.d. Cited as DAR 1987b in text. *Year-End Accomplishment Report, 1987*. Quezon City: DAR.

——. ——. N.d. Cited as DAR 1988 in text. *Accomplishment Report 1988*. Quezon City: DAR.

——. ——. 1989a. *Administrative Order No. 6: Rules and Procedures on Land Valua-*

tion and Compensation. 1988 series. Quezon City: DAR. Mar. 8. Reprinted in
Manila Chronicle, Mar. 13, 1989.

———. ———. N.d. Cited as DAR 1989b in text. *1989 CARP Accomplishment Report.*
Quezon City: DAR.

———. ———. N.d. Cited as DAR 1990 in text. *Comprehensive Agrarian Reform Program, 1990 Year-end Accomplishment Report.* Quezon City: DAR.

———. ———. N.d. Cited as DAR 1991 in text. *1991 Accomplishment Report.* Quezon
City: DAR.

———. ———. N.d. Cited as DAR 1992 in text. *1992 Accomplishment Report.* Quezon
City: DAR.

———. ———. 1993a. *Executive Report: 1993 Year-end Review.* Quezon City: DAR.
Dec. 23.

———. ———. N.d. Cited as DAR 1993b in text. *1993 Accomplishment Report.* Quezon
City: DAR.

———. ———. 1993c. *The CARP 2000: Medium-Term Development Plan (1993–1998).*
Quezon City: DAR. Aug. 4.

———. ———. N.d. Cited as DAR 1993d in text. *CARP 2000: MTDP (Year of the ARC).*
Quezon City: DAR.

———. ———. 1993e. "Setting the Record Straight." Mimeograph. Quezon City:
DAR. July 26.

———. Department of Justice (DOJ). 1973. *Opinion No. 35.* Quezon City: DOJ.
Feb. 27.

———. Department of Local Government and Community Development
(DLGCD). 1975. *Annual Report on Cooperative Development, 1974–1975.* Quezon City: Bureau of Cooperatives Development.

———. ———. 1976. "The New Cooperatives Development Program." Mimeograph.
Quezon City: Bureau of Cooperatives Development.

———. ———. 1979. *Annual Report of the Bureau of Cooperatives Development for CY
1978.* Quezon City: Bureau of Cooperatives Development.

———. ———. N.d. "Overview on the Philippine Cooperatives Development Program." Mimeograph. Quezon City: Bureau of Cooperatives Development.

———. Director of Lands. 1951. *Lands Journal* 3 (Sept.). Manila: Republic of the
Philippines.

———. ———. 1956. *Annual Report.* Manila: Republic of the Philippines.

———. Inter-Agency Task Force on Agrarian Reform (ITFAR). 1987a. "Accelerated
Land Reform Project: A Project Proposal." Mimeograph. Manila, Jan. 23.

———. ———. 1987b. "Accelerated Land Reform Project: A Project Proposal." Revised draft. Mimeograph. Manila, Mar. 13.

———. ———. 1987c. "Proposal for Rehabilitation of Negros." Mimeograph. Quezon
City: Apr. 27.

———. ———. 1987d. "Accelerated Land Reform Project: Program Brief." Mimeograph. Manila, Apr. 27.

———. National Census and Statistics Office (NCSO). 1985a. *1980 Census of Agriculture: National Summary,* vol. 1: Final Report. Manila: NCSO.

——. ——. 1985b. *1980 Census of Agriculture: Negros Occidental*. Vol. 1: Final Report. Manila: NCSO.

——. ——. 1985c. *1980 Census of Agriculture: Batangas*. Vol. 1: Final Report. Manila: NCSO.

——. ——. 1985d. *1980 Census of Agriculture: Bukidnon*. Vol. 1: Final Report. Manila: NCSO.

——. ——. 1985e. "Family Income and Expenditure Survey." Manila: NCSO.

——. ——. 1988. "Integrated Survey of Households." Manila: NCSO.

——. National Economic and Development Authority (NEDA). 1986a. *Policy Agenda for People-Powered Development*. Manila: NEDA.

——. ——. 1986b. *Medium Term Development Plan, 1987–1992*. Manila: NEDA.

——. Presidency. Office of the Press Secretary. 1989. *Winning the War Against the Insurgency: Issues and Answers* 1, no. 5. Manila, Apr.

Philippines, Republic of the (ROP), and United States Agency for International Development (USAID). 1989. *Grant Agreement between the ROP and the United States for the Agrarian Reform Support Program*. Manila, Aug. 28.

Picornell, Ramon, Jr. 1985. "An Update of Experiences in Operating RO-RO During Crop Year 1984–85." *Philippine Sugar Technologists Proceedings*, pp. 84–107.

Picornell, Ramon, Jr., Roberto B. Dumatol, and Tranquilino Espinosa. 1984. "The Development of Central Azucarera de Don Pedro's Cane Distribution Program." *Philippine Sugar Technologists' Proceedings*, pp. 192–204.

Pilapil, Eduardo P. 1987. "Transcript of the Meeting of the Committee on Agrarian Reform with the Members of the Cabinet Action Committee re Draft of the Executive Order on Agrarian Reform Program." Remarks of Congressman Eduardo P. Pilapil. Mimeograph. Manila, July 17.

Piven, Francis F., and Richard A. Cloward. 1977. *Poor People's Movements: Why They Succeed, How They Fail*. New York: Vintage Books.

Po, Blondie, and Cristina Montiel. 1980. *Rural Organizations in the Philippines*. Quezon City: Institute of Philippine Culture, Ateneo de Manila University.

Polanyi, Karl. 1944. *The Great Transformation*. New York: Rinehart.

Pomeroy, William. 1978. "The Philippine Peasantry and the Huk Revolt." *Journal of Peasant Studies* 5, no. 4 (July): 497–517.

Popkin, Samuel L. 1979. *The Rational Peasant: The Political Economy of Rural Society in Vietnam*. Berkeley: University of California Press.

——. 1981. "Public Choice and Rural Development: Free Riders, Lemons, and Institutional Design." In Clifford S. Russell and Norman Nicholson, eds., *Public Choice and Rural Development*, pp. 43–80. Washington, D.C.: Resources for the Future.

Porter, Gareth. 1986. "Philippine Catholics: Hierarchy and Radicals." *Christianity and Crisis* 46, no. 9 (June 16): 203–6.

——. 1987a. "Counterinsurgency in the Philippines: Aquino Was Right." *SAIS Review* 7, no. 2 (Summer–Fall): 93–108.

——. 1987b. "Philippine Communism After Marcos." *Problems of Communism*, 36, no. 5 (Sept.–Oct.): 14–35.

Powelson, John P., and Richard Stock. 1987. *The Peasant Betrayed: Agriculture and Land Reform in the Third World*. Cambridge, Mass.: Lincoln Institute.

Prosterman, Roy L., and Jeffrey M. Riedinger. 1987. *Land Reform and Democratic Development*. Baltimore: Johns Hopkins University Press.

Prosterman, Roy L., and Timothy M. Hanstad. 1988a. "Analysis of Republic Act No. 6657, The Philippine Land-Reform Law: Can an Effective Land Reform Result?" Memorandum. Seattle: University of Washington School of Law.

——. 1988b. "Whether Failure Is Inevitable Under the New Philippine Land-Reform Law." Memorandum. Seattle: University of Washington School of Law.

——. 1990. "China: A Fieldwork-Based Appraisal of the Household Responsibility System, with Recommendations for the Future." In Roy L. Prosterman, Mary N. Temple, and Timothy M. Hanstad, eds., *Agrarian Reform and Grassroots Development: Ten Case Studies*, pp. 103–36. Washington, D.C.: Lynne Rienner.

Przeworski, Adam. 1986. "Some Problems in the Study of the Transition to Democracy." In Guillermo O'Donnell, Philippe C. Schmitter, and Laurence Whitehead, eds., *Transitions from Authoritarian Rule: Comparative Perspectives*, pp. 47–63. Baltimore: Johns Hopkins University Press.

Putzel, James. 1988. "Prospects for Agrarian Reform Under the Aquino Government." In Mamerto Canlas, Mariano Miranda, Jr., and James Putzel, *Land, Poverty and Politics in the Philippines*, pp. 37–60. Quezon City: Claretian.

——. 1992. *A Captive Land: The Politics of Agrarian Reform in the Philippines*. Quezon City: Ateneo de Manila University Press.

Pye, Lucian W. 1966. "Party Systems and National Development in Asia." In Joseph LaPalombara and Myron Weiner, *Political Parties and Political Development*, pp. 369–98. Princeton: Princeton University Press.

Quisumbing, Ma. Agnes R., and Ma. Concepcion J. Cruz. 1986. "Rural Poverty and Poverty Programs in the Philippines." In *Agenda for Action for the Philippine Rural Sector*. Los Baños: University of the Philippines.

Race, Jeffrey. 1972. *War Comes to Long An*. Berkeley: University of California Press.

Rafael, Vicente L. 1988. *Contracting Colonialism: Translation and Christian Conversion in Tagalog Society Under Early Spanish Rule*. Quezon City: Ateneo de Manila University Press.

Ranger, Terence. 1983. "The Invention of Tradition in Colonial Africa." In Eric Hobsbawm and Terence Ranger, eds., *Invention of Tradition*, pp. 211–62. Cambridge: Cambridge University Press.

Recto, Claro M. 1946. *Three Years of Enemy Occupation*. Manila: People's Publishers.

Remmer, Karen L. 1985–86. "Exclusionary Democracy." *Studies in Comparative International Development* 20, no. 4 (Winter): 64–85.

——. 1986. "The Politics of Economic Stabilization: IMF Standby Programs in Latin America, 1954–1984." *Comparative Politics* 19, no. 1 (Oct.): 1–24.

Research Conference Board. 1988. *Political Monitor*, Oct. 16, p. 13.

Resurreccion, Lyn. 1990. "If There's Any Doubt (in CARL), We Should Decide in Favor of the Farmers." *Philippine News and Features* 6, no. 30 (Feb. 18): 3–6.

Reuters News Service. 1993. "Ramos Vows to Complete Land Reform by Term's End." June 9.

Revilleza, Rodolfo P. 1976. "A Farm Practice Report on San Antonio Farms in Lian, Batangas." B.S. thesis, University of the Philippines, Los Baños.

Reyes, Wilfredo G. 1993. "NUC: Poor Implementation of CARL a Primary Cause of Domestic Conflict." *Business World*, Sept. 21, p. 12.

Richards, Alan, and John Waterbury. 1990. *A Political Economy of the Middle East: State, Class, and Economic Development*. Boulder, Colo.: Westview Press.

Richter, Linda K. 1982. *Land Reform and Tourism Development: Policy-Making in the Philippines*. Cambridge, Mass.: Schenkman.

Riedinger, Jeffrey M. 1989. "Hacienda Luisita Stock Distribution Analyzed." Mimeograph. Princeton University, Sept. 25. Reprinted *Newsday*, Dec. 18, 1989.

——. 1990a. Letter to Corazon Paredes Del Rosario. Princeton University, Jan. 31, 1990. Reprinted as "Letter from Princeton," *Newsday*, Feb. 9, 1990.

——. 1990b. "Philippine Land Reform in the 1980s." In Roy L. Prosterman, Mary N. Temple, and Timothy M. Hanstad, eds., *Agrarian Reform and Grassroots Development: Ten Case Studies*, pp. 15–47. Boulder, Colo.: Lynne Rienner.

——. 1991. "Redistributive Reform in Transitional Democracies: Philippine Agrarian Reform." Ph.D. diss., Princeton University.

——. 1994. "Innovation in Rural Finance: Indonesia's *Badan Kredit Kecamatan* Program." *World Development* 22, no. 3 (1994): 301–13.

Rivera, Temario C., Merlin M. Magallona, Rigoberto D. Tiglao, Ernesto M. Valencia, and Alex R. Magno. 1982. *Feudalism and Capitalism in the Philippines: Trends and Implications*. Quezon City: Foundation for Nationalist Studies.

Rocamora, J. Eliseo, and Corazon Conti-Panganiban. 1975. *Rural Development Strategies: The Philippine Case*. Quezon City: Institute of Philippine Culture, Ateneo de Manila University.

Rodriguez, Joel I. 1987. *Genuine Agrarian Reform*. Quezon City: National Council of Churches in the Philippines.

Roett, Riordan. 1986. "The Transition to Democratic Government in Brazil." *World Politics* 38, no. 2 (Jan.): 317–82.

Rondinelli, Dennis A. 1979. "Administration of Integrated Rural Development: The Politics of Agrarian Reform in Developing Countries." *World Politics* 31, no. 3 (Apr.): 389–416.

Ronquillo, M. 1988. "Exemption of 50-ha. Estates Proposed." *Philippine Daily Inquirer*, June 14.

Rood, Steven. 1992. "Non-Government Organizations and the 1992 Philippine Elections." Paper presented at the 44th Annual Meeting of the Association for Asian Studies, Washington, D.C., Apr. 2–5.

Rosenberg, David. 1990. "The Philippines." In Barry M. Schutz and Robert O. Slater, eds. *Revolution and Political Change in the Third World*, pp. 160–91. Boulder, Colo.: Lynne Rienner.

Roth, Dennis M. 1977. *The Friar Estates of the Philippines*. Albuquerque: University of New Mexico Press.

——. 1982. "Church Lands in the Agrarian History of the Tagalog Region." In Alfred W. McCoy and Ed. C. de Jesus, eds., *Philippine Social History: Global Trade and Local Transformations*, pp. 132–53. Quezon City: Ateneo de Manila University Press.

Roxborough, Ian. 1988. "The Dilemmas of Redemocratization." *Government and Opposition* 23, no. 3 (Summer): 354–67.

Rueschemeyer, Dietrich, and Peter B. Evans. 1985. "The State and Economic Transformation: Toward an Analysis of the Conditions Underlying Effective Intervention." In Peter B. Evans, Dietrich Rueschemeyer, and Theda Skocpol, eds., *Bringing the State Back In*, pp. 50–55. Cambridge: Cambridge University Press.

Rutledge, Ian. 1977. "Land Reform and the Portuguese Revolution." *Journal of Peasant Studies* 5, no. 1 (Oct.): 79–97.

Ruttan, Vernon W. 1966. "Tenure and Productivity of Philippine Rice Producing Farms." *Philippine Economic Journal* 5, no. 1, pp. 42–63.

——. 1977. "The Green Revolution: Seven Generalizations." *International Development Review* 19, no. 4 (Dec.): 16–22.

Rutten, Rosanne. 1982. *Women Workers of Hacienda Milagros: Wage Labor and Household Subsistence on a Philippine Sugarcane Plantation*. Amsterdam: Anthropology-Sociology Center, University of Amsterdam.

——. 1992. "'Mass Surrenders' in Negros Occidental: Ideology, Force and Accommodation in a Counterinsurgency Program." Paper presented at the Fourth International Philippine Studies Conference, Canberra, July 1–3.

Sabino, Mr. 1987. "Transcript of Hearing of the Senate Committee on Agrarian Reform." Testimony of Mr. Sabino, Sugarcane Landowner. Mimeograph. Aug. 14.

Sacerdoti, Guy. 1986a. "Shadow of the Past." *Far Eastern Economic Review*, May 29, pp. 42–43.

——. 1986b. "Cory's Basic-Law Makers." *Far Eastern Economic Review*, June 5.

——. 1986c. "Reds See Their Missed Chances." *Far Eastern Economic Review*, June 12.

Samson, Josephine A. 1991. "Agrarian Reform and Market Formation in the Philippines." *Journal of Contemporary Asia* 21, no. 3: 344–70.

San Andres, Ricardo R., and Jeanne Francis I. Illo. 1978. "Beyond Share Tenancy: A Socioeconomic Study of the Effects of Agrarian Reform Programs in the Bicol River Basin, Camarines Sur, 1974 and 1977." Mimeograph. Quezon City: Institute of Philippine Culture, Ateneo de Manila University.

Sanciano y Goson, Gregorio. 1881. *El progreso de Filipinas: Estudios economicos, administrativos y politicos*. Madrid.

Sandoval, Pedro R., and Benjamin N. Gaon. 1971. *Agricultural Land Reform in the Philippines: Economic Aspects*. Los Baños: College of Agriculture, University of the Philippines.

——. 1972. "Some Effects of Land Reform in the Philippines." *Journal of Agricultural Economics and Development* 2, no. 1 (Jan.): 235–42.

Sandoval, Romulo A., ed. 1986. *Prospects of Agrarian Reform Under the New Order*. Quezon City: Urban-Rural Mission, National Council of Churches in the Philippines.

Sa-Onoy, Modesto P. 1987. "Burning Issue." *Visayan Daily Star*, June 9.

Sarrosa, Edgar G. 1987. Transcript of hearing of the senate committee on agrarian reform. Testimony of Edgar G. Sarrosa, President, Negros Prawn Producers Marketing Cooperative. Manila: Aug. 18. (Senate transcript incorrectly identifies witness as Mr. Larrosa; House transcripts and NPPMC documents identify witness as Mr. Sarrosa.)

Sawit, Mr. 1987. "Transcript of Hearing of the Senate Committee on Agrarian Reform." Testimony of Mr. Sawit, President, Central Azucarera de Tarlac Planters Association, and Managing Director, Paniki Sugarmills Cooperative Marketing Association. Mimeograph. Aug. 14.

Schieck, Frederick. 1981. "Statement of Frederick Schieck, Acting Assistant Administrator, Asia Bureau, Agency for International Development." *Hearings of the Subcommittee on Asia and Pacific Affairs, House Foreign Affairs Committee*. Washington, D.C. Mar. 31.

Schluter, M. 1971. "Differential Rates of Adoption of the New Seed Varieties in India: The Problem of the Small Farm." USAID Research Project Occasional Papers, no. 47. Ithaca, N.Y.: Department of Agricultural Economics, Cornell University.

Schönherr, S., and E. S. Mbugua. 1974. "New Extension Methods to Speed Up Diffusion of Agricultural Innovations." Institute for Development Studies Discussion Papers, no. 200. Nairobi: University of Nairobi.

Scott, James C. 1972a. "Patron-Client Politics and Political Change in Southeast Asia." *American Political Science Review* 66, no. 1 (Mar.): 91–113.

——. 1972b. "The Erosion of Patron-Client Bonds and Social Change in Rural Southeast Asia." *Journal of Asian Studies* 32, no. 1 (Nov.): 5–37.

——. 1976. *The Moral Economy of the Peasant: Rebellion and Subsistence in Southeast Asia*. New Haven: Yale University Press.

——. 1985. *Weapons of the Weak: Everyday Forms of Peasant Resistance*. New Haven: Yale University Press.

Scott, James C., and Benedict J. Kerkvliet. 1973. "The Politics of Survival: Peasant Response to 'Progress' in Southeast Asia." *Journal of Southeast Asian Studies* 4, no. 2 (Sept.): 241–68.

——, eds. 1986. *Everyday Forms of Peasant Resistance in South-east Asia*. London: Frank Cass.

Scott, William Henry. 1982. "Filipino Class Structure in the Sixteenth Century." In id., *Cracks in the Parchment Curtain*. Quezon City: New Day Publishers.

Sebastian, Roberto. 1987. "Transcript of Hearing of the Senate Committee on Agrarian Reform." Testimony of Roberto "Bobby" Sebastian, Pilipino Banana Growers and Exporters Association. Mimeograph. Manila, Sept. 4.

Seligson, Mitchell A. 1993. "Thirty Years of Transformation in the Agrarian Structure of El Salvador." MS. Pittsburgh: University of Pittsburgh.

Shaplen, Robert. 1986. "Reporter at Large: From Marcos to Aquino." *New Yorker*, Aug. 25, Sept. 1.

——. 1987. "Reporter at Large: The Thin Edge." *New Yorker*, Sept. 21, 28.

Shoesmith, Dennis. 1985. "The Church." In R. J. May and Francisco Nemenzo, eds., *The Philippines After Marcos*, pp. 70–89. New York: St. Martin's Press.

Sicam, Paulynn P. 1988. "Government Can't Afford to Give Lands for Free." *Manila Chronicle*, Jan. 31, p. 11.

Sidell, Scott. 1987. *The IMF and Third World Political Instability*. London: Macmillan.

Simon, Lawrence R., and James C. Stephens, Jr. 1981. *El Salvador Land Reform, 1980–1981: Impact Audit*. Boston: OXFAM America.

Simons, Lewis M. 1987. *Worth Dying For*. New York: Morrow.

Sin, Jaime Cardinal. 1988. "The Meaning of EDSA: Two Years After." Homily. Manila, Feb. 25.

Sionil, Francisco Jose. 1984. *Po-On*. Manila: Solidaridad Publishing House.

——. 1986. "Editor's Notes." *Solidarity*, no. 106–7, p. 2.

Sison, Jose Maria. 1968a. *Rectify Errors and Rebuild the Party*. In ROP, *So the People Will Know*, pp. 99–152. Quezon City: Department of National Defense, 1970. Reprint, London: Filipino Support Group, 1976.

——. 1968b. *Programme for a People's Democratic Revolution in the Philippines*. Ratified by the Congress of Re-Establishment of the Communist Party of the Philippines, Dec. 26, 1968. Palimbagang Anak-Pawis, 1977. In ROP, *So the People Will Know*, pp. 32–80. Quezon City: Department of National Defense, 1970.

——. 1970. *Philippine Society and Revolution*.

——. 1974. *Specific Characteristics of Our People's War*.

——. 1986. "Economic Development." Seventh in lecture series on Philippine Crisis and Revolution. Quezon City: Asian Center, University of the Philippines.

Skocpol, Theda. 1979. *States and Social Revolutions: A Comparative Analysis of France, Russia, and China*. Cambridge: Cambridge University Press.

Social Weather Stations. 1988a. *October 1987 Public Opinion on Land Reform*. Manila. SWS Survey Bulletin. Quezon City.

——. 1988b. *October 1987 Survey Data on Ownership of Agricultural Land*. Manila: SWS Bulletin Series 1988, no. 3. Quezon City.

——. 1988c. *March 1988 Public Opinion on Congress and on Land Reform*. Manila: SWS Bulletin Series 1988, no. 6. Quezon City.

——. 1988d. *March 1988 Perceptions of Metro Manilans on the Communist Insurgency*. Manila: SWS Bulletin Series 1988, no. 19. Quezon City.

——. 1988e. *March 1988 Perceptions of Metro Manilans on the Possibility of Filipinos Losing Faith in Peaceful Means of Promoting Democracy*. Social Weather Bulletin Series 1988, no. 21. Quezon City.

Starner, Francis L. 1961. *Magsaysay and the Philippine Peasantry: The Agrarian Impact of Philippine Politics, 1953–1956*. Berkeley: University of California Press.

——. 1969. "The Landed Interests and the Enactment of Land Reform Bill of 1955." In Jose V. Abueva and Raul P. de Guzman, eds., *Foundations and Dynamics of Filipino Government and Politics*, pp. 230–34. Manila: Bookmark.

Steinberg, David Joel. 1967. *Philippine Collaboration in World War II*. Ann Arbor: University of Michigan Press.

——. 1982. *The Philippines: A Singular and a Plural Place*. Boulder, Colo.: Westview Press.

——. 1986. "Tradition and Response." In John Bresnan, ed., *Crisis in the Philippines: The Marcos Era and Beyond*, pp. 30–54. Princeton: Princeton University Press.

Stepan, Alfred. 1971. *The Military in Politics: Changing Patterns in Brazil*. Princeton: Princeton University Press.

——. 1978. *The State and Society: Peru in Comparative Perspective*. Princeton: Princeton University Press.

——. 1988. *Rethinking Military Politics: Brazil and the Southern Cone*. Princeton: Princeton University Press.

Stephens, Evelyne H. 1990. "Democracy in Latin America: Recent Developments in Comparative Historical Perspective." *Latin American Research Review* 25, no. 2, pp. 157–76.

Stern, Steve, ed. 1987. *Resistance, Rebellion, and Consciousness in the Andean Peasant World: Eighteenth to Twentieth Centuries*. Madison: University of Wisconsin Press.

Stiglitz, Joseph E. 1974. "Incentives and Risk Sharing in Sharecropping." *Review of Economic Studies* 41 (Apr.): 219–55.

Stinchcombe, Arthur L. 1961. "Agricultural Enterprise and Rural Class Relations." *American Journal of Sociology* 67, no. 2 (Sept.): 165–76.

Stokes, Bruce. 1978. *Local Responses to Global Problems: A Key to Meeting Basic Human Needs*. Washington, D.C.: Worldwatch Institute.

Sturtevant, David R. 1976. *Popular Uprisings in the Philippines, 1840–1940*. Ithaca, N.Y.: Cornell University Press.

Szanton, David L. 1971. *Estancia in Transition: Economic Growth in a Rural Philippine Community*. IPC Papers, no. 9. Quezon City: Institute of Philippine Culture, Ateneo de Manila University.

Szanton, M. Cristina Blanc. 1979. "The Uses of Compadrazgo: Views From a Philippine Town." *Philippine Sociological Review* 27, no. 3 (July): 161–80.

Tadem, Eduardo C. 1980. "Philippine Rural Development: Corporate Farming or Land Reform." Paper presented at the Philippine Sociological Society National Convention, Nov. 27–28. Quezon City.

——. 1986. "A Step Forward for Land Reform: But There Are Loopholes." *Philippine Daily Inquirer*, Aug. 22.

——. 1987. "Directions in Philippine Agrarian Reform." *New Asian Visions* 4, no. 1: 19–30.

——. 1993. "Agrarian Reform Implementation in the Philippines: Disabling a Centerpiece Program." In J. Ibarra A. Angeles, ed., *International Conference on Agrarian Reform: Proceedings and Documentation*, pp. 79–109. Quezon City: Secretariat, International Conference on Agrarian Reform held Jan. 28–Feb. 2, 1991.

Tadeo, Jaime. 1986. "Reflections on Genuine Land Reform." In Romulo A. Sandoval, ed., *Prospects of Agrarian Reform Under the New Order*, pp. 11–22.

Quezon City: Urban Rural Mission, National Council of Churches in the Philippines.

Tai, Hung-chao. 1974. *Land Reform and Politics: A Comparative Analysis.* Berkeley: University of California Press.

Takahashi, Akira. 1969. *Land and Peasants in Central Luzon.* Tokyo: Institute of Developing Economies.

Takigawa, Tsutomu. 1974. "A Note on the Agrarian Reform in the Philippines Under the New Society." Discussion Paper 74-17. Quezon City: Institute of Economic Development and Research, University of the Philippines.

Tancangco, Luzviminda G. 1988. "The Electoral System and Political Parties in the Philippines." In Raul P. de Guzman and Mila A. Reforma, eds., *Government and Politics of the Philippines*, pp. 77–112. Singapore: Oxford University Press.

Tanchoco-Subido, Chita. 1978. "Small Farmer Credit Policies and Programs in the Philippines." Mimeograph. Los Baños.

Tangbawan, Romy. 1988a. "Farmers Group to Occupy Big Estates." *Malaya*, March 29.

——. 1988b. "Farmers Confiscate 11-ha. Laguna Land." *Malaya*, May 18.

Tangbawan, Romy, and Florencio Narito. 1989. "Three More Land Scams Exposed." *Malaya*, June 20.

Taussig, Michael T. 1980. *The Devil and Commodity Fetishism in South America.* Chapel Hill: University of North Carolina Press.

Tejam, Catalina S. 1988a. "National Leadership Support and Initiative: Towards an Economically Viable CARP." *Intersect* 2, no. 6 (June): 6–7, 13.

——. 1988b. "The Dawn and Death of Agrarian Reform in the Philippines." *Intersect* 2, no. 9 (Sept.): 4–5.

Third World Studies Center. 1988. *Marxism in the Philippines.* Quezon City: University of the Philippines Third World Studies Center.

Thomas, Scott. 1987. "Success or Failure in the Philippines?" *SAIS Review* 7, no. 2 (Summer–Fall): 109–25.

Thompson, E. P. 1966. *The Making of the English Working Class.* New York: Vintage Books.

Thompson, Mark R. 1989. "Cory and 'the Guy': Reformist Politics in the Philippines." Field Staff Reports, Asia, 1988–89, no. 16. Universities Field Staff International.

——. 1990. "The 'Little Left' in the Politics of the Philippines." Field Staff Reports, Asia, 1989–90, no. 17. Universities Field Staff International.

Tiglao, Rigoberto. 1989. "Caught in the Act." *Far Eastern Economic Review*, July 13, p. 15.

——. 1992. "Repeat Offenders: Agrarian Reform Programme Fails in Its Objectives." *Far Eastern Economic Review* Feb. 6, pp. 16–17.

Time. 1987. "Cory: Aquino Leads a Fairy-Tale Revolution, Then Surprises the World with Her Strength." Jan. 5, pp. 18–25, 27–31.

Tiongson, Mari L., Aurora Regalado, and Ramon San Pascual. 1988. "Agriculture in the 70's and 80's: TNC's Boon, Peasants' Doom." In *Sowing the Seed: Proceedings of the International Solidarity Conference for the Filipino Peasantry, Oct. 11–21, 1986*, pp. 22–49. Quezon City: KMP.

Trimberger, Ellen. 1978. *Revolution from Above: Military Bureaucrats in Japan, Turkey, Egypt and Peru.* New Brunswick, N.J.: Transaction Books.

Tucker, Robert C., ed. 1978. *The Marx-Engels Reader.* 2d ed. New York: Norton.

Union Communal Salvadoreña. 1981. "El Salvador Land Reform Update: Land to the Tiller Program." Mimeograph. San Salvador.

United States Agency for International Development (USAID). 1975. *A Study of Philippine Farmer Organizations.* Manila: Agrarian Reform Division, USAID.

——. 1989. *Project Assessment Document: Agrarian Reform Support Program.* Manila: USAID.

Valenzuela, Arturo. 1978. *The Breakdown of Democratic Regimes: Chile.* Baltimore: Johns Hopkins University Press.

Van Atta, Donald, ed. 1993. *The "Farmer Threat": The Political Economy of Agrarian Reform in Post-Soviet Russia.* Boulder, Colo.: Westview Press.

van der Kroef, Justus M. 1988. "The Philippines: Day of the Vigilantes." *Asian Survey* 28, no. 6 (June): 630–49.

Viewpoints. 1987. "Barking up the Wrong Tree, Putting the Cart Before the Horse." 2, no. 14 (Aug.): 5.

Villacorta, Wilfrido V. 1983. "Contending Political Forces in the Philippines Today: The Political Elite and the Legal Opposition." *Contemporary Southeast Asia* 5, no. 2 (Sept.): 185–204.

Villalobos, Marty (pseud.). N.d. "Where the Party Faltered: An Analysis of the Snap Polls and the February Uprising." Unpublished paper.

——. 1986. "On the Insurrectional Strategy." Unpublished paper (March 30).

Villegas, Bernardo. 1986. "The Economic Crisis." In John Bresnan, ed., *Crisis in the Philippines: The Marcos Era and Beyond*, pp. 145–75. Princeton: Princeton University Press.

Von Oppenfeld, Horst, Judith Van Oppenfeld, J. C. Sta. Iglesia, and P. R. Sandoval. 1957. *Farm Management, Land Use and Tenancy in the Philippines.* Quezon City: University of the Philippines.

Von Pischke, J. D., Dale Adams, and Gordon Donald. 1983. *Rural Financial Markets in Developing Countries: Their Use and Abuse.* Baltimore: Johns Hopkins University Press.

Walinsky, Louis. 1977. *Agrarian Reform as Unfinished Business: The Selected Papers of Wolf Ladejinsky.* New York: Oxford University Press.

Wallace, J., and R. Beneke. 1956. *Managing the Tenant-Operated Farm.* Ames: Iowa State College Press.

Wang, In Kuen. 1987. "Korean Rural Development Experience with Special Reference to Land Reform and *Saemaul Undong.*" In *Agrarian Reform: Experiences and Expectations*, pp. 55–71. Agrarian Reform Symposia, Apr. 22–23 and May 23. Manila: Center for Research and Communication.

Warren, James. 1982. "Slavery and the Impact of External Trade: The Sulu Sultanate in the Nineteenth Century." In Alfred W. McCoy and Ed. C. de Jesus, eds., *Philippine Social History: Global Trade and Local Transformations*, pp. 415–44. Quezon City: Ateneo de Manila University Press.

Warren, Kay. [1978] 1989. *The Symbolism of Subordination: Indian Identity in a Guatemalan Town.* 2d edition. Austin: University of Texas Press.

Warriner, Doreen. 1969. *Land Reform in Principle and Practice*. Oxford: Clarendon Press.

Waterbury, John. 1983. *The Egypt of Nasser and Sadat: The Political Economy of Two Regimes*. Princeton: Princeton University Press.

Weber, Max. 1978. *Economy and Society*. Berkeley: University of California Press.

Weede, Erich. 1983. "The Impact of Democracy on Economic Growth: Some Evidence from Cross-National Analysis." *Kyklos* 36, no. 1, pp. 21–39.

Wickberg, Edgar. 1964. "The Chinese Mestizo in Philippine History." *Journal of Southeast Asian History* 5, no. 1 (Mar.): 62–100.

Wise, William M. 1987. "The Philippine Military After Marcos." In Carl H. Landé, ed., *Rebuilding a Nation: Philippine Challenges and American Policy*, pp. 435–48. Washington, D.C.: Washington Institute Press.

Wolf, Eric R. 1957. "Closed Corporate Peasant Communities in Mesoamerica and Central Java." *Southwestern Journal of Anthropology* 13 (Spring): 1–18.

———. 1969. *Peasant Wars of the Twentieth Century*. New York: Harper & Row.

Wolters, Willem. [1983] 1984. *Politics, Patronage and Class Conflict in Central Luzon*. The Hague: Institute of Social Studies, 1983. Quezon City: New Day Publishers, 1984.

Wong, Susan E. 1987a. "The Congressional Battle over Agrarian Reform." *Intersect* 1, no. 2 (Sept.): 9–10.

———. 1987b. "Tent City for Agrarian Reform." *Intersect* 1, no. 2 (Sept.): 11.

———. 1987c. "The Agrarian Reform Debate in the Senate." *Intersect* 1, no. 3 (Oct.): 1, 4.

———. 1987d. "Lobbying for Agrarian Reform." *Intersect* 1, no. 3 (Oct.): 12, 14.

———. 1988a. "Whence Agrarian Reform in the Philippines." *Intersect* 2, no. 4 (Apr.): 1–4.

———. 1988b. "Agrarian Reform Express." *Intersect* 2, no. 4 (Apr.): 6.

World Bank. 1985. *The Philippines: Recent Trends in Poverty, Employment, and Wages*. Report No. 5456-PH. Washington, D.C.: World Bank.

———. 1986. *World Development Report 1986*. Washington, D.C.: World Bank.

———. 1987a. *Agrarian Reform Issues in the Philippines: An Assessment of the Proposal for an Accelerated Land Reform Program*. Washington, D.C.: World Bank.

———. 1987b. *The Philippines: A Framework for Economic Recovery*. Washington, D.C.: World Bank.

———. 1987c. *World Development Report, 1987*. Washington, D.C.: World Bank.

———. 1989. *World Development Report, 1989*. Washington, D.C.: World Bank.

Wurfel, David. 1962. "The Philippine Elections: Support for Democracy." *Asian Survey* 2, no. 3 (May): 25–37.

———. 1969. "Individuals and Groups in the Philippine Policy Process." In Jose V. Abueva and Raul P. de Guzman, eds., *Foundations and Dynamics of Filipino Government and Politics*, pp. 208–23. Manila: Bookmark.

———. 1977. *Philippine Agrarian Policy Today: Implementation and Political Impact*. Institute of Southeast Asian Studies Occasional Papers, no. 46. Singapore: Institute of Southeast Asian Studies.

———. 1979. "Elites of Wealth and Elites of Power: The Changing Dynamic: A

Philippine Case Study." In *Southeast Asian Affairs, 1979*, pp. 233–45. Singapore: Institute of Southeast Asian Studies, Heinemann Educational Books.

——. 1983. "The Development of Post-War Philippine Land Reform: Political and Sociological Explanations." In Antonio J. Ledesma, Perla Q. Makil, and Virginia A. Miralao, eds., *Second View from the Paddy: More Empirical Studies on Philippine Rice Farming and Tenancy*, pp. 1–14. Quezon City: Institute of Philippine Culture, Ateneo de Manila University.

——. 1988. *Filipino Politics: Development and Decay*. Ithaca, N.Y.: Cornell University Press; Quezon City: Ateneo de Manila University Press. Page citations are to the latter edition.

Youngblood, Robert L. 1981. "Church-Military Relations in the Philippines." *Australian Outlook* 35, no. 3 (Dec.): 250–61.

——. 1982. "Structural Imperialism: An Analysis of the Catholic Bishops' Conference of the Philippines." *Comparative Political Studies* 15, no. 1 (Apr.): 29–56.

——. 1987. "The Corazon Aquino 'Miracle' and the Philippine Churches." *Asian Survey* 27, no. 12 (Dec.): 1240–55.

——. [1990] 1993. *Marcos Against the Church: Economic Development and Political Repression in the Philippines*. Ithaca, N.Y.: Cornell University Press, 1990; Quezon City: New Day Publishers, 1993.

Interviews

Abad, Florencio B., congressman, June 21, 1989; executive director, KAISAHAN, Feb. 7, 1991; Jan. 15, 1992; Mason Fellow, Harvard University, Mar. 25, 1994.

Adriano, Fermin, Luzviminda Cornista, Filomena Javier, Linda Peñalba, Ma. Agnes R. Quisumbing, Agnes Rola, and Rene Talatala, Institute of Agrarian Studies, University of the Philippines, Los Baños, Mar. 20, 1986.

Adversario, Jose, community agrarian reform officer (CARO), Department of Agrarian Reform, Camarines Sur, Jan. 29, 1992.

Alunan, Eduardo M., vice president, Rafael Alunan Agro-Development, Inc., Bacolod, Negros Occidental, June 16, 1986.

Alvarez, Heherson, senator. Manila, Feb. 24, 1989; Feb. 20, 1991; Jan. 22, 1992; Nov. 23, 1992.

Aquino, Agapito, senator. July 13, 1989; Feb. 7, 1991; Jan. 14, 1992.

Bacsain, Ed., Kilusang Magbubukid ng Bicol, Jan. 25, 1992.

Banzuela, Raul Socrates C., department head, agrarian reform and rural development department, PhilDHRRA, Feb. 10, 1992; Feb. 22, 1994.

Beebe, James, USAID, Manila, Mar. 21 and June 26, 1986.

Belarmino, Sofie, Delia Locsin, Peter Lopez, Vicky Rallos, and Ramon Villanueva, First Farmers Human Development Foundation, Inc., June 17, 1986.

Benedicto, Emilio M., Jr., sugarcane landowner, Bacolod, Negros Occidental, June 18, 1986.

Bercaro, Arthur, chairperson; Wilson Latoza, staff; Rodolfo Sepida, staff; Small Farmers Association of Negros (SFAN), Mar. 2, 1989.

Bernas, Joaquin G., S.J., president, Ateneo de Manila University, Quezon City, July 10, 1989.

Biadora, Daisy T., community agrarian reform officer (CARO), Department of Agrarian Reform, Negros Occidental, Feb. 12, 1991.

Blackton, John, deputy mission director, USAID, Manila, July 27, 1987; Oct. 7, 1988; Mar. 17 and June 16, 1989.

Bosworth, Stephen W., U.S. ambassador to the Philippines, Manila, Mar. 19, 1986.

Bueno, Luis B., Jr., provincial agrarian reform officer (PARO), DAR, Palawan, Feb. 4, 1992.

Bulatao, Victor Gerardo J., assistant secretary for support services, DAR, Mar. 15 and June 27, 1989; executive director, KAISAHAN, Feb. 16, 1994.

Cabezon, Virgilio E., assistant secretary, DAR, Feb. 11, 1992.

Cherniguin, Serge, NFSW, Bacolod, Negros Occidental, Mar. 3 and July 5, 1989.

Cornista, Luzviminda, Institute of Agrarian Studies, University of the Philippines, Los Baños, June 13 and 24, 1986; Feb. 23, 1989.

Cornista, Luzviminda, Mariano Garcia, Filomena Javier, Linda Peñalba, and Rene Talatala, Institute of Agrarian Studies, University of the Philippines, Los Baños, Mar. 24, 1986.

Dago-ob, Gerundio, deputy secretary-general, NFSW, Bacolod, Negros Occidental, Oct. 25, 1988.

de la Cruz, Zoilo V., president, National Congress of Unions in the Sugar Industry of the Philippines (NACUSIP); Jeremias Montemayor, president, Federation of Free Farmers; Ken Philipps, Asian American Free Labor Institute; Abelardo Resurreccion; Eligio J. Tavanlar; Nilo Tayag; and A. Valerio, Quezon City, June 13, 1986.

Dumankas, Eric, deputy to the governor, Negros Occidental; Pacifico R. Burgos, assistant executive director, Negros Economic Development Foundation (NEDF); Ramon Alisan, Jr., NEDF; Dr. Florintina Romero; and Luis Ballon, June 17, 1986.

Empestan, Fr. Romeo, director, Diocesan Pastoral Center, Bacolod, Negros Occidental, July 5, 1989.

Espallardo, Efren, NFSW, Bacolod, Negros Occidental, Mar. 6, 1989.

Estacio, Edgardo R., national vice president, NFSW, June 16, 1986.

Fortich, Antonio, bishop, Catholic Church, Bacolod, Negros Occidental, June 16, 1986; Oct. 22, 1988; July 5, 1989.

Gallardo, Leonardo, president, Negros Economic Development Foundation, July 3, 1989; Feb. 11, 1991.

Garilao, Ernesto D., secretary, DAR, Nov. 25, 1992.

Gillego, Bonifacio H., congressman, Quezon City, Oct. 7, 1988; Feb. 22 and June 17, 1989; Feb. 6, 1991; Jan. 21 and Nov. 20, 1992; Feb. 17, 1994.

Guanzon, Romeo G., congressman and president, NFSP, Bacolod, Negros Occidental, June 19, 1986; July 1, 1989.

Illo, Jeanne F. I., Institute of Philippine Culture (IPC), Ateneo de Manila University, Oct. 11, 1988.

Jimenea, Pedro, and Edgardo Gison, officials, NACUSIP, Bacolod, Negros Occidental, Mar. 1, 1989.

Jones, Clayton, correspondent, *Christian Science Monitor*, Oct. 10, 1988; June 21, 1989.

Juico, Philip E., secretary, DAR, Oct. 14, 1988.

Julayco, Mabini H., president, Hawaiian-Philippines Sugar Workers' Union, Mar. 13, 1989.

Juliano-Soliman, Corazon, and Felipe S. Ramiro, Jr., staff, CPAR, June 30, 1989.

Korten, Frances F., program officer, Ford Foundation, Feb. 6, 1991; Jan. 14 and Feb. 10, 1992.

Lacson, Daniel L., Jr., governor, Negros Occidental, June 19, 1986; Mar. 10, 1989.

Lagman, Edcel C., chairman, Committee on Agrarian Reform, Philippine House of Representatives, Mar. 15, 1989.

Lara, Cynthia, Philippine Peasant Institute, Feb. 21, 1989; Management and Organizational Development for Empowerment (MODE), Feb. 24, 1994.

Lara, Francisco, Jr., project development director, Philippine Peasant Institute (1989–91) and executive director, MODE (1992–present), Feb. 21, 1989; Feb. 19, 1991; Nov. 27, 1992; Feb. 24, 1994.

Leong, Benjamin T., secretary; Dorothy Tadeo, undersecretary; Renato B. Padilla, undersecretary, DAR, Feb. 22, 1991.

Lim, Evelyn, media consultant/television producer for the Office of the President, July 28, 1987.

Locsin, Eduardo E., president, Chito Foundation, Bacolod, Negros Occidental, June 16, 1986; July 5, 1989.

Locsin, José Marie, and Margarita Locsin, sugarcane landowners; Roger Z. Reyes, Ernesto Treyes and Eutiquio Fudolin, attorneys, Sugar Industry Advisory Council, Bacolod, Negros Occidental, June 14, 1986.

Lopez-Gonzaga, Violeta, University of St. La Salle, Bacolod, Negros Occidental, June 17, 1986; Oct. 28, 1988; Mar. 3 and July 4, 1989; Feb. 12, 1991.

Mananzan, Sister Mary John, vice president, St. Scholastica's College, and chairperson, General Assembly Binding Women for Integrity, Equality, Law and Action (GABRIELA), Feb. 22, 1989.

Mariano, Rafael, acting chairman, KMP, Feb. 8, 1991; Jan. 21 and Nov. 24, 1992.

Martokoesoemo, Soeksmono, director for Agriculture, and E. F. Tacke, assistant director for Agriculture, Asian Development Bank, Mar. 25, 1986.

Merrill, David, and Tom Muncy, Philippine desk officers, USAID, Apr. 15, 1986.

Miranda, Mrs., social services officer (SSO), and Mr. Yongque, director, Social Services Office, DAR, Negros Occidental, Feb. 12, 1991.

Modina, Rolando B., executive director, Agency for Community Education and Services Foundation (ACES), Oct. 17, 1988.

Montemayor, Jeremias, president, FFF, June 13, 1986; Feb. 18, 1991.

Moore, Ralph R., Economic counselor, U.S. embassy, Manila, June 26, 1986.

Morales, Horacio R., Jr., chair, Philippine Rural Reconstruction Movement (PRRM), Oct. 14, 1988; Mar. 16, 1989.

Nolan, Ramon, former executive secretary, NFSP, and former director, Philippine Sugar Quota Administration, July 8, 1989.

Obias, Fanny G., legal officer, DAR, Camarines Sur, Jan. 26, 1992.

Orbos, Oscar M., congressman and LDP deputy secretary, Oct. 6 and 12, 1988; June 22, 1989; presidential executive secretary, Feb. 21, 1991.

Ortigas, Gaston, dean, Asian Institute of Management, Oct. 21, 1988; June 22, 1989.

Pelaez, Emmanuel N., Philippine ambassador to the United States, July 16, 1986.

Potente, Baltakar N., national vice president, PAKISAMA, Feb. 27, 1989.

Quisumbing, Ma. Agnes R., Department of Economics, University of the Philippines, June 24, 1989.

Racelis, Mary, Ford Foundation, Manila, Nov. 27, 1992; Feb. 24, 1994.

Ramiro, Felipe S., Jr., Congress for a People's Agrarian Reform, Oct. 14, 1988; Feb. 21, 1989; Feb. 19, 1991; Jan. 21, 1992.

Reuyan, Eliezer, community agrarian reform officer (CARO), DAR, Camarines Sur, Jan. 29, 1992.

Rojas, Enrique D., executive vice president, NFSP, Bacolod, Negros Occidental, June 17, 1986. Guests: Joey de la Paz, Antonio de Leon, José Mari Miranda, Willy Cimafranca, Carmelo Locsin, Emilio H. Hernay, Modesto P. Sa-Onoy, and Mr. and Mrs. Sevarino.

Salcedo, Martha Carmel, secretary, Committee on Agrarian Reform, Philippine House of Representatives, Mar. 15, 1989.

San Antonio, Zues Angelo, PhilDHRRA, Jan. 24, 1992.

Schieck, Frederick, mission director, USAID, Mar. 17 and June 11, 1986.

Serrano, Isagani, vice president, Philippine Rural Reconstruction Movement (PRRM), Feb. 21, 1991; Jan. 13 and Nov. 27, 1992; Feb. 21, 1994.

Soliman, Hector, undersecretary for Legal Affairs, DAR, Feb. 22, 1994.

Starke, Hortensia L., congresswoman and president, New Alliance of Sugar Producers, Manila, June 23, 1989.

Starke, Hortensia L., congresswoman; Eduardo M. Alunan, vice president, Rafael Alunan Agro-Development; and Teresita Montilla Araneta, Bacolod, Negros Occidental, June 16, 1986.

Tadeo, Jaime, president, KMP, July 11, 1989.

Tadeo, Jaime, Gino Lopez, and Felicisimo Patayan, members of the KMP National Executive Committee, Feb. 22, 1989.

Talatala, Rene, Institute of Agrarian Studies, University of the Philippines, Los Baños, Mar. 20, 1986.

Tavanlar, Dr. Eligio J., retired UN consultant on agrarian reform, June 13, 1986.

Tumbado, Samuel P., development cooperation and advocacy staff; Chie T. Nuuan, area coordinator; and Lally Balcueva, project development officer, Philippine Rural Reconstruction Movement (PRRM), Camarines Sur, Jan. 24, 1992.

Valenzuela, Edgardo T., Asian NGO Coalition for Agrarian Reform and Rural Development (ANGOC), Oct. 21, 1988.

Villarosa, Tadeo, consultant to NFSP and First Farmers' (Milling) Association, Bacolod, Negros Occidental, June 19, 1986.

Vistan, Deogracias N., president, Land Bank of the Philippines, June 23, 1989; Feb. 20, 1991.

Wong, Susan E., Institute on Church and Social Issues, Oct. 12, 1988.

Index

In this index an "f" after a number indicates a separate reference on the next page, and an "ff" indicates separate references on the next two pages. A continuous discussion over two or more pages is indicated by a span of page numbers, e.g., "57–59." *Passim* is used for a cluster of references in close but not consecutive sequence.

Abad, Florencio B., 150, 166, 181–88 *passim*, 192f, 295n71
Abandoned lands, *see* Idle lands
Acuña, Arsenio R., 38, 285n95
Administrative Order No. 6 (1992), 179
Administrative simplicity, 98f, 269n86
Adriano, Fermin, 279n57, 294n66
African agriculture, 73, 81, 238n7
Agoncillo, Teodoro, 251n49
Agrarian reform, 58; agricultural yields and, 2, 11, 97, 101–4, 110, 119, 154, 168f; definition of, 2, 71f, 104, 122–25, 141, 225; economic development and, 2, 119, 142, 146; rural unrest and, 2f, 6, 11, 13, 86, 88, 94, 120f, 146, 217, 238n12; history in the Philippines, 9, 75, 217, 220; in Asia, 9, 93, 121, 154, 157f, 188, 231, 245n50; in Latin America, 10, 116, 239n16, 278n51; landowner responses to, 75, 88f, 99f, 128–34, 149, 156–60 *passim*, 182, 186f, 225; income inequality and, 103f, 169; symbolism of, 118, 180f; international influence, 121f, 279n57; politics of, 131f, 188, 191, 216f, 230, 238n11. *See also* Genuine agrarian reform; *specific legislation, Philippine presidents, and programs by name. See also under* Democracy

Agrarian structure, 72–77
Agrarian unrest, *see* Rural unrest
Agricultural credit, 39f, 75, 81, 83, 98, 118f, 141, 168, 173, 215, 291n41
Agricultural extension, 83, 118f, 143, 173
Agricultural Land Reform Code (1963), 91, 281n67
Agricultural prices, 81, 168
Agricultural Tenancy Act (1954), 87f
Agriculture, 5, 221; yields, 2, 78–81, 100, 216, 229; population, 72f, 259n5; Philippine, 73, 80f. *See also* Economies of scale
Alunan, Eduardo M., 38f, 258n4, 262n31, 269n88
Alvarez, Heherson T., 282n74; Senator, 117, 131f, 152, 165, 301n22; Minister of Agrarian Reform, 125f, 183, 274n21, 289n16, 289n18
Anderson, Benedict, 110, 148, 278n48
Anticipatory land transfers, 160, 218
Aquino, Agapito "Butz," 28f, 152
Aquino, Benigno "Ninoy," Jr., 1, 26ff, 94, 108, 136, 242n28; agrarian reform and, 116, 278n43, 293n49
Aquino, Benigno, Sr., 22, 241n17
Aquino, Pres. Corazon C., 1, 16, 70, 114, 214, 273n12; and democracy, 3, 105f,

Library of Congress Cataloging-in-Publication Data

Riedinger, Jeffrey M.
    Agrarian reform in the Philippines : democratic transitions and redistributive
reform / Jeffrey M. Riedinger
        p. cm.
    Includes bibliographical references and index.
    ISBN 0-8047-2530-6 (acid-free paper)
    1. Land reform—Philippines. 2. Agriculture and state—Philippines. 3. Philippines—
Politics and government—1986– . 4. Democracy—Philippines. I. Title.
HD1333.P6R54   1995
333.3′1599—dc20   94-44005
                                                                   CIP

⊗This book is printed on acid-free, recycled paper.

Agrarian Reform in the Philippines